The Cambridge Companion to

THE AGE OF AUGUSTUS

The age of Augustus, commonly dated to 30 B.C.–A.D. 14, was a pivotal period in world history. A time of tremendous change in Rome, Italy, and throughout the Mediterranean world, many key developments were under way when Augustus took charge, and a recurring theme is the role that he played in shaping their direction. *The Cambridge Companion to the Age of Augustus* captures the dynamic and richness of this era by examining important aspects of political and social history, religion, literature, and art and architecture. The sixteen essays, written by distinguished specialists from the United States and Europe, explore the multifaceted character of the period and the interconnections among social, religious, political, literary, and artistic developments. Introducing the reader to many of the central issues of the Age of Augustus, the essays also break new ground and will stimulate further research and discussion.

Karl Galinsky is professor of classics at the University of Texas at Austin. The author of several books, including *Augustan Culture*, and numerous scholarly articles, he has received awards for his teaching and research, including fellowships from the National Endowment for the Humanities, the Guggenheim Foundation, and the von Humboldt Foundation.

THE CAMBRIDGE COMPANION TO

THE AGE OF AUGUSTUS

Edited by

KARL GALINSKY

University of Texas at Austin

CAMBRIDGE
UNIVERSITY PRESS

CAMBRIDGE UNIVERSITY PRESS
Cambridge, New York, Melbourne, Madrid, Cape Town, Singapore,
São Paulo, Delhi, Dubai, Tokyo, Mexico City

Cambridge University Press
32 Avenue of the Americas, New York, NY 10013-2473, USA

www.cambridge.org
Information on this title: www.cambridge.org/9780521003933

First published 2005

A catalog record for this publication is available from the British Library

Library of Congress Cataloging in Publication data

The Cambridge companion to the Age of Augustus / edited by Karl Galinsky.
p.   cm. – (Cambridge companion to the classics)
Includes bibliographical references and index.
ISBN 0-521-00393-8 (pbk.) – ISBN 0-521-80796-4 (hardback)
1. Rome – History – Augustus, 30 B.C.-14 A.D.   2. Augustus, Emperor
of Rome, 63 B.C.-14 A.D.   3. Rome – Civilization.
I. Galinsky, Karl, 1942-   II. Series.
DG279.C35   2005
937'.07 – dc22   2005010513

ISBN 978-0-521-80796-8 Hardback
ISBN 978-0-521-00393-3 Paperback

Additional resources for this publication at www.cambridge.org/9780521003933

Contents

ILLUSTRATIONS

Color Plates

Color plates follow page 260.

CONTRIBUTORS

ALESSANDRO BARCHIESI is Professor of Latin Literature at the University of Siena at Arezzo, and at Stanford. He has published widely on the major Augustan poets in various contexts, cultural and literary. He is currently working on two books, entitled *Virgilian Geopoetics* (based on his 2001 Gray Lectures at Cambridge, UK) and *Copies without Models. Hellenization and Augustan Poetry* (from his 2002–3 Jerome Lectures in Ann Arbor and the American Academy in Rome). He is editor of the Florence-based journal *Studi Italiani di Filologia Classica.*

RICHARD BEACHAM is Professor of Theatre History at the University of Warwick. He is the author of *The Roman Theatre and Its Audience* (Harvard, 1992), and *Spectacle Entertainments of Early Imperial Rome* (Yale, 1999). He is currently working on Vol. 2 of *Spectacle Entertainments*, and, together with Dr. Hugh Denard, on *Performing Culture: Roman Pictorial Arts and the Ancient Theatre*, both to be published by Yale University Press. Together with Professor James Packer, he is directing the first scientific survey and analysis of the Theatre of Pompey at Rome.

JOHN R. CLARKE is Annie Laurie Howard Regents Professor of History of Art at the University of Texas at Austin. He is the author of numerous scholarly articles as well as five books on Roman art and culture, including *Roman Sex* (2003), *Art in the Lives of Ordinary Romans: Visual Representation and Non-elite Viewers in Italy, 100 B.C.–A.D. 315* (2003), and *Looking at Lovemaking: Constructions of Sexuality in Roman Art, 100 B.C.–A.D. 250* (1998).

WALTER EDER is Professor of Ancient History at the Ruhr University at Bochum, Germany. His numerous publications are about both Greek and Roman history and constitutional history in particular. He is the editor of *Staat und Staatlichkeit in der frühen römischen Republik*

(1990) and *Die Athenische Demokratie im 4. Jahrhundert v. Chr.* (1995), and coeditor of the lexicon *Der Neue Pauly.* He is currently at work on a comparative study of Greece and Rome with the tentative title *Die geteilte Antike.*

DIANE FAVRO is Professor of Architecture and Urban Design at UCLA and the author of *The Urban Image of Augustan Rome* (Cambridge, 1996). She served as President of the Society of Architectural Historians from 2002 to 2004 and currently is Associate Director of the Cultural Virtual Reality Lab at UCLA, which is modeling the ancient Roman Forum. Among her current projects are articles on ancient urban icons and city boundaries, and a book on Roman architecture with Fikret Yegul for Cambridge University Press.

KARL GALINSKY is Floyd Cailloux Centennial Professor of Classics and University Distinguished Teaching Professor at the University of Texas at Austin. He has published extensively on the Augustan poets and Augustan art and directed numerous projects, including seminars on the Augustan age, for the National Endowment for the Humanities. He is the author of *Augustan Culture: An Interpretive Introduction* (Princeton, 1996; paperback ed. 1998).

JASPER GRIFFIN is Professor of Classical Literature and Public Orator at Oxford University. His interests and publications range widely over both Greek and Roman literature. Some of the books he has written are *Homer on Life and Death* (Oxford, 1980); *Latin Poets and Roman Life* (London, 1985); and *Virgil,* 2nd ed. (Bristol, 2002). He has also edited Book 9 of Homer's *Iliad* (Oxford, 1995) and is the coeditor of *The Oxford History of the Classical World* (Oxford, 1986).

ERICH S. GRUEN is Gladys Rehard Wood Professor of History and Classics at the University of California, Berkeley. He is the author of many important books especially on Republican Rome, including *The Last Generation of the Roman Republic* (Berkeley, 1974); *The Hellenistic World and the Coming of Rome,* 2 vols. (Berkeley, 1984); *Studies in Greek Culture and Roman Policy* (Leiden, 1990); and *Culture and National Identity in Republican Rome* (Ithaca, 1992). His most recent book-length study is *Diaspora: Jews amidst Greeks and Romans* (Cambridge, Mass., 2002).

DIANA E. E. KLEINER, Dunham Professor of History of Art and Classics at Yale University, has explored art at all levels of Roman society from aristocrats to slaves and has helped define the significant contribution made by Roman women. She is the author of *Roman Sculpture* (Yale, 1992, paperback ed. 1994) and editor (with Susan B. Matheson) of *I, Clavdia: Women in Ancient Rome* (Yale University Art Gallery, 1996) and *I, Clavdia II: Women in Roman Art and Society* (Austin, 2000). Her latest book, *Cleopatra and Rome*, will be published by Harvard University Press in October 2005.

NICHOLAS PURCELL has been Fellow and Tutor in Ancient History at St John's College, Oxford, and University Lecturer in Ancient History in the University of Oxford since 1979. His numerous publications reflect his interest in the economic, social, and cultural history of the Greek and Roman worlds, and especially in the city of Rome and its region, and in problems that concern the Mediterranean area in a broad sense. His Jerome Lectures will be published as *The Kingdom of the Capitol*.

JOHN SCHEID, a native of Luxembourg, has been Professor at the Collège de France since 2001. From 1983 to 2001 he was Directeur d'études at the École Pratique des Hautes Études in Paris. He has directed excavations of Roman religious sites at La Magliana (Rome) and Jbel Oust (Tunisia). His numerous publications on Roman religion include, most recently, *La réligion des Romains* (Paris, 1998), translated into English as *An Introduction to Roman Religion* (Bloomington, 2003), and *Réligion et piété à Rome* (Paris, 2001).

SUSAN TREGGIARI is the Anne T. & Robert M. Bass Professor Emerita in the School of Humanities and Sciences, Stanford University, and a member of the Sub-faculty of Ancient History, University of Oxford. Her publications include *Roman Freedmen During the Late Republic* (Oxford: Clarendon Press, 1969, re-issued, 2000); *Roman Marriage. Iusti coniuges from the Time of Cicero to the Time of Ulpian* (Oxford: Clarendon Press, 1991, paperback edition, 1993); and *Roman Social History* (London: Routledge, Classical Foundations, 2002).

ANDREW WALLACE-HADRILL is Director of the British School at Rome. His multifaceted scholarship on the Roman Republic and Empire encompasses historiography, art, architecture, social and intellectual history, literature, and numismatics. Besides numerous articles he is best known for *Suetonius: The Scholar and His Caesars* (London, 1983), *Augustan Rome* (London, 1993), and *Houses and Society in Pompeii and*

Herculaneum (Princeton, 1994). He is currently completing books on *Cultural Change in Roman Italy* and on *A Pompeian Neighbourhood (Reg. 1, Ins. 9)*. In addition, he directs the Herculaneum Conservation Project.

L. MICHAEL WHITE is Ronald Nelson Smith Professor of Classics and Director of the Institute for the Study of Antiquity and Christian Origins at the University of Texas at Austin. Specializing in the social context of Jews and Christians in the Roman world, he currently directs excavations at the site of the Synagogue of Ancient Ostia. He is the author of *The Social Origins of Christian Architecture* (Harrisburg, 1996–97) and *From Jesus to Christianity* (San Francisco, 2004). He is coeditor of *Early Christianity and Classical Culture* (Leiden, 2003) and is series editor for Religion and Society in the Ancient World (University of Texas Press).

PETER WHITE is Professor of Classics and of New Testament and Early Christian Literature at the University of Chicago. His published work focuses mostly on interrelationships between Latin literature and Roman society during the Late Republic and Early Empire, and includes the book *Promised Verse: Poets in the Society of Augustan Rome* (Cambridge, Mass., 1993). He is currently writing about the correspondence of Cicero.

GREG WOOLF has been Professor of Ancient History at the University of St Andrews in Scotland since 1998. He is the author of *Becoming Roman. The Origins of Provincial Civilization in Gaul* (Cambridge, 1998) and editor of *Literacy and Power in the Ancient World* (with Alan Bowman) (Cambridge, 1994), *Rome the Cosmopolis* (with Catherine Edwards) (Cambridge, 2003), and the *Cambridge Illustrated History of the Roman World* (Cambridge, 2003). He is currently working on a book on imperialism and culture in Roman antiquity.

Preface

It is a pleasure to contribute this volume to the newly expanded series of *Cambridge Companions*. Like its predecessors, it is not an attempt at an encyclopedic *vade mecum*. Instead, it aims to provide an accessible and yet sophisticated discussion of some paradigmatic aspects of this incredibly rich period. More is involved than a distillation of recent and older scholarship; while being duly informative, we have also tried to break some new ground and point the discussion in new directions. I will comment on this some more in the Introduction.

I would like to thank the sterling group of contributors who enlisted in this effort. It has been exciting to be their first reader (with the privilege of becoming a discussant) and I can only hope that other readers will benefit as much from their expertise and acuity as I have. I also wish to thank Beatrice Rehl for her constructive support and advice ever since the project's inception; my graduate student Dan Hanchey for meticulously checking the final version (and there were several prior incarnations) of the various chapters; and Dr. Darius Arya for help with the increasingly complicated task of obtaining illustrations and permissions. The color reproductions have been made possible by a generous grant from one of Maecenas' descendants, Mr. Mark Finley, and from the Floyd A. Cailloux Centennial Professorship endowment at my university, which also aided work on this volume in many other ways.

Austin
September 23 MMIV

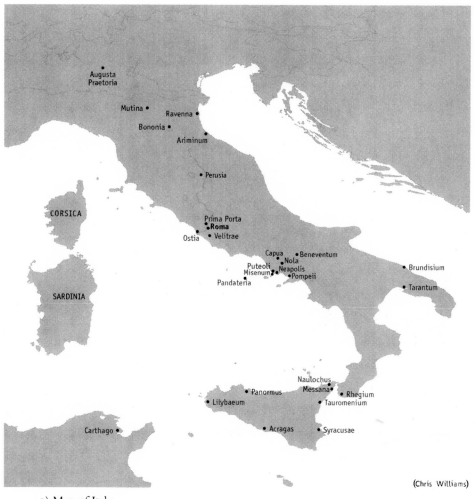

1) Map of Italy

2) Map of major cities in the Augustan empire

Pantikapeion • • Phanagoreia

Chersonesus •

Troesmis •

Tomis •

Danube

Serdica •

• Narona

• Nicomedia

• Philippi • Nicaea • Ancyra

Pella • Cyzicus

Apollonia • • Thessalonica

• Alexandria

• Pergamum

Nicopolis • Smyrna

Actium • Samos • • Sardis

• Delphi Priene • Ephesus

Patras • • Athens Miletus • • Aphrodisias

Corinth Cos •

Olympia • • Limyra

Sparta • Rhodos •

• Gythion

• Cnossus

• Gortyn

CYPRUS

• Salamis

• Heliopolis

Berytus •

Tyrus • • Damascus

Caesarea •

• Jerusalem

• Cyrene

Alexandria • • Nicopolis

Tigris

Euphrates

• Antiochia

• Laodicaea

0   500 km

(Chris Williams)

3) The provinces of the Augustan empire

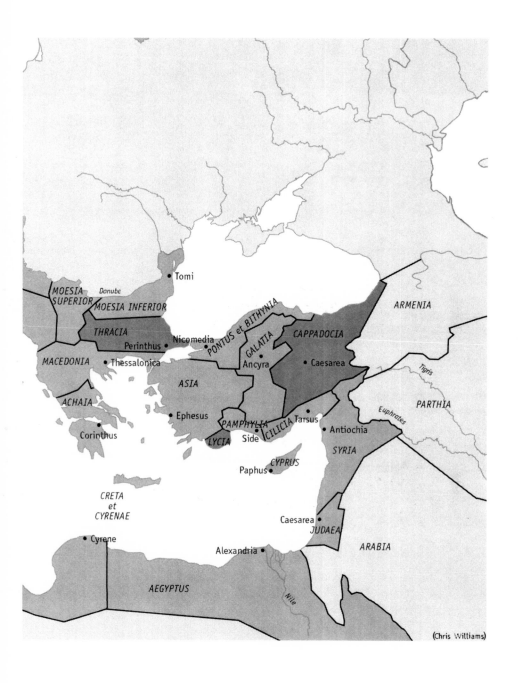

(Chris Williams)

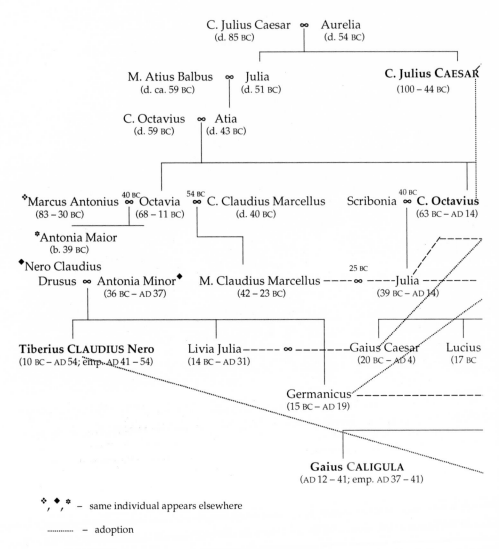

C. Julius Caesar ∞ Aurelia
(d. 85 BC)   (d. 54 BC)

M. Atius Balbus ∞ Julia   C. Julius CAESAR
(d. ca. 59 BC)   (d. 51 BC)   (100 – 44 BC)

C. Octavius ∞ Atia
(d. 59 BC)   (d. 43 BC)

❖Marcus Antonius ∞ Octavia ∞ C. Claudius Marcellus   Scribonia ∞ C. Octavius
(83 – 30 BC)   40 BC (68 – 11 BC)   54 BC (d. 40 BC)   40 BC (63 BC – AD 14)

❖Antonia Maior
(b. 39 BC)

◆Nero Claudius
Drusus ∞ Antonia Minor◆   M. Claudius Marcellus ––––– ∞ –––– Julia –––––––
(36 BC – AD 37)   (42 – 23 BC)   25 BC   (39 BC – AD 14)

Tiberius CLAUDIUS Nero   Livia Julia ––––– ∞ –––– Gaius Caesar   Lucius
(10 BC – AD 54; emp. AD 41 – 54)   (14 BC – AD 31)   (20 BC – AD 4)   (17 BC

Germanicus ––––––––––––––––
(15 BC – AD 19)

Gaius CALIGULA
(AD 12 – 41; emp. AD 37 – 41)

❖, ◆, ❋ – same individual appears elsewhere

.... – adoption

4) Genealogical chart of the family of Augustus

The Julio-Claudian Family

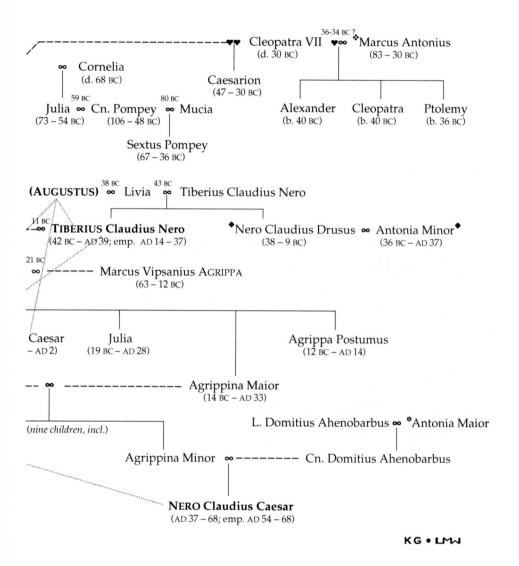

Cleopatra VII (d. 30 BC) ∞ Marcus Antonius (83 – 30 BC) 36-34 BC ?

Cornelia (d. 68 BC)

Caesarion (47 – 30 BC)

Alexander (b. 40 BC)   Cleopatra (b. 40 BC)   Ptolemy (b. 36 BC)

Julia (73 – 54 BC) ∞ Cn. Pompey (106 – 48 BC) ∞ Mucia   59 BC   80 BC

Sextus Pompey (67 – 36 BC)

(AUGUSTUS) ∞ Livia ∞ Tiberius Claudius Nero   38 BC   43 BC

TIBERIUS Claudius Nero (42 BC – AD 39; emp. AD 14 – 37)   11 BC

Nero Claudius Drusus (38 – 9 BC) ∞ Antonia Minor (36 BC – AD 37)

∞ Marcus Vipsanius AGRIPPA (63 – 12 BC)   21 BC

Caesar – AD 2)   Julia (19 BC – AD 28)   Agrippa Postumus (12 BC – AD 14)

∞ Agrippina Maior (14 BC – AD 33)

(nine children, incl.)

L. Domitius Ahenobarbus ∞ Antonia Maior

Agrippina Minor ∞ Cn. Domitius Ahenobarbus

NERO Claudius Caesar (AD 37 – 68; emp. AD 54 – 68)

KG • LMW

History/Politics	Finances/Expenditures	Buildings/Art/Literature
70–30 B.C.		
		70 Birth of Vergil
63 23.9 Birth of C. Octavius		65 Birth of Horace
		59 Birth of Livy
		ca. 48 Birth of Propertius
44 15.2 Caesar declared dictator for life		
15.3 Death of Caesar, Octavian named heir	Octavian seizes war (against Parthians) treasury and tax collections from province of Asia	
Oct./Nov. Octavian raises private army and marches on Rome	Victory Games for Caesar (financed by Octavian); comet appears	
	First payment of 300 sesterces (HS) each to 250,000 plebeians under Caesar's will	
43 19.8 Octavian made consul	Proscriptions (300 senators, 2,000 *equites*)	Death of Cicero
Triumvirate with Mark Antony and Lepidus	Special payment of 2,500 *denarii* to each of Octavian's soldiers	Birth of Ovid
42 Battle of Philippi; death of Brutus and Cassius	Settlement begins of veterans in Italy; land confiscations	Temple of Divus Iulius begun
		Temple of Mars Ultor vowed
40 Perusine War		42–39 Vergil's *Eclogues*
Treaty of Brundisium		41–30 Horace's *Epodes*
Official declaration of Caesar as *divus*		39–29 Vergil's *Georgics*
Octavian takes name of *Imperator Caesar divi filius*		
37 Extension of triumvirate for 5 years		
Antony from now on mostly in east		
36 Battle of Naulochus; death of Sextus Pompey		Temple of Palatine Apollo begun
Defeat of Antony in Parthia		
35 Livia and Octavia granted *sacrosanctitas*		
	33 Rebuilding of Rome begun under Agrippa's aedileship; largesses to urban populace; games	Horace, *Satires* I
31 2.9 Battle of Actium		Horace, *Satires* II
30 1.8 Conquest of Alexandria; suicides of Antony and Cleopatra	700 million HS for land purchases for veterans	
29 B.C. – A.D. 14		
29 11.1 Closing of Temple of Janus	Largesse of 400 HS to 250,000 plebeians and of 1,000 HS to 120,000 soldiers	Dedication of Temple of Divus Iulius and of Curia Iulia
13-15.8 Triple triumph of Augustus (Dalmatia, Actium, Egypt)		Vergil begins *Aeneid*
28 Re-establishment of government by laws	Restoration of 82 temples	Temple of Palatine Apollo dedicated
		Mausoleum begun
		Propertius, Book I
27 13-16.1 return of powers to SPQR; Octavian named "Augustus"		26 Suicide of Cornelius Gallus
	24 Largesse of 400 HS to 250,000 plebeians	
23 Augustus seriously ill	60 million HS: 12 distributions of grain to 250,000 plebeians	Horace, *Odes* I–III
Augustus granted *tribunicia potestas* for life; official beginning of his reign		
Death of Marcellus		Propertius, Books II and III
22 Famine in Rome; refusal of dictatorship		
21 Augustus becomes member of Arval Brotherhood		
20 Return of standards by the Parthians		Horace, *Epistles* I; *Art of Poetry*
		19 Deaths of Vergil and Tibullus
18 Julian laws on marriage and adultery		
17 Secular Games		Horace's *Carmen Saeculare*
	16 Gladiatorial games of Drusus and Tiberius	
	14 160 million HS: land purchases for	Propertius, Book IV; death of Propertius

5) Timeline

	colonies in the provinces	
		13 Ara Pacis begun Horace, *Odes* IV Theater of Balbus dedicated
12 Deaths of Lepidus and Agrippa Augustus becomes *pontifex maximus*		
	11 Largesse of 400 HS to 250,000 plebeians	Theater of Marcellus dedicated
8 Organization of Rome into 14 regions and 265 *vici* Reorganization of cult of *Lares Com-* *pitales*		9 Ara Pacis dedicated Death of Horace; *Epistles* II published posthumously
7 *Fasti* of the *vicomagistri* begin 6 Tiberius withdraws to Rhodes	400 million HS for veterans (until 2 B.C.) 170 million HS paid into *aerarium militare* 5 240 HS each paid to 320,000 plebeians	
2 Augustus acclaimed as *pater patriae* Julia exiled	Naumachy with 3,000 combatants Recipients of grain dole reduced to 200,000	Dedication of Forum of Augustus and Temple of Mars Ultor
A.D. 2 Death of Lucius Caesar Tiberius returns to Rome 5-9 Famines in Rome; reorganization of grain supply 6-9 Pannonian revolt	Largesse of 240 HS to 200,000 plebeians	A.D. 1 Ovid, *Art of Love* 6 Temple of Castor and Pollux dedicated 8 Ovid exiled; publication of *Metamorphoses* and *Fasti*
9 Revision of laws on marriage		10 Temple of Concordia Augusta dedicated 12 Basilica Iulia rededicated as Basilica of Gaius and Lucius
14 Death of Julia 19.8 Death of Augustus (in Nola) 3.9 Livia declared Livia *Augusta* 17.9 Augustus declared *divus* Tiberius elevated to *Augustus*	96 mill. HS: largesses to people and soldiers under Augustus' will	

5) (*continued*)

INTRODUCTION

Karl Galinsky

The age of Augustus continues to fascinate. For good reason: it was unquestionably one of the pivotal periods of western history, if not world history. Its monuments and art still vividly speak to us today as do its writers: Vergil, Horace, and Ovid in particular. At center stage, of course, is the young heir of Caesar, only eighteen years old at the time his adoptive father was cut down. A charismatic personality, maybe; a flamboyant one, no; but surely one as multifaceted as the arts, politics, and social developments of the time and, certainly, the Roman empire that he accumulated, tirelessly expanded (we should not be fooled by his parting admonition to Tiberius), helped shape, and unified – which does not mean homogenized – to an unprecedented degree. In structural and material terms, a basis was laid for the system called the principate that lasted for more than 200 years; the birth of Christ during his era may convince even agnostics of divine foresight.

Great periods in world history and their leading figures are destined to keep attracting attention and undergo changing evaluations. There is more to that than the perpetually grinding mills of the scholarly (re)interpretation industry, spurred on by the usual academic rewards. Even outside this sphere, the process of reception is ever changing and shaped by multifarious factors, consumers, and producers. Every age brings its own perspectives to those before it. Such perspectives tend to be far from monolithic because they often reflect contemporary tensions. In "Augustan" England, for instance, Augustus' reputation fluctuated like a cork on the tide of violent crosscurrents – political, literary, and cultural (Weinbrot 1978).

In the end, however, the basic reasons for the multiple reactions to, and assessments of, the Augustan age are, to borrow Gibbon's famous phrase (no matter that it did not motivate him on to write a shorter work) about the fall of the Roman empire, "simple and obvious." They are its endemic richness of events, characters, ideas, inspirations, dynamics, and contradictions, all amounting to significant and palpable change. A central issue, therefore, is how to define and assess this change. A related and, citing Gibbon again, obvious question is: "What did Augustus have to do with it?" Sure, this all happened on his watch, but what precisely was his role? Was he instigator or catalyst, or was he channeling an already strong flow of history and giving it some direction and definition? We confront the time-honored question of what shapes the course of history and culture broadly defined, events or individuals? Clearly, there is a dynamic between the two.

Speaking of definitions and directions: the aim of this *Companion*, therefore, is not only to inform the reader of where things are at in terms of previous scholarship but to provide some new departures and directions that can, and should, be developed further. I would like to outline some central ones.

Augustus did not simply step into history as if on a blank slate that needed to be inscribed. Events were already in the making, as they always are. The dominant approach to that issue in the last century was that of Syme whose *Roman Revolution* (1939) was written explicitly to hold up a mirror to its own time when autocrats like Hitler, Mussolini, Franco and Stalin loomed large. On this view, Octavian engineered a bloody, military coup against the old order to seize power, and that power was defined mostly in political terms. Accordingly, the Augustan literati were viewed as mere mouthpieces of the political regime. Happily, Syme did not treat Augustan art and architecture, but he did not need to in order to make his point: Mussolini did it for him.

Today, this view of power is too limited. One aspect of power, as Foucault (1971) has argued, is that power is an outcome of knowledge. As for Rome, we are looking at key areas such as control over the calendar. More is involved than a mere reckoning of time: the calendar determined the flow of public life and, through the annual *Fasti*, marked identity by singling out individuals for the offices they held and their activities. There was a great deal of latitude for those who knew how to handle such matters or, at any rate, handled them. They were, of course, members of the nobility and they often proceeded at will. The calendar reform of Caesar marks the arrival of expert professionals. They bring their knowledge to regularizing a haphazard system, and they are employed and appropriated by the new leader of the state. The process continues under Augustus with the additional dimension that, like control over the calendar, *Fasti* are not a privilege anymore that is limited to the aristocracy, but spring up all over for local festivals, magistrates, and functionaries, including freedmen and slaves. As Andrew Wallace-Hadrill summarizes: "In slipping from the nobility, Roman time becomes the property of all Romans" (p. 61). Far from being isolated, this occurrence is part of a broader phenomenon: one of the defining aspects of the Augustan reign is precisely the opening up of formerly restricted opportunities to a much larger segment of the populace. A shift to autocratic government is accompanied by an authentic involvement of much wider strata of the population.

Is this a paradox? Only if one thinks in terms of traditional academic dichotomies, which have had their heyday especially in the interpretation of Augustan poetry. It is clearly relevant, however, to consider Vergil's *Aeneid* against this background: with all its sophistication this was a work that was accessible not only to the élite, but its popular reception was strong and immediate, as we know from inscriptions in Pompeii, theatrical performances, and everyday utensils such as lamps (Horsfall 1995; Galinsky 1969). Similarly, the age witnessed an efflorescence of the art of freedmen. I will return to this aspect again.

Knowledge was power and, as Wallace-Hadrill demonstrates in detail, professional experts had increasingly begun to replace Roman aristocrats as purveyors of knowledge. The development was well under way in vital areas of the Roman state. Religion (with an obvious connection to the calendar) is a prime example: the polymath Varro's compendium on *Human* [i.e. Roman] *and Divine Antiquities* was a landmark and not by coincidence dedicated to the *pontifex maximus* Julius Caesar. Similarly, law and public speaking passed from the realm of the nobles to that of professionals at Cicero's time, and the shift of authority over that all-controlling entity, language, began even sooner. The list does not end here, but one more of its facets deserves mention because it also is a good example of the many interconnections between the chapters of this book. That is the construction and reorganization of the cityscape of Rome. It is one of the dominant images of the period, familiar from the well-known dictum of Augustus that "he left the city, which he found made of bricks, sheathed in marble" (Suetonius, *Aug.* 28; characteristic of Augustan multiple meanings, the phrase follows upon Augustus' claim to have built "the new state" on a secure foundation [*fundamenta*] – architecture is both reality and metaphor). As Diane Favro illustrates, the new urban plan had clear and orderly rationales. The Augustan organization of the city into fourteen *regiones* (see Fig. 40 on p. 244) was part of this concept, but it also had the effect of making the city more knowable. Again, professionals, such as surveyors and census officials, did the work and, as Wallace-Hadrill points out, the result was a city that was under control because, in contrast to its late Republican predecessor, it was clearly known.

There is a further connection. One of the defining building types was the theater. Pompey had broken the barrier and, once again, there were social implications. The nobility in Rome had resisted such buildings, which came to exist in Italy by the second century B.C., because the theater, as Cicero makes clear, was a venue for the true will of the Roman people at all levels of society. The rapid diffusion of the Theater of Marcellus (Fig. 9 on p. 165) as a model in Italy and the provinces, therefore, has more than architectural and aesthetic reasons. And the phenomenon provides an additional perspective on the embedding of the spectacular and theatrical in many aspects of Augustan public and private life, as discussed by Richard Beacham, including wall paintings in Augustus' house (see Plate III) that are one of the subjects of John Clarke's chapter. I invite, nay, urge the reader to make such connections throughout this *Companion* (cf. Alessandro Barchiesi's remarks on p. 281); the headings in the Table of Contents do not imply compartmentalization.

In this context of the transformation of power a useful distinction comes to mind that is currently employed by modern analysts of global power and security, including the so-called *Pax Americana*. They differentiate between the "hard power" of military dominance and the nonmilitary "soft power" of culture in its various aspects (cf. Nye 1990). Augustus based his power on both. The professionalization of major areas of cultural activity intensified during his reign and he appropriated its practitioners; it might be helpful to consider the Augustan writers in this larger context, too, rather than from the usual perspective of "patronage" and the like (cf. Peter White's chapter for a critique of such approaches). The paradigm shift had been in the making; the loser was the former ruling class; and these developments, and not just the loss of political power, are behind the laments about the "decline" of the Republic.

Other developments had been under way that were resulting in profound change and received further articulation under Augustus. One is that the stage was far larger than Rome and Italy. Syme (1939) observed astutely that the victory of Augustus in essence was the victory of the nonpolitical classes of Italy who had been burned by decades of civil war, which was fomented by ambitious members of the governing class, and who just wanted to get on with their lives. No doubt that was a factor, but Augustus played to a larger gallery. That was the Mediterranean world, the site of Roman provinces and client states, and of immense social, economic, and political change that had been developing for over a century. The chapters by Nicholas Purcell and Greg Woolf address this issue from perspectives that are different as well as complementary. In his article on Augustus in the third edition of the *Oxford Classical Dictionary* (1996, 218), Purcell summarized the achievement of Augustus by saying that it "lay in the flexibility with which he and his advisers responded to a period of striking social change in the Mediterranean world, the legacy of the Roman/Italian diaspora of the previous century." His chapter in this volume is an extended demonstration and, like Woolf's, extends the horizon from which it is vital for us to consider the Augustan age. For it is too limiting to view the Roman empire under Augustus, let alone the Roman empire after him, predominantly in terms of Roman civil and military functionaries sent out from the center while neglecting the many interactions – cultural, religious, economic, and social – that were reciprocal and had their own dynamics.

Who were the diaspora Romans? One trait they shared is that they were entrepreneurial, taking advantage of the opportunities Rome's expansion offered. They were a heterogeneous bunch, including Roman citizens who had emigrated and their descendants, freedmen (and their descendants), and locals who had been granted Roman citizenship. They were an important constituency – not necessarily the glue that held the empire together, but clearly a binding link and vital connection between these lands and Rome. Their Roman-ness can be defined in various ways. Purcell, for one, sees their identity as depending "far more on their relationship to Roman power than on any cultural ties." Their ethnicities and cultures reflected those of the entire Mediterranean; what made them "Roman" was their relation with the powers that were at Rome, which gave them privileged status. The presence of a monarch provided a much clearer focus for that relationship, and Augustus evolved into the patron of patrons. We are looking not at an administrative structure but at a dynamic system that is akin to what we would call networking today. And the case can be made that the true locus of action had shifted to the diaspora because "it was in that world that the political outcomes of the age were determined"; it was no accident that Caesar, Augustus, and Tiberius "spent formative years in the currents of the diaspora" (Hadrian later would outdo them all). This view by Purcell finds its complement in Woolf's observation that "Roman civilization, having been taken on by the provinces, no longer belonged to the City of Rome." We are back to the topic of the vast expansion of opportunities in a multitude of areas (except for governance at the top) with the concomitant diminution of the exclusiveness of traditional *loci*.

Besides the diaspora Romans, the main beneficiaries were the provincial élites; there is, of course, an overlap between the two. They took the initiative in becoming "Roman," a notion that was not static but kept evolving, thus assuring the longevity of the Roman empire. As Woolf points out, it was relatively easy to achieve this identity as "habits of dress, speech, manners and conduct were more important than descent" – a good example of "soft" power. Aspects of "real" power were the other part of the equation, such as Augustus' strong emphasis on the protection of private property in general and of the propertied classes in the provinces in particular. He systematically buttressed a system that had already evolved in the towns of Italy and in the successor states to Alexander in the Greek east. It is on such local and regional but widespread foundations that the *Pax Augusta* came to rest; it did not automatically kick in after Antony's and Cleopatra's defeat at Actium in 31 B.C. Augustus' behavior clearly indicates that he both recognized the importance of the diaspora and could rely on a stability that was not located at, and emanated from, the center alone: he was away from Rome for long stretches of time in the 20s and 10s B.C., and not only for military campaigns.

The complex of issues we have surveyed also provides some answers to the question about Augustus' role amid a world of developments and changes that were well underway. In other words, events or the man? The parameters are evident: not everything that happened under Augustus happened because of Augustus (John Clarke takes up this issue in an entirely different context, that of marked shifts in Roman painting). But just as clearly, he left his imprint, and already his contemporaries could speak of their times as "your age" (*tua, Caesar, aetas*: Horace, *Odes* 4.15.4). In this case, and his *modus operandi* was not always the same, Augustus found a parade that was already marching and placed himself at its head – one of the classic definitions of leadership as it recognizes the fluid interaction between leaders and followers: "Leadership, unlike naked power-wielding, is thus inseparable from followers' needs and goals" (Burns, 1978, 19). And we can add an even more traditional metaphor: Augustus navigated on the stream of history and was successful because he did not oversteer. He saw himself that way (*Res Gestae* 34): not as one wielding *potestas* ("power") but as exerting *auctoritas* ("influence").

Reacting to conditions that were not of his own making was nothing new to Augustus. In his early incarnation as Octavian he faced such situations, starting with the murder of Caesar, as a way of life, and he reacted forcefully; Walter Eder well surveys this stage and the next. Similarly, when it came to his plans to establish the principate securely, and with it his succession, Augustus had to revise his expectations again and again (see Erich Gruen's discussion). In all these situations – transformation of knowledge, social change in the diaspora and the provinces, ascent to and maintenance of power, succession – Augustus maneuvered adroitly. But while the last two of these have received plentiful emphasis (which does not mean they cannot be analyzed afresh, as they are here) and shaped much of our view of Augustus and his time they do not rise to the same level of interaction as the others. They were, to be sure, more than mere technical or tactical problems and their solution was important. It is, however, Augustus' attention to the other areas, those of ongoing cultural and social change, that best explains the fundamental impact of the Augustan age on later ages. In Susan Treggiari's (1996b, 902) succinct formulation: "The Roman world was opened up both physically and mentally."

We can make a connection here with one of the salient characteristics of Augustan poetry and art. They were sophisticated and carefully crafted – definitely not pop art, but nonetheless with tremendous popular appeal that is well documented. When one divides the number of days Vergil worked on the *Aeneid* by the number of lines in the poem one arrives at about three lines a day, not exactly the speed of composition of modern best-selling authors, and the figures for Horace's lyric poetry are similar. But the genius of the *Aeneid*, as we saw earlier, was precisely to reach out to readers (at the time more were listeners than readers) of all kinds, and anyone could find meaning in the story, regardless of background and education. Similarly, as Diana Kleiner explains, an Augustan monument like the Ara Pacis "displayed an uncanny ability to invest the major themes of his principate with multiple meanings so that everyone could find significance in them." Sophisticated scholars and interpreters that we are, we take it all for granted, but it is useful, as always, to think of potential alternatives. Why not simply erect a monument with a statue of the Goddess of Peace (we know her image from coins)? Or design a straightforward historical frieze featuring Roman soldiers, as on the Column of Trajan – after all, in Augustus' famous formulation, "peace was achieved through victories" (*Res Gestae* 13: *parta victoriis pax*)? More important, the deliberate polysemy of works like the *Aeneid* and the Ara Pacis can be apprehended not only in general terms of viewer or reader response, but in the context of an Augustan milieu that was inclusive rather than exclusive.

Another corollary of the themes I have sketched is the brittleness of periodization. The precise temporal distinction between Republic and Empire is modern; it did not exist for Augustus' contemporaries. Instead, they saw a sea of flux without a big marker that shouted "Actium!" (cf. Gurval 1995). Many of the defining trends, as we have observed, were already well underway, and similar considerations are relevant when we look, for instance, at the "Augustan" poets. As Jasper Griffin points out, the activity of Horace, Vergil, and others antedates the Augustan age – when exactly did they become "Augustan"? And what exactly does that mean – some kind of realignment, as discussed here by Peter White, and what was its nature? As for Augustus, we all know that he became "Augustus" on January 16, 27 B.C. But while he shed the excesses of bloodlust, revenge, ruthless carnage and civil war mayhem of the "Octavianic" period, the break was less total in more benign areas such as his shaping of Roman religion. As John Scheid demonstrates, there was considerable continuity, and the essential elements of his policy had already been forged in his pre-Augustan years. These findings converge with a similar argument recently advanced by Fergus Millar (2000, 30), namely "that many of the most decisive steps – and even more important, the most decisive aspects of fundamental alteration of mentality and political awareness – had already taken place" before 27 B.C. As illustrated in Eder's essay and others, there was transformation, there was experimentation, and there were certain phases we can distinguish, but, as in all things Augustan, we need to stay away from facile dichotomies.

Certainly, there was no rigid "ideology." There was a sense of purpose and direction, and there were ideas, ideals, and values that, again, were shared, articulated, and debated by many participants rather than Augustus alone. However imperfect their implementation may have been at times, they resulted in lasting inspirations that are another legacy of this remarkable age. I have dealt with such matters and others in some detail in *Augustan Culture* (1996) and, therefore, see no need for a repeat, even if updated ("with consideration of the bibliography that has appeared since 1995," of course). In fact, several (well-meaning) friends, colleagues, and publishers asked why I would undertake the present volume – had I not covered the subject already? The answer is easy: as I said at the time, the book was meant to be an introduction (even if it ran to 474 pages) and not an exhaustive, let alone definitive (as if there were such a thing), treatment. There are so many different ways to look at the Augustan age, and there were (and still are) plenty of aspects left for discussion. Even Syme, whose *Roman Revolution* was a hundred pages longer, never intended his book to be the last word, although admiring epigones assiduously tried to award it that status. Instead, Syme would always stress that "there is work to be done." The maxim would have pleased Augustus.

PART I

POLITICAL HISTORY

I: AUGUSTUS AND THE POWER OF TRADITION

Walter Eder

(Translated by *Karl Galinsky*)

REPUBLICAN OR MONARCH?

When Augustus on his deathbed pointedly asked whether he had played the "farce of life" (*mimum vitae*; Suet., *Aug.* 99) well and asked for applause, he did not say what role he had in mind. Was it that of world ruler and *imperator*, who more than any Roman before him had enlarged and secured the boundaries of the Roman empire? Or did he want to be applauded as "prince of peace," who after the turmoil of protracted civil wars brought the Romans the calm of the *Pax Augusta*? Did he think of his efforts on behalf of morality and religion or of his reputation as "Father of his Country" (*pater patriae*) and his unceasing care for peace, liberty, and prosperity of his "children"? But there was one thing he surely did not mean: the role of a monarch.

True, he had never restricted himself to the role of "Grey Eminence," content with operating in the background. Rather, he always sought recognition for his accomplishments and assiduously saw to raising his and his family's profile in both Rome and the provinces through the media of architecture, literature, and art. At the same time, he had also renounced all insignia of personal power: no scepter, no diadem, nor the golden crown and purple toga of his adoptive father. He knew well that as son of the deified Caesar and as Augustus ("The Revered One") he was endowed with a special aura and that his military, political, and financial resources elevated him beyond the reach of his fellow citizens. The more evident, however, his power became in the state during the fifty-seven years of his rule, the more resolutely he opposed the appearance of being a monarch.

It is not only the much cited next to the last chapter of the account of his deeds, the *Res Gestae*, that attests his political moderation when Augustus programmatically makes the point that he possessed no more official power (*potestas*) than his colleagues in the magistracy (*RG* 34). Even more significant are the numerous passages where Augustus lists carefully everything he had renounced: he refused several triumphs (*RG* 4) and the dictatorship, which the Senate and the People offered him in 22 B.C., and he rejected the offer to become consul for life (*RG* 5). No less than three times, in 19, 18, and 11 B.C., did Augustus not follow the unanimous wish of Senate and People to be appointed sole and plenipotentiary guardian of law and order (*RG* 6: *curator legum et morum summa potestate solus*). The reason, he states, is that he would not "accept any office inconsistent with the custom of our ancestors" (*contra morem maiorum*) and, therefore, not fitting for a republic or, for that matter, his republic (*RG* 6). Similarly, he declined (*recusavi*) the offer of the people to become *pontifex maximus* while the incumbent, Lepidus, was still alive (*RG* 10). Further, he refused to have his name immortalized on the Capitoline Temple and the Theater of Pompey although he had restored both at great cost (*RG* 20), and he purchased the land for his forum and the Theater of Marcellus in a regular way instead of simply confiscating it (*RG* 21). Finally, he declined to accept the "gold for crowns" (*aurum coronarium*) which the Roman citizens of Italy had offered him (*RG* 21) and he emphasizes that he organized only four games (*ludi*) in his own name in contrast to twenty-three for others (*RG* 22).

This long list of *res non gestae* ("deeds not done") in the *Res Gestae* could serve only to profile the *princeps* as the incorruptible guardian of tradition who took care, even against the will of Senate and People, not to contradict the constitution of the fathers. Should Augustus have been the only one not to see that "Rome was generally accepting of an autocrat" and the monarchy needed neither being masked nor "the semblance of a republican façade" (Zanker, 1988)? Didn't his subjects, who were supposedly hungry for a monarchy, have to be rather disappointed when it became clear to them that the author of the *Res Gestae*, which were exhibited in front of his huge Mausoleum on the Campus Martius, began with the "liberation of the republic from the tyranny of a faction" (*RG* 1) and ended with the transfer of his power to the Roman Senate and People (*RG* 34), and clearly wanted to be remembered as a great statesman in the tradition of the old *res publica*? Some monarch indeed!

Surely, a state cannot be simply regarded as "republic" because its most powerful man does not want to look like a monarch. For the same reason, however, we should hesitate to characterize the *res publica* of Augustus as "monarchy." It is noticeable that the ancient historians tend to speak of a monarchy the further removed they are from Augustus' own times. Two hundred years later it was clear to Cassius Dio that after Actium (31 B.C.) one could consider Augustus' rule as a *monarchia*. For Suetonius and Plutarch, Augustus was already the second monarch, Julius Caesar leading the way. Tacitus strikes more of balance when he connects the first *princeps* with the dominating ruler personalities of the declining Republic. Even while he does not share this view, he shows some understanding why Augustus' contemporaries might not have needed at all to feel they were living under autocratic rule. He respects as "insightful" (*prudentes*) both those who argued that Augustus did not rule as a king or dictator, but as *princeps* reestablished the *res publica* as a state of laws, and those who trashed his character and left no doubt about his "lust for domination" (*cupido dominandi*; *Ann.* 1.9–10). That Tiberius' "court historian," Velleius Paterculus, cannot detect unrepublican behavior in Augustus and Tiberius is unsurprising. More telling is the absence of any indication in the work of Livy, Augustus' contemporary and "republic specialist," that there was a new departure.

Augustus himself refused to denote the new state of affairs (*novus status*), which he considered to be *optimus status*, with a uniform name, nor did his contemporaries search for a label from the repertory of known forms of government. They found it all the easier not to do so because the spectrum of what could be considered "republican" had always been extraordinarily wide. The reason was that the Roman Republic in its heyday was based on the consensus of the powerful and boiled down to a system of traditional concepts and principles that could be adapted time and again to changing realities. The Republic derived its stability not from legal norms, but from a balance of societal power, namely the calibrated cooperation between Senate, People, and magistrates. It was a balance that constantly renewed itself through the social dynamics of *clientela* and *amicitia*, and not on the basis of rigid legal norms. The situation changed during the second century B.C. when the consensus on political guidelines and standards started eroding and *mores* (customs) were increasingly being replaced by *leges* (laws), but this did not change the flexible conceptualization of the constitution. On the contrary, the gradual identification of *mores* and *leges*, clearly evidenced by Cicero's treatise *On Laws*, made it easier during the crisis of the Republic to incorporate even substantive governmental changes into the republican tradition so long as they were based on formal "legal" models and the authority of an individual could be justified by the function of his accomplishments for the *res publica*.

Augustus capitalized on this by insisting on his *auctoritas* (Galinsky, 1996, 10–41). For this power, which was both concrete and creative, least disturbed the formal constitutional structure of the *res publica*. His contemporaries, however, well recognized the unique character of the epoch, which could be neither a "republic" because of the extraordinary *auctoritas* of the *princeps* nor, according to the will of this very *princeps*, a monarchy. Hence their name for it, *Saeculum Augustum* ("the Augustan Century"), though not *Saeculum Augusti* ("The Century of Augustus") pointed forward by suggesting the novelty of this "august age" and, at the same time, looked back to a blessed past that was being revived in the golden age, *aurea saecula*, of the present.

Similar perspectives informed the work of the two most astute modern scholars of the period, Theodor Mommsen and Ronald Syme. Mommsen recognized the special character of the new order, for which he coined the term "principate." He tried to do justice to its peculiarity from the perspective of constitutional law, with the term "dyarchy," that is, rule by two, so as to identify the juxtaposition of Senate and *princeps*, whom he saw in the role of both magistrate and "trustee of the community." In this way he (re)connected the principate formally with the Republic while acknowledging its new character. Syme, too, stayed with the term "principate" ("To be sure, the State was organized under a principate – no dictatorship or monarchy"; Syme, 1939, 516). According to him, the special character of the period was that "the principate, though absolute, was not arbitrary. It derived from consent and delegation; it was founded upon the laws" (Syme, 1939, 516). To Syme, the connection with the Republic was evident in the way Octavian/Augustus ascended to power. He made his way with a clique of "adherents and partisans" and this "composition of the oligarchy of the government" constituted "the binding link between Republic and Empire" (Syme, 1939, vii). It stands to reason, however, that the method would also affect the result, that is, the Augustan principate, and we therefore can view the principate, in accordance with Syme's logic, as binding link between republic and monarchy.

The special character of this transitional epoch stands out most clearly when we, like Syme, change the perspective: we must not view the principate in retrospect as a finished product or "system" whose "republican" and "monarchic" components need to be painstakingly analyzed. Rather, and this is the principal theme of this chapter, we must look at the road that the creator of this multifaceted social and political order had to take. No doubt, ever since his adoption the young Octavian had two firm goals of which he never lost sight: to assume, like his father, the dominating position in the state and hold on to it, and nevertheless not come to the same end as his father. That road, however, was by no means clear. The fact that he finally did reach both goals gives rise, in retrospect, to the deceptive impression that a predetermined road map existed. Most details, however, could not be planned in advance because the principate, to quote Rilke, was formed "growing out of plans, but not planned." From the start, Octavian had to slip into many roles. Hardly ever was he able to choose one freely, but he had to react to conditions that were often not of his own making. Often enough chance was his helper − call it luck, if you will − but he always knew how to use changing political constellations with the assurance of genius and, often, ruthlessness. He was a master at coping with contingencies. But we can recognize an abiding component of his actions: his respect of the power of republican traditions. He recognized their importance at the latest after his first, and failed, attempt to gain power by marching on Rome like his father. Moreover, he viewed these traditions not as an obstacle but an opportunity.

Augustus himself singles out the two spheres of action where he followed tradition. He does so in the two final and culminating chapters of the *Res Gestae*, which were meant as a summation. In Chapter 34, he refers to the reconstitution of the *res publica* as a state governed by laws with particular emphasis on the equal *potestas* of all magistrates, and in Chapter 35 he proudly proclaims his acclamation, on the basis of the broadest possible consensus, as *pater patriae* and, therefore, the change from *res publica* to fatherland (*patria*). "State governed by laws" and "Fatherland" certainly were not altruistic goals of Octavian but means to the end of winning and securing his personal power. The means, however, could fulfill the end only if they were used with continuity and conviction and made the "republican" position of the creator of order seem credible. Nor did Augustus pursue these goals simultaneously and with equal intensity. During the first phase, he focused primarily on the value of formally restoring republican institutions within whose frame-work room was left for a powerful individual. During the second phase he left this formal level and created the idea of a fatherland in which the legacy of the past was fused with patriotic pride in the present. The divide between the two phases comes approximately around 19 B.C., when the last gap in the *princeps'* formal constitutional capacities was closed by the conferment of the *imperium consulare*, the wide range of consular powers, without Augustus' actually having to hold that office.

FROM HIGH TREASON TO LEGAL GOVERNMENT

This happy end could not have been foreseen by him or his contemporaries. The nineteen-year-old Octavian showed little sympathy for the rules of the *res publica* when he recruited on his own initiative an army from Caesar's former legionnaires, confiscated the tax revenues from the province of Asia with no justification whatever, and marched on Rome in a state of high treason. His first speech in Rome, in an assembly convened by a friendly tribune of the people, gave no premonition of anything good. The message that he wanted to liberate the state from the tyranny of Antony and, at the same time, "to strive for the honors of my father" (Cicero, *Att.* 16.16.3) was contradictory and showed little political savvy. How could this Caesar wannabe, who held no office, possibly succeed against Antony, the incumbent consul and Caesar's loyal follower, and even save the Republic?

Once, however, Octavian had decided – against the advice from several friends – to accept Caesar's testament the only escape that was left was to the front. Antony was a dangerous opponent. He had not hesitated to eliminate an alleged son of Marius who had become popular with the people after Caesar's death, and Octavian had good reason to fear Antony might inflict the same fate on him. It did not help him much that Antony was generally unpopular because of his maneuvering between Caesarians and Caesar murderers. Octavian did not command the allegiance of credible Republican eminences either. It was, therefore, a special stroke of luck when Cicero, after long hesitation, yielded to Octavian's urging: Cicero was able to move the Senate to award the youngster an official military command (*imperium pro praetore*) and thus rid him of the odium of high treason, admit him to the Senate and grant him special privileges for candidacy for higher office. By integrating Octavian, Cicero saw an opportunity to give the Senate a sword in its fight with Antony. The elder statesman's notion, however, that he would be able to guide the young man with his republican spirit and vouch for his good "republican" behavior turned out to be a complete illusion. Rather, Octavian's actual military power was the driving force behind the developments. On the other hand, the attentive young man could not fail to recognize the opportunities that the traditionally flexible boundaries of the republican constitution could offer an ambitious political climber. This epiphany, then, had probably more to do with the nature of the constitution than with Cicero, and it pointed to a possible way for Octavian's political future. He never again reiterated his goal to attain the honors of his father. Nor could he forget that his *imperium pro praetore*, which Cicero justified with examples of youthful heroes of the Republic (Scipio Africanus, Flamininus, and Pompey), became the springboard for his career. It led to his first acclamation as *imperator* and, with some pressure from his soldiers, the consulate, which put him in a position to force Antony to make him a partner in the triumvirate with Lepidus (end of 43 B.C.).

That still left him far removed from the power he dreamed to seize. He was the lowliest member of the triumvirate and his task to find lands for veterans in Italy was a quick way to make enemies because of widespread expulsions and confiscations. His weak role at the battle of Philippi (42 B.C.) was not apt to increase his standing. Further, Antony's wife and brother capitalized on the tensions between the triumvirs and the disturbances in Italy by attempting to cut out Octavian altogether (Perusine War, 41–40 B.C.). Here, however, Octavian asserted himself with such merciless methods – after the town fell, he supposedly butchered its ruling council and 300 senators at the altar of his recently deified father – that war threatened to break out between him and Antony. Only the refusal of their soldiers to fight each other forced the Treaty of Brundisium (fall 40 B.C.). It superficially divided the spheres of interest between Antony in the East and Octavian in the West. In reality, however, and despite the marriage of Octavian's sister Octavia (cf. Chapter 9 by Diana Kleiner, this volume), the lines were drawn even more sharply than before.

Octavian, who from 38 B.C. (and maybe 40 B.C.) appropriated the title "Imperator" as his first name (*praenomen imperatoris*) and thus, as Imperator Caesar, referred to his only dynastic legitimation, was sole ruler not even in the West. He had to put up with Lepidus in Africa and acknowledge Sextus Pompey's dominion over Sicily, Sardinia, Corsica, and the Peloponnese in the Treaty of Misenum (39 B.C.) after Pompey's son had blockaded Italy and caused a famine. Only after Antony withdrew his protection from this antagonist because he urgently needed troops from Octavian for his Parthian campaign was Sextus' fate sealed. In the Treaty of Tarentum (37 B.C.) Antony supplied 120 ships for the fight against Sextus Pompey and received the promise, which Octavian never kept, that 20,000 soldiers would be sent.

Even before his victory over Sextus Pompey the junior triumvir, who up to now had broken treaties and shown utter ruthlessness, displayed surprising sensibilities for republican legality: he insisted that the assembly (*comitia*) in Rome officially ratify the extension of triumviral power that had been agreed on privately in the Treaty of Tarentum; and he alone, not Antony, henceforth called himself correctly *triumvir iterum* ("triumvir for a second time"). His endeavor to rid himself of the accusation of being an autocrat became even clearer after his victory in 36 B.C. He proclaimed that the civil wars had ended and his readiness to give up his power as triumvir if Antony did the same; Antony did not accept that offer. At the same time, he arranged it so that Lepidus, who had tried to claim Sicily for himself, was stripped of his triumviral powers by the correct formality of a *lex de imperio abrogando*, though he allowed him to retain the post of *pontifex maximus*. He proceeded pointedly to restore law and order in Italy: taxes were remitted; slaves in Sextus Pompey's army were returned to their masters or, if that proved impossible, crucified, but they were not made loyal clients of Octavian, despite a precedent under Sulla; banditry, which had increased due to confiscations and proscriptions, was eliminated; and 20,000 veterans were discharged and settled in Italy, this time without expropriating the original owners.

A return to the constitution of the Republic seemed feasible. That it did not materialize was due to Antony who – without divorcing Octavia – threw himself into the arms of the foreign queen Cleopatra. The following years had to show who was the better Roman. The heir of Caesar changed from ruthless powermonger to defender of Roman ideals and protector of Rome in the imminent conflict with the powers of evil in the East, Antony and Cleopatra. The construction of the Apollo Temple of the Palatine, begun in 36 B.C., could be interpreted as profiling the Julian family but also as rejection of Antony's oriental and Dionysiac affectations. And one did not have to leave it at allusions because Antony's actions provided enough grist for Octavian's mills. Antony's plan for reordering the East was based on the traditional system of client states under Roman supremacy, but his investiture of Cleopatra as "Queen of queens" and of her children as regents in parts of the Roman empire could with ease be propagandistically distorted into "donations" and thus as robbery of Roman possessions.

The struggle for Rome had begun as Octavian's representing himself as guardian of Rome started having an impact on his opponents. In the best Republican tradition, generals who were closer to Antony than Octavian began to adorn the city with spoils from their triumphs:

Pollio restored the Atrium Libertatis and established in it the first public library; Sosius began the construction of another Apollo Temple; and Ahenobarbus even repaired a temple of Neptune, the protective deity of Sextus Pompey. But everyone's worst suspicions seemed to be confirmed when Antony celebrated his triumph over the Parthians not on the Capitoline in Rome, but with foreign customs in Alexandria, and recognized his children with Cleopatra as legitimate. When he went on to proclaim Caesar's and Cleopatra's son Caesarion (officially: Ptolemy XV Kaisar) as the legitimate heir of the Deified Julius and thereby weakened the legitimacy of "Imperator Caesar" the final conflict between the triumvirs seemed inevitable.

Neither of the two, however, pounced immediately. Octavian, at the onset of second consulate in January of 33 B.C., attacked Antony vitriolically and Antony answered with some heavy accusations of his own, but a propaganda war was the only outcome. Besides, Octavian found himself in a favorable situation in early 33 B.C.: while still in possession of his triumviral *potestas* he was basking in the fresh glory of military successes in Illyria, whereas Antony's Parthian triumph could be downplayed as undeserved and un-Roman. Surprisingly, Octavian's friend Agrippa agreed to hold the office of aedile, a step down from his former consulship, and did not spare his private resources to restore the aqueducts to working order, build a new one, care for their upkeep, and organize lavish games during which he did not stint with distributions of money and foodstuffs to hundreds of thousands of citizens. What were the plans? In early 32 B.C., however, the situation seemed to reverse itself: it now was the (absent) Octavian who came under heavy attack in the Senate, especially from Sosius, who was consul that year and Antony's partisan. Sosius drew especially on a letter from Antony, whom he praised extravagantly. He did not, however, actually read from the letter and, in a later session of the Senate, did not yield to Octavian's urging to do so. Octavian, in turn, answered with sharp accusations against Antony and Cleopatra and offered to present evidence in another session.

For the moment that remained an empty threat. The consuls and some 300 senators hurriedly made for Ephesus to join Antony, but the muddle cleared only a few months later when two close allies of Antony changed sides and informed Octavian that Antony's will was being kept by the Vestals. Seizing this testament was an enormous breach of law, a relapse into the worst days of Octavian's beginnings. But just the few excerpts that were read out aloud in the Senate appeared to justify the deed because they confirmed the rumors about the *fatale monstrum*

Cleopatra (Horace, *Odes* 1.37.21), who had cast her spell over Antony and was soon going to rule over Rome with him. Now things happened in quick succession: the Senate cancelled all of Antony's powers; all of Italy demanded Octavian as a leader in the war and swore – voluntarily, it was alleged – an oath of allegiance, with the western provinces joining in (*RG* 25); and the protector of the Roman west stepped up to confront the danger from the East, ostentatiously declaring war on Cleopatra as fetial priest by reviving the almost forgotten ritual of tossing a spear into the symbolic "enemy ground" near the Temple of Bellona. Of course the war was aimed at Antony, but it could not be presented as civil war.

Enough questions remain. Why did Octavian in his pursuit to declare war leave himself at the mercy of a mere accident that played the testament of his adversary into his hands? Why didn't he simply start the war by deploying his legions while Antony had already begun to transfer his troops to Greece? His soldiers and veterans had followed him when he was an illegitimate warlord, procured his first consulate for him, and most recently lent their help with the "voluntary" oath of allegiance in Italy. Couldn't they be expected to follow him now?

It is certain that Octavian did not have formal triumviral *potestas* since the beginning of 32 B.C. That, however, does not explain anything because the same was true of Antony, who did not hesitate to lead his troops against Italy, and we can hardly assume that veterans and soldiers in the West thought along more "legalistic" lines than their counterparts in the East. The problem becomes even more complicated when one follows the plausible assumption that Octavian after 33 B.C. was definitely not without *imperium*. The main reason is that he was granted *imperium* for his campaigns in Illyria, which he finished in 34 B.C., and he did not have to relinquish it until he celebrated his triumph in 29 B.C. (Girardet, 1990). In that case, we cannot interpret Octavian's being seated between the two consuls in 32 B.C. as the coup of a *privatus* without *imperium* and *potestas*. And that raises the question all the more urgently: Why did Octavian not force the necessary declarations of war from the Senate just as he had done in the case of his consulate ten years earlier? Had his sense of obligation to act as guardian of Roman culture and, therefore, its traditions reached the point that he could not pull back from his role as savior of the "Republic" without losing credibility?

There cannot be a definite answer to that in view of the inseparable mix of propaganda and tactics that characterized these years. It is telling, however, that after the victory over Antony, when Octavian literally was *mon-archos*, sole ruler, and not constrained by tactical reasons to play the role of staunch Roman and Republican, he did everything he could to emphasize exactly this role in order to make people forget the time before Actium. The power struggle between Antony and Octavian had been decided, but now the real difficulty arose: who was going to rule Rome, the victor or the Senate and the People. Like his father, Augustus was "in complete control of all affairs" (*RG* 34). Because he did not, however, want to share his father's fate, he decided seemingly to share the power: the Senate and People were to decide who from now on would rule res *publica* and empire and what role in all this would be granted to the savior of liberty.

Therefore the period between his triumphal reception in Rome (mid-29 B.C.) until the resignation of his comprehensive powers on January 13, 27 B.C. was shaped by his effort to return to an ordered state of affairs. Even before then, in 29 B.C., Octavian had the Temple of Janus closed, solemnly promised a policy of peace, and backed it up by the discharge of many soldiers and the return of the province of Asia to the Senate. In the same year he paid out 400 sesterces each to 250,000 citizens and 1,000 sesterces each to 120,000 veterans in the colonies. Simultaneously he spent 700 million sesterces for purchasing land for his soldiers and thereby distanced himself programmatically from the hateful method of confiscation. The expenditures for the restoration of 82 temples and the costs of games celebrating his victory also were incurred during that year and the next. In sum: with a total of about one billion sesterces he had proven that he cared for the people of Rome and was serious about his "disarmament policy" and his respect for the ancient gods of Rome or, in a different view, had tried to buy his recognition as First Citizen and greatest benefactor.

In 28 B.C., Octavian moved away from his "Octavianic" phase by drawing even closer to Republican norms. He had eighty silver statues that were dedicated to him melted down, made his name gradually disappear, and stopped using his special powers. He shared his sixth consulate with his colleague Agrippa who was granted the same number of *fasces*, twelve. Agrippa also was his colleague as censor when more than 4 million citizens were counted. The uncertainty among new citizens and supporters of Antony came to an end, and the citizenry was constituted anew. A first cautious *lectio senatus* ("scrutiny of the Senate") rid that body, which numbered about 1,000, of some 200 unworthy and insignificant members and raised its prestige. The end of the year saw the emphatic end of this chapter as Octavian declared all unconstitutional acts from his triumviral period as invalid (Dio 53.2.5; Tacitus, *Ann.* 3.28.3) and proclaimed on a gold coin (*aureus*) that he restored law and justice to the Romans (LEGES ET IURA P[opulo]

R[omano] RESTITUIT; Plate I). That meant the laws of the old Republic. He struck the same note when he emphasized later that he avenged Caesar's murder "through tribunals established by law" (*RG* 2) and that "exemplary practices of our ancestors which were disappearing in our time were brought back into use by new laws passed on my proposal" (*RG* 8; transl. Brunt-Moore). Evidently he wanted the *res publica* to be understood as a state governed by laws and not as a state in which the word of the *princeps* simply was law.

But where in this republican, if not Republican, environment was there a place for the *de facto* ruler of the Roman world? In the famous Senate meeting of Jan. 13, 27 B.C., in his seventh consulate, Octavian staged the solemn ceremony of his return to the state of laws. He renounced all remaining powers and left the decision about the future shape of the *res publica* to the Senate and People of Rome. Formally, the senate was the arbiter of the exercise of power, but its decision was not free; in actuality the power remained with Augustus, who was inundated with honors, yet more was involved than a mere usurpation. At a superficial glance, the Senate now was enabled, as before, to decide on awarding honors and special powers and on the allocation of provinces. After years of protracted civil war this was certainly not business as usual, nor was it unusual business. We would be wrong to dismiss all this as a pure formality because form was a decisive element in the late Republic. With the exception of some unusual honors everything remained within the Republican framework. The award of the honorific name "Augustus" was truly unique as it approximated its bearer to Romulus, famous for his *augurium* at the city's foundation, and elevated him above human norms, but after all, one was dealing for the first time with the son of a *divus*. Other departures were the affixing of Apolline laurels to his private residence and the award of the golden shield and its display in the Curia, but the words inscribed on it – *virtus, pietas, clementia,* and *iustitia* – were strongly reminiscent of traditional values. Finally, the conferment of the *corona civica* ("civic crown") in grateful recognition of saving the citizens from deadly peril was completely in the Republican tradition.

Similarly, even a republic-minded senator could get along with the division of the provinces. About half of the empire, including the granary of Africa and the strategically important provinces of Illyria and Macedonia with their several legions, remained in the hands of Senate and People, keeping Augustus from a military monopoly. Moreover, it had been customary since Pompey to grant, at times, immense military empowerments to outstanding individuals in order to secure peace in the empire. Finally, it was not alien to republican thinking to give members of the upper classes the opportunity to demonstrate their achievements for the *res publica* with a conspicuous display of military might or pomp and thus to confirm their special *dignitas*. So long as Augustus kept to republican precedents like Pompey and Caesar in the administration of his provinces through *legati* of consular or praetorian rank and one could see his powers as emanating from the *imperium* he held as the annually elected consul one could easily imagine that one was living in a republic.

There was only one problem: Augustus' continuous tenure of the consulate. More was involved than a blemish that contradicted the principle of annual change. Rather, the condition hindered the work of the Senate, which felt unsure of its footing especially when this permanent consul, who possessed paramount *auctoritas*, was absent from Rome. And it irritated the *nobiles* because the blockade of the position led to a logjam of potential candidates. Upon his return in 24 B.C., Augustus, who since the end of 27 B.C. had campaigned in Spain and Gaul, carefully undertook to optimize the compromise of 27 B.C. Money flowed again, as it had during Agrippa's aedileship in 33 B.C. and the years preceding the reconstitution of his powers in 27. Once more he paid out 400 sesterces each to 250,000 citizens, followed by extensive distributions of grain and oil. In a smartly designed scenario a proven Republican was to be elected as Augustus' consular colleague, and in the following year Augustus was to retire completely from the consulate. The first step succeeded. Piso, Augustus' favorite Republican, who must have known all about these plans, was duly elected consul for 23 B.C. But then Augustus fell gravely ill.

On his supposed deathbed he showed himself as a Republican. He handed over all his official papers to his co-consul Piso and his signet ring to Agrippa. His nephew Marcellus, the putative successor, came away empty-handed. There was no better way for Augustus to demonstrate that he knew and shared the opinions and concerns of the *nobiles* (Badian 1982). We can suspect Augustus the actor behind all this, but we cannot overlook the fact that Augustus emphatically conducted himself as "republican" especially when that mask was of little use to him, for example, near death in 23 B.C. and after his death by means of the *Res Gestae*. Why would a monarch want to go down in history as the savior of the Republic, especially since a way had been found that assured him plentiful recognition of his special achievements in the *res publica*?

To everyone's surprise, Augustus recovered. He gave up the consulate and held it only twice more, in 5 and 2 B.C. As a substitute he received a military command with a time limit. That was the "greater" (*maius*) *imperium proconsulare*, and Augustus evidently was interested in not making its renewal not appear as a matter of course. And he made sure he was in Rome when it came up for renewal and prepared for it in 13 B.C. by lavish donations to the veterans.

A second pillar of his power was, since 23 B.C., the full power of the tribune of the people (*tribunicia potestas*) and, in particular, the right to call the people's assembly and the Senate into session and introduce legislation (*ius cum plebe agendi, ius cum senatu agendi*). Augustus thereby was given back powers that he had relinquished with the consulate. The *tribunicia potestas* became the core of the principate. Augustus listed it permanently in his official title from 22 B.C. and used it to count his years of service. Paradoxically, it was exactly his exercise of this *potestas* that was in most open contradiction with tradition. The office was rarely held by patricians and the separation of the office and its powers was unprecedented. Repeated tenure of the tribunate was identified in the Republic with a cardinal, anti-republican sin, *adfectatio regni* ("striving for kingship"), even if Augustus could argue that he was not actually holding that office. At the same time, the tribunate had never enjoyed special prestige among the *nobiles* and seemed superfluous to many. Only later observers, like Tacitus, may have realized that more was involved here than currying favor.

The resulting compromise appeared brilliant but was not without its dangers. Augustus had deliberately draped himself in a republican mantle, and because he needed to protect it, he could not damage it but had to give it permanent luster. But this radiance could dazzle and make the mantle appear more important than the wearer. A superficial look at this institutional arrangement could raise the illusion that one could manage without a *princeps*. Further, the years following 23 B.C. gave rise to the concern that Augustus, by giving up all offices, had taken one step too far back into the Republic: the machinery of the *res publica* proved not to be up to the task. A famine in 22 B.C. even led to the demand by the urban plebs that Augustus should become dictator in order to take charge of the grain supply. Augustus theatrically refused this request when he felt the Senate's opposition. Instead, like Pompey, he took over the care for the grain supply (*cura annonae*) by virtue of his proconsular *imperium* and ended the crisis with suspicious speed.

In 21 B.C., Augustus went to the East. The following years reminded Rome of the good and bad days of the Republic: even before his departure Augustus had arranged for the election of two censors, the first election in twenty years. Governors of the province of Africa celebrated triumphs in 21 and 19 B.C. and maximized this opportunity of splendid self-display for *nobiles*. And Augustus returned two of his provinces to the senate. The two censors, however, started quarrelling, and the attempt of Egnatius Rufus, who was very popular with the people, to be elected consul, contrary to all rules, immediately after his praetorship led to major disturbances. The Republic was still very much alive, but it was the Republic of Clodius to which nobody wished to return. Despite repeated entreaties, Augustus hesitated for a long time to interfere – too long, in fact, not to be suspected to have risked the escalation of the troubles deliberately in order to remind especially the *nobiles* that the new order of the *res publica* needed him. He therefore could count on widespread acceptance when, decked out in the glory of the military standards returned by the Parthians, he reestablished order with a strong hand. Egnatius was accused of conspiracy and executed. The grant of an *imperium consulare* for life supplemented the settlements of 23 B.C. and thereby closed the last gap in his powers that was caused by his abdication of the consulate.

After these corrections Augustus had found his final place in a *res publica* that was formed as a state governed by laws. He got everything without having to give up anything. Formally speaking, Augustus in 19 B.C. was, just as in 44 B.C., a *privatus* without an office and with a great army, but now he was situated in a *res publica* whose political mechanisms were overshadowed by his *auctoritas*. The question remained: was the idea of a state grounded in laws enough in the long term to make this superior *auctoritas* bearable?

THE ROAD TO THE FATHERLAND

Augustus did not trust this state of affairs, however tranquil it appeared to be. Proving himself as savior in crises which he connived at or even manufactured was not a means, repeatable at will, for proving his indispensable *auctoritas*; people's confidence in his power and his acceptance by all could easily vanish in the process. Hence Augustus looked for a way to continue remaining at the center and yet to deflect from his own personality. He outlines the result in the concluding chapter of the *Res Gestae* (35) that reports on his proclamation as *pater patriae* in 2 B.C.: "The senate and the equestrian order and the whole (*universus*) people of Rome gave me the title of Father of my Country." Here Augustus deliberately deviates from the formula "The Roman Senate and People" (SPQR) by listing the equestrian order besides the Senate and by characterizing the *populus Romanus* as *universus*. With this the distance between upper and lower strata stays intact, but the mention of the equestrian order as the middle link effaces the harsh divisions within the sociopolitical structure and makes all Romans appear as members of a *populus Romanus universus*. To all of them Augustus had given not only the cold shell of a *res publica* founded on laws but the security of a fatherland.

The proclamation as *pater patriae* marks the terminus of the road to the common fatherland. The various stages of this journey, however, stand out less distinctly than the steps he took during the first phase, the process of his integration into the *res publica*. That is only natural as ideologies take shape beneath the surface and develop their effectiveness precisely because convictions and feelings tend to present themselves almost of their own accord. But after 19 B.C. we can uncover some tendencies in the *princeps'* behavior that point in a new direction. Whereas he had undertaken a conspicuous building program in the 30s and 20s to demonstrate his palpable connection with the city of Rome and had converted the city into the impressive capital of world empire (cf. Diane Favro's Chapter 10, this volume), he now increasingly showed concern for the morals of the Romans and their *Romanitas*. Already as censor in 19 B.C. he tried, by invoking time-honored Roman models, to curb ostentatious displays of luxury. In the following year he intruded deeply on the private lives especially of the upper classes by passing old-fashioned laws regulating marriage and morals, and he held to them despite only modest success. The lavish Secular Games of 17 B.C. clearly signaled his aim to meld the *populus Romanus* with the *domus Augusta* into one family. In an intricately thought-out scenario Augustus combined, with the participation of all social orders and strata, the great past of Rome with expectation of a happy future. In the prayer to the Fates (*Moirai*) he linked the fate of the Romans, whom he always names first, with his own (*CIL* VI 32323). The symbolic intensification of the myth of the state continued in 16 B.C. with the restoration of the Temple of Quirinus, the deified Romulus.

Thereafter the signals grow less distinct. His election as *pontifex maximus* after Lepidus' death in 12 B.C. could not be planned, but Augustus used the occasion adroitly to show off the general respect in which he was held in Italy and to combine his position as *pater familias* with the official task as guardian of the traditional Roman religion.

From that time the eternal fire of the Hearth of the State, symbolized by the goddess Vesta, was kept burning under Livia's supervision in a part of his house, which he had declared to be public property. In the pictorial program of the Ara Pacis, dedicated in 9 B.C. (see Chapter 9 by Diana Kleiner, this volume), he once more takes up the theme of the unity of Rome, Italy, and his person, and at about the same time he appears, by means of the representation of the *genius Augusti*, as collective *pater familias* on the numerous shrines of the Lares throughout Rome. The step from *patronus* to *pater patriae* was only a question of being properly staged at Rome; outside of Rome that step had been taken since 5 B.C. at the latest (Strothmann, 2000, 183f.).

On February 5 of 2 B.C., the festival of Concordia, this process that had been in the works for many years, reached its carefully arranged finale with the dedication of the Forum Augustum. Immediately adjacent to the forum of Augustus' deified father and with the Temple of Mars Ultor towering over it, the sculptural world of the Forum demonstrated the achievements of the Roman people through the statues of its distinguished ancestors (*summi viri*) and the sublime ancestry of Augustus' family. Both these strands converged in the honorific monument, voted to him by the Senate, which stood in front of the temple. As in a huge Lararium, the ancestors of the Romans shared a splendid ambience with the ancestors of their *pater*, just as he shared the *patria* with his fellow citizens. As has been correctly observed (Zanker, 1988), this world of images was definitely worthy of a monarchy, but it was not intended to embellish and celebrate a monarchy. Rather, it was to highlight the majesty of Rome and her greatness that had been for centuries in the making, and to promote civic consciousness and patriotism. That explains the "autonomous" process of the willing acceptance and spread of a supposedly monarchic program (Zanker, 1988): it was not a yearning for a monarch that drove this development but the natural readiness for patriotic pride.

Augustus himself points us in that direction. By making the title *pater patriae* the crowning finale of the *Res Gestae*, he points to the decisive importance he wants us to attach to the title and the idea behind it: he had arrived at the peak of his *auctoritas* because he had transcended the state of mere laws with an ideology of patriotism and thereby had ensured acceptance for himself on a higher level. This creation of a Roman patriotism was to be considered his real achievement. A Roman self-consciousness, the myth of the state, was to characterize people's existence and obviate unwelcome questions about the legal role of the *princeps*. This is also indicated by Augustus' expressly calling for a national consciousness of Roman values, as reported by Suetonius (*Aug.* 40, transl. Graves):

> Augustus thought it most important not to let the native Roman stock be tainted with foreign or servile blood, and was therefore very unwilling to create new Roman citizens, or to permit the manumission of more than a limited number of slaves. . . . Augustus set himself to revive the ancient Roman dress and once, on seeing a group of men in dark cloaks among the crowd, quoted Vergil [*Aen.* 1. 282] indignantly: "Behold the conquerors of the world, all clad in Roman gowns!" and instructed the aediles that no one should ever again be admitted to the Forum, or its environs, unless he wore a toga and no cloak.

With this, solidarity, if not uniformity, was emphasized on the home front and, at the same time, so was demarcation from the world on the outside. It was every Roman's calling to rule over that world because this was the traditional task of a superior people:

> tu regere imperio populos, Romane, memento!
> Roman, remember by your strength to rule the earth's peoples!
> (Vergil, *Aen.* 6.851)

All Romans could identify with this task even if they left the actual governing to the *princeps*. After all, the Senate and the toga-clad People had commissioned him to do so. The nation of Romulus, *gens Romula*, was special because its guardian (*custos*) was someone special. Commingled in this concept of "We, the People," which united the most powerful and the least significant *civis Romanus*, were, as in any patriotic ideology, parasitic claims to the achievements, past and present, of great ancestors along with the conviction that as a contemporary Roman, however minimal one's own contributions, one came to share in their achievements.

The endeavor to have as many citizens as possible participate in the life of the *princeps* and the state was a common feature of Augustus' religious policy, his building program, and his support of the arts. None of these aspects can be neatly separated from the other during this second phase. Augustus was visible everywhere, but he did not impose. While his house on the Palatine stood between the hut of Romulus and the

Temple of Apollo, it remained modest. Augustus was a member of all venerable priestly brotherhoods (*sodalitates*), but he took his place beside the descendants of Rome's most important families; in the procession on the Ara Pacis he does not tower over his entourage (Fig. 28). In the Forum Romanum he set some clear architectural accents, but he showed consideration for prior structures. In numerous corners of the city the shrines of the Lares at the crossroads (*Lares compitales*), many of which were embellished by Augustus, attested the presence of the *princeps* through his *genius* rather than by his representation as a ruler. In literature, too, a concept of Roman culture comes to the fore that is removed from its political ambience and from any glorification of personal power. The object of that pride is Rome.

The final words of the *Res Gestae* were chosen well. They were directed at the senatorial upper classes whose members shared directly in shaping the government of a world empire due to their military positions; at the equestrians, whom he involved increasingly in the administration of that empire; and at the entire people, who either directly guaranteed this rule by serving in the military legions or as populace of Rome, which could identify with *res publica* and *patria* by virtue of the "tribune of the people" and the *princeps* Augustus. Participation in the tasks of the *res publica* was not limited to citizens and the city of Rome, as even the new citizen, the freedman, now had the opportunity to identify intensely with the *res publica Romana* by serving as a functionary of the cult of the Lares at the crossroads or in the society of the Augustales.

With the title *pater patriae* Augustus had definitively become First Citizen and father of a sole Roman family. In 27 B.C. Augustus had shared power with the Senate and the People; he now shared the fatherland with all members of Roman society. In his contest with Antony, Augustus had made Rome's cause his own; now Rome had become the cause of all Romans. His unassailable position at the top was swathed in the aura of patriotic ideology. Above the *princeps* there now ranked the idea of the fatherland where the First Citizen was simultaneously first among equals (*primus inter pares*) beside other citizens, and that also made his surpassing *auctoritas* easier to bear for the upper classes. Some conspiracies appear to have continued, but the position of the *princeps* was not in serious jeopardy: he was intertwined with the machinery of the state financially, militarily, and administratively. His achievements, styled initially as the First Citizen's helpful activities for the *res publica*, had become objectified and increasingly became a matter of course during this second phase.

Above all, the "Fatherland" now protected the *princeps* as he was the incarnation of the *patria*. Each attack on his person now amounted to an attack on the fatherland, and each opinion that diverged from the will of the *princeps* now could be denounced as unpatriotic: criticism of Augustus now affected the *maiestas* of the *princeps* as well as the *maiestas* of the *populus Romanus*, and vice versa. Augustus succeeded in silencing partisan strife and opposition by invoking patriotism. The appeal to the tradition of the republican "state based on laws" on the one hand, and its ideological elevation to a common "Fatherland" on the other allowed him to rule like a monarch and to die peacefully like a republican.

It was the role of the republican for which he desired applause. True, it was a role, but a role he had not only played but lived out all his life. For only the power of tradition enabled him to transform a republic safely into a principate.

SUGGESTIONS FOR FURTHER READING

On the political history of Augustus' time see the detailed and balanced chapters of Christopher Pelling (triumviral period) and J. A. Crook (30 B.C. to A.D. 14) in the second edition of *The Cambridge Ancient History*, vol. X (1996); also, the concise treatments by Wallace-Hadrill (1993) and Bringmann and Schäfer (2002). Good discussions of important individual aspects are found in Millar and Segal (1984) and Raaflaub and Toher (1990). Ramage (1987) is a pioneering discussion of the importance of the *Res Gestae*. On Antony's policy and conduct in the East see Schrapel (1996); on the ideology of the *pater patriae* Strothmann (2000); and on Augustus' relations with the plebs Yavetz (1988). Galinsky (1996) offers a successful synthesis of the political, literary, artistic, and religious dimensions of the Augustan principate.

Brunt's (1988) thorough presentation of the central issues of the late Republic and Syme's (1939) astute analysis of the political ascent of Octavian/Augustus provide a deeper understanding of the transformation from Republic to Empire.

2: AUGUSTUS AND THE MAKING OF THE PRINCIPATE

Erich S. Gruen

Tacitus elected to begin his *Annals* with the death of Augustus. The free state was already dead – long since. "How many were left who had even seen the *res publica*?" (*Ann.* 1.3). Augustus' own longevity had enabled him to outlast almost all whose memories might stretch back to the Roman Republic. Nearly half a century had elapsed since the battle of Actium, sixty-three years since Caesar had crossed the Rubicon. Tacitus sums it up with typically concentrated force at the beginning of the *Annals*: "Augustus subjected all to his power – under the name of *princeps*" (*Ann.* 1.1). The contrast between word and fact, a Tacitean trademark, appears here in the very opening lines. Tacitus makes the same point elsewhere: "Augustus gave us the institutions under which we gain use of peace – and a *princeps*" (*Ann.* 3.28). The cynical attitude affected the view of the great eighteenth-century historian Edward Gibbon, who wrote "Augustus was sensible that mankind is governed by names. Nor was he deceived in his expectation that the senate and people would submit to slavery, provided they were respectfully assured that they still enjoyed their ancient freedom." It did not happen in a day or a year. Augustus, says Tacitus, grew ever greater in small steps, gradually usurping for himself the functions of senate, magistrates, and laws (*Ann.* 1.2). Such was the Augustan principate, in Tacitus' jaundiced view.

But what does it mean to speak of the "principate"? The Latin word *principatus*, in reference to a form of government, was common enough in Tacitus' day, the early second century CE. Augustus, however, did not use the term in that fashion, nor did any of his contemporaries. To be sure, he referred to himself as *princeps*. And others too, like the poets Horace, Propertius, and Ovid, referred to him as such.

But *princeps* was a term much in use in the Republic as well, a designation of influential figures, a sign of esteem and authority. Augustus had no monopoly on it in his own day. Horace could address him as "greatest of the *principes*" (*Odes* 4.14.6). But the notion of *principatus* as designating a type of regime is not to be found in Augustus' autobiographical memoir, the *Res Gestae*, nor in the works of contemporary writers.

The distinction is critical. Augustus never occupied a post called the Principate, nor did he exercise an office to which the title *princeps* was attached. He had been appointed *triumvir* for ten years with the purpose of restoring the state torn by civil strife (*RG* 7.1). He continued to wield this virtually untrammeled authority in the course of his war with Antony and Cleopatra, and in the mop-up operations that followed. He acknowledges the fact unabashedly in the *Res Gestae*: "I had total power in all matters" (*RG* 34.1). No reason not to acknowledge it. That was a revolutionary era, dominated by civil war and the almost constant threat of upheaval. Institutions may have survived but military might ruled. The worst was over by 28 and 27 BCE. Augustus yielded up supreme power, or so he asserts. "I transferred the *res publica* from my power to the discretion of the senate and people of Rome" (*RG* 34.1).

Augustus, of course, did not exactly retire into private life to cultivate his garden in 27. Whatever formal powers he resigned in that year, he retained the substance of most of them. With the approval of the senate, he held command over the Iberian peninsula, all of Gaul, Syria, Egypt, and Cyprus, for a ten-year term (Dio 53.12.4–7, 53.13.1). That meant unquestioned control over almost the entire military establishment. The ten-year limit was renewable – and would be duly renewed. Augustus furthermore continued to hold one of the two consulships, Rome's chief magistracies in the Republic, each year, and would do so for some years to come. Honors were showered upon him, including, not least, the name of Augustus itself, a designation which, according to our source, implied a status somewhat more than human (Dio 53.16.8).

The settlement in 27 was in no meaningful sense a restoration of the Republic. Nor was it ever claimed to be by Augustus or any spokesman for him. The phrase *res publica restituta*, often conveyed in modern studies, appears on no official documents and is celebrated by no poet or prose writer of the era. The poet Ovid, in fact, put the matter succinctly and accurately: *res est publica Caesar* ("Caesar Augustus *is* the state"; *Trist.* 4.4.13–16). The accumulation of powers and their exercise over an extended period of time was unprecedented and hardly compatible with the principles of the Roman Republic.

It must be emphasized, however, that this was indeed a collection of powers and honors. Each was voted or acquired *ad hoc* and piece-meal. They did not amount to a position, an established institution, a principate. Augustus made a point of shunning that concept. It smacked too much of despotism. He declined the earnest appeals of the populace when they entreated him to take on the dictatorship. He even tore his clothes, went down on his knees, and bared his breast to insist that he wished no such post (Suet., *Aug.* 52; Dio 54.1.4). The histrionics were calculated but meaningful. Augustus refused to take the office of censor for life, when that, too, was offered him (Dio 54.2.1). And he firmly turned down a proposal that he hold the consulship in perpetuity (*RG* 5.3). Indeed he asserts in the *Res Gestae* that he accepted no office in violation of ancestral practice (6.1). The pattern is clear. Augustus disassociated himself from anything that resembled an institutionalizing of his role. Institutionalizing would run the risk of giving offense, stirring resentment, and possibly provoking conspiracy, especially within the senatorial class. As Dio Cassius reports, with regard to Augustus' declining of the dictatorship, he already had more power than the old dictators, so why engender jealousy and hatred by taking the position (54.1.5)? Augustus was *princeps*. But he did not hold a *principatus*.

This presented a major dilemma for the regime. None can doubt that Augustus sought a genuine stability in the empire, best provided by a solitary hand at the helm. He certainly expected that his work would be carried on after his death. Suetonius quotes an Augustan edict announcing the *princeps'* desire that when he died the foundations of the state that he had laid down should remain on track (Suet., *Aug.* 28). And in a famous letter written to his grandson Gaius, Augustus expresses the hope that his grandsons would grow to manhood and succeed to his position (Gellius 15.17.3). But here is the central paradox. If Augustus did not hold an official position, apart from annual consulships to which he was elected, and did not possess legal privileges apart from those bestowed upon him *ad hoc* and individually, then how could he assure the stability of his achievement, the continuity of his work, and the succession to a "principate" that did not exist? On the one hand, he wished to avoid the suggestion of institutionalized one-man rule; on the other, he expected his system to endure. The difficulty created by two policies that pulled in opposite directions needs to be confronted. How to resolve the tension? How to perpetuate a principate without admitting that there was a principate?

The year 23 BCE created a crisis. And it also brought Augustus' dilemma into sharp relief. The *princeps* resigned his consulship in the summer of that year, a post to which he had been elected for nine years running (Dio 53.32.3). And he was not to hold it again, except on rare, honorific occasions. The senate, in turn, gave him the right to retain his *imperium* (his military authority), so as to avoid the tedious constitutional exercise of having to lay it down and get it renewed every time he crossed the *pomerium* (the sacred boundary of the city). More significant still, the compliant senators augmented the force of Augustus' *imperium* abroad by making it superior to that of governors in any subject territory, even those outside his own extensive provincial commands of Gaul, Spain, Syria, Egypt, and Cyprus – an extraordinary authority conventionally known as *maius imperium* ("greater power"). That did not exhaust the novel measures. The Roman senate accorded Augustus the right to wield the responsibilities of a tribune for life (*RG* 10.1; Dio 53.32.5). He could not hold the tribunate itself, for it was closed to patricians, a status that Augustus had acquired upon adoption by Julius Caesar. But the award gave him the equivalent of a tribune's authority. The *princeps* placed special weight on that distinction. Coins (Fig. 1) and official documents begin the numbering of his years in 23 BCE by the registering of his *tribunicia potestas* (tribunician power).

What does all this mean? Common interpretation has it that the settlement of 23 represents a retreat on Augustus' part, that resignation of the consulship diminished powers that he previously wielded, even that a secret coup d'état had thwarted Augustus' plans for a dynastic succession. All of that is speculation, unfounded and implausible.

Resignation of the consulship hardly constituted a political setback. Dio Cassius provides a perfectly reasonable motive for that deed: Augustus wished to open the post for additional members of the nobility (53.32.3). Two consuls held office as chief executives of the state each year, occasionally succeeded by two others in the course of the year. (The suffect consulship carried slightly lesser status.) By occupying one of the two prime consulships annually, Augustus had, in effect, blocked the aspirations of several Roman aristocrats who had hoped to rise to that distinction. Resignation of the office in 23 opened it to more claimants. Not that this was pure concession to senatorial sentiments. Augustus retained key influence in the recommending of individuals to the consulship. The gesture, in fact, allowed him to exercise wider patronage within the senatorial class.

FIGURE 1. Roman bronze coin (*as*) issued A.D. 11–12. The obverse shows Augustus, CAESAR DIVI F(ILIUS) AUGUSTUS. The SC on the reverse signifies the Senate's privilege to strike bronze coinage. The legend PONTIF(EX) MAX(IMUS) TRIBUN(ICIA) POT(ESTAS) XXXIIII denotes his priestly office and illustrates the reckoning of his reign from his assumption of the tribunician power in 23 B.C. Photo: Numismatik Lanz, courtesy Dr. Hubert Lanz.

Augustus may have technically relinquished the specific privileges that attached to the consulship. But this entailed no lapse in authority. Special grants issuing from the senate restored most of those privileges to Augustus immediately: the right to retain his *imperium* when going in and out of the city, the right to convene the Senate, and the prerogative to bring any motion he wished before that body (Dio 53.32.5, 54.3.3). The authority inherent in the *maius imperium* which he now obtained certainly enhanced rather than reduced his power. Augustus implemented this widespread power without delay. In 22 and 21 he traveled to Sicily, Greece, and Asia Minor, areas technically under the control of other governors, settled disputes, restructured territorial arrangements, exercised punitive jurisdiction, and generally threw his weight around (Dio 54.6.1, 54.7). This was anything but a retreat from his previous ascendancy.

How then does one account for the "settlement of 23"? Augustus had just recovered from a serious illness. It can hardly be a coincidence that the new constitutional arrangements followed closely on the heels of his recovery. He had indeed been ill during the previous year in Spain as well (Dio 53.25.7, 53.28.1). And it is noteworthy that, after his recuperation at that time, the Senate freed him from "all compulsion of the laws" (Dio 53.28.2). Given the context and circumstances, that presumably means he would be immune from prosecution. The senatorial measure suggests strongly that Augustus in 24 was already planning to resign the consulship and seeking a guarantee that he would not be vulnerable to judicial attack. (The consulship carried with it the privilege of immunity from criminal charges.) Augustus foresaw potential problems along these lines.

The illness in 23, however, was far more serious. Augustus for a time gave up hope of survival (Dio 53.30.1). His doctor had to apply drastic measures: frigid baths and potions that might have made the remedy seem worse than the disease. But the treatment worked and the *princeps* regained his health. In the throes of what Augustus considered to be his final hours, he made hasty, spur of the moment dispensations. He turned over state papers to his fellow-consul Calpurnius Piso. And he handed his ring to Agrippa, his coeval and closest collaborator (Dio 53.30.1–2). What he conspicuously did *not* do was to appoint a successor. Some were surprised, even shocked by this, according to Dio Cassius (53.30.1–2, 53.31.2). They had expected the designation of young Marcus Marcellus, a favorite of the *princeps*, his son-in-law as well as his nephew. Marcellus was moving up the ladder of offices, indeed speeded on his way by the benefactions of Augustus. He held the aedileship in that year, with municipal responsibilities for the city of Rome, he held a place among men of praetorian standing in the senate, and he had acquired the right to seek consular office ten years before the legal age (Dio 53.28.3). Marcellus, it must have appeared, had all the marks of a future *princeps*. And yet Augustus refrained from bestowing any formal blessing upon him. The omission does not reflect a loss of stature, let alone a fall from favor, as some have thought. Rather, it points to a more fundamental fact: Augustus had made no provision for a successor.

The *princeps*, it seems, had never designed a blueprint for this purpose. That may cause surprise to moderns, looking back on the situation, accustomed to thinking in terms of a Julio-Claudian dynasty, a hereditary regime, an ongoing principate. But none of that existed in 23 BCE. Augustus indeed was committed to avoiding any overt signs of an institutionalized position subject to inheritance. Tongues wagged in aristocratic circles, and not all the talk was favorable. Suspicions arose that the *princeps* harbored dynastic schemes in secret. Nothing else can readily explain the remarkable act of Augustus immediately upon recuperation from his near-fatal ailment. He brought his will into the senate house, offered to break the seal, and read it aloud to the assembled *patres*, thereby to prove that it contained no provision appointing a successor to his rule (Dio 53.31.1). Of course, the will would contain clauses that bestowed property and possessions to designated heirs. That legacy stands in a very different category from the transfer of political power. Few had forgotten that the will of Julius Caesar had adopted Octavian as son and heir, thus laying the foundation for his rise to preeminence – even without the conferral of official position. Augustus felt impelled to squelch such talk and lay the matter to rest. The senators, of course, hastened to exhibit their loyalty to and trust in the *princeps*. They insisted that he had no need to read the will. His word sufficed.

The episode brings into sharp relief the dilemma delineated above. Augustus had resolutely resisted any implication that he occupied a throne that could be passed on to an heir. To act differently would only invite opposition, dissent, and possibly upheaval. He enjoyed exceptional powers that had been voted to him alone, and not to an institution. The institution did not yet exist. Augustus underscored the fact by his dramatic proposal to disclose his testamentary dispositions in public. At the same time, however, the events of 23 must have driven home a lesson to the *princeps*. He had stared death in the face and had only just escaped. Had he perished in that year, the results could have been calamitous. No provision had been made for a smooth transition, no steps taken to assure continuity in governance of the realm. The clashing ambitions and bloody strife that followed Julius Caesar's assassination could easily have been replayed. The quandary stood forth most boldly. To designate a successor might engender hostility and provoke resistance menacing to the stability of the regime. But to make no plans for the future risked worse consequences: ruinous domestic discord and civil war.

Those circumstances supply the context for the constitutional settlement of 23. Augustus acquired the authority of a tribune without the office. Why? Was this compensation for resigning the consulship? Surely not. He got more than enough compensation in the form of specific privileges and substantial power accorded by senatorial vote. Did he need it as a constitutional vehicle for sponsoring legislation? Hardly. That function could always be performed through the agency of others, as indeed it frequently was in the later years of Augustus' life. Did it provide a means to exercise *intercessio*, a veto to cancel senatorial decrees or actions of the popular assembly? *Tribunicia potestas* contained that prerogative. But nothing in the evidence suggests that Augustus ever issued a veto. Had it been needed, *intercessio* could always be implemented by other tribunes at Augustus' instigation. Did its value consist in cultivating a pose as champion of the people? This seems reasonable on the face of it, a useful device to advance the *princeps'* popular image. But against whom would he need to champion the *plebs*? In the age of the Roman Republic, tribunes might challenge the policies and practices of the Senate. Those days were long since past. And Augustus certainly did not set himself up as an opponent of the Senate. He may well have wished to exhibit his affection for the *plebs*, a serviceable posture. But did he need the *tribunicia potestas* for that purpose? Augustus had provided tangible benefits to the *plebs* on many prior occasions. He paid out handsome largesse prompted by the provisions of Caesar's will (*RG* 15.1). He authorized lavish expenditures after his victory over Antony and Cleopatra on gladiatorial games, gifts to *plebs* and veterans, land distribution, and building programs that provided employment (*RG* 15.1–3, 21.3, 22.1). As recently as 24 BCE he made a donative of 400 sesterces per man out of his own pocket. In the very year of 23, prior to the constitutional settlement, he purchased vast amounts of grain and allocated portions to each member of the *plebs* (*RG* 15.1). All this was done *before* he obtained the authority of the tribune. Augustus did not require the official conferral of that distinction in order to demonstrate his affection for the *plebs*. A noteworthy fact deserves emphasis. Augustus' own references to the *tribunicia potestas* in his *Res Gestae* do not associate it in any way with advocating or advancing the interests of the Roman *plebs*.

We need to look elsewhere for explanation. The most striking feature of the tribunician authority is not how Augustus exercised it – for he does not seem to have exercised it very much at all. The institution itself represented the truly dramatic shift. *Tribunicia potestas* signified the possession of official authority without the holding of office. Augustus carried the powers of the tribune, but was not and, as a patrician, could not be a tribune. The principle contained a marked novelty, in some ways the sharpest break with the constitutional underpinnings of the Republic. The magistracies of the Republic, however extensive their powers, worked within two fundamental restraints: the concepts of annuality and collegiality. A Republican official could hold a particular office only for a year (under normal circumstances), and, after stepping down, would be held accountable for all actions taken by him during that year. And for every Republican official there stood at least one colleague with functions and powers equal to his own, one who could, in theory at least, veto any of his deeds, rendering them null and void. Augustus himself, when he held a consulship year after year, had to submit to annual election (formality though that may have been) and to share office with a fellow consul whose power within that office duplicated his own (*RG* 34.3).

The *princeps'* new position after 23 escaped those Republican constraints. As possessor of tribunician authority without the tribunate, he had no fellow tribunes who could veto or curb his activities. He had no annual office from which he was required to step down and for which he would be held accountable. Both collegiality and annuality were waived. The award of *maius imperium* can be seen in a comparable light. Augustus had obtained an official *provincia* in 27 BCE. Vast and powerful though it was (Spain, Gaul, Syria, Egypt, and Cyprus), it depended upon a formal grant of the Senate, as customary under the Republic, and it had an explicit ten-year limit. That chronological terminus was unaffected by anything that happened in 23. The *provincia* was renewed when the grant expired in 18, and renewed again thereafter at intervals of five or ten years (Dio 53.16.2, 54.12.4–5, 55.12.3, 56.28.1). The *maius imperium* by contrast had no such restrictions. It empowered Augustus to intervene and exercise his *imperium* in any area of the Roman empire, without time limits, and with authority superior to that of any governor to whom a province had been assigned. In short, Augustus now possessed an *imperium* independent of magisterial office and independent of any specified *provincia*. Like his tribunician power, this authority outstripped precedents, untrammeled by conventional Republican practices. Augustus' position after 23 was far more extraordinary and, in principle, far more potent than before.

Why did he assume this new and awesome status? He surely did not require the powers obtained in 23 to intimidate others, to work his will against opposition, or to implement measures otherwise outside his jurisdiction. As noted above, he made little active use of his *tribunicia potestas*. Nor did he find much reason to exercise the *maius imperium*. One can point to the adjudication of some disputes in Sicily, Greece, and Asia Minor in 22 and 21, and the institution of criminal procedures and regulations in Cyrene in 6 and 4 BCE. But comparatively minor actions of this sort hardly explain the motives for acquisition of an authority so sweeping as that contained in *maius imperium*. The explanation must lie elsewhere.

It should perhaps be sought in the very dilemma noted earlier: the need to assure continuity in the system – without direct acknowledgment that there was a system. The one use which Augustus certainly did make of the tribunician power – and it may have been almost the only one – was to number his years by it. This, as we have seen, he did regularly after 23, on edicts, official documents, coins, and in the *Res Gestae*.

But this alone is significant, unprecedented, and worthy of close attention. It represents an implicit, indeed an explicit, acknowledgment that Augustus' powers did not rest on magisterial offices that were subject to annual review and election, or on specific provinces with territorial boundaries and time limits requiring renewal. Augustus here underlined continuity. Piecemeal appointments and extensions of command would still occur. But the tribunician years rolled on, uninterrupted, symbolic of stability and a continuum.

More important still, the new concept of power divorced from office enabled Augustus to take a critical step. He could now move toward assuring a smooth transfer of authority after his death and a perpetuation of his work, while avoiding the pitfalls of appointing a successor and the overt appearance of a hereditary monarchy. Magisterial office was transitory. Augustus' resignation of the consulship acknowledged that principle. And magisterial office could not be inherited, shared, or divided. But power without office, a novel concept, carried none of that baggage. Unencumbered by traditional limitations, it contained a flexibility that permitted the *princeps* to mold it to his design. In particular, it supplied a means whereby he could associate others with himself. A telling item brings this feature to the fore. On the one occasion in the *Res Gestae* where Augustus actually speaks with any concreteness about the *tribunicia potestas*, he describes it as a power for which he five times requested and received from the Senate a colleague (*RG* 6.2; cf. Suet., *Aug.* 27.5).

Association in the tribunician power eventually became tantamount to identification of a successor. Tacitus describes it as the "designation of supreme rank" (*summi fastigii vocabulum*). He proceeds to remark that Augustus selected Agrippa as the "partner of his power" and, after Agrippa's death, chose Tiberius for that role, "lest there be any doubt about his successor" (*Ann.* 3.56). But Tacitus wrote more than a century after the shaping of Augustus' system. From his distant vantage point the outcome was clear and the principate a long established fact. That analysis, however, overlooks the subtle difficulties faced by Augustus in 23 and the years immediately following.

Augustus designated no successor in 23 – or indeed at any time thereafter, despite repeated modern assertions to the contrary. The proposal to read his will, thus to prove that no heir had been marked out for his position, demonstrates this with all desired clarity. What would it mean to designate a successor? There was as yet no such institution as the "Principate," so that there was nothing to which a successor could succeed. No one could inherit a magistracy, nor could the specific honors bestowed on Augustus for his virtues and accomplishments pass automatically to another. What could be done, however, was to associate a partner, albeit a junior partner, in powers independent of magistracies and of Republican conventions. Herein lay the instrument whereby to resolve that dilemma confronting the *princeps*.

Augustus, however, drew back from taking that step in 23. It would have been premature. The situation was too delicate, the time not yet ripe. Rumors had circulated of a prospective blood-line dynasty, rumors which Augustus had been at pains to discredit. He could not give even the appearance of preparing such a dynasty by indirect means. The *princeps* took tribunician authority and *maius imperium* in that year, but shared them with none other. That would have been too obvious and too offensive, aggravating rather than soothing hostile suspicions. Marcellus was young and inexperienced, as yet untried with major responsibilities. And Marcellus died of illness in that very year, not long after the new settlement (Dio 53.30.4; Velleius 2.93.1).

Augustus looked to Agrippa, his helpmate for the past two decades, the husband of his niece. Indeed he had already looked to Agrippa before the death of Marcellus in 23. Augustus posted him to Syria, there to supervise the affairs of the East (Dio 53.32.1). Two years later he returned to Rome, where he was wed to Augustus' daughter Julia, the widow of Marcellus (Tac., *Ann.* 1.3; Suet., *Aug.* 63; Dio 54.6.5; Velleius 2.93.2. Cf. Susan Treggiari's discussion on p. 140).

The *princeps* had stability uppermost in mind. Agrippa possessed experience and influence. Any future issue of the marriage would not only be Augustus' grandchildren but would carry the blood of Agrippa, a powerful guarantee against civil strife. As Tacitus put it, Agrippa would serve, like Marcellus before him, as bulwark of the regime (*Ann.* 1.3). Agrippa proceeded to active duty in Gaul and Spain in 20 and 19 BCE, where his stern administration and military success brought pacification of troublesome areas (Dio 54.11).

Five years had elapsed since the settlement of 23. Augustus had not shared his powers, and had made no move to elevate a successor. The *tribunicia potestas* and *maius imperium* belonged to him alone, special distinctions awarded to an individual of exceptional stature. And the Senate had conferred still a further distinction in 19. They accorded him the power of a consul for life, with the right to hold the *fasces*, the emblems of consular authority, and sit on the symbolic chair between the two current occupants of consular office (Dio 54.10.5). This marked another instance in which the *princeps* obtained functions and trappings belonging to an office without holding the office itself. The time now did seem ripe, the crisis of 23 long past, and Agrippa's abilities further demonstrated by additional accomplishments abroad. In 18 Agrippa obtained *tribunicia potestas*. He very probably received *maius imperium* then as well. Dio's account implies as much. And a papyrus discovered a generation ago appears to confirm it (Dio 54.12.4; Koenen [1970] 226).

This did not deliver Rome into a dual principate, as is sometimes thought. Even in a formal sense, distinctions existed between the two men's positions. Augustus' prerogatives held without time limit, Agrippa received them for a five-year period, duly renewed in 13 (Dio 54.12.4, 54.28.1). Augustus still enjoyed a unique position, none to challenge him. But a significant change had occurred. Agrippa now carried the distinctions of *maius imperium* and *tribunicia potestas* as well, and would continue to carry them should Augustus die. The change could not be missed. Agrippa too began to number his tribunician years immediately. They would run consecutively from the year 18.

Augustus, moreover, looked ahead to another generation. Two boys were born to Agrippa and Julia, Gaius in 20 BCE, Lucius in 17 BCE (Dio 54.8.5, 54.18.1). Augustus promptly adopted them both as his own sons (Dio 54.18.1; Suet., *Aug.* 64). It would be anachronistic to regard such moves as "succession policy" or to label Agrippa at this point as "regent" for the heirs-apparent. Augustus could no more declare or suggest a hereditary monarchy now than he could before. The boys, if ever to reach supreme power, had a very long road ahead. If the *princeps'* health should fail, only Agrippa possessed the authority to hold the empire together. The future of the young sons would be his responsibility and his decision. But Augustus had made provision for stability and continuity.

As fortune would have it, Agrippa's health failed first. Augustus returned to Italy from Greece in 12 BCE to find his long-time associate dead (Dio 54.28.2–3). The carefully orchestrated plan temporarily foundered. But Augustus had someone else to turn to: his stepson Tiberius. Tradition has been unkind to that individual. Sources portray Tiberius as dour, grim, morose, misanthropic, and even henpecked by his mother. Tales of friction between Augustus and Tiberius, indeed mutual dislike, made the rounds. Doubtless the sour disposition of Tiberius did not find favor with the *princeps*. But there can be no question about his abilities. Tiberius, born in 42, had served his stepfather well, and had been advanced and groomed by him in unmistakable fashion. Tiberius fought under Augustus in Spain between 27 and 24 BCE, receiving important responsibilities already as a teenager. He became the *princeps'* quaestor in 23, a prosecutor of conspirators in 22, Augustus' deputy in 20 to recover the captured military standards from Parthia (a critical public relations move), and he installed a new ruler in Armenia (Suet., *Tib.* 8–9; Dio 53.26.1, 53.28.3, 54.9.4–6; Velleius 2.94.3–4, 2.122.1).

Tiberius' career moved from strength to strength. He secured the right to stand for office five years before the legal age, held the praetorship in 16 BCE at the age of twenty-six, accompanied Augustus to Gaul, fought in Raetia in 15, and reached the consulship two years later (Dio 54.19.6, 54.22.1–5, 54.25.1; Velleius 2.95.1–2; Suet., *Tib.* 9). If the *princeps* had reservations about Tiberius' personality, he did not allow them to get in the way of his rapid advancement. Trained in civic and military duties, experienced, mature and in his thirtieth year, Tiberius stepped easily into the place vacated by Agrippa as mainstay of the regime and guarantor of its continuity. A successful campaign in Pannonia in 12 proved his mettle once more (*RG* 30.1; Dio 54.31.2; Velleius 2.96.1–3; Suet., *Tib.* 9). In the following year he received as bride Augustus' daughter Julia, now widowed a second time. Tiberius did not welcome the prospect. He was obliged to divorce his wife Vipsania, an act he performed with great reluctance. Report had it that he pined away for Vipsania, that whenever she appeared in the palace he burst into tears (Suet., *Tib.* 7). The promiscuous Julia was not his type. But however much Tiberius may have longed for his former mate, he carried out his responsibilities to the regime with dutiful deference. Tiberius had amply demonstrated skill and loyalty. He was now both stepson and son-in-law to Augustus, and stepfather to the *princeps'* grandchildren, the most prominent figure in the realm after Augustus. And he had still heavier duties in store: campaigns against Pannonians and Dalmatians in 11 and 10 BCE, command of armies on the Rhine in 8, and a second consulship in 7 (Dio 54.34.3–4, 54.36.3–4, 55.6.1, 55.8.1; Velleius 2.97.4).

An important fact, however, requires emphasis. The *tribunicia potestas* and the *maius imperium* that Augustus had bestowed upon Agrippa lapsed at the latter's death in 12 BCE. Augustus did not transfer them to Tiberius or to anyone else at that time. Why? One explanation best accounts for that omission. Augustus remained most sensitive to the potential criticism that he was setting the stage for a monarchical dynasty. He studiously avoided even the appearance of such a scheme. An automatic transfer of the extraordinary distinctions from Agrippa to Tiberius on the death of the former would point unavoidably to a royal succession. Augustus shrank from the move. Let Tiberius earn his distinctions, as Augustus had done, and as Agrippa had done. Then they could come as reward for service and accomplishment, not as rights belonging to the heir of a throne. Augustus, it appears, still grappled with that dilemma that had plagued him for more than a decade: how to perpetuate his system without making it appear that he was installing a sequence of rulers. His apprehensiveness on this issue can be illustrated in more than one way. Twice he exhibited annoyance with the populace for the untimely and premature honors they showered upon his young grandsons (Dio 54.27.1, 55.9.1–4; Suet., *Aug.* 56.2; Tac., *Ann.* 1.3). And when the Senate voted a triumph for Tiberius in 12 BCE, Augustus refused to let him conduct it, though conceding triumphal honors instead (Dio 54.31.4).

Augustus nurtured the development with care and prudence. By 6 BCE Tiberius had established his worthiness at home and abroad. The *princeps* could now confer upon him the *tribunicia potestas* as token of his achievements rather than as overt mark of a successor (Dio 55.9.4; Velleius 2.99.1). Even then, however, he withheld the *maius imperium*. Augustus moved with patient steps to avoid offense and resentment. Not for nothing did he acquire the label of *festina lente* (make haste slowly). Tiberius received the tribunician authority for a five-year term, as Agrippa had before him, renewal to come thereafter – if earned. The *princeps* had restored the situation that once held prior to the death of Agrippa. He once again enjoyed an associate in his extraordinary powers, one who would presumably retain them even after the *princeps* was gone. Continuity seemed assured.

But suddenly things went sour. Tiberius ceased to cooperate. He stalked off to the island of Rhodes and withdrew altogether from public life. The reasons defy analysis. Speculations flew about, reported by our sources in various inconsistent or contradictory accounts. Did Tiberius wish to avoid obstructing Gaius and Lucius, in fear of their wrath, anger at their promotion, or desire to leave the field clear to them? Did he flee the sight of Julia, out of disgust for her infidelities, or to indulge his own secret lusts? Did he go to prove that he was indispensable, or out of weariness to gain rest from incessant labors? All these motives and more receive mention in our evidence (Suet., *Tib.* 10–11; Tac., *Ann.* 1.4, 1.53, 4.57; Velleius 2.99.2; Dio 55.9.5–7). The riddle will not receive any definitive resolution. Whatever the reason, Tiberius' retirement spoiled Augustus' blueprint, enraged and exasperated the *princeps*. Now, and not before, Augustus determined upon rapid acceleration for the careers of Gaius and Lucius, who had barely entered their teens. Gaius, just fifteen years old, became consul-designate five years in advance in 5 BCE, and his brother received a similar honor three years later (*RG* 14.1–2; Tac., *Ann.* 1.3; Dio 55.9.4, 55.9.9–10). The *princeps* plainly hastened a process that he had previously stalled, lest the final threads of continuity be snapped. He was himself rapidly approaching his sixty-third year, the so-called *klimakterikon* (a potentially fatal year in astrological speculation), and not at all sure of surviving it.

Tiberius eventually altered his resolve to stay on Rhodes. He sought permission from Augustus for a return to Rome. Significantly, the request came in 1 BCE, just as the tenure of his tribunician power had run out. Tiberius wrote that, since Gaius and Lucius had now grown to manhood and could safely hold second place in the empire, he would return as a private citizen and thus escape suspicion of rivalry with them (Suet., *Tib.* 11). That missive may supply a clue to his original motive for withdrawal. Uncomfortable with the tribunician power and hesitant to stand on the verge of stepping into Augustus' place, Tiberius pronounced himself ready to return when that power lapsed and others had been groomed for it.

Augustus, however, proved to be unforgiving. He withheld permission. Tiberius, in the *princeps'* view, had willfully upset his scheme and forced him to hurry the advance of untested youths on whom he could not yet rely (cf. Dio 55.10.18). Nor was Augustus prepared even now to bestow the *tribunicia potestas* and *maius imperium* upon either of his grandsons. For the third time since 23 BCE he held those powers without an associate. Augustus still steered clear of the impression that they were tantamount to royal succession. Gaius and Lucius, like Agrippa and Tiberius before them, would have to prove themselves worthy to the senate and people of Rome, and thus earn the distinctions. Unfortunately for the *princeps*, they did not live long enough to do so. Lucius perished in 2 CE, Gaius two years later (Dio 55.10a.9; Velleius 2.102.3). Augustus frustrated his own plans by sheer longevity.

Now in his late sixties, Augustus had to revise his expectations yet again. But he determined to pursue the scheme adumbrated in 23. Tiberius, and he alone, survived as hope for the future. "Everything converged upon him," says Tacitus (*Ann.* 1.3). He had gained leave to return to Rome in 2 CE, on the importuning of his mother Livia – but with the understanding that his public career had come to a halt (Suet., *Tib.* 13). The deaths of Gaius and Lucius, however, created an altogether new situation, thrusting Tiberius back into the limelight.

Augustus adopted him as his own son in 4 CE. Indeed he engineered a series of adoptions. The *princeps* took as his sons both Tiberius and Agrippa Postumus, the last surviving male issue of Agrippa and Julia (Suet., *Aug.* 65; *Tib.* 15; Dio 55.13.2; Velleius 2.103.2–3). And Tiberius himself, on Augustus' request, adopted his own nephew Germanicus (Suet., *Tib.* 15; Dio 55.13.2; Tac., *Ann.* 1.3, 4.57).

Why this elaborate set of adoptions? Did Augustus endeavor to hedge Tiberius about with rivals and potential claimants on power? Hardly a likely proposition. That could only promote divisiveness. If anything, the reverse was true. The combined adoptions displayed to all the unity of the family (for the concomitant expressions in portraiture see Kleiner on pp. 212–17). Agrippa Postumus might well inherit the popularity that his brothers had enjoyed. Augustus, we might surmise, would not wish to see this turned against Tiberius. Making them both adoptive brothers seemed a neat solution. As for Germanicus, the request that Tiberius adopt him looks like an Augustan scheme to assure successors of his choice for the next two generations. But that impression may miss the real point. Augustus concerned himself not with setting out a sequence of rulers but with uniting Germanicus to Tiberius, thus to reduce the likelihood of factions within the household. The Temple of Concord, restored and dedicated to Concordia Augusta a few years later in 10 CE, reinforced the message. A comparable purpose would also best explain the notorious phrase in Augustus' will stating that he had adopted Tiberius because "cruel fortune" had robbed him of his grandsons (Suet., *Tib.* 23). A similar statement appears in the *Res Gestae* (14.1). Augustus could hardly have intended such words to undermine Tiberius' position. More probably the *princeps* here issued an indirect appeal to those who had placed their hopes in Gaius and Lucius to rally around Tiberius. The adoption of Tiberius, as Augustus himself said, was done *rei publicae causa* ("for the good of the state"; Suet. *Tib.* 21.3; Velleius 2.104.1).

The adoptions themselves were all private family affairs. They served to consolidate the house of the Julio-Claudians. But they did not mark out succession to a throne. More to the point, Tiberius once again acquired the privilege of *tribunicia potestas* (Tac., *Ann.* 1.10; Velleius 2.103.3; Suet., *Tib.* 16; Dio 55.13.2). It bears reminder that five years had passed with no associate of Augustus in that privilege. Augustus had made it abundantly clear that he was not anointing a royal heir but announcing confidence in a valuable helpmate now restored to his good graces. Tiberius expressed reluctance in public to take on the *tribunicia potestas* (Velleius 2.103.3). Perhaps, in view of his earlier

FIGURE 2. The so-called Gemma Augustea. Sardonyx cameo (10 × 23 cm), approx. A.D. 10. In the upper register, Augustus and the goddess Roma are seated and receiving Tiberius, who is descending from his chariot on the far left. In the lower register, Roman soldiers are erecting a trophy amid defeated barbarians. Augustus' birth sign, Capricorn, is shown between his head and Roma's; Tiberius', Scorpio, is engraved on the shield hanging from the trophy on the far left (right beneath him). Vienna, Kunsthistorisches Museum. Museum photograph.

behavior, the reluctance was genuine. But he accepted the role *rei publicae causa*.

The place of Tiberius as central figure in the regime next to Augustus henceforth went unquestioned. Agrippa Postumus, described by our sources as a vulgar young man, brutal and brutish, and of depraved character, soon fell from Augustus' favor. He was banished in 7 CE with an armed guard placed around him, an exile made permanent by senatorial decree, and the *princeps* officially disowned him (Velleius 2.112.7; Tac., *Ann.* 1.3–4, 1.6; Suet., *Aug.* 51, 65; *Tib.* 15; Dio, 55.22.4, 55.32.2; Pliny, *NH* 7.150). Tiberius, by contrast, exercised the highest responsibilities. He conducted campaigns in Germany from 4 to

6 CE, and suppressed rebellious Pannonians from 6 to 9, followed by an elaborate triumph (Velleius 2.104–116; Dio 55.13.1a, 55.28–34, 56.11–17; Suet., *Tib.* 16–17). He went on to further campaigns on the Rhine in 10 and 11, and enjoyed yet another triumph in 12 (Velleius 2.121.1–2; Suet., *Tib.* 18–20; Dio 56.23–25). Whatever Augustus' innermost feelings toward his adoptive son, the public association remained close and conspicuous (Fig. 2). And, if the *princeps'* letters to Tiberius, as preserved by Suetonius, are genuine, there were warm personal feelings as well (Suet., *Tib.* 21).

The accomplishments of Tiberius, when added to his previous service, fully justified further distinctions. In 13 CE his *tribunicia potestas* reached its tenth year, and was duly renewed. And in the same year Tiberius acquired the privilege hitherto withheld: an *imperium* equal to that of Augustus in all provinces and over all armies – in short, the *maius imperium* (Velleius 2.121.1; Suet., *Tib.* 21). Tiberius now fully occupied the place once held by Agrippa. That elevation, however, had come in slow and painful steps, with care to avoid the impression that a monarchical system demanded them.

In the end, Augustus had successfully resolved his dilemma. By sharing powers that were not tied to office or subject to annual review, he had raised first Agrippa and then Tiberius to a position nearly comparable to his own during his lifetime. Hence he dodged the criticism of installing a dynasty, while assuring that his own death would not interrupt the continuity of the system. Augustus never designated a successor to his powers, not even (especially not even) in his will. The will bequeathed his name and most of his estate to Tiberius – but no constitutional powers (Suet., *Aug.* 101; *Tib.* 23; Tac., *Ann.* 1.8; Dio 56.32.1). It did not have to. Tiberius already had them. It is no coincidence that Tiberius' first acts upon the death of Augustus in 14 CE – and before the will was disclosed – were to issue commands to the praetorian cohorts and to the armies abroad by virtue of his *maius imperium*, and to summon the Senate into session by virtue of his *tribunicia potestas* (Tac., *Ann.* 1.7; Suet., *Tib.* 23–24; Dio 57.2.1). Those acts made public affirmation that the powers belonged to Tiberius independently of the fallen *princeps*. Augustus' prior planning had borne fruit. He had refrained from the offensive and unpopular step of appointing an heir to his position, while at the same time obviating the risk of leaving the state without firm and experienced leadership. When Augustus died, his principate, if such it may now be termed, died with him. But Tiberius' principate, thanks to the foresight of his stepfather, was already underway.

SUGGESTIONS FOR FURTHER READING

Augustus' gradual translation of a republican form of government into monarchical power has received much attention in the scholarship. The classic account by Syme (1939), while disputable in individual matters, remains fundamental – and required reading on the subject. Crook (1996) and Kienast (1999) provide sensible overviews. On the Augustan era as a bridge between Republic and Empire, see Eder (1990), and the same author's contribution to this volume. Augustus' "succession policy" is treated by Corbett (1974) and Bowersock (1984). On the tangled constitutional issues, see Chilver (1950), Salmon (1956), Fadinger (1969), and Lacey (1996).

PART II

INTELLECTUAL AND
SOCIAL DEVELOPMENTS

3: *MUTATAS FORMAS*: THE AUGUSTAN TRANSFORMATION OF ROMAN KNOWLEDGE

Andrew Wallace-Hadrill

In nova fert animus mutatas dicere formas / corpora
("My mind impels me to tell of forms changed to
new bodies"; Ovid, *Met.* 1.1–2)

Ovid's extraordinary tour-de-force in representing all of mythology, indeed the whole history of the world from creation to the deification of Caesar, as a seamlessly interconnected series of transformations, offers a vision rooted in contemporary Augustan experience.[1] The transformational skill with which Augustus constructed his new order out of the elements of the old order is conceptually parallel to the processes, which Ovid loves to describe, by which Daphne's metamorphosis from human to tree happens gradually, almost organically, using individual elements of the old body to fashion a new body.[2]

It is hard for us to find the appropriate language in which to characterize the impact of Augustus. If we speak of a 'Roman Revolution', we not only inescapably evoke the revolutions of the modern world, and their social antagonisms rooted in the specific circumstances of capitalism, but we also represent the outcome in a way that does violence to the ideology of the players themselves. 'Metamorphosis', unlike 'revolution', allows some space for the Augustan claim to be restoring and adding to Roman tradition. But terminology is not the issue. That the reign of Augustus represents a major rupture in political systems is beyond dispute. The much larger issue is how political revolution (or transformation) ripples outward in its effect on society and culture.

Or rather, since even this formulation attributes an apparent primacy to politics, and a secondary role to culture (a Marxian 'epiphenomenon'), the challenge is to understand how political revolution may be read as one component of more fundamental and comprehensive shifts in the formation and reproduction of social and cultural forms. Anyone who has tried to engage with this evasive set of issues is bound to take as their starting point Michel Foucault's redefinition of power as an outcome of knowledge. Foucault's vision is of European history as a succession of epistemological systems, whereby different ways of knowing the world underpin the power systems they both engender and reflect. Inescapably, the great revolution at the centre of his thinking is the French Revolution: the shift from the *ancien régime* to republic is viewed as a transformation of ways of knowing.[3] A particularly fruitful application of Foucault's approach is Roger Chartier's discussion of the transformation of the intellectual and cultural bases of French society that underpin the Revolution, with its emphasis on the shift of authority in society.[4] The present chapter is an essay in applying a similar approach to Rome.

As a starting point, it is helpful to return to that core issue of Roman social history, patronage. Patronage was the concept invoked by Mattias Gelzer to explain the political dominance of a relatively narrow group of families which he termed the nobility, a system which he saw as characterizing the Republic, and which was by definition terminated by the victory of Augustus.[5] We must now concede that Gelzer's idea of a dominant élite was too rigid, and that his analysis of the function of patronage was too mechanistic. But when we dismantle patronage as the explanation of the power of the republic on nobility, the question becomes the more pressing as to the basis of the dominance of the republican élite. John North has suggested that we should look again at the role of religion and ritual power in sustaining this dominance.[6] The suggestion is persuasive, but is surely only one part of the answer. If, with Foucault, we see religious power as a discourse that forms only a part of an entire epistemological system, we may suggest that the dominance of the republican élite was due to their control of a system of knowledge, that their loss of control was due to the collapse of that system of knowledge, and that the Augustan revolution consists of the construction of a new epistemological system, made, through a metamorphosis which it would take an Ovid to describe, from the transformation of existing elements.

'Patronage' is inadequate as an explanation of the republican system because it fails to account for how a restricted group was able to maintain its hold on the minds of the voters. The 'nobility' was less tightly defined than Gelzer suggested,[7] and was subject to the constant percolation of new recruits, as Hopkins' (1983) statistics showed. We should also allow for the extent to which the image of the Roman nobility was a myth produced by the very people who challenged it, oversimplifying a complex and fluid system in order to discredit it. But though the contrast is relative rather than absolute, the rates of promotion of new men accelerate dramatically from Augustus on, bringing the expanding ripples of provincial recruitment that was one of Syme's central themes (cf. also N. Purcell's chapter, this volume). In both cases, 'insiders' in the sense of members of families which have penetrated to the inner circles of power exercise influence over the recruitment of 'outsiders'. Under the Republic, the insiders use their influence over the voters (whatever we attribute this to) to restrict the recruitment of outsiders and protect their own interests. Under the 'court society' of the Empire,[8] where office is a benefice distributed from the centre, the emperor has a clear interest in avoiding the entrenchment of any social group, and actively promotes expanding recruitment; members of court circles facilitate this process through their role as 'brokers', promoting the interests of their own networks.[9]

That transformation constitutes a radical reorientation of Roman identity and Roman culture, even if the components are familiar and traditional. Because in both cases we see an 'élite' and see the operations of 'patronage', we are inclined to stress the continuity. But it is as delusory as any Ovidian metamorphosis. In the republican system, constitutional power lies with the citizen body, but social power lies with those who are in possession of the knowledge through which the system functions. That knowledge can be transmitted from generation to generation, and enables the survival of a quasi-hereditary élite. In the court society of the Empire, the ruler controls power and knowledge. Of course he is partly dependent on the existing élite, but it is greatly in his interest that knowledge and authority should not become entrenched within one social group.

The model here offered proposes a fundamental shift in the location and structure of knowledge, and specifically of the knowledge which constitutes Roman society. The republican 'nobility' (by no means a hermetically sealed group, but certainly a restricted one with a limited rate of replacement) are those who control the vital forms of knowledge of what it is to be Roman. The forms of knowledge are multiple, but closely interconnected and comprehensive. Religion is part of it, but a part interlinked with all other aspects of Roman custom and practice, of *mores*. It is a knowledge of time and space, or rather *Roman* time and *Roman* space, of religious rites and human practice, of law and morality, of language and public discourse. We perceive the system in the moment of its collapse in the late Republic, as players complain of a world disintegrating into perceived disorder. And it is that contemporary perception of collapse that creates the authority that underpins the new system. Augustus is specifically invited to reconstruct Roman *mores*, and in doing so he creates a new order that deprives the nobility of anything but the vestige of authority, and in 'professionalizing' knowledge, both opens access to a new empire-wide élite, and retains ultimate authority for the ruler. The metamorphosis is not the work of the sole agency of Augustus, achieved in a moment: Ovid knew that transformation was long drawn out. Augustus tapped into deep changes that took place over the course of a century, and in proclaiming the demise of one paradigm was able to formulate a new one.[10]

TIME

The reform of the Roman calendar by Julius Caesar (in 46 BCE) and by Augustus (in 9 BCE) is paradigmatic of this shift.[11] Ways of marking time are also powerful ways of marking identity. The French Revolution, for instance, within a year imposed a radical new calendar, numbering the years of the Revolution from September 22, 1792, renaming all months, decimalizing them as thirty days in length, and substituting weeks with ten-day cycles. The experiment lasted fourteen years.

The subtlety (and durability) of the Augustan metamorphosis lies in the perpetuation of most features of the republican calendar, combined with a pervasive incorporation of the imperial presence.[12] The year still takes its name from the consuls. The month names are those of the Republic, with the one significant exception that Sextilis is now named for Augustus, as Quintilis for Julius, both on the occasion of their calendar reforms. The cycle of republican (and pre-republican) religious festivals is preserved, if not actually reinvigorated, though alongside the old festivals there is a heavy presence of celebrations of imperial occasions, parading as an extension rather than a substitution of tradition.

The Roman calendar reform is therefore of a quite different order from that of the French Revolution, which sought to mark republican time in every possible way as an abandonment of the time of the *ancien régime*. Rather than parading change, it masks it, or re-presents republican time in such a way that imperial time seems its natural and organic extension. But the rupture is there. The significant reform is that of Julius Caesar as dictator, who removes from the *pontifices* the power to 'intercalate' additional days at the end of February, in order to bring the calendar back into line with the solar year, and introduces the system of four-yearly leap years which survives with only minor subsequent adjustments. From one point of view, the reform is no more than a technicality, for which the credit should go to the group of leading philosophers and mathematicians, led by Sosigenes, to whom Caesar entrusted the calculations,[13] together with his successor Facundius, who in 9 BCE enables the correction necessitated by the confusion between a four- and three-yearly cycle.

But Roman accounts make clear that the reform is political. The contemporary perception of the situation before the reform is one of corruption. For Cicero, intercalation was an institution "wisely set up by Numa which has disintegrated thanks to the negligence of subsequent *pontifices*." That negligence, as Cicero himself was well aware, was also the outcome of numerous pressures on the college of *pontifices*, and the interests at stake were not only the anxieties of those like Cicero who did not wish their term of provincial office prolonged, but political (intercalated days were extra days for meetings of the assembly) and financial (the *publicani* were accused of bribery). In the short term, Caesar's reform removed from the game a tool of political manipulation which has been used by his enemies. But it also constituted a more fundamental attack on the authority of the *nobiles* who controlled the priesthoods.[14]

Intercalation was more than an archaic privilege. It was part of the fact that the entire calendar was an expression of the power of the priesthood. The calendar defined when certain words could be spoken in public (*fasti*), when not (*nefasti*), when assemblies could be held (*comitiales*), and when by contrast the gods should be worshipped. It was the business of the *pontifices* to know when Romans should act and how, to know the rhythms of life that would secure divine approval. Caesar's reform denied the *pontifices* that knowledge, and transferred the knowledge of the year to the rational calculations of the mathematician. The authority of the *pontifices* had been compromised by the perceived neglect, openness to improper influence, and inability to deliver a calendar that meets consensus and constitutes order.

Conversely, the use of 'professionals' to correct the calendar is a political use of the professional authority of experts who enjoyed widespread esteem to trounce the authority of the traditional priestly caste. Both Caesar and Augustus turn the calendar into an expression of the new order. One sign of that is the proliferation of the documents, usually as inscriptions, but also in painted form, which we refer to as 'Fasti'. They consist of two types of list: the first is that of the high officials who mark the years, the consuls, supplemented by *triumphatores*, dictators and others, the second is the calendar of months and days. Many monuments combine the two types.[15]

Both types of Fasti, but especially the calendars of months and days, have a marked concentration under Augustus and Tiberius, to the extent that calendars inscribed in marble rather than painted on walls are scarcely found at any other period. Behind the Augustan proliferation of monthly calendars in marble lies not only the confidence that the cycle of the year and its festivals is completely predictable, but the opportunity it offers for displaying the festivals and anniversaries of the imperial house. The mechanism is not of centralized propaganda machine, but of competitive flattery: senators, local town councillors, members of colleges, and corporations competed in their zeal to display their loyalty.[16] To inscribe the Roman calendar was a statement of loyalty to the Roman system, and the acknowledgement of the emperor as the central feature of that system. That was why Ovid could not embark on a poetic Fasti without knowing that his own zeal would be at every point under scrutiny.[17]

The enormous success of this imperial appropriation of Roman time can be illustrated by its wide diffusion beyond the inner circles of power. The Fasti of Praeneste, despite their 'official' appearance, must have been a local commission. The lists of consuls, of which only two small fragments survive, were found together with lists of the local magistrates of Praeneste, inscribed in the same style, and it surely follows that the monument was locally commissioned, mirroring a metropolitan model.[18] At a local level, Roman time becomes local time by the juxtaposition of Roman magistrates with local ones. The same phenomenon is seen in the Fasti of Venusium and of several other Italian towns, where the lists interleaf Roman magistrates and local magistrates under each year.[19]

The monthly calendar is likely to be part of the same commission.[20] We learn from Suetonius' *Lives of Grammarians* that it was Verrius Flaccus, the most distinguished grammarian/antiquarian of the Augustan age, and tutor to Augustus' own grandchildren, who was responsible for their publication, and who was celebrated by an honorific statue nearby.[21] Verrius Flaccus encapsulates to perfection the process by which Augustus made Roman time his own. We need not think in terms of the emperor distributing copies of the 'official' calendar to local centres like

Praeneste. They are willing enough to do it under their own impulse, and buy into the system by synchronizing Roman time with Praenestine time (and local festivals, especially that of Fortuna Primigeneia, are registered on the calendar along with Roman ones, just as local magistrates). But who better to turn to for an authoritative version of the calendar than the great expert of the age, whose tutorship on the Palatine gave the ultimate stamp of approval to his scholarly learning? What substitute in terms of authority could the college of the *pontifices* now offer? Roman time has definitively slipped beyond the grasp of the nobility.

And in slipping from the nobility, Roman time becomes the common property of all Romans. It is not only town councils throughout Italy which enthusiastically inscribe the Fasti. Two remarkable examples show the habit reaching the level of freedmen and slaves. One is the calendar of the local magistrates of a *vicus*, a city ward, in the Testaccio area of Rome near the Via Marmorata.[22] Here the monthly calendar was inscribed on two faces of a marble panel, the six months in six vertical columns on each side. Beneath the first six months are listed the *fasti* of the consuls from 43 BCE, the year of Augustus' first consulship (Hirtius and Pansa are passed over in silence) down to the end of his reign and slightly beyond. Beneath the second are listed, after the names of the consuls, the four *vicomagistri* of each year, from the first year when Augustus presented them the 'Lares Augusti'; that year (7 BCE) is dated by Augustus' eleventh consulship and seventeenth year of tribunician power. The adulation of Augustus is unconcealed, but the important point is that, at the level of the parish pump, local officials of freedman status could also make Roman time their own. Trimalchio too had a calendar painted on his walls.[23]

Equally remarkable are the Fasti from Antium, put up by the slaves of the imperial household.[24] The inscription comes almost certainly from the imperial villa at Antium, beloved of Nero, where the household slaves have set up a *collegium*, apparently with the approval of the local council, which periodically requests a contribution, made by one of the officers of that year. The inscription has the familiar combination of monthly calendar and lists of magistrates. Spanning a period from the 30s to the 50s CE, for each year are given the names of the two consuls, followed by the slaves who held office that year: Eros glutinator (the man who glued together papyrus rolls), Dorus atriensis (the doorman), Anthus topiarius ('Flower the gardener'), Primus subvilicus (the sub-bailiff), Claudius Atimetus *a bybliothece* (the librarian, a freedman), take their proud places in the roll of annual honour. On the one hand, the wealth, power and self-confidence of the imperial court and its staff

are evident; on the other, the success of Augustus in opening access to
Roman time to all those who would be loyal to him.

Religion and Tradition

On the model here proposed, calendar reform, while on the surface a
technical matter of sorting out a confused traditional practice, entailed
a far deeper shift of social authority and control of knowledge: from a
republican society in which a 'nobility' maintained its preeminence by
a superior knowledge of Roman discourse – in this case, through the
right of the pontifical college to 'know' the year – to a court society in
which knowledge, far from being concentrated in a single power group,
was diffused among experts, whose authority was endorsed by the ruler.

One way to interpret this transformation is as a process of structural
differentiation. A ruling élite upon which are concentrated the functions
of priests, politicians, legal authorities, advocates, and military leaders
is replaced in a larger and more complex society by a broader élite in
which functions are more specialized.[25] It is part of a much larger and
slower transformation of the Roman world. But though it is true that
a long-term tendency is at work, we may be struck by the success with
which the nobility clung to their monopoly of functions until the very
last stages of the Republic. The *pontifices* of Cicero's day may have been
partly discredited, but they retained control of the calendar, and used
it as vigorously as ever. It took a violent act of political change, the
establishment of Caesar as dictator, to wrest the control from them.

Time is no more than an instance of a far-reaching sea-change
affecting all aspects of Roman custom, religion, and tradition. I wish to
underline the common theme that affects diverse areas: the perception
by late republican Romans, including many nobles, that the nobility has
lost its grip of matters for which it was supposed to be responsible, and
that this is part of a deep malaise affecting the state, and the representation
of the Augustan regime as having addressed these issues in setting up a
new order.

Religion

Perhaps the most familiar example is the picture of 'decline' of Roman
religion in the late Republic, followed by Augustan 'revival'. To translate
the laments of Cicero and Varro of negligence and the celebrations by
Augustan authors of the revival of neglected practices into a story of

a profound decline of a religious system may be to fall too naively for the rhetoric of the sources: religion was as central as ever to Roman public discourse in the late Republic. But, leaving aside the intractable question of what identifies a religion in true 'decline', we can focus on the issue of the authority of the priestly caste.

When Polybius identified religion as the single element which most contributed to the superiority of the Roman constitution (6.56), it was an instrument of social control, a means of keeping the unruly desires of the populace (*plêthos*) under control by fear. Fear of the gods is exactly what the Epicurean Lucretius sought to dispel, but Polybius (who acknowledges the philosophical arguments) asserts its social utility. In the same spirit, Cicero justified the practice of augury in terms of the benefit of the state. The thesis that religion and control of priesthoods was as much a foundation of the social dominance of the nobility as patronage is indeed attractive. As Cicero put it (albeit addressing the college of *pontifices* in flattering terms):

> Among the many things, gentlemen of the pontifical col-
> lege, that our ancestors created and established under divine
> inspiration, nothing is more renowned than their decision
> to entrust the worship of the gods and the highest inter-
> ests of the state to the same men – so that the most emi-
> nent and illustrious citizens might ensure the maintenance
> of religion by the proper administration of the state, and the
> maintenance of the state by the prudent interpretation of
> religion.[26]

The great importance of priesthood to the nobility is underlined by the scrupulous care with which families shared out this privilege, ensuring both that no more than one member of any *gens* was member of any priestly college, and that nobody held more than one priesthood.[27]

But if it is plausible that the tenure of priestly office was one of the means by which a group of families shored up their social dominance, it follows that doubts about their competence must have eroded that respect. Cicero, himself an augur, and a sceptic about the philosophical underpinnings of the practice of augury, is the more damaging when he suggests the nobility are culpable of a deep negligence (*De natura deorum* 2.9–10):

> But by the negligence of the nobility (*negligentia nobili-*
> *tatis*) the discipline of augury has been dropped, and the

true practice of auspices spurned, and only its appearance retained. And so most functions of the state, including warfare on which its safety depends, are administered without auspices. . . . By contrast, religion had such force for our ancestors, that some of them ritually veiled their heads and vowed their lives to the immortal gods for the republic.

That claim of neglect parallels the complaint that the calendar had fallen into confusion through neglect; that neglect had allowed temples to fall into decay, and priesthoods into desuetude, and set the stage for Augustus' claim to reverse the neglect. Such allegations deliberately overlooked the historical record of Roman religion for constant innovation and self-renewal, and attributed too much significance to the antiquarian unearthing of obscure rituals. The crucial point, however, is that such allegations were made, and were potentially devastating not for the practice of religion, but for the credibility of the *nobiles*.[28]

DIVINATION

One area of religious practice in which the shift from traditional to scientific discourse is especially marked is the set of practices by which the will of the gods was 'known'.[29] To simplify a complex story, the Republic is characterized by forms of divination aimed at establishing the will of the gods with regard to the state, as opposed to the prediction of the future with regard to the individual. The traditional forms of divination were under the control of the priestly colleges: the *augures* as authorities in reading the flight of the birds, the *XVviri sacris faciundis* authorities on the Sibylline books and prodigies and portents, while the *haruspices* stand slightly apart as Etruscan (hence non-Roman) experts in the reading of entrails whom the *pontifices* called in for advice. The forms of 'knowledge' of divine will are firmly under the control of the political class, and are essentially non-scientific, though there is evidence that haruspicy, distinctive in depending on a class of experts, developed under the influence of Hellenistic astrology, and came in the first century BCE increasingly to play a role as offering an individual a way of foreseeing the future.

In the course of the first century, the emphasis shifts dramatically toward predictive sciences. The central argument of Cicero's *On Divination*, over whether it is philosophically tenable to hold that the future can be predicted, is interesting not for its implications about belief in traditional religion (the arguments for and against are, after all, carefully balanced), but for its implications about the expectations for divination.[30] Cicero can maintain that the debate does not affect the function of augury as a powerful mechanism for keeping the Roman state in balance. The opponent, however, with which Cicero does not openly engage is astrology, with its offer of rational predictions of the future of each individual derived from the inherent logic and order of the universe. It was exactly in this period that astrology established widespread credibility among leading Romans, and that Roman experts emerged alongside the Greek practitioners, like Cicero's friend Nigidius Figulus.

The triumph of Augustus is also the triumph of astrology: his own publication of his horoscope and the widespread diffusion of his sign of the Capricorn are already evidence of the stamp of official approval; and the Horologium erected in the Campus Martius, even if Buchner was overoptimistic in some of his hypotheses, was a monumental expression of the victory of Augustus as the will of a divine universe, written in the stars. From Augustus onward, astrology and other predictive sciences (including physiognomics and the interpretation of dreams) flourish, and traditional divination disappears below the horizon. A form of knowledge predicated on the application of rational principles to a highly complex body of material by professionals displaces the traditional forms of knowledge embedded in the ruling class.[31]

TRADITION AND ANTIQUARIANISM

The perceived neglect of religious practice was part of a perceived neglect of Roman traditional practice in general. The key figure here is M. Terentius Varro (himself a *nobilis*), whose 30 books of *Antiquities Divine and Human* established themselves at once as the definitive text of what 'the Roman way' was. It is important that Varro, while distinguishing religion from other aspects of Roman *mores*, nevertheless sees them as related parts of a complex: a coherent set of practices that distinguished the Roman way in religious and non-religious life. We may juxtapose Augustine's account of how Varro saw his purpose with Cicero's reception.

According to Augustine (*Civ. Dei 6.2.48*):

He (Varro) feared that the gods should perish, not by an enemy invasion, but by the negligence of citizens, and he claimed that this was the doom from which he was rescuing them, and that it was a more useful service that things should be stored away and preserved in the memory of good men through books of this type, than when Metellus is said to have rescued the sacred objects of the Vestals from burning, or Aeneas to have saved the *penates* from Troy.

How bold that claim was is made apparent by the importance Vergil attributes to Aeneas's rescue of the *penates*. He presents himself as a saviour, a refounder, not a mere antiquarian who has rediscovered some quaint ceremonials in some old manuals. Particularly significant is his reference to the memory of good men, for memory is precisely the mechanism by which 'knowledge of tradition' is transmitted. The fallibility of memory both ensures that traditions can modify and transform, and be subject to dispute. Argument over true 'ancestral practice' was a staple of political discourse (the classic example being the contest between Caesar and Cato over clemency versus severity as the true Roman tradition). Argument over ancestral practice in religion was equally legitimate. Yet if the 'memory of good men' was now to be informed by an antiquarian book, it deprived the ruling class of the chance of establishing their authority by winning such argument.

Cicero's own eulogy of Varro conceded his claims (*Academica Posteriora* 1.9):

> When we were like strangers abroad and lost in our own city, your books led us back home, so to speak, so that at last we were able to recognise who and where we were. You revealed the age of our native land, its divisions of time, the rules of sacrifices and priesthoods; discipline at home and at war; the location of regions and places; and the names, types, functions and causes of all matters human and divine.

The great Augustan 'reinvention of tradition' is preceded by the Varronian invention of the loss of tradition. The Roman as peregrine in his own city has suffered a catastrophic collapse of identity. The 'knowledge' of what it is to be Roman has disintegrated, leaving him reliant upon Varro's writings for a rediscovery. But the nobility were distinguished precisely by their ancestors, and their ability to remember them. Polybius' description of a Roman noble funeral with its display of wax masks and recitations of speeches of the good deeds of the ancestors is a powerful insight into how social prestige was maintained (Flower 1996). But if the men with the *maiores* could no longer reliably guide the Romans as to the *mores maiorum*, and no longer were the guardians of Rome's collective memory, what credibility did they have?[32]

It may well have been a false perception to see adherence to Roman secular custom as in decline in the late Republic, just as much as religious practice: in both religious and non-religious spheres, Romans demonstrated an admirable capacity to innovate and change, and one has only to read the contemporary speeches to see that in both spheres there continued to be an obsessive concern to justify action by reference to tradition. But that is why the misperception (if such it was) carried such weight. It was inherently an expression of collapse of confidence in the ruling class to exercise its function of defining the Roman social order. That is the vacuum into which the Augustan court flowed.

VIRTUE AND PHILOSOPHY

Mores, social custom, was coterminous with morality. The Ennian line,

> moribus antiquis res stet Romana virisque
> (Rome is founded on her customs and men of old)

asserts that Rome's success was based both on its respect for tradition (*mores maiorum*) and on its morality. The ideological role of *virtus* is critical for the nobility. Public office was a reward for *virtus*, and nobility was the recognition of the *virtus* of holders of public office. Roman education was based on the imitation of *exempla*; the descendants of nobles had both the obligation and the privileged opportunity to reproduce the *virtus* of their ancestors. That, as nobles of the late Republic explicitly told Sallust, was the effect of seeing the images of their ancestors. But the same Sallust analysed the collapse of the Republic as a collapse of morality; *virtus* replaced by ambition and greed. The rhetoric is the same as the claims of 'new men' that they, not their noble competitors, are the true possessors of *virtus* (how many times does Cicero assert that he reached high office through his virtue, not the commendation of dusty ancestral busts?).

Here too we see one form of 'knowledge' displaced by another. The superior knowledge of virtue of the ruling class is based on the claim that they reproduced through imitation the virtues of their ancestors. But simultaneously, widespread contact with Greek philosophy by members of the ruling class introduced an alternative or parallel moral discourse. The competing philosophical schools had an enormous amount to say about what virtue was and how it was transmitted; and while nobles had a headstart in extending their patronage to philosophers who reassured them that Roman virtue made sense in philosophical terms, the same philosophers, notably the Stoic Posidonius, helped to articulate the analysis that the political crisis was the outcome of a collapse of public morality.[33]

PUBLIC SPEECH

If knowledge of religious and secular tradition and morality may appear to us to impact only tangentially on political life, other areas of knowledge were manifestly at the core of the public activity of the ruling class. What has been taken as the classic image of patronal power is the description, placed by Cicero in the mouth of the orator Crassus, of the nobles, who

> in the old days either strolling thus (i.e. across the Forum) and sitting at home on the chair of state were approached to be consulted not only on matters of civil law, but also about marrying off a daughter, buying a farm, cultivating the land, in fact on any matter of duty or business.
>
> (*De oratore* 3.133)

But interestingly, it is not a norm but a lost ideal he describes. The discussion, already distanced by being placed in the mouths of a previous generation, addresses precisely the issue of the knowledge (*scientia*) of a Roman public figure, and the impact on it of Greek learning and its tendency to specialization. Crassus is sustaining the unity of knowledge, and holding up as a model the men of a generation before himself whose knowledge was not specialized but wide-ranging. He cites the memories of his own father and father-in-law of Sextus Aelius, and his own observation of Manius Manilius, whom he had seen so wandering in the forum and offering advice to all comers.

Crassus makes clear that the ideal has not survived the importation of sophisticated foreign learning ('hanc politissimam doctrinam transmarinam atque adventiciam'). He draws a contrast between Cato as the universal man, equally adept at civil law, at oratory, at political life and military action, as one who 'knew everything which in those days could be known or learnt' (135), and the young men of today who 'approach public life naked and unarmed', and think themselves clever if they have mastered a single area of knowledge – military, legal (let alone pontifical law), and rhetorical, little knowing 'the kinship among all the skills and virtues' (136).

This Crassus would certainly agree that knowledge (*scientia*) should lie at the basis of the power of the ruling class, and believes that at some point in the past the various forms of knowledge were united in practice in a social élite. He also sees Greek learning as making a fundamental impact in its tendency to make knowledge more complex and hence specialist. Even so, Cicero must have been conscious of his exaggeration: Caesar proved every bit as successful as Cato in uniting the diverse forms of *scientia*, and doubtless Cicero would like us to think of himself. But the discussion makes clear that certain forms of *scientia* were fundamental to Roman public life, namely law, oratory and military science. The claim that each of these became more specialized and restricted can be substantiated.[34]

LAW

Knowledge of the civil law was essential for a public figure. Servius Sulpicius Rufus, the dominant jurist of Cicero's generation, said he was told by Mucius Scaevola the *pontifex* that ignorance of the law was disgraceful in one who was a patrician, a noble, and an advocate (Pomponius, *Digest* 1.2.2.43). True, the same Servius was beaten to the consulship by Licinius Murena, and when Cicero defended Murena against the charge of bribery, he took the opportunity to downplay the importance of jurisprudence. The two skills that paved the road to the consulship were military and oratorical; the jurist was too much of a backroom boy, an orator manqué (Cicero, *Mur.* 29). He can mock the pettifogging nature of jurisprudence, and suggest that the profound obscurity of legal language is a plot to make lawyers powerful, frustrated that their old ploy of ruling on which days public business could or could not be done had been foiled by the scribe Cn. Flavius in his publication of the *fasti* (*Mur.* 25). But this is only to express in a different way the shared awareness that legal, just like religious, knowledge (the calendar) was a pillar of the power of the ruling class.

In a different context, at a different time, Cicero expressed the profoundest respect for Servius' knowledge, and lamented the passing of an era (*Off.* 2.19.65):

> Among the many excellent practices of our ancestors was the high respect they always accorded to knowledge and interpretation of the corpus of civil law. Until the present age of confusion (*hanc confusionem temporum*), the *principes* kept this profession exclusively in their hands; but now, with the collapse of every other grade of social distinction, the prestige of this science has been destroyed – and that in the lifetime of one (Servius) who equals all his predecessors in social standing, and excels them all in science.

This squares exactly with what Crassus says about Greek learning and specialization, and even with Cicero's own mockery in the *Pro Murena*. Jurisprudence has shifted its social location, from a necessary skill of a nobility which dominates all forms of knowledge, war, law, religion, and public speaking, to the specialist activity of a subset, who talk a legal language that seems obscurantist to the ordinary Roman.

As Bruce Frier (1985) has shown, it was precisely Mucius Scaevola the Pontifex and Servius Sulpicius (patricians and nobles both) who transformed Roman jurisprudence into a legal science and a distinct profession. Their voluminous publications made it what Crassus would call a *politissima doctrina*. But that in turn put a premium not on noble birth but on mental agility, the ability to master a complex discipline; as the complexity of the discipline rises, so the social status of its practitioners drops.

Jurisprudence happens to be an especially sharp example of the transformation, completed, as Cicero observes, within his own lifetime. Chronologically, it stretches back at least to Mucius the Pontifex, to the generation of Crassus at the turn of the second and first centuries BCE. The last great proponent of the 'patrician–noble' style, Servius, dies at the very end of the Republic, on the verge of the final civil war. Caesar and Augustus did nothing to engineer the change, but their new order exploited it: Caesar's plan to publish a code of Roman law would have been, in Cicero's vivid description of the publication of the *fasti*, 'to poke out the eyes of the crow' in ensuring that no social group had a monopoly of knowledge. Augustus' approach was not codification, but continuous modification. Under Augustus and his successors, the profession of jurist flourished as never before, and the deep imperial involvement in ruling on the law gave jurists a key role in the imperial *consilium*. The court of Augustus relied on the authority of experts like Capito and Labeo, but their authority was unconnected with high social standing.[35]

PUBLIC SPEAKING

Similar processes are surely at work with oratory, at least from Cicero's perspective the key tool of public life. The *De oratore*, and several of Cicero's other rhetorical treatises like the *Brutus*, are centrally concerned with the issue of whether oratory should be seen as a specialised technique of speaking, or as a much broader set of social skills. Cicero's tendency is to argue for the broad vision, the Catonian *vir bonus dicendi peritus*, a 'good man' in the broad sense of one with all the social skills of the citizen, with a specific skill in speaking. That is also the ideal of the *Brutus*, which sees the history of Roman speaking as coterminous with the history of Roman politics: the orators are the leading politicians, because public speaking is the vital tool of politics.

But the pressures in the direction of highly specialised skills of rhetoric are obvious, and Cicero himself has a responsibility exactly parallel to that of Servius in the law for being the practitioner whose example (in his published speeches), and whose detailed contributions to the theory of rhetoric transformed the practice of oratory at Rome. The easiest way to see the transformation is in the history of its teachers. Here we have the particularly helpful insight offered by Suetonius' *Lives of the Grammarians and Rhetors* (Kaster 1988). The theme is the professional teaching of grammar (i.e., Latin language and literature) and rhetoric, and the dramatic rise in social significance of these disciplines. Both are seen by Suetonius as late-comers, and make a tentative appearance in the mid-second century BCE. The teaching of rhetoric, he maintains, arrived late and in the teeth of opposition, and he cites a senatorial decree of 161 expelling philosophers and rhetors from Rome.

He then cites the edict of the censors Domitius Ahenobarbus and Licinius Crassus (92 BCE) which laments the arrival of men calling themselves *Latinos rhetores*, and the way young men waste whole days hanging around listening to them. They are banned in a memorable assertion of traditional values (25):

> Our ancestors established what manner of things they wished
> their children to learn and what manner of schools they

wished them to attend. These novelties, which do not accord with received and traditional practice (*consuetudinem et morem maiorum*), neither meet our approval nor seem right.

The same edict is cited by Cicero in the work already discussed, for the censor Crassus is the great orator whom Cicero portrays as enemy of Greek specialization. Cicero had to deal with the fact that one of his greatest predecessors was author of this remarkable ban, and he embraces the paradox by setting his dialogue in the year after Crassus' censorship. He has Crassus grudgingly admit that Greek teachers of rhetoric at least had some learning, whereas the Latin teachers contributed nothing but daring, a 'school for impudence' (*De Or.* 3.70).

The motives for the edict, political or otherwise, have been much debated. What is clear is that the Roman traditional practice, by no means so fixed as the censors suggest, was based on the system still advocated by Cicero of *tirocinium fori*, of following an established speaker and learning by example in practice. It therefore favoured a pattern of transmission of knowledge within the ruling class. Greek rhetorical instruction was probably well established by 92 (though scarcely a 'school established by our ancestors'), and by definition was limited in access. The arrival of rhetorical instruction in Latin offered the potential of greater accessibility, and the *impudentia* is the threat of pushy newcomers (Corbeill 2001).

The motivation of the censors scarcely matters. The real question is the effect of the availability of teachers of rhetoric in Latin. The most palpable effect was the rise of the practice of declamation, not only in the use of the declamatory exercises of *controversiae* and *suasoriae* in training young orators, but the use of these exercises as performances. Suetonius demonstrates the rising prestige of rhetoric from the prestige of those who declaimed. The real take-off of the practice is in the 40s, and the remarkable compilation of the elder Seneca shows the new phenomenon at the heyday of its fashion under Augustus. Already under the early empire, it became a topic to blame declamation for the decline of true oratory, and Tacitus in the *Dialogus* is the heir of Crassus, the orator who blames the teaching of rhetoric for a supposed crisis in oratory.[36]

The point is that oratory follows the same paradigm as other branches of knowledge. The republican model, or at least the model which Cicero projects on the past, is of public speaking transmitted as part of a bundle of knowledge of Roman ways (with law and religious law in close association) within a relatively closed ruling class.

Specialization gathers pace throughout the first century BCE, with Cicero himself as the outstanding example of the potential of oratory as a special skill to bring rapid social promotion to a new man. Once declamation settles in as a standard practice, especially under Augustus, the nature of public speaking has changed.

Declamation becomes a language in its own right, a specialised discourse, with its own extensive complex of rules and tricks and 'colours'. It is a discourse accessible only to those who have undergone the demanding training. They do indeed constitute an élite, but an élite defined and constituted by the process of education itself. That is a different *sort* of élite from an hereditary nobility that maintains its social advantage by keeping knowledge, as far as it can, within itself. Such an élite suits a court society, which constantly recruits to its ranks from outside: enough to recall the success of the elder Seneca from Corduba, who documents the fashion for declamation, and whose son's skill in rhetoric carried him to the inmost circle of the court.

LANGUAGE

The teacher of rhetoric comes as a package deal, as Suetonius documents, with the grammarian. The 'guardian of the language' (*custos Latini sermonis*) also has a vital social role.[37] As Suetonius shows, the learned study and teaching of the Latin language arrives late, taking its impulse from Greek exemplars in the mid-second century. But it leads to a decisive shift of authority over the language of the public life. The public speaker, to carry conviction, must speak good Latin. But how can you tell what proper, correct Latin is? The debate was launched at the end of the second century by Aelius Stilo, who got his name for his 'stylistic' support to his noble patrons in their speech writing. As Greek theory taught, there was a choice between the principles of anomaly, based on standard usage, *consuetudo*, however illogical or anomalous that might be, and that of analogy. Analogy assumed that usage should be dictated by *ratio*, the set of logical rules ensuring that words of similar formation behaved in similar ways in similar circumstances. Neither Stilo, nor more importantly Varro, whose *de Lingua Latina* preserves much of this debate, ever fully came down on one side or other: they knew that it must be a continuous tussle between received usage and systematic rules. But in the very process of launching the debate, they constituted the grammarian as the new figure of authority.

Here, too, Cicero proves a key witness of the shift:

> Hitherto, pure Latin was not a matter of reason and science (*rationis et scientiae*) but of good usage (*bonae consuetudinis*). I pass over Laelius and Scipio; in that period men were praised for their pure Latin as for their innocence (though there were those who spoke badly). But virtually everyone in those days who neither lived outside this city, nor was tainted with domestic barbarity, used to speak correctly. But this has been corrupted in Rome as in Greece. Both Athens and this city have received a flood of people from a diversity of origins whose language is polluted (*inquinate loquentes*). This is why our talk needs purging, and some sort of rationality needs to be applied by a touchstone, which cannot be changed, nor are we to go by the perverted rule of usage.[38]

This revealing passage exposes the link between demographic and linguistic change. Of course, second-century Rome was not a haven of true-born native Romans, all speaking a consistently pure tongue. What is more probable is that the élite from which the speakers were drawn was small and homogeneous enough to be able to impose its own linguistic authority. To revert to our paradigm, a nobility which gave itself the authority to 'know' the Roman way, 'knew' the Latin language as the rest of Roman usage (*consuetudo*). What Cicero is observing is that this authority had collapsed. A flood of 'outsiders' in Rome, and not just servile immigrants, but members of the municipal élites like Cicero himself, wanted to make the Latin language their own, and turned to Varro and to the growing profession of grammarian to get clear rulings.

That process had an enormous impact on Latin, turning it from a local dialect, unstable, shifting, and contradictory, into a fixed literary language with high levels of consistency over region and over time (Adams 2003). The revolution takes place over the first century, and is one to which the nobility again willingly contributed. One of the champions of strict analogy (too much so for Cicero's taste) was Julius Caesar, who penned a treatise *de analogia* while on campaign in Gaul, "amid volleys of javelins about declinations of nouns, amid trumpets and tubas about aspirations and rational rules." We can see, in Fronto's (p. 221 N) word-play, the analogy between the imposition of military order on barbarians, and the imposition of linguistic order ('barbarism' was the standard grammarian's term for erroneous language). Both projects are imperialist: if the Gauls speak a form of Latin today, it is because Caesar fought on both fronts.

War

It would be neat to be able to turn at this point to Roman military science and point toward a parallel paradigm shift. Law, public speaking, and military science were the routes which Cicero identified as giving access to the consulship. It is not difficult to characterise the Roman republican nobility as above all a military élite, and to suggest the majority of élite education until the mid second century was military, acquired above all through experience.[39] One might therefore take the line that what constituted the nobility was not knowledge, but action in the field.

But warfare is a form of knowledge as much as religion or language (Cicero could speak of *scientia rei militaris; Imp. Cn. Pomp.* 28), and we must suppose that in this field too there was a vast development toward specialization. While in the second century *all* those wishing to hold office were required to undertake ten seasons of campaign, in the first the requirement lapsed, with the precedent set by Cicero.[40] That means that by a parallel process, while military service and public speaking had been a common grounding, each was becoming a specialist field. The rise of Marius, *novus homo*, is the rise of a specialist general adapted to new forms of warfare in new conditions: long campaigns abroad with large armies, complex logistics, and sophisticated equipment (siege engines, etc.). The Hellenistic kingdoms had transformed the technology of warfare as much as any other branch of science; and even if Plutarch could represent Marius as lacking in culture and Hellenism, his military science, starting with radical military reform, was irreproachable.[41] Warfare-like rhetoric became the topic of treatises and manuals, from Cato's *De re militari*, through Frontinus' *Strategemata* to Vegetius' *Epitoma rei militaris*.[42]

However, it would give the wrong emphasis to suggest that the important change is a transformation of Roman warfare into a form of military science. The point is not that generals became more 'rational' or 'scientific', but that the knowledge of war, which had to some extent characterized the entire republican ruling class, became progressively restricted to a separate set of 'military' experts. Just as Marius' reforms marked a decisive step from citizen militia to professional army, and Augustus' reforms completed the process of professionalization, the same period marks the emergence of those who we may call *viri militares* as a specialist class, though these are easier to recognize among the equestrian officers than the senatorial élite.[43] War has passed from the field of general knowledge to that of specialists.

THE CITIZEN AND SPACE

The idea of a paradigm shift applies as much to the Roman construction of the physical, as of the intellectual world. Space, as much as time, is a social construct. How the Romans knew, mapped, and built their spatial world was subject to the same process of transformation. Nicolet's study (1991) of the mapping of urban and imperial space has thrown into relief the cognitive change that comes to a head with Augustus: mapping from being an irrelevance becomes an obsession. We can trace the development, moving from the centre outwards.

CITY

How was republican Rome knowable to its users in terms of urban space? Since the city is the space of the citizen, the divisions of the citizen body were also divisions of space, with the four city tribes instituted by Servius Tullius (Suburana, Palatina, Esquilina, Collina) corresponding, as Varro explains, to four regions of the city, and the 26 (later 31) rustic tribes to divisions of the territory of Rome.[44] But though Varro uses these four 'regions' to articulate his account of the names of places in Rome, they had no significance in the administration of the republican city, and locality had parted company with tribal membership so that by the late Republic the urban tribes were used as the dumping ground of new citizens and the urban plebs; they did not even cover all the territory within the Servian walls, excluding both Capitoline and Aventine. A more detailed topographical landscape was provided by religious festivals. The Septimontium was the festival of the several *montani* of the seven hills, but though Varro seems to include Capitoline and Aventine in his list, the Augustan jurist Antistius Labeo preserved a very different list which may indeed preserve a memory of a pre-Servian city, indeed several layers of memory.[45]

Montes ('hills') and *pagi* ('districts') seem to have been living fossils in the late Republic, and it is no coincidence that we know about them now through the antiquarian writers of the first century BCE. There is nothing to suggest that there were alternative discourses available to map the republican city. It was a city which could be known through ritual, and by the distribution of its citizens in their tribes, both practices in the hands of the nobility.

The Augustan reorganization of Rome created a city that was defined and knowable in a fundamentally different way. The division into 14 *Regiones* (Fig. 40), with the subdivision into an expandable number of *vici* ('quarters'; we cannot say how many Augustus set up, only that under Vespasian there appear to have been 265) was systematic and comprehensive. Every corner of the city could be defined and listed in terms of *regio* and *vicus*. There was a ritual element, thanks to the cult of the Lares Augusti at the Compitalia; though in the hands of the freedmen *vicomagistri* it was anything but noble. There was also an administrative function, and the initial impulse for Augustus' reorganization is given as the need to provide against fires. The *vici* provided the framework for census-taking, and the census of inhabitants *vicatim* by *domus* and *insula*, introduced by Caesar in his dictatorship, provided a detailed knowledge of the inhabitants of the city unimaginable to previous censors, and a powerful enough instrument to enable a reduction of the dole list from 320,000 to 150,000. The extensiveness of the imperial knowledge of the capital is evidenced by the fourth-century Regionary Catalogues: though they present problems of detail, they reflect the possibility of establishing the detailed statistics of the housing stock of the city.

A vital tool of such knowledge was cartography. The plan of the city inscribed on marble at the end of the second century CE, fragmentary though its state is, bears witness to the same capacity to document all aspects of the urban fabric, not just public monuments and public property. The knowledge goes down to the level of the individual private property, and the individual shop. Fragments of earlier versions show that the initiative went back at least to Augustus, though it should not be ruled out that this too goes back to Caesar.[46]

The city known and displayed, measured by professional surveyors, listed by census-officials, is a city (unlike that of the late Republic) under control. The cohorts of the City Prefect or the Prefect of the Firewatch depended for their effectiveness on this detailed information, and on the willing collaboration of the local officials of the *vici*. The manifest 'rationality' of the system makes us ask why such measures were not introduced before. But it is not a mere exercise of rationality and administrative efficiency; it is part and parcel of a paradigm shift, from a knowledge conceived in traditional and ritual terms to the professionalized knowledge under imperial surveillance. That emerges too from the abortive attempts in the late Republic for the city to emerge as one of *vici: populares* like Clodius could see such local divisions as a basis for articulation of their own support among the urban masses, and the Senate could only see such alternative articulations of power as subversive, and repress them.

CONSTRUCTING THE URBAN LANDSCAPE

If we can see Augustus' reorganization of the city not just as an act of administrative convenience, but as the outcome of a new way of knowing and controlling the city, this may help us to take a fresh look at the history of architecture in the metropolis. That the face of Rome is transformed under Augustus is common ground (cf. Diane Favro's Chapter 10 in this volume): we witness the passage from the undignified jumble of winding streets and the cacophony of competing buildings to a series of monumental complexes that draw on the current language of Hellenistic urbanism, and render the city worthy of the dignity of the capital of an empire.[47] The outcome, the importation of a rationalist model of urban order from the Greek East, is of a piece with other aspects of the Augustan revolution we have been examining. But it certainly cannot be explained in terms of a late dawning of awareness in Rome of such a model, which had been spreading in other centres in central Italy for at least two centuries. The delay is deliberate and conscious, and cannot be disengaged from structures of social power.

Augustus' claim to be saving Rome from long neglect – 82 temples repaired at the very moment of the launching of the new order in 28 BCE – was manipulative, not merely a boast of his own contribution, but an attempt to discredit the 'neglect' of the old order.[48] Naturally there had been intense building activity throughout the first century BCE, as it is part of a natural rhythm for older buildings to fall into disrepair while new ones spring up around them. The problem was rather that since republican temple-building was typically the outcome of the individual initiative, above all of the successful general expending his spoils of war (*manubiae*), so maintenance and reconstruction depended on individual initiative.

One could therefore present the shift as a shift of authority from the dispersed authority of a ruling élite, which is interested only in its own competitive monuments, to the central authority of the ruler concerned with the image of his capital. The ideology of the *monumentum* as the 'memory' of the name of the builder fits with this. To know the buildings of republican Rome was to know the identity of the dominant families who built it, and to participate in its collective memory. One of the most significant shifts of Augustus' reign, after an initial encouragement to the élite to maintain their family monuments (the Aemilii and the Basilica Aemilia were both the model and the end of a tradition), the imperial family itself establishes a stranglehold over the naming of metropolitan buildings, and even introduces a new ideal of modesty by which the builder suppresses his name.[49]

But the argument may be carried one step further. The shift is not only in who builds, but in what type of monument is built. The staple of republican public building is the temple, though basilicas, porticoes, and also utilities like roads and aqueducts play a significant role. Imperial Rome is familiar for monumental complexes, baths, amphitheatres, theatres, and new imperial *fora*. In contrast to Augustus' emphasis on the restoration of sacred buildings, it is the Republic which is characterised by frenetic temple building, and the Empire by secular building. What is at stake is not the construction of piety, but of Roman social order.

Pompey's theatre is rightly taken as an important turning point. According to the well-known narrative, the building of any permanent theatre in Rome had been vigorously opposed by the Senate since the second century BCE, and Pompey was able to overcome opposition only in the mid 50s by presenting his theatre as an adjunct to the temple of Venus.[50] Without entering the debate on the reasons for the ban on stone theatres, we can say that the issue is about Roman perceptions of the relation between theatres and social order. Cicero's presentation of the theatre as the place where the true will of the Roman people in all its social ranks is manifested ties in both with the Augustan legislation on seating at theatres and with the details of Roman theatrical building (cf. Richard Beacham's Chapter 7 in this volume).

But if the theatre (or even better, amphitheatre) was where the emperor 'built' his people, assembled it, distinguished its ranks and conditions, knew and controlled it, the contrast is that the republican nobility did not wish the citizen body to be constructed in this way. They accepted that the privilege could be granted temporarily to a member of the élite to do so for a festival, but not in permanence, as a *monumentum*. The parallels between Pompey's theatre and the sanctuary complexes of central Italy make the refusal more marked. Though Tertullian represented the combination of theatre with temple as a pretext, the form of the Pompeian complex, with temple, theatre, and portico, has long been seen to be akin to the great second-century complexes of Hercules at Tivoli, of Fortuna Primigeneia at Praeneste, of the Samnites at Pietrabbondante, and, we may now add, of the northern

Campanians at the recently discovered temple-theatre complex on the dorsal ridge of Pietravairano.[51]

The magnificence of these sites makes it the more likely that the new model was one of which the Roman élite was well aware, but did not wish to appropriate. That evidently has a political dimension, in resistance to the rise of autocracy. But it is also rooted, if the suggestions above hold, in an epistemological system. A city which could only be known through ritual, through a multiplicity of places which preserved the memory of the past, which was not susceptible to an overall rational system, gave way under Augustus, following Pompey's model, to a city which was multiply ordered and displayed, whether overall in its marble plan, or in the microcosm of individual monumental complexes which replicated the good order of the knowable citizen body.

EMPIRE

Finally, the shift can be seen at level of empire as well as city. The first great mapping and display of the *imperium Romanum* of which we know is Agrippa's Porticus Vipsania (Nicolet, 1991, 95–122). It is the product on the one hand of Greek geographical science, and on the other of a new concept of the Roman empire as bounded and definable. *Imperium sine fine* ("Empire without end"; Vergil, *Aeneid* 1.279) is indeed a republican ideal of empire, not in the sense of an infinite empire covering the entire world, but of an empire not defined by physical boundaries. It is precisely Augustus who leaves to his successor an empire confined within limits, limits which not only restrain the ambition to conquer (cf. Woolf, p. 121), but which place a territorial marker between us and them.

The shift of conception has been recognised in the changing definition of a *provincia*: from the theatre of war in which a magistrate is instructed to operate, to a bounded territory within which his jurisdiction holds sway.[52] That shift took place progressively in the second and first centuries BCE, but the decisive change is in Augustus' act of return to the Senate of provinces, not all, but certain provinces within known boundaries. The charge of infringing on the *maiestas populi Romani* is swiftly levelled against the magistrate who exceeds his boundaries (so the case of Murena in 23 BCE): only the emperor, the successor to the unbounded *imperium maius* of Pompey, can enjoy power without limits. Known boundaries supported the imperial order, so that we see on the one hand a proliferation of territorial limits (Italy subdivided into eleven regions, just as Rome into fourteen), and on the other a proliferation of detailed descriptions of the landscape of empire, from Strabo to the elder Pliny. It is not that the rationalist instruments of geographical knowledge were absent before Augustus; but rather that the previous order did not see such knowledge as the means to maintain order.

CONCLUSION

This essay has attempted to trace a consistent pattern of changes in a wide variety of fields. Many of the shifts in Roman intellectual life and material culture have in the past been attributed to 'Hellenization', as if culture obeyed its own autonomous rules of contact and assimilation irrespective of political and social change. The present argument neither explains political by cultural change, nor the opposite. It attempts to show that the two processes of change were deeply enmeshed with each other, indeed were one and the same process.

The increasing dissatisfaction with terms like 'Hellenization' and 'Romanization' to characterize and explain the cultural changes associated with Roman conquest (cf. the next two chapters by N. Purcell and G. Woolf in this volume) has led to the suggestion that in what has been called 'Romanization,' we see another aspect of the Roman Revolution.[53] That theme would lead far beyond the bounds of the present chapter. But that Roman culture was an epistemological system, a way of knowing, is exactly the argument of this chapter. In so much as the Roman Empire was a system of knowledge, the impact of Rome on the people it ruled led not just to one revolution, but to a continuous process of change: the outcome was perhaps not one great knowledge, but a multiplicity of knowledges that linked and interconnected, in tension and mutual influence.[54] The Roman culture which the Augustan 'revolution' reformulated was one which Ovid would recognize as perpetuating itself in its self-renewal or metamorphosis.

SUGGESTIONS FOR FURTHER READING

No single work covers exactly the range of topics here addressed, though Moatti (1997) covers some similar ground. The issues of political and cultural revolution were addressed by Habinek and Schiesaro (1997); the transformation of culture under Augustus is explored by

Galinsky (1996) and, from the aspect of visual language, by Zanker (1988). On intellectual life in the late Republic, Rawson (1985) is fundamental. On 'Hellenization' and Roman identity, see Gruen (1990) and (1992). For the political background, Brunt (1988), Hopkins (1978a) and (1983), Millar (1998) and (2002). On religion, Beard, North, Price (1998), on geographical space Nicolet (1991) and Horden and Purcell (2000).

NOTES

1. At the editor's request, I offer a recast version of my essay, '*Mutatio morum*: the idea of a cultural revolution' in Habinek and Schiesaro (1997) 3–22, though I have tried in the process to carry the arguments there a step further in the light of subsequent discussion. The comments of Nicholas Purcell, Peter Wiseman and Greg Woolf have been particularly helpful. I am grateful to Rosie Harman for invaluable help with bibliographic research.

2. Galinsky (1999); also my essay, 'Augustus' *Metamorphoses*', *JACT Review* ser. 2 no. 4 (Autumn 1988) 18–23.

3. Foucault (1971) and (1977).

4. R. Chartier, *The Cultural Origins of the French Revolution*, trans. L. G. Cochrane (Durham and London 1991).

5. Gelzer (1969).

6. North (1989) and (1990).

7. Brunt (1982); Hölkeskamp (1987); Burkhardt (1990).

8. See my discussion in *CAH* 10 (1996) 283–308; Winterling (1999); Pani (2003).

9. Cf. Saller (1982) and (1989).

10. Moatti (1997) traces a similar transformation, underlining its duration.

11. On the Roman calendar, Michels (1967); Radke (1990); Rüpke (1995); Beard, North, Price 2 (1998) 60–77.

12. Wallace-Hadrill (1987).

13. Plutarch *Caesar* 59.5; Pliny *NH* 18. 211ff. draws on the three treatises of Sosigenes.

14. On that control, see Beard, North and Price 1 (1998) 99–108.

15. The classic edition is that of A. Degrassi in *Inscriptiones Italiae* vol. XIII. It is unfortunate for the understanding of how the two types of Fasti relate that he splits into two volumes the Fasti of the magistrates (fasc.1, Rome 1947) and the calendars ('Fasti Anni Numani et Iuliani', fasc.2, Rome 1963).

16. Cf. Wallace-Hadrill (1986).

17. See the discussions of the *Fasti* in *The Cambridge Companion to Ovid*, ed. P. Hardie, (Cambridge 2002), esp. A. Schiesaro, "Ovid and the professional discourses of scholarship, religion, rhetoric," pp. 62–75; C. Newlands, "*Mandati memores*: political and poetic authority in the *Fasti*," pp. 200–216; also B. Boyd, "*Celabitur auctor*: the crisis of authority and narrative patterning in Ovid *Fasti* 5," *Phoenix* 54 (2000) 64–98.

18. Degrassi observes the relationship, but does not print the local magistrates, who are published in *CIL* XIV, 2964–9.

19. Venusium, Degrassi, *Inscr. It.* XIII, 2, no. 8 (249–56), compare no. 5 (173–41) Ostia, no. 7 (243–48) Cupra Maritima; no. 10 (259) Luceria; no. 12 (261) Nola;

no. 13 (263) Volsinii; no. 14 (264–5) Teanum; no. 15 (266–8) Interamnum; no. 16 (269–70) Cales.

20 Degrassi, *Inscr. It.* XIII, 2, no. 17 (107–145). His publication separates the two lists between two volumes while admitting the link.

21 Suetonius *de Grammaticis et Rhetoribus* 17, with the commentary of R. A. Kaster (Oxford 1995) 190–6.

22 Degrassi, *Inscr. It.* XIII,1, no. 20 (279–90) and vol. 2, no. 12 (90–98); discussed by J. Rüpke in *La Mémoire perdue. Recherches sur l'administration romaine* (Rome 1998) 27–44.

23 Petronius, *Satyricon* 30, noted by Degrassi, *Inscr. It.* XIII, 2, 217. Note also the Fasti of the *vicomagistri* of Pompeii, dating back to Caesar's dictatorship: Degrassi, *Inscr. It.* XIII, 1, no. 17 (271–2).

24 Degrassi, *Inscr. It.* XIII,1 no. 31 (320–34). Cf. no. 23 (294–5), the *fasti* of a burial college of Augustan date, with freedmen and slaves as officers, no. 25 (302) from Tusculum, of Augustan date with slave *magistri*, and no. 28 (309–10), Fasti Lunenses, of a servile college of Tiberian date.

25 So, e.g., Beard, North, Price 1 (1998) 149.

26 Cicero, *De domo sua* 1; see Beard, North, Price 1 (1998) 115; 2.197f.

27 Beard, North, Price 1 (1998) 99–108; J. A. North, "Family strategy and priesthood in the late Republic," in *Parenté et stratégies familiales dans l'antiquité*, ed. J. Andreau and H. Bruhns (Rome 1990) 527–43.

28 Similarly Moatti (1997) 30–44.

29 Liebeschuetz (1979) 7–29; North (1990) 49–72; Barton (1994) 27ff.

30 Beard (1986) 33–46.

31 On the evidence of Suetonius, in striking contrast with republican historiography, see Wallace-Hadrill (1983) 189–97.

32 See Hölkeskamp (1996) 301–38; Moatti (1997) 101–37.

33 Moatti (1997) 44–6.

34 For what follows, cf. Hopkins (1978a) 74–96, who looks at the army, education, and law from the point of view of structural differentiation. My emphasis on an epistemological paradigm shift does not contradict or substitute the thesis of differentiation.

35 Cf. Moatti (1997) 137–9, 186–8.

36 Bonner (1969).

37 Seneca, *Ep. mor.* 95.65 for the expression, taken up in the title of the perceptive study of Kaster (1988).

38 Cicero, *Brutus* 258. The reference to Athens evokes the parallel debate on pure Attic, which goes back at least to Ps-Xenophon, *Constitution of Athens* ii.8.

39 Harris (1979) 10–15.

40 Harris (1979) 257.

41 But note the observations of A. K. Goldsworthy, *The Roman Army at War 100 BC–AD 200* (Oxford 1996) 116–70 on the low level of theorization of Roman military training.

42 On Roman military manuals, B. Campbell, "Teach yourself how to be a general," *JRS* 77 (1987) 13–28.

43 The doctrine of a distinct career path for senatorial *viri militares* was questioned by B. Campbell, "Who were the *viri militares*?," *JRS* 65 (1975) 11ff.; cf. Campbell (1984) 325ff.

44 Varro, *Ling. Lat.* 5.41–56, with the detailed discussion of Fraschetti (1990) 132–203.

45 Fraschetti (1990) 134 ff.; A. Carandini, *La nascita di Roma. Dèi, Lari, eroi e uomini all'alba di una civiltà* (Rome 1997) 267–456.

46 On marble plans before the Severan one, see now E. Rodríguez-Almeida, *Formae Urbis Antiquae: le mappe marmoree di Roma tra la Repubblica e Settimio Severo* (Rome 2002).

47 For a classic formulation, Zanker (1988) 18–25. On Augustan Rome, see now Haselberger (2002).

48 Beard, North, Price 1 (1998) 120–5.

49 Eck (1984) 129–67, esp. 140–2. On the Basilica Aemilia, Tacitus, *Ann.* 3.72.

50 Much discussed since Hanson (1959).

51 Coarelli (1987). For Pietravairano, *Lo Sguardo di Icaro. Le collezioni dell'Aerofototeca Nazionale per la conoscenza del territorio*, ed. M. Guaitoli (Rome 2003) 295.

52 Nicolet (1991) 191f.; Richardson (1991).

53 Woolf (2001) 173–86.

54 Following Horden and Purcell (2000).

4: ROMANS IN THE ROMAN WORLD

Nicholas Purcell

INTRODUCTION

During the period of the Roman conquest of the Mediterranean basin, a singular form of deracinated but coherent society came into being. Starting as mercenaries, even pirates, and moving seamlessly into the world of commerce and ultimately the management of Roman provinces, a whole diaspora of mobile, opportunistic Italians outside Italy – men and women, slaves and free, very rich and grindingly poor – had come into being by the beginning of the first century B.C. Their identity was not much shaped by a sense of a common homeland, because Italy itself was so heterogeneous and – especially at this time – changing so fast. The changing fortunes of this loose collectivity have resisted generalization because of its erratic and labile distribution in space and time. Yet it can claim to be one of the great diasporas, to be compared with the archaic Phoenician and Hellenic diasporas, or that of the Hellenistic Jews. It was maintained through common interaction with the Roman state, especially through military service, and through a growing feeling of shared advantage over non-Romans. It was therefore indeed neither a simply colonial nor a truly ethnic phenomenon: but in it lie clues to the dynamic of Roman imperial power, and to the cultural weave of the empire itself, east and west, of the provinces and, in many respects, of Italy too. These – besides free-born Romans they included grantees of citizenship, and freedmen and their descendants – were the people who formed the Roman core of provinces and who bound client-kingdoms into the fabric of the *imperium*.

The diaspora also had a lasting effect on the imperial system itself. Even if the *princeps* appears more preoccupied with the inner circles of status, at Rome and within Italy, the Romans of the wider world were a gallery to which Augustus had to play too, and arguably the most important for the development of the discourses of power, legitimacy, and political expectation which were to be characteristic of the imperial future. The Augustan age (by which they numbered several hundred thousand) might even be regarded as an acme in the fortunes and self-consciousness of the scattered Romans of the Empire, and a particular phase in its relationship with the societies on which it so variously abutted. For all that, it is very curious how most scholarship on the subject has stopped at Actium, precisely the moment when they become historically most significant! Even if the diaspora did rapidly lose its identity in the Augustan age (which is very doubtful), that process would demand analysis and explanation.

Most Romans in the provinces in this age are simply names to us, accidentally preserved in the inscriptions of the towns where they resided for short or long periods. The systematic study of names, ono-mastics, is a painstaking discipline, which has only in the last generation accumulated the critical mass to make a large contribution to history. Nomenclature clearly identifies certain aspirations to Roman-ness, but remains an ambiguous window on a blurry world. It is a better guide to community than it is to culture: claiming to be in some sense a Roman was more likely to be a political statement than an ethnic one. Romans were not like other outsiders. They were privileged citizens of the Power that ruled the world. Much of what we normally call 'Roman culture' can be interestingly illuminated by this exercise, but it is not my aim to offer another discussion of 'Romanization'. Indeed, what is most distinctive about the people in this chapter is the structures with which they interacted. Their choices of religion, clothing, tableware, recreation, language, and food were extremely diverse, like their places of residence and their genetic origin. What linked them, in East and West, across the Mediterranean, was the aspiration to, or the deployment of, certain types of political relationship with the imperial state.

The Italians overseas first became spectacularly visible in 88–7 B.C., when King Mithridates of Pontus ordered massacres of the Romans resident in the areas under his control, expressly including wives, children and freedmen of Italian birth. The Romans of the next generation remembered the episode with understandable horror (Cicero, *Imp. Pomp.* 11), and, as is often the case with massacres, it is im-possible to discover the real death-toll, which is estimated in surviving accounts at 80,000 to 150,000. Three important facts emerge: Romans in this broad sense were very numerous; they were frequently hated by the people among whom they lived; and the event became a landmark in how the Romans of the provinces related to their neighbours.

A mere antipathy toward aliens, even ones tainted by association with a rapacious and implacable empire, is not a sufficient explanation. The historian Memnon put it rather differently: the presence of Romans scattered in the cities was a major obstacle to Mithridates' plans (*FGH* 352.22.9). These people mattered politically in their communities, as is too rarely allowed. City-government in Greek is *politeia*: and this word always means both constitution and citizenship. Negotiating and regulating the boundaries between various sorts of insiders and outsiders was one of the main functions of public institutions. This delicate and ever-shifting task was immensely complicated by the fact that encoded in the balances and accommodations between groups within each community were the parameters of interrelationship *between* communities. The status of an outsider-group was both a matter of anxious concern for the internal workings of the state, and a symbol of the relationships – economic, political, military, social – which bound individual communities into wider networks. This status and its vicissitudes were expressed in the conventional languages of public esteem: honour, benefaction, rhetoric, religion, and history.

This is why the legal and customary skeins which tied Roman outsiders to hundreds of local communities mattered so much. The language of *politeia* here served to express the relations of the community with the imperial state which had gradually, by conquest, diplomacy, edict, and judgement, acquired the supreme disposing power in all matters of intercommunity negotiation. It is hardly surprising that unfortunate Roman outsiders lent themselves to being used for statements of hatred and rejection of that disposing power, arbitrary, oppressive, excessive, and corrupt as it usually was. After the defeat of Mithridates, the fates of Romans, the behaviour of city-officials, and the new arrangements for Roman outsiders in communities became more than ever the primary language for statements about the status and privileges of those communities in relation to the ruling power. The Mithridatic war thus placed the Roman diasporas centre-stage in the spectacle of intercity competition and the quest for status, honour, and prosperity. Their fortunes became the gauge of loyalty. Exact and detailed record of how each community had behaved before, during, and after the conflict was therefore essential, and remained so until the *domus Augusta* took over as the principal currency of pro-Roman zeal.

"After the [Mithridatic] war" and its travails, the first normal chief magistrate, or "crown-wearer" (*stephanephoros*) in the city of Priene in

Asia was A. Aemilius Zosimus (*Inschr. von Priene* 112–14). His activities are recorded in a dossier of inscriptions whose passionate detail confirms the gravity of the moment. He is a Roman citizen, and that is vital to his rôle in post-Mithridatic Priene. His activities as a benefactor are noteworthy, and give the flavour of the time. He gave feasts to certain significant groups: to all the full citizens by their 10 tribes; to all the Romans and to the resident Athenians (first in the list, as befitted the city which had refounded Priene in the fourth century and lent it its civic organization), Thebans, Rhodians, Milesians, Magnesians, Samians, Ephesians and a few selected Trallians. The benefactor articulates the web of mutual admiration in which cosmopolitan Priene was located. Cities did not vie for their place in the pecking order singly; they had their friends and their rivals, in a kind of stylized remnant of the days of military alliances and local war. It was, however, as *grammateus* (secretary) of the city of Priene, that Zosimus, no mere figurehead benefactor, made his most important mark: he archived public documents on papyrus and parchment, the multiple copies on different materials being clearly intended to prevent loss of the records to decay. After Mithridates, it was crucial to be able to provide evidence of claims about honours and immunities, special relationships, and past favours. This evidence went on being vital in the ceaseless negotiation of advantage with the Roman state. In the Augustan period we see a Roman proconsul of Asia investigating a dispute using just this kind of document, dating from just the same tense Mithridatic aftermath – and discovering that in the city of Chios Roman citizens were in certain respects subject to local law in ways which they were clearly not elsewhere. Zosimus bridged the void between Roman and non-Roman communities. The decisions of men like him, and their recording, shaped the East which Augustus was to rule.

The Hellenistic world had been united by the web of inter-community diplomacy. Cities and other collectivities needed to argue their case: they needed plausible reasons for advancing their superiority, such as literary fame, religious distinction, all the claims of history, geographical advantage, distinguished citizens. And all these one-upmanships had to be expressed in the languages of classical literary form: local history, poetry, and above all oratory. A historical memory was essential, and all dealings with Romans might find a relevance at some point. But it was the vicissitudes of resident Romans that struck the most resonant chords: the archive-conscious Zosimus minutely details the place of honour accorded to them in all his benefactions. As Cicero put it of a Greek city in Sicily: "The witnesses are the public records – the great city of Lilybaeum – and a very worthy and numerous community of resident Roman citizens" (*Verr.* 2.5.10). It was precisely as living, witnessing record that the Romans of the diaspora mattered.

The wars of 49–31 B.C. catalysed the diplomatic world of the whole Mediterranean with a new alignment in relation to Roman power as Mithridates had done before in the East. In times of divided loyalty, taking sides is the most important political decision, and the record of the process is vital. In the Mediterranean world in the first century B.C., scattered Romans played a pivotal part in such decisions from the Mithridatic disaster on. The last set of similar decisions was to be taken in the stand-off which was won by Augustus.

THE NATURE OF A DIASPORA

An inscription from Cyzicus on the Sea of Marmara offers one of those sweet novelistic vignettes that so enliven history (*IGRR* IV 1375). Soterides, a eunuch priest of the Great Mother, describes how he prayed to the Goddess on behalf of his *sumbios* (a word more usually employed of a spouse) in the difficult days of the Civil War of 49–46 B.C. The partner has a very Italian-sounding name – Marcus Stlaccius, son of Marcus – and he is described as a flautist, presumably another ritual rôle in the cult of Cybele. He has gone to war in the quadrireme *Saviour Goddess*, one of the 12 ships from Asia which joined in Caesar's expedition to Africa in the war of Zama. The ship was captured and its crew enslaved, and the Goddess revealed to Soterides in a dream that Marcus was one of those who had been taken prisoner. Alas, we do not know what happened next . . . but the inscription is a very valuable illustration. Here, in a rich and important coastal city, there were many Roman citizens of Italian stock. One of them, and a Greek Cyzicene, have the closest of relationships in the cult *par excellence* of northwest Anatolia. But their destiny was shaped by events on a Mediterranean scale: the Roman civil wars between 49 and 31 B.C. were essentially wars within and concerning the Roman diaspora. Tacitus announced that the inner secret of imperial power, that emperors could be made elsewhere than Rome, was revealed in A.D. 69–70; but it had actually been clear since the Peace of Dardanus, which ended the second Mithridatic war, and made Sulla's fortune.

War and its necessities were responsible for much of the shape that the diaspora took. Roman commanders and their staffs, with armies of Romans, Italians, and other allies, were always, as the agents of *imperium*, the most conspicuous 'Romans in the Roman world'. Their relations with the communities in which they found themselves were difficult and burdensome. The provision of winter quarters, for instance, was one of the principal matters for negotiation between local élites and the ruling-power, a field in which Roman sympathizers or resident Romans, and local benefactors, might play a vital rôle in reducing the hardship faced by a city. Soldiers, who before Augustus did not join up for fixed periods of years, had access to a wide range of opportunities for social and economic betterment in the lands whose rule by Rome they had been involved in maintaining. Ex-soldiers settling in the provinces did much to maintain Roman communities well before the Caesarian and Augustan veteran-settlements, the *coloniae*.

Not all Roman soldiers in the late Republic were fighting for Rome. We find Romans in Ptolemaic forces in the third century B.C.; but even at the very end of Hellenistic Egypt one Lutatius Crispus is on view at Cretan Gortys, 'soldier of the Ptolemies', foreign representative (*proxenos*) and citizen (*InscCret* IV 215). We should recall this when considering the position of Roman commanders such as Antony and their soldiers between provinces and independent royal territories, cities, and temple-states, in the ambiguous years of the civil war and triumvirate. The situation was further complicated by the recruitment of substantial numbers of Romans of the provinces – men like Stlaccius of Cyzicus – to the armies of the warring generals of 49–31. And throughout this period, Rome depended on non-Roman manpower, the highest reward for which was Roman citizenship. The showcase example is the package of privileges given by Augustus to reward a naval captain from north Syria, Seleukos of Rhosos (Sherk, 1984, no. 86). But this is only a customized version of general procedure, which became more and more regular until Claudius as censor undertook the complete institutionalization of citizenship on discharge for allied troops. Men like Seleukos in the next generation are found as equestrian officers in the *auxilia* and in the legions: the pattern so familiar in the West by which local notables were promoted in this way is found in the East, too. A luminous instance is L. Antonius Zeno, member of a dynasty of Anatolian magnates given the citizenship by Antony, and military tribune of the 12th legion Fulminata: a dedication to him from Tralles (*AnnEp* 1987.929) describes him as 'honoured by the most manifest of Gods, Augustus, with the right of wearing royal purple throughout the world, and formerly High Priest of Augustus in the province of Asia.' Or take a case from lower down the social scale, and a little later: a freed slave of the emperor who became a captain in the Roman naval squadron of the Sea of Marmara shows us the self-conscious pride of a new Roman of the late first century A.D. He made a dedication with his four sons, unlike him subject to no stigma of servile origin, the Tiberii Claudii (Quirina) Maximus, Sabinus, Lupus, and Futurus, their names redolent of hope for social promotion and solid Roman tradition: but the god could hardly have been more local, the Greek-Thracian hybrid Zeus Zbelsourdos (McCrum and Woodhead, 1961, 164). The citizenship with which the loyal were rewarded meant little at Rome (Roman citizens, for instance, could not vote unless they came to Rome): it was in the company of, and by comparison with, other sorts of Romans *in the provinces* that it was worth having. Service in the army no doubt led to cultural change; but most of all, it also led to political opportunity, as successful soldiers settled, equipped with entrées to chains of patronage leading up through society and across wide distances, joining more Roman to less Roman, providing new arenas for influence.

It is quite wrong to compartmentalize military, political, economic, and social history. Maintaining Rome's military mission involved the provision of money, food, clothing, transport, and military and naval supplies. The contractors followed the legions. The traders followed the contractors. Roman technical personnel worked on civilian architecture and engineering. Service of the ruling power gave certain people a status in which their activities were more than merely private, somehow analogous to the standing of the state. This ambiguity must have been particularly acute with those Romans who (though technically acting as private agents under contract to the state) had the authority of the conquerors behind them in collecting Rome's tribute and taxes. A very prominent part was played by financiers in the Roman diaspora. But just as this financial activity shaded into other forms of profiteering, so other economic activities crossed civic boundaries and were shaped by the networks of influence which resulted from Roman conquest. One of the principal commodities that enriched businessmen was people, the enslaved: that so many people were for sale was also the product of war. The political connection *was* profitable, whether one was buying up slaves for resale, negotiating fiscal advantages, trading in staple food-stuffs, or calculating the advantages of euergetistic investment. The successful opportunism of the 'Romans' of the Mediterranean world is one of their salient characteristics: their communities in the African cities of Thapsus and Hadrumetum, having made the wrong choice in the civil war, were forced to pay colossal but very revealing fines (Caesar, *Bell. Afr.* 97: 2 million and 5 million sesterces respectively). Hence their status and the appeal of belonging, however dubious the qualification;

hence envy and sometimes violent antipathy; and hence ultimately the obsolescence of the social form, as being Roman lost cachet during the empire of the mid-first century A.D.

Meanwhile, however, the quasi-public economic life of diaspora Romans is visible to us through the medium of civic inscriptions. Romans in every part of the Roman world were quite unabashed to use the language of public epigraphy to describe themselves as 'businessmen', *negotiatores* or *pragmateuomenoi* – a term which covered a multitude of overlapping activities: "To the God Augustus, this is dedicated, under the Curatorship of L. Fabricius, by the Roman Citizens who do business at Thinissut," says an inscription from Africa (Ehrenberg-Jones 106 = *ILS* 9495). These men are happy to boast of the details of their trade: Timotheus, freedman of an Italian-sounding Aulus Capreilius, coins a new word to describe his activities as a slave-trader at Amphipolis: "dealer in bodies." Such groups (perhaps originally for military reasons) also often specialized in craftsmanship, and gathered in centres where raw materials were available, such as the metals of Noricum in the eastern Alps. Here communities of Roman settlers formed the proto-urban settlement at the Magdalensberg, and later constituted the nucleus of the properly chartered town of Virunum. They gave buildings to cities, which, alongside the repertoire of traditional civic architecture, included *macella*, specialized retail outlets for investment agriculture: at Mantinea in the Peloponnese, the city and the 'Romans who do business in it' honour, in wonderfully flowery language, Euphrosynus son of Titus and his wife Epigone for building a lavish one from scratch 'sketching out its free-standing ornament of workshops' (*Syll.* 3 783).

The economic main chance was pursued through the establishment of nets of links between centres of communication, production, and exchange, which owed everything to the maintenance of stability under Roman rule, and which in turn promoted the cohesion of the diaspora – a diaspora, it must constantly be reiterated, of the highly mobile. Onomastics suggest rough outlines of certain economic networks in this age, tying the 'Romans who do business' together and to the communities of Italy. There is not space here to give more than a single example. The Faenii of Capua and Puteoli are widely attested as having an interest in the perfume business. When a freedwoman at Gytheion in the Peloponnese bears the name Faenia Aromation, 'Faenia Perfume', it is not hard to spot a link: the tie of the ex-slave to her former owner that passes on the family name. How many removes there are between free-born members of the original Faenius family and Aromation we can never know.

The economic activities of the people of the diaspora were immensely important, but still more so is the fact that they themselves tirelessly proclaimed through their use of the medium of civic inscriptions: they had a distinctive place in the world of influence, status and politics. Opportunism and self-defence set up and maintained structures of power and dependence. To the peoples of the East, outsiders using Roman names and operating in some more or less privileged relation to Roman power were naturally known by a single designation, whatever their relationship to the Roman citizenship: they were *Rhomaioi*, Romans.

These Roman outsiders, with their connections with the wealthy or the ambitious in other centres of the provinces or in the ports of Italy, and their connection with the conquering power, were individually conspicuous (and vulnerable, as was clearly seen in 88–7 B.C.). Either deliberately or through the perceptions of the host community, they came to acquire a certain critical mass and to be identified as a more formal category of Residents. Everywhere, in kingdoms as well as in cities, it was as Residents that the peoples of the East were most likely to meet, and to picture, Romans. There is one ringing testimony to this: in the gathering of all the peoples at the first Pentecost of the Christian tradition, the ruling power is represented by precisely *epidemountes Rhomaioi*, Romans who are for the time being resident among us – theologically the finest hour of a great historical structure (*Acts* 2.11). The label became a title, its connotations became more and more formal, until the Resident Romans formed collectivities – very numerous, and especially frequent in cities with economic advantages such as ports or crossroads, and in some cases numbering many scores, if not hundreds, of individuals – all over the Roman world. These communities enjoyed benefactions and honours, and acquired rights and privileges under local law, such as the right to own land, or even to hold office.

Take this example from Hadrianic Apamea Cibotus, in central Anatolia on the great highway between Asia and Syria:

> The Council and People of Apamea and the Resident Romans honour Ti. Claudius Piso Mithridatianus (son of Ti. Claudius Mithridates) of the *tribus* Quirina, Priest for life of Zeus Kelaineus, head of the *ephebeia*, head of the Gymnasium, Clerk of the Market in an Assize-year, all at his own expense – the statue was set up by the craftsmen of the Leatherworkers' Street.
>
> (*IGRR* IV 790)

Two communities join to honour a man whose names suggest a grant of citizenship to a forebear from Claudius and a proud Anatolian clan. His involvement in the economic life of this rich city is apparent, and his commitment to its ancient institutions (he went on to be High Priest of Asia in A.D. 128, *IGRR* IV 780): services all the more valuable in the year when the governor of Asia held his assizes in the city. Roman and non-Roman met on uneasy terms in places where great profits were to be had and where the official presence of Rome was heavy. The date at which five Romans (with names typical of diaspora families) first held civic office at Apamea is known: A.D. 45/6 (*IGRR* IV 792). This was a very conspicuous engagement in the affairs of the host community.

It is not difficult to imagine the common bonds that linked Romans in the age of Mithridates. But the separations which originated in defensiveness continued for longer than is sometimes imagined. Roman status, until at least the middle of the first century A.D., was a matter of seriously discrepant privilege. It is hardly surprising, in this context, that the resident Romans are so prominent in assize-centres such as Apamea. We can readily imagine the dilemmas faced by governors called upon to adjudicate in disputes involving the property of Romans. Cicero's defence of a governor of Asia vividly illustrates the controversies and conflicts that arose from Roman landowning (*Flacc.*, 70–83, 84–9). As a governor himself, he wrote to ask a fellow-governor to intervene on behalf of the interests (*negotia*) of one L. Genucilius Curvus at Parion on the Hellespont (he was having trouble realising privilege decreed by the city in relation to his estates; *Fam.* 13.53). Both those who sought uninhibited opportunities and those who defended themselves against exploitation needed Cicero and his peers as their patrons. And the very large sums of money that might be involved made the relationships still more complex. The unjust authority of Romans was a real grievance to *peregrini* in regard to local institutions too. One of Augustus' Cyrene edicts addresses the quite disproportionate position 'Romans' had acquired on the panels of local judges – to their great benefit. Violence against Romans did not die with Mithridates. We should recall the episodes for which free cities were punished – in Cyzicus in 20 B.C., Roman citizens were beaten and killed in rioting (Dio 54.7); and in A.D. 43 in Rhodes Roman citizens were crucified (Dio 60.24).

Recognized, conciliated, lionized, hated as collectivities in the cities, groups of Roman citizens in the formal sense might think of themselves as microcosms of the self-conscious Roman citizen-community as a whole. Their self-estimation was supported by magistrates at Rome, who allowed, or encouraged, through patronage, no doubt, and with patronage's usual rewards in mind, the recognition of some of these groups of citizens as formal collectivities under Roman law, Associations of Roman Citizens (*conventus civium Romanorum*). The 'worthy and numerous community of citizens' at Lilybaeum in Sicily of which we have heard Cicero speak in 70 B.C. is one of the first examples known, and others are attested in the West over the next thirty years, and in the East from the Augustan period.

The institution of the *conventus* enabled Roman communities to adopt something of the style of a formal body politic. This enabled them in some cases to assume almost parallel status with the host cities or even, in regions with weaker civic traditions, to form the senior partner, as in the late Republic at the points on the coast of Dalmatia where important routes from the Balkan interior debouched. Formal or informal, these arrangements were often very long-lived. We can often see social continuity over generations, and indeed an upward social mobility on the part of the Roman residents, which was undoubtedly linked with the increasingly close symbioses between Romans and locals through cultural assimilation, civic rights, and intermarriage. The heterogeneity of the 'Romans' themselves, the mix of freedman and free, Romans enfranchised, manumitted and born, from different parts of the diaspora rather than from Italy, highly mobile and very opportunistic, made them easier to integrate. The identity of diaspora Romans depended far more on their relationship to Roman power than on any cultural ties. And privileged status could be maintained while worshipping non-Roman gods, speaking Punic or Greek, or living in the style of a non-Roman city. So the apparent assimilation of Roman-ness by what surrounded it is never puzzling. A schematic separation of real Roman outsiders from genuine indigenes has lured many into a too polar approach to the composition of these cities' populations as seen from the inscriptions. The difference in status between groups within the population and between cities continued to make a real difference: Roman-ness continued to be distinctive in its relation to power, whatever it may have meant in cultural terms. These groupings continue to play an important part in the mediation of Roman power to the provinces and in the dialectics of the nascent imperial system.

Coherence in the diaspora was the product of resemblance between the radii, the myriad relationships which tied individuals and groups across the world to the centre. It did not derive from the Roman state and its policies. For all their vital practical significance in times of civil war, Romans overseas did not constitute a suitable arena for overt public ambition. We need to appreciate the contempt (mixed with fear) of the Romans for their Empire. The Romans of this period regarded Romans overseas as settlers, like the émigrés who had long ago founded new cities of Greeks and Phoenicians around the Mediterranean. A striking passage of a history written in the reign of Tiberius attacked the proposal of Gaius Gracchus 150 years before to establish cities of Romans beyond the peninsula (Velleius 2.7). Carthage, Massalia, Syracuse, and Byzantium all had grown more powerful than their mother-cities: the Romans before Gracchus had been wise in insisting that all Roman citizens should return from the provinces to Italy for the census. The Augustan marriage laws, we may also note, explicitly rank the Romans of the provinces below those of Italy, who are in turn less deserving than those of the capital, in the privileges allotted to procreation (Justinian, *Inst.* 1.25 pr.).

These caveats help us to reassess another, rather more famous, kind of Association of Roman Citizens: *coloniae* (rather than *conventus*) *civium Romanorum*, in which, typically, discharged citizen-soldiers from the legions were given the institutions of a city, and the agrarian base from which to make themselves into a prosperous citizen-community. The apparent simplicity of 'colonization' is compromised by the existence of too many other official manifestations of Roman-ness. Overlooking or underestimating these has often been the cause of misconstruing the meaning of the *coloniae*. Whole cities of Romans in peregrine provinces must be seen alongside groups of Romans in peregrine cities. The foundation of *coloniae* was a conspicuous, prestigious, and expensive, action; but despite the link with imperial authority, we should not be tempted to see it as a 'colonizing effort.' It was rather the insertion of another strategy of status, another deployment of favour, another rearrangement of rights and privileges, into the geography of Romans overseas. These Romans being everywhere, one thing that might happen is that they were formed into a whole city, a new nucleus and standpoint for the footloose conquerors of the world. The early history of Roman overseas *coloniae* suggests an eye for the commercial and agrarian opportunities very suitable to the age of rapid growth of the diaspora. When Julius Caesar radically revived the idea of extra-Italian *coloniae*, moreover, the flagship examples were not veteran settlements at all. The best-known of these new cities is the community he created on the site of the ancient *polis* of Corinth. *Colonia Laus Iulia Corinthus*, the Settlement at Corinth "Praise of the Julii," was peopled with freedman craftsmen from Rome, probably because of the long association of the site with the profits to be acquired from commerce (Strabo 8.381).

The revived Corinth was in many ways like a more splendid and larger version of a *conventus civium Romanorum*, fitting excellently well into the networks of the Roman diaspora, and like them intended to splice Roman institutions into the civic frameworks of the provinces: it attracted, moreover, new settlers from the existing diaspora communities. A set of honorary decrees of the federation of cities in Lycia, in what is now southwest Turkey, in Claudius' reign praises a wealthy citizen lady of Corinth for her hospitable reception of prominent Lycians exiled from their communities in a period of civil strife. "Junia Theodora, daughter of Lucius, a fair and goodly Roman lady from among those settled at Corinth" is how the Lycians ceremoniously describe her (*SEG* 18, 1962, 143). We cannot tell how she came to have such close ties with Lycia, but it is overwhelmingly likely that they were through the economic networks with which Corinth had been refounded in her grandfather's time.

Many of the Caesarian and Augustan foundations are manipulations of the geography of the diaspora. The *conventus* cities of Dalmatia were replaced by *coloniae*. Parion, the major centre of Roman activity on the Hellespont, found itself turned within a few years into a Roman *colonia*, so apt did it seem to Roman interests. Our typical picture of the *colonus* is a veteran. A small fragment of the register of lands assigned in the *colonia* of Ilici in southern Spain reveals a more complex picture: there are a few Italians, but also some Romans of Spain, men from the north African coast opposite, and one man from the Balearic islands. Rather than simply moving Italians into the provinces, *coloniae* rearranged the diaspora. Some of the strangest *coloniae*, the chain of ports along the coast of the Maghreb, were not in a province at all, but the client-kingdom of Mauretania. But this is anomalous only if we see all these cities as tools of Roman government, as part of the provincial system. As privileged communities of Romans at large in the world, they might naturally be located in many different relationships to the geography of Roman power, and to the settlement patterns of the area. Thus most *coloniae* were free-standing cities; but some in the Anatolian interior appear to be uneasily twinned with existing settlements, just as if they were inflated *conventus civium Romanorum*. And in all new cities, we must remember the maintenance of part at least of the previous population as subordinates. Turning the tables on the usual arrangement where the Romans are the outsiders, however honoured, a *colonia* is a city in which it is the non-Romans who are the 'residents'. It has often been claimed that the Roman *coloniae* of the East were not very active or successful at propagating any distinctively Roman culture. They were not intended to do so, any more than were privileged individual Romans in peregrine communities: they were signs of the favour, power, and prestige of Rome.

The *coloniae* of Caesar and Augustus must also be understood alongside the equally radical extension to the provinces on a large scale of the old Italian institution of the *municipium*, in which a different kind of interaction between Roman citizens and non-Romans was established – different mainly in that although they had offices and used laws derived from the Roman tradition, and some of their élite were citizens, most of the population remained peregrine in status. This accommodation between Roman and non-Roman was known by the historically evocative term of the 'Latin right', a kind of mirage of the Roman citizenship. Take the instance of Nemausus (now Nîmes):

> Nemausus is the chief city of the Arekomiskoi, and is much inferior to [the *colonia* of] Narbo in respect of the numbers of outsiders and traders in its population, but superior in the political sense: for it has subject to it 24 villages of the same people, all distinguished for populousness, and possesses what is called 'Latium', which means that those who are elected to the magistracies of aedile and quaestor become Romans. As a consequence, the people is not under the direct control of the governors sent from Rome.
>
> (Strabo 4.1.12)

Here something of what no doubt happened in practice in cities with large communities of Romans and a high exposure to Roman power, such as Apamea or Ephesus, was codified: the rules and customs of the élite Roman society were made available for others to observe and imitate if they wanted. The principal difference was that here the majority of the Roman group was enfranchised at the establishment of the city: often explicitly as an act of reward for loyal military service, so that this collective enfranchisement too has parallels in the promotion of individuals. The result was another institutional framework for the juxtaposition and interrelationship of a Roman community with non-Roman neighbours. The establishment of formal Roman legal and customary institutions in the provinces should be seen as part of the spectrum of rights and perquisites enjoyed by the Romans of the diaspora. Whole cities of Romans in peregrine provinces, and cities where groups of non-Romans are given the rights of Romans, must be seen alongside groups, whether formal or informal, of Romans, whether by birth, manumission or enfranchisement, in peregrine cities.

New cities were also founded to magnify Roman glory, with resident Romans in them, but without any distinctive status under Roman public law. Augustus' own memorial to Actium, the city of Nicopolis, was no chartered town, but still a very Roman city. And the same could be said of cities founded in the Augustan spirit by loyal kings: the Caesareas in Palestine and Mauretania. Existing cities could be transformed by their adaptation as provincial centres, as was Ephesos in Asia, where a vocal and visible community of Romans of various kinds made it one of the most Roman of cities in the east in the first centuries B.C. and A.D. When Horace hails Augustus as "father of cities" (*pater urbium*; *Odes* 3.24.27), it is as a founder rather than a 'Romanizer' that he is being praised. The title knows no distinction between Roman and other towns: the founder of the city-form, the benefactor, the saviour, of cities in the Hellenistic style, is a rôle which draws on a range of urban institutions and a repertoire of meanings which far transcends Roman identity. The multiplication of characteristically Roman cities derived significance from the rest – from the assertive and self-conscious place they took among other kinds of city.

How the emperors themselves viewed their empire is revealed in the language of official documents, where the world is envisaged as a collectivity of fragments. Among these, Roman cities are naturally prominent: first the scattered *coloniae* and *municipia* of Italy, then those of the provinces, and finally peregrine communities. Just as ambassadors from non-Roman cities wove the webs of Hellenistic diplomacy, so ambassadors representing Roman cities take home messages from the magistrates at Rome or the representatives of the emperor. This collectivity of Roman towns was a product of Augustan bureaucratic and legal practice, created within a world of cities by piecemeal articulation rather than by grand constructive *fiat*.

But the latent 'Roman' identity of these groups was nonetheless given a wholly new form, meaning, resolution, and urgency by its infusion with the ideology of the Augustan regime. No such single focus had been available before: nascent monarchy, however, found one of its most receptive audiences in these milieux, and derived some of its centralizing self-definition and normative character from its influence on this strangely configured world. At the same time it further sharpened the self-awareness of the Romans of the empire whose sense of who they were was now strongly bolstered by their mutual attention to a single highly effective source of images, ideas, reassurance, favours, and opportunities.

AUGUSTUS' DIALOGUE WITH THE ROMANS OF THE ROMAN WORLD

It has been central to the argument so far that the Romans of the diaspora mattered – disproportionally to their numbers or activities – because as Romans they enjoyed a different, and privileged, position in the increasingly complex topography of patronage within the empire. The Romans of the provinces had a number of advantages in mediation with the powerful Romans on whose decisions everything depended. First, when they were strongly Roman by origin, upbringing, social connections, or culture, they participated from within in the patronage structures characteristic of Roman society: a minor banker might have an inherited equestrian patron. Second, they were often engaged as agents or partners in the economic enterprises which lay at the heart of so many situations in which patronage was called for. Third, as the Roman state became more complex institutionally, and as law and legal bureaucracy expanded, they offered particular interpretative and advisory skills. The rules that were worth knowing about were specially concerned, of course, with the law of persons, and the demarcation of precisely the boundary between Roman and non-Roman, and they went beyond the literally legal.

Certain patterns of relation with Rome through 'big men' emerge. Sometimes the relationship was direct: the hereditary *clientelae* of prominent Romans in the provinces formed one meeting-point between provincial and Roman. We have noted other attempts to pursue this form of backing at Parion and Buthrotum. From the second century we find Greek cities recruiting prominent patrons and – notably – calling them by the Roman term. More often the mediation of Roman or non-Roman clients of the great must have been employed. Locals honoured by Rome played their part alongside the Romans of the provinces. Pompey's ally Theophanes of Mitylene, and Caesar's dependents Balbus of Gades or Theopompus of Cnidos, are the most visible of a very extensive series. Such men were often naturally well inclined to other kinds of locally resident Roman. They need to be seen not merely as favoured outsiders operating at Rome, but as participants in the world of Roman-provincial interaction in their home community. The "Romans who do business in all the cities of Laconia" did very well from the local magnate Eurycles of Sparta (*SEG* 11.924), who also made a point of making the *colonia* of Corinth the setting for generous self-display.

Eurycles is a key to a vital transition (for his connection with Herod see M. White's Chapter 16 on p. 376). The local power of a Theopompus or a Theophanes was no doubt a reflection of the supereminent station of a Pompey or a Caesar. But Eurycles was something new: son of an individual executed by Antony as a pirate, owner of the island of Cythera – the key to the sea-routes of southern Greece – great landowner in Laconia, he was a classic beneficiary of the opportunities of the times. But it was as representative (*epistates*) of Augustus that he experienced a standing and an impunity (up to a point) that made him a different kind of local authority. The existence of a super-patron in the Roman world gave new effectiveness to those who represented him in the communities of the provinces.

Who was whose patron mattered. Not only was the game of competition and rivalry within and between cities a source of considerable disorder, but the wealth disposed of by the Romans of the diaspora and their local relatives and allies gave them important advantages, which was only enhanced by the new implication of linkage with the supreme authority of Augustus. Augustus saw to it that he became the patrons' patron, arbiter throughout the world of the law of persons. We have seen in L. Antonius Zeno – once again – a conspicuous instance of how this involved parallel wielding of the instruments of status within the diaspora – grants of citizenship, promotion to high military rank – and of the older emblems of power in the Hellenistic world: only Augustus could have aspired to being able to grant the right of wearing royal purple throughout the world, with all the seniority to mere royalty and cosmological inclusiveness that the grant implies. Both types of preferment are fascinating, but it is their deployment *in tandem* that is so distinctive of Augustus' rule. With Augustus, promotions to Roman status became much more common, but quite rapidly, like other aspects of the law of persons, became the business of the emperor. Romans in the community – whatever their history – acquired a new cachet in the maintenance of the community's relationship with the *domus Augusta*. They became experts at a new kind of relationship, which had the benefit of being largely symbolic.

The Roman businessmen of Cos took it upon themselves to honour their host-community for being well-disposed toward them, and for their proper devotion to the divinized Julius Caesar (*AnnEp* 1947.55). One of the ways in which Roman citizens might seem to be different was their engagement with the distinctive practices of Roman religion, and Roman magistrates had long cultivated Rome's reputation for punctilio in relations with the divine. You turned to a Roman to discover how to get on your side the gods who had helped them to conquer the world – and all the better, now, if the god was one of the Romans' own rulers. Religion had of course long shaped the honours, immunities and privileges for which communities vied. Roman governors had come to regulate the form and membership of festivals and leagues, the standard organisms of inter-city relations.

It is therefore arresting that Octavian, resident on Samos in the winter of 30/29 B.C., made a novel statement to the people of Asia in the language of cult. He enacted that the Romans of Asia and Bithynia might set up sacred precincts to Julius Caesar and to Rome, and that they should do so in the foremost cities of those provinces, Ephesus and Nicaea respectively; while "the non-Romans who knew themselves as Hellenes" might worship him, and that they should do so in what were by implication the second cities of the provinces, Pergamum and Nicomedia. In the former a full sacred festival was authorized in his honour (Dio 51.20.7–9). Who received the greater honour? The Greeks, licensed to worship the living ruler? Or the Romans, whose quite distinct religious preferences and obligations are being carefully prescribed? History, patriotism, and power may be thought to outweigh the condescending permission to subjects to live up to their cultural stereotype, but the subtlety of the balances is great and the whole a very characteristic piece of Augustan equivocation. Directly after Actium, Octavian was already acting as the organizer of what was Roman wherever it was found, and its demarcation, in law and custom, from what was around it: the aim was the more precise definition of the restored body politic, and the establishment of an unprecedented power for himself as the arbiter of these matters. Both aims depended on the Roman diaspora: through it he could dispose of the hierarchies of cities and the claims of local prestige anywhere in the world.

The fusion of Roman and non-Roman in exhibitions of loyalty and devotion to the emperor's divinity is not limited to the ancient cities of Greece and Ionia. In the interior of the Maghreb, in just the same way, "the Associations of Roman Citizens and of Numidians who dwell at Masculula" honour the deified Augustus (*ILS* 6774/5; Ehrenberg-Jones 111). And in remote mountainous Anatolia it is spectacularly visible in the oath sworn in Paphlagonia in 3 B.C. (Sherk, 1984, 105), where the inhabitants of this far-flung territory and the Romans who do business among them appear side-by-side as equipollent parts of the body politic, as we have seen elsewhere, and take their oath in shrines of Augustus, in front of the altars of his cult. It was as natural for Romans in the community to be involved in the more dilute patronal relations of the imperial age as in the direct pursuit of powerful help in the past. At Assos, the city and the Roman *negotiatores* – the same pair – combined to honour Livia Hera the new Augusta, benefactress of the Cosmos, and were quick to swear a delighted oath of loyalty to Gaius Caligula (*IGRR* IV 249–51): they voted as the necessary ambassadors to Rome the most distinguished Greeks and Romans of the community, three Assians and C. Varius C.f. Vol. Castus, who travelled to Rome and sacrificed to Jupiter Capitolinus, the god of the Roman citizen collectivity, on behalf of his city. Meanwhile in Gaul, spontaneously or by design, the highly organized Resident Romans of the province under their *summi curatores* took as their stage the great altar in the suburb of the *colonia* of Lugdunum at the Confluence of the Rhône and the Saône, where the conquest of Gaul and its loyalty to the imperial system were celebrated by the assembled indigenous peoples of the Three Provinces. *Coloniae* in general became regular showcases for cultic and other displays of loyalty – but once again only as the brighter stars in much more extensive constellations.

The Rome of Augustus' childhood was still traumatised by the dilution of the citizen body that followed the Roman–Italian War. Scarcely an ethnic concept even before, 'Roman' now had become so vague a label that identity was a real problem. Links to the centre were vital, and for a dispersed citizenry religious expressions of unity had a powerful role to play. Even the communities of Italy were too numerous and too far flung to find it easy to practice collective action. The taking of an oath, the sharing of a festival, offered a remedy. The vows of Italy for the health of Pompeius just before the civil war represent a landmark (Dio 41.6.3–4).

Augustus himself, like so many Romans, had been a resident Roman in a peregrine city. Toward the end of 45 B.C. he travelled to the city of Apollonia, on the Adriatic coast of Epirus, an ancient settlement of the Corinthians, in the heart of the area in which élite Romans had been busily investing. One account of his time there suggests that his purpose was educational (Nicolaus, *Augustus* 37–47); another has him supervising the training and exercising of recruits from Macedonia (Appian, *Civil War* 3.9): the mix of associations is eloquent. As a relative of the Dictator, he received frequent formal visits from other prominent Romans abroad, and was lionized by the Apolloniates, who no doubt (like so many other cities) regarded any contact with potentially powerful Romans as worth some opportunistic affection, in which the town-council and the citizen-body both joined enthusiastically. They had their reward, as the city later gained a very favoured position from the successful Octavian. This biographical detail is more than anecdotally relevant to our theme. Caesar, Augustus, Tiberius, all spent formative periods in the currents of the diaspora, in part because it was, as we have seen, in that world that the political outcomes of the age were determined. Augustus' long and frequent stays on Samos, in the heart of the Roman networks of the Aegean, have no parallel in later imperial history.

The competences of people in authority are determined by the issues to which they find themselves devoting their time. Their agendas, and so eventually their job-descriptions, are shaped not by planning or prescription, but by the incremental drifts of the matters which occupy their attention, prompt their consideration and elicit their responses. The office of proconsul in the late republic was shaped by the disputes and petitions which succeeded in involving him, and therefore especially by those which had a greater call on his time, and it was natural that issues involving Roman citizens had a certain advantage. Through this effect, the collectivities of Romans in the provinces moulded governors' behaviour and the evolution of the office of proconsul. And ultimately, by extension, this unplanned configurative influence, acting on institutions like weathering on rocks, helped shape the office of that super-proconsul, the Roman emperor, too. The Roman diaspora gave Augustus another stage, and his acting cemented the audience together.

Like Sulla and Vespasian, Augustus won his power in the Roman diaspora, where he could equally have lost it. Lessons learned there about recruitment, taxation, loyalty, and the relations of Rome with local élites formed his behaviour, which would have been quite different if Italy had really been what mattered most. He chose to assert the overarching importance of Italy and Rome, and with such success that we can all too readily join him in downplaying Antony's world, the world of Romans in a peregrine empire. But that policy itself shows how important this world was: as Velleius said, the danger was that the settlers become more significant than the mother-city.

The Roman diaspora, seen in this way as a mediator of authority, is a vital missing link in the study of the social and political encounters between ruler and ruled in the Roman empire. In West and East alike, the presence of such substantial and varied groups of Romans of different kinds entailed a different kind of dialogue from one conducted by subjects with representatives of a distant power. It is becoming orthodox to claim that the heterogeneity of the Empire trumps the familiar east-west divide. The Roman diasporas deserve greater emphasis in explaining how this heterogeneity worked. Their study helps us avoid the variety of Romanocentrism which puts overwhelming emphasis on the city of Rome or Italy, their institutions and inhabitants. Indeed, they help us understand the Roman-ness of the centre from a usefully different perspective. The dialogue of Roman and non-Roman and the tricky adjudication of emphases must involve local Roman-ness too. It is, equally, true that our account of Greekness in the Flavian and later ages needs to be rewritten in the light of the recognition that Roman–Greek interaction in the preceding two centuries had been so varied and so complex. Yes, Hellenism in a certain sense is triumphant: but its victory is different when it is read as a victory over the diaspora, rather than one over the distant western Italian urban Roman overlords. No bipolar account of the interplay of Hellenic and Roman as cultural systems can work. It is in these webs of ambiguous identity at the local level that we must seek for the secret of understanding and explaining the Roman empire, its robustness and its transience.

SUGGESTIONS FOR FURTHER READING

For a general survey of cultural contact in the Roman world of the time of Augustus see MacMullen (2000). On the linguistic frontiers of Roman culture, Adams (2003). The special problems of Roman relations with Greeks in the eastern Mediterranean are discussed by Susan Alcock, "Preface: East is East?", in Alcock (1993) v–viii; R. M. Errington, "Aspects of Roman Acculturation in the East under the Republic," in P. Kneissl and V. Losemann, eds., *Festschrift für Karl Christ zum 65. Geburtstag* (Darmstadt 1988) 140–157, and Woolf (1994). The economic aspects of these contacts are helpfully presented for the crucial case of Delos by N. K. Rauh, *The sacred bonds of commerce: religion, economy, and trade society at Hellenistic and Roman Delos, 166–87 B.C.* (Amsterdam 1993). The classic study of the evidence for Romans in the east is J. Hatzfeld, *Les trafiquants italiens dans l'Orient Héllénique* (Paris 1919); recent discoveries in this field are presented, for instance, in Rizakis (1996) and there are other examples in the bibliography.

5: PROVINCIAL PERSPECTIVES

Greg Woolf

WRITING THE PROVINCES INTO A VERY ROMAN REVOLUTION

Augustus and the City of Rome stand at the heart of all histories of this period. Augustus and his image builders put them there. The contributions made by others were limited in fact, and effaced from memory unless they could be grouped around the person of the emperor. The other great cities of the Mediterranean – Athens and Alexandria above all – were plundered and marginalised. Augustus wrote his name all over the City and transported the City out to the world. His *Res Gestae et Impensae* lists wars won abroad and money spent at home, that is in Rome. Most modern accounts have followed this steer in stressing the complexity and importance of the accommodation that Octavian/Augustus achieved with the senatorial and equestrian élites of the City and of Italy (Syme 1939, Eck 2003). Others have explored how he constructed the new order – symbolic, political, religious, moral, military, and economic – out of the traditional symbols, words, rituals, spaces, and institutions of Republican Rome (Galinsky 1996, Nicolet 1991, Zanker 1988).[1] We slip, in our usage, easily from Rome the City to Rome the Empire and back again. *Urbs* obscures *Orbis*.[2]

Yet Roman history in the lifetime of Augustus is no longer the history of one city. Well before Actium the Roman People, so prominent in Augustan writing, referred to a citizen body that incorporated virtually all the free inhabitants of the Italian peninsula and many beyond it (cf. Purcell, previous chapter in this volume). Roman power extended even farther, embracing not just the scatter of Mediterranean provinces but also allied cities and the kings and tribes beyond and between them. The history of this great area cannot simply be an appendix to debates in the Senate on tribunician power, or subtle monumentalisation of the

Campus Martius. What this chapter offers is not a complementary picture of the provinces in the age of Augustus. Instead, it asks how we might write the history differently if we did not start from Rome and the first emperor.

So how do the provinces figure in conventional narratives? In the provinces, there were reserves of manpower and wealth for warring dynasts, and also places to which they might absent themselves when life in Rome was difficult. In the provinces were the armies, ostensibly pursuing the historic destiny of the Roman people, in fact ever ready to march against the City, as they had under Sulla. In the provinces, monarchy dared speak its name and the divine qualities of generals and emperors could be recognised. Tacitus, in his ironized sketch of Augustus' reign, represented the provincials as indifferent to the collapse of a free Republic that had enslaved them:

> Nor did the provinces mind this state of affairs. They were distrustful of the power of the senate and the people because of the struggles of the powerful and the greed of the magistrates. The laws offered them no help because they were perverted by violence, favouritism and, most of all, by bribery.
>
> (*Annals* 1.2)

Many studies present the provinces as laboratories of autocracy in which Rome's rulers learned quite what they might get away with in the City itself (e.g., Millar 1977). But most of all provincials are represented as cannon fodder, collateral damage, second and third murderers in dramas where Romans get all the best parts.

Analysis in these terms does have something to be said for it. Empires might be defined, in part, as hegemonic systems organised so that some places matter much more than others. Just as today's developing world is dependent on decisions taken in the capitals − financial and political − of the West, so the provinces looked to Rome, trying to guess the outcome of power struggles within the imperial court. Rome, after Actium and maybe even earlier, was not really a capital city any more. The centre of power was the person of the emperor, wherever he was at the time. But the City's magnificent monuments, the games and triumphs, the distributions of gold and grain, the court poets and the gladiators, were largely paid for by the provinces, and they advertised to provincials the splendours of the empire (Edwards and Woolf 2003). The advancement of Rome as the unrivalled cultural capital served to mark other centres as 'provincial'. The provincialisation of non-Roman cultures was an artefact of Roman power and – to the extent that it was successful[3] – there is no point ignoring it.

It is important then, that we resist our natural temptation to knock the first emperor off his pedestal and turn our backs on the centre. It is not possible to write un-Augustan narratives of Mediterranean history in which the City of Rome is decentred. The mass of epigraphical finds from all over the empire have made clear that there were no places, no matter how remote, where the identity of this latest Roman dynast was genuinely a matter of indifference. Perhaps the slaves and peasants of the Mediterranean world did not know that Actium was 'a secular miracle.' Maybe women did not have a 'Roman revolution' of their own. But the danger of the revisionist agenda is that we may become seduced into a dialogue with Augustus over his own world-historical importance, a dialogue that in the end can only confirm his status.

What historians can do is experiment with looking at familiar events in a broader perspective, one that prioritises the political and cultural convulsions experienced right across the Mediterranean world and its continental hinterlands. There is, however, a serious methodological problem that we cannot dodge. Rome's wider environment was indeed characterised by major changes in the reign of Augustus. But that reign was extremely long even if counted only from Actium (and why should we accept his own, politically necessary, dismissal of his career as triumvir?).[4] The time span involved has made it easy for historians to connect all kinds of change with his political ascendancy. But correlation is not explanation, and demonstrating temporal coincidence is not the same as showing causal connections. Much of what happened 'in the age of Augustus' was rooted in longer term processes (cf. Wallace-Hadrill and Purcell, this volume). Territorial expansion, the growing infatuation of the Roman aristocracy with Greek aesthetic forms, the growth of the citizen body and the accelerating rate at which old families were replaced with new ones within the élite are just some examples.

Augustus and his spokespersons were well aware of these processes, and (for their own purposes) often stressed the elements of continuity in his reign. Historians since antiquity have often convicted Augustus of making fraudulent claims in this respect. But neither Augustus nor his critics lived with our conventional periodisation of Roman history into 'Republic' and 'Principate'. And much did continue unchanged. Slavery, family structure, the organisation of intellectual knowledge, law, language, religion, and moral discourse are just the most obvious realms where there was no great discontinuity. Who are we to decide that the political freedom of senators should be the touchstone of continuity? Continuity, to be sure, might mean remaining unchanged or it might mean continuing to change in a direction unaffected by the regime change. But maybe it is pointless expecting Augustus to single-handedly divert history. Augustus took advantage of some tides in the affairs of men, and perhaps he steered some changes. Virtual historians can wonder about the sort of epic Virgil might have written for a victorious Antony, or what role the Senate might have played in a principate founded by a Caesar who escaped assassination. Our task is to see how our understanding of the historical Augustus changes if his career is set against a wider backdrop than that of Rome and its (new) past.

Momentous cultural changes were certainly occurring across the Roman world in the last decades of the last century B.C. and in the first decades A.D. Archaeologists working on the western provinces often term these changes 'Romanization.'[5] The term is less commonly used in Rome's eastern provinces, but those societies too were undergoing major transformations (Woolf 1994). Italy was changing at least as fast (Keay and Terrenato 2001). The term 'Hellenization' is sometimes used of areas like central Asia Minor and Egypt in this period. The education and physical environment of the élite of Rome were preoccupied with things Greek (Wallace-Hadrill 2000). For Italy, cultural change is sometimes expressed as Romanization, sometimes as Hellenization. Neither term is very satisfactory as it is easily understood to mean the spread of unified and well-defined cultures at the expense of others. No such cultures existed. But there really were major changes in intellectual life, literature, rhetorical culture, domestic architecture, public monuments, sculpture, painting, tableware, diet, dress, styles of hygiene, sexual custom, and much else across the entire Empire. In some places Greek identity was sought and claimed, in others Roman, and in yet other areas one or both those labels were regarded as culturally prestigious. Both in Rome and in Greek centres, processes of canon-formation were at work during this period reclassifying certain periods and works as classical.

Only in Rome itself were these processes highly politicised. Historians are still unsure how best to describe this process. 'Augustan culture' has been used (e.g., Galinsky 1996), and the idea of a 'Roman cultural revolution' has been floated (Wallace-Hadrill 1989 and in this volume; Habinek and Schiesaro 1997; cf. Woolf 2001) to describe similar changes. What both those terms share is a commitment to understand in similar terms literary, intellectual, and artistic changes. This is certainly to be preferred to analyses that restricted themselves to the relationship between, say, poetic production and the politics of the court. But despite classicists' traditional strengths in combining different media and thinking in an interdisciplinary way, it is not easy to make the connections between all these changes in a convincing manner. More difficult yet is the task of integrating political change into the picture. Traditionally, political change has been allowed to set the agenda and provide the periodization. When Paul Zanker's fundamental work *Augustus und die Macht der Bilder* (literally *Augustus and the Power/Might of Images*) was translated into English it was given the title *The Power of Images in the Age of Augustus*. But Augustus is not just a temporal reference, anymore than he was the prime-mover. His reign was neither simply coincidental to, nor was it the main cause of these changes. The shift to autocracy at Rome, in other words, was *just another component* of the cultural transformation of the Mediterranean world: it needs to be understood in those terms.

Characterising this transformation is not easy, but here are some of the major trends underway at the turn of the millennia. It was an age of urban expansion (Hopkins 1978; Jones 1987; Woolf 1997). Cities grew where they were already well established, and new ones were founded. This was true whether the cities were Greek *poleis*, the administrative centres of Egyptian nomes, Roman colonies, iron age hillforts in Gaul, or Anatolian temple states transformed or replaced by new foundations. It was a world where the rich were becoming richer and the poor poorer, a process that went hand in hand with the rich entrenching their power in local communities. Again the local details differ enormously. The metropolite class emerges in Egypt, democracy finally expires in the Greek world, tribal warlords are replaced with municipal landowning élites in the West (Bowman and Rathbone 1992; Alcock 1993; Quass 1993; Brunt 1976). It was a world where the rich built, privately of course, but also on a grand public scale, mostly in the cities, but also in great sanctuaries. A mass of monumentalization characterises the period. In Italy one stimulus was the end of senatorial building in the City of Rome, where it became futile and dangerous to compete with the emperor (Eck 1984). In Gaul monument building perhaps replaced leading warbands as a means of aristocratic display (Goudineau and Rebourg 1991; Woolf 2000). Much municipal building in the West asserted compliance with Roman custom and ideal. Greek cities around the Aegean world started competing with each other to develop the most splendid public buildings in a new style that made heavy use of the fabulously expensive marble (Millar 1993). By all these routes the empire of the Principate became profoundly urban in a way the empire of the Republic had not been. The vast mass of the population still lived in the countryside, but their lives revolved around the cities which in turn were built on their labour.

Underpinning this expenditure by the landowning classes who now dominated the political establishment were changes in production. Much of their wealth certainly derived from accumulation of property, but these quantitative changes made possible qualitative ones. Technological innovations and knowledge spread throughout the Roman world, from hydraulic engineering to kiln manufacture, from the cultivation of fruit trees to the construction of mosaics, from navigation to medicine and astrology and the use of slavery and Roman law to organise these activities. Equally important, the growth in the wealth of the wealthy gave some the chance to invest in new technologies. The immense production of the red-gloss potteries in north Italy and then of their provincial offshoots attests to high level of capital investment. The final component in this cycle of growth was the increase in the size of the market for agricultural and other produce. Urbanisation, along with the existence of a standing army paid well above subsistence levels, made it worthwhile to intensify the production of olive oil in Spain and Africa, of wine in Italy, of grain in Africa, Egypt, and Sicily and so on.

A different kind of economic growth was generated among the upper classes of the empire as common cultures began to emerge creating a set of élite values that transcended the divide between Greek and Latin literary culture. The diet of the well off was broadly similar across the empire. They shared a taste in domestic architecture, created large slave households partly staffed by highly specialised (and expensive) personal attendants. The powerful hunted, at great expense, employed entertainers and teachers, patronised and sometimes competed in athletic and musical competitions. These converging cultures of consumption were created at great cost. Olive oil was used everywhere even though olives could not grow in many parts of the empire. Wine replaced beer even where vines could not be cultivated. Papyrus, flax, and marble were available everywhere but at a cost that reflected the expense of transporting them from the few areas that could produce them. Political stability made these exchanges easier, and perhaps more profitable, but the quest for luxury was well established among the last generation of the Republic's aristocracy (Edwards 1993). If this commerce de luxe cost some of the rich a great part of their fortunes, it made others very wealthy. There were no rich merchant classes in the Roman world and, although they often concealed their involvement, rich aristocrats capitalised and profited from these trades.

Only a few of these changes can plausibly be attributed to the person or policies of Augustus and his followers. Many developments – the growth of the Italian pottery industry and of Italian agriculture for instance – were already underway in the middle of the last century B.C. (Woolf 1992). Yet this was the world from which Augustus' regime emerged, and these were the energies which it had to harness, or else resist.

PRINCEPS AND PRINCIPES

Let us begin, then, with politics. Josephus offers one provincial angle on the events of the period in Judea:

> In the fifteenth year of his reign [Herod] restored the existing Sanctuary and round it enclosed an area double the former size, keeping no account of the cost and achieving a magnificence beyond compare. This could be seen particularly in the great colonnades that ran around the entire Temple and the fortress that towered over it to the north. The former were completely new structures, the latter an extremely costly reconstruction, as luxurious as a palace, and named Antonia in honour of Antony. His own palace, built in the Upper City, consisted of two very large and very lovely buildings which made even the Sanctuary seem insignificant: these he named after his friends, one Caesareum, one Agrippeum.
> (Josephus, *Jewish War* 1. 40, trans. G. A. Williamson)

Herod did not confine his munificence to Jerusalem (see Fig. 57 on p. 370 and Chapter 16 by Michael White). Josephus goes on to tell how he built a city named Sebaste (the Greek equivalent of 'Augusta') with walls two miles long, settled 6,000 colonists in it, gave them land, a charter, and in the centre built a vast shrine dedicated to Caesar (cf. Fig. 60 on p. 373). Later "when Caesar had enriched him with the addition of greater lands" Herod built another shrine to him in Paneum, at the source of the Jordan. Other buildings dedicated to the same friends were constructed in Jericho, and in other places. In fact, concludes Josephus:

> I cannot think of any suitable spot in his kingdom that he left without some tribute of esteem for Caesar. When he had filled his own country with temples, these tributes

overflowed into the province and in city after city he erected a Caesareum.

Herod was not an isolated case. The great city of Caesarea in Mauretania, modern Cherchel, was constructed by King Juba, another prince closely linked to the house of Augustus. Neither Herod nor Juba were Greek by descent, although Greek culture was for them (as for Augustus) a natural medium of display. Their activities can be compared to those of Eurycles, the tyrant of Sparta (cf. pp. 101 and 376), and to the building programmes of tribal chiefs in Gaul, the Alps, and southern Britain:

> Each of the allied kings who enjoyed Augustus' friendship founded a city called 'Caesarea' in his own domains; and all clubbed together to provide funds for completing the Temple of Olympian Zeus in Athens, which had been begun centuries before, and dedicating it to his Genius. These kings would often leave home, dressed in the togas of their honorary Roman citizenship, without any emblems of royalty whatsoever, and visit Augustus at Rome, or even when he was visiting the provinces; they would attend his morning audience with the simple devotion of *clientes*.
> (Suetonius, *Aug.* 60; trans. R. Graves with adaptations).

Herod, Juba, and Eurycles (and more names could easily be added) illustrate the collusion of interests on which Roman Peace rested. If Augustus was *patronus* to their *clientes*, each played the role of Augustus within their own communities. Most early empires worked largely through a collusion between the imperial élites at the centre and local élites who do their bidding in return for support against their local rivals and subordinates (Alcock *et al.* 2001). Augustan propaganda represented this collusion as a harmonious order comprised of friendships focused on the emperor. He also arranged for these princes to be linked by intermarriage, and their children, often raised in Rome alongside members of the imperial family, sometimes took on Roman names.

On closer examination these relations seem a little less harmonious. These kings were more often termed "friends" than "clients," but "friendship" in Augustus' *Res Gestae* is generally something that Augustus claims he has compelled foreigners to seek. There was indeed a long Republican tradition of granting lesser allies the title "friend and ally of the Roman people" and bestowing on them honorary symbols of office and togas. Sallust has Scipio advise a young Jugurtha to seek the friendship of the Roman people rather than individual Romans (Sallust, *Jugurtha* 8.2). Suetonius is correct to refer to these friendships as orientated toward Augustus himself, whether or not they really performed a version of the Roman client's *salutatio*. But Augustus was not always the first (or last) friend they made at Rome. Herod had already built his Antonia before he began work at Caesarea Maritima (see Fig. 58 on p. 371) and he also built monuments to Agrippa, a potential successor to Augustus. The network of friendships that bound together the Augustan Mediterranean was just the latest in a series of similar alliances.

The persistence of this pattern emerges from the case of Caius Iulius Rufus, one member of a family that dominated the new town of Saintes at the western terminal of one of the major trunk roads that Agrippa built across Gaul. That family was responsible for most of the earliest monuments there and also for the building of an amphitheatre at Lyon at the federal sanctuary of the three Gallic provinces. Rufus' most impressive surviving monument is an arch that once stood at one end of the bridge that carried the Agrippan road across the Charente into the town. On the arch stood statues of Tiberius, the emperor, and of his two sons Drusus and Germanicus. An inscription celebrated Rufus' descent from a father Caius Iulius Catuaneunius, his grandfather Caius Iulius Agedomopas and his great grandfather Epotsorovidus. The inscription is often cited as an example of the gradual Romanization of names and families, but in A.D. 18 or 19 what it proclaimed was the antiquity of that dynasty's prominence of the Santones, way back beyond enfranchisement – probably by Caesar – to a pre-conquest chieftain. How should we read the relationship between the two dynasties displayed on the arch? A simple equation, Rufus is to the Santones what Tiberius is to the Romans? Alliance? A statement about the importance of descent? Even a claim that for all his Roman name, the Roman arch and his loyalty to the *princeps* – the inscription adds that he had been elected priest of Rome and Augustus at the altar at Lyon by the delegates of the Gallic communities – nevertheless it was Epotsorovidus' blood that gave Rufus real title to dominate Mediolanum of the Santones?

It would be easy to press further back, to that generation of friends of Pompey, scattered from Spain to Syria, or further forward in time to Claudius' reign and Togidubnus, king and representative of Rome in the southern British tribe renamed the Regnenses. But the pattern is clear enough. Shifting alliances between dynasts at the centre and dynasts in the provinces are a constant in the history of Roman power. And even in Augustus' reign there were disruptions. The tangled history of the Euryclids of Sparta is a good illustration. The exact details of their intrigues, that involved Herod's family as well as Augustus', are unclear, but it looks very much as if rival groups in the Greek East took sides in the quiet contest between Gaius Caesar and Tiberius over who would succeed Augustus (Bowersock 1984). Eurycles' family fell from grace and were then restored to favour, following the shifting balance of power in the centre. In every city and in every royal house there were friends-in-waiting ready to exploit any collapse in the relations of the *principes*.

What emerges from this is a picture of an empire that was no unified whole, but rather a political field in which conflicts increasingly resonated with each other. The energy on which these conflicts depended did not come only from the centre. Nor were moves toward peace only the product of Augustan statesmanship. The level of stability in the system certainly increased over time, and Roman generals and princes played a major part in building alliances. Yet Herod and Juba, Eurycles and Rufus and the rest had their own interests to consult, their own reasons for seeking stability. The efforts made by each of these *principes* to entrench their power preserved the power of all of them. Many, like Herod, had achieved local stability before Rome did and so were courted by successive Roman dynasts.

It is not only modern historians who have succumbed to write the history of the political unification of the Mediterranean world from a Roman perspective.[6] Polybius found it difficult to write a 'universal history' without doing so. Appian's history was organised as a series of Roman wars, classified by the opponents. His civil war narrative, in which conflict begins with the Gracchi and spreads to include Italy and eventually the entire Mediterranean world, provides a prototype for modern accounts. But we cannot explain either the repeated civil wars of the last century B.C. or the century of peace that followed Actium simply as a by-product of Roman domestic politics. Drawing the provinces into civil wars certainly expanded the scale of those wars, and drawing them into the settlements that followed helped solidify the peace. But it was political processes at work across the Mediterranean world that allowed all these areas to be drawn into war and peace. *Pax* – meaning security and order rather than tranquillity (Weinstock 1960) – might be dubbed *Romana* or *Augusta*, but many parties were involved in its creation.

This process had begun long before Augustus. The coalition of interests among the rulers of the Mediterranean world built upon an earlier entrenchment of the power of the wealthy at the expense of other classes. That development had been underway in the city states of Italy and the Greek world for the last three centuries B.C. and was closely linked to the rise of imperial powers. Rome and the other Hellenistic empires had tended to favour the wealthy in the cities in which they dwelt. Popular assemblies had survived in many cities, Rome included, but had less and less power. The reasons for this trend, too broad to interest all but the bravest ancient historians (e.g., Veyne 1976, and de Ste. Croix, 1981, 518–37) are uncertain. Perhaps hegemonic powers found it easier to deal with stable predictable oligarchies than volatile democracies. Wealthy and educated individuals were often the most successful representatives of their cities at the courts of kings and Roman generals. Parallel processes are familiar to scholars of other imperial systems (Alcock, 1993, 72–80). The rise of oligarchy was not driven by ideological agendas, but had an ideological component that can be inferred from the way Cicero writes of the fundamental importance of property rights or from a widespread anxiety (among the rich) about debt-abolition programmes.

When, after Actium, Octavian was able to distance himself from the *popularis* programmes and slogans of Julius Caesar he moved much closer to Cicero's view that the protection of the propertied classes was the foundation of political stability (Nicolet 1984). Once again, this should not be understood only in terms of the domestic experience of the city of Rome. Augustus aligned himself with broader trends of Mediterranean history. The fact that he did so contributed to his success, at home and also in the wider Roman world.[7]

THE EXPANSION OF ROMAN POWER

The pacification of the world is one narrative that Augustus offers us in his *Res Gestae*. Another is the story of its conquest. Neither Augustus nor his provincial subjects could ignore this central transformation of the world. The eighty years or so of Octavian/Augustus' lifetime coincided with the period in which Roman imperialism was at its most ferocious. This was the time of Rome's greatest conquest (and greatest defeats). Most of the eventual empire was conquered and turned into provinces by Pompey, Caesar, Augustus, and their agents.

The great victories of the second century B.C. which left Rome without a rival in the Mediterranean world had often resulted in great hegemonic power and booty, but in little territorial gains. At Octavian's birth, Rome controlled almost nothing beyond the Mediterranean coastal plain, and not all of that. Romans were just beginning to think of their *imperium* as a vast expanse of space, rather than as mastery over defeated peoples (Nicolet 1991; Richardson 1991). By Augustus' death, Roman armies had fought in Ethiopia and Arabia, had penetrated Europe to the Elbe and exercised control in some form or other of all regions south of the Danube and west of the Rhine, north of the Sahara and west of the Euphrates. Roman explorers had gone even further. Embassies had been apparently received from India and other distant lands. The horizons of the Roman world had changed. Within those horizons the provinces were more numerous, were managed with more uniform systems, and were more securely held. With hindsight it seems a watershed had been passed: Rome had moved from greedy and unstable conquest state to tributary empire. When Tiberius is reported as telling a rapacious governor that he wanted his sheep "shorn, not flayed" it is easy to recall all those other periods of imperial consolidation, from the reign of Darius I in Persia to late Victorianism.

Some provincial writers certainly claimed that their world had been transformed, culturally and politically. Dionysius of Halicarnassus, writing in Augustan Rome, argued that Roman conquest had rescued Greek rhetorical culture from itself. Rome had redirected the cities back to their ancient classical standards and set them an example of leadership:

> [Rome's] leaders are chosen on merit and administer the state according to the highest principles. They are thoroughly cultured and in the highest degree discerning, so that under their ordering influence the sensible section of the population has increased its power and the foolish have been compelled to behave rationally. This state of affairs has led to the composition of many worthwhile works of history by contemporary writers, and the publication of many elegant political tracts and many by no means negligible philosophical treatises; and a host of other fine works, the produce of well-directed industry, have proceeded from the pens of Greeks and Romans, and will probably continue to do so.
>
> (Dionysius of Halicarnassus, Preface to *On Ancient Orators* 3; Loeb transl.)

Dionysius' analysis has been much discussed (e.g., Gabba, 1991, 23–59) and has formed the basis for modern studies of 'Augustan Classicism' (e.g., Zanker 1988 with Galinsky, 1996, 332–363, and Wallace-Hadrill, 1997, 10–11). The association of the creation of a new political and moral order with a revision of the literary canon is striking, as is the powerful appropriation of a commonplace Roman rhetoric of imperialist legitimation to Dionysius' critical and stylistic ends.

No provincial witness offers better testimony to Rome's transformative power than does Strabo, another Greek, and one whose own political connections went back to the Pompeian Mediterranean, but who also wrote in Augustus' Rome and lived to eulogise Tiberius. Throughout his text he juxtaposes life before, with life after the Romans took control. Alexandria, he writes, has opened up now that the Romans have taken over from the Ptolemies (2.3.5); the Romans are now teaching the naturally barbarous peoples of Europe to live civilised lives (2.5.26); Cadiz has been made prosperous by the bravery of its sailors . . . and the friendship of the Romans (3.1.8); Turdetania trades easily now with Rome and Italy thanks to the recent peace and the eradication of piracy (3.2.5); Rome has civilised the Turdetanians (3.2.15) the Artarbians (3.3.5), the Cavares (4.1.12) . . . the list goes on. At the other end of the Mediterranean the Romans have brought an end to Spartan helotage (8.5.4), have restored Corinth (8.6.21), brought about the end of Athenian democracy (9.1.20) and Cretan piracy (10.4.9). The chronology is deliberately vague: "then . . . now" or "up until the rule of the Romans" are characteristic phrases. But the sense of a world being transformed by Roman expansion is powerfully conveyed.[8]

At the centre of the work, Strabo concludes his account of Italy with a whistle stop tour of Rome's conquest of the world leading up to a panoramic view of the (Tiberian) present in all the continents of the Roman world (6.4.2). The war against the Germans has already produced triumphs. Africa, once ruled by many kings, is now safe in the hands of Juba. Asia, too, has been ruled through kings, some rebellious ones have been deposed, and all territory west of the Phasis and the Euphrates has been subjected to the Romans and rulers appointed by them. The Armenians and their neighbours are to be conquered in due course. The same applies to the tribes north of the Danube up to the lands of the nomads who are not worth conquering. The Parthians, the only plausible rival to Rome, "have nevertheless yielded so far to the pre-eminence of the Romans" and have returned the trophies they captured from earlier Roman generals. Phraates has entrusted his children and grandchildren to be raised in Rome and the emperors appoint Parthian kings. Even Italy has found peace from civil strife and Rome has pulled back from the brink:

But it would have been a formidable task to administer so great a dominion otherwise than by turning it over to one man, as to a father. In any case, never have the Romans and their allies thrived in such peace and plenty as that granted them by Caesar Augustus from the time he assumed the absolute authority, and is now afforded them by his son and successor Tiberius, who is making Augustus the model of his administration and decrees as are his children Germanicus and Drusus who are assisting their father.

(Strabo, *Geography* 6.4.3)

Somehow "the world conquered" is combined with the vision of relentless further expansion and both are attributed to Augustus' genius.

We should be sceptical. The panegyrical tone is not the only cause for alarm (if it is so obvious, why make such a noise about it? If the succession Augustus to Tiberius to Germanicus plus Drusus is so smooth why say so?).[9] We also need to consider how far Augustus' world conquest was begun by others, how far his long reign coincided with world conquest, and how great his impact on it was. After all, Octavian certainly did not initiate this last phase of major Roman expansion, however much it was promoted in the middle part of his reign, and in the years before his death it slowed to a crawl, whatever Strabo says (Gruen 1996).

Expansion was not anyone's grand strategy. The Republican empire was created by competing aristocrats harnessing the energies of a society increasingly geared to constant warfare (Hopkins 1978; Harris 1979). The only central institutions were those of the city of Rome. The Senate pooled and transmitted experience of the provinces without the aid of administrators. Senators and *equites* staffed ineffectual corruption courts. Senior magistrates let out public contracts to private individuals to supply all the infrastructure needed from road building and army supply to tax collection. The provinces were even less institutionalised. Much of the territory that obeyed Roman orders was not part of a formal province. There were few regular governors, fewer garrisons, only a handful of public slaves. Roman rule often meant little more than obeying the commands of the most powerful Roman in the vicinity (cf. Purcell in this volume). Pompey made and broke kings, abolished and amalgamated kingdoms, founded cities, gave provinces constitutions and his men extravagant rewards. Much depended on his personal prestige and connections. This pattern endured until late in Augustus' reign.

Modest institutionalisation was underway long before Augustus took control of expansion. The pace of territorial acquisition from the

60s onward, together with some spectacular Roman disasters prompted by inconsistency at the centre and corruption and incompetence at the edge, forced Rome's leaders to develop a more sustainable administrative apparatus. Most of it did take its final form in the reign of Augustus. Key components included a huge expansion of the number of territorial provinces; the creation of a standing army; the recruitment of more senators and also members of Rome's second aristocracy – the *equites* – to share the burden of government; and major changes in the way taxes were collected, passing much of the burden onto provincial propertied classes (Bowman 1996). Accompanying these changes was the elaboration of an ideology of empire that represented Rome as having a divine mandate to rule the world.

Tracing the precise chronology of these changes is not easy. Pompey created provinces that were more systematically ordered than ever before. Caesar pioneered the transfer of land-tax collection to the cities from the contractors. Both used senatorial lieutenants to help administer large provinces. Equestrian officers became prominent in the civil wars, which had also seen the emergence of armies that were in effect professional troops. Not long before Octavian's birth, Cicero's speeches in support of Pompey's super-commands provide evidence of an emerging consciousness of empire, and of the paucity of instruments available at Rome for managing it (Steel 2001). Caesar's *Gallic War*, written in the 50s B.C., testifies to changing attitudes to conquest. Each campaign is justified individually – as Romans had always claimed that each of their wars were just – yet Caesar also boasts of being the first to lead Roman armies beyond the Ocean and the Rhine (Brunt 1978). From Pompey on, all successful Roman generals were fascinated with the person of Alexander the Great (cf. Fig. 53 on p. 342). They founded cities named after themselves. They were hailed in language usually reserved for Hellenistic monarchs or the gods. Conquests were expressed in terms of great geographical features, the Pyrenees and the Alps, the Gulfs of the Ocean, the great rivers at the edge of the Roman world.

The Augustan regime did build on these foundations. The *Res Gestae*, Virgil's *Aeneid*, and the images of the globe that appear again and again on Augustan coins and monuments, offer the first explicit claims about Rome's divine mandate to conquer the world. But we know little of the process by which institutional change progressed. Were there great rationalising planning meetings, of the kind Dio imagined in the debate he staged between Agrippa and Maecenas about the nature of the principate? Or do we observe not much more than an intensification of the kind of large-scale problem solving conducted by Pompey? The latter seems more probable. The continued importance of client princes in his scheme of things, the diversity of taxation systems, the mutinies that followed his death, all show the limits of any Augustan 'system.' The last chapter (101.4) of Suetonius' *Life of Augustus* records how he included with his will a brief account of the empire:

> How many soldiers there were under arms and where they were stationed, how much money was in the *aerarium*, how much in the other treasuries and what tax revenue was still owing. He added to it the names of the freedmen and slaves from whom fuller accounts might be asked.

This was one limit of the Augustan reorganisation of the provinces: like any Republican magistrate he had managed public affairs through his most trusted household staff.

One major contribution we can be sure Augustus made to Roman expansion was to slow it down: although he had conquered more territory than any other Roman leader before him, and duly highlighted this in the preface to the *Res Gestae*, caution gradually replaced the bold enterprise of his predecessors. Military defeats have been blamed for the end of expansion, but late Republican disasters like those suffered by Crassus and Antony in their invasions of Parthia had not derailed conquest. Second century A.D. authors under the spell of Trajan blamed the end of conquest on the emperors' laziness and/or vice. Modern attempts to produce a rational explanation for the location of the empire's frontiers have not been convincing. Most do not rest on geographical or ecological limits, do not coincide with the limits of prehistoric social systems and have no strategic rationale. It is far more likely that, just as conquest was at first driven by political competition, so the end of competition had made the costs and risks of territorial expansion seem no longer worth it.

PROSPERITY

So Greater Rome rolled out, powered by forces Augustus had not set in motion. But if he neither invented nor accelerated Roman imperialism, he benefited from its results. So did many others. One of the remarkable features of this last phase of Roman expansionism was the very large numbers of people who shared in its profits. The populace of the city had their building, their dole, and their games, paid for first by the booty of captured Egypt and then by the great revenues Augustus enjoyed privately and the state enjoyed publicly as a result of conquest. But the profits were much more widely spread.

One consequence of the low level of institutionalisation of the empire was that it depended for its success on a series of social institutions most of which pre-dated empire, but which assumed new roles as Rome acquired hegemony over the Mediterranean world. Among the institutions that were especially important were citizenship and slavery, both of which led to a steady expansion in the numbers of Romans. Closely linked to citizenship was an evolving notion of Roman identity in which habits of dress, speech, manners, and conduct were more important than descent. This made it relatively easy to become Roman (Woolf 1998). The family, extended by patronage and slavery, came to perform many of the organizing functions that are performed in modern societies by companies, corporations, or associations. Education, once a means of concentrating cultural capital in the hands of the wealthy, became a means of socializing new Romans and creating a common culture for imperial élites.

The beneficiaries of many of these institutions were first of all members of the Italian aristocracies. Agricultural intensification, first undertaken to take advantage of the growing market in the City, was expanded to supply the overseas colonies and the provinces with Italian products. The same techniques allowed the new Roman owners of provincial land to intensify its productivity. Viticulture was extended to new areas for example, Roman systems of water management were applied in much of the west, new milling and pressing technology was widely disseminated. Expansion probably provided much of the capital for this process. Italy itself was probably never richer than at the turn of the millennium, a period when the taste for Italian produce had become generalised, but the techniques to satisfy that demand had not yet become naturalised in the provinces.

Many Italians shared in this prosperity. The new civic monuments built in southern Gaul resemble those built in the Po Valley the generation before, those in Africa have more in common with southern and central styles. Architects and workmen must have moved out in pursuit of new contracts (Ward-Perkins 1970). Ceramic production, when it spread to Gaul, was brought by Italian firms. Italian entrepreneurs had been operating under the umbrella of empire from at least the second century B.C. throughout the Mediterranean (cf. Purcell, this volume). The numbers will have increased as the sphere of Roman military and political interventions increased. Many followed armies to buy booty from soldiers, and to sell them other goods. Some doubled as tax-farmers, some sought out and exported to Rome objects of special value such as Greek statuary. There is extensive archaeological evidence for a large scale trade in Italian wine in Gaul: papyri suggest Egypt also imported it. The grain trade grew in importance as the total number of urban mouths increased. Most sinister of all was the slave trade. Many slaves were prisoners of war, but not all. Some were probably enslaved within Europe by tribes beyond the frontier who sold them on to Roman buyers. Parallels have often been drawn with the slave trade from Dahomey to the Americas. A casual mention in Cicero's speech *For Quinctius* (24) reveals a caravan of slaves being transported from Gaul to Italy.

Most of the traders involved were not of high status but in some cases the very rich were certainly involved. Only they had the capital to invest (or the social credit with which to borrow it) in large scale intensification in Italian viticulture, in developing ranches in the provinces like those discovered on the Crau plain, in setting up the transport infrastructure that made it worthwhile growing large surpluses of olives in Spain and Africa, in building kilns capable of firing thousands of vessels at very high temperatures and so on. Archaeological evidence of massive investment in agricultural and non-agricultural production all over the empire at the turn of the millennium is building up. It is difficult to imagine who but the very richest could have been involved. Patronage and a series of legal instruments developed in the early second century are the most probable means by which these ventures were organised.

Other Romans lived permanently in the provinces. The process began in the second century B.C. when settlements like Gracchuris were created in Spain, allegedly for the descendants of soldiers and local women. The redistribution of provincial land to Roman and Italian settlers was debated from the late second century B.C. and a few colonies were actually created then. But the great period of overseas settlement followed Caesar's defeat of Pompey. Once most Italians were Roman citizens the political costs of settling soldiers or the overspill population of the city of Rome in the peninsula became too high. As with more recent imperialisms, the settlers were often concentrated in territories that most resembled their home country. So the Mediterranean coasts of Tunisia, Spain, and Gaul were colonised intensively while their continental hinterlands received fewer colonies. There were exceptions: strategic reasons determined the location of some colonies, for example, those of southern Asia Minor (Levick 1967).

But the growing taste for Italian produce and what we might loosely term Roman style goods was not confined to expatriate communities. Most early public building in the West was funded by local notables, men like Rufus in Gaul (Mierse 1990). It is very difficult to find much public building on Roman lines before the mid-first century B.C. but there is enough to show that it was not an innovation of Augustus' reign. By the middle of the next century, however, the townscapes of southern Spain, north Africa, southern Gaul, and Italy were furnished with grandiose public monuments. In a few cities in the interior there was building on a grand scale from the same period. In most of these areas the monumental centres were not complete until the late first century A.D., but there were colonies like Aosta and Lyon to imitate, and the great cities built by the friends of Rome and Augustus. The catalogue of cities named, or incorporating names like Augusta, Augustodunum, Augustonemetum, Caesarodunum, Caesaromagus and Caesarea is enormous: they would be joined by Tiberias and Germanicopolis (and they followed in the tradition of Pompey's Magnopolis).

Generally, but not always, public monuments were developed ahead of private housing. But the same élites had engaged with a broad range of Roman culture from the turn of the millennium. Their children were taught Latin in model schools, reading Horace and Terence, Virgil and Cicero just as they did in Italy. They purchased Italian foodstuffs and learned how to produce them at home. They ate their food off Roman style ceramics, a change which shows the adoption of Roman styles of cuisine and manners. Perhaps these new habits were still markers of élite culture in the Augustan period. Many would soon be generalised.

What led to these shifts in taste? It was not characteristic of the Republican empire, it cost provincial élites a great deal to satisfy and enriched many Italians of various statuses. At least part of the answer seems to be that Roman society was quite easily penetrated by those whose loyalty to Rome was supported by civilised credentials. Roman writers from Lucretius on had developed a particularly Roman version of a civilizing myth by which barbarians might be softened and refined by training and the acquisition of virtue. It would obviously be ridiculous to say that local chiefs in Spain started using *terra sigillata* to support applications for citizenship. But in an empire where patronage was often an essential prerequisite for success, in which education indoctrinated the young into absolutist views of civilisation and morality, in which Roman military success seemed a proof of the superiority of Roman ways, it is maybe not difficult to imagine the seductions of Roman culture. The Republican empire had come less close to the lives of provincials. Government had been less intensive, settlers fewer, the tentacles of the Italian economy had been fewer and shorter. General enfranchisement had only reached the Alps under Caesar.

These processes must have contributed to the success and stability of the new order in all sorts of ways. Even today, regimes have an easier time when the economy is booming. With Italian landowners richer than ever before, it was the perfect time both to purge the Senate with minimum protest and to find new recruits. While provincial élites were investing so heavily in becoming Roman, some loyalty and displays of enthusiasm might be counted on (Ando 2000). The prosperity of Italy and the growing prosperity of the provinces must have made it easier to increase the revenues of Rome and also the profits that accumulated from Augustus' considerable personal property. It was, in short, a good time to found a world-empire.

ROME'S LAST CULTURAL REVOLUTION?

Universities and schools today teach Latin off much the same texts as were used in classrooms of Gaul and Italy, Africa and Spain toward the end of Augustus' reign. Why?

Once upon a time it would have been fashionable to answer that "Golden Latin" was intrinsically better than what had gone before and from what followed, that generations of discerning readers had recognised this quality, and so that "our" "Classics" had come down to us authorised by centuries of refinement. Today we understand much more about the processes of canon-formation, how books slip in and out of fashion. It is apparent that Roman writers were actively engaged in debating which texts were central and which secondary, within a Latin classics defined during the lifetime of Augustus. Horace's *Letter to Augustus* has been read as an overt attempt to redefine the canon of 'Great Works.' Less controversially, it has been shown that a vast quantity of Latin verse set out more subtly to reinterpret and unseat what it claimed as vulgar unpolished precedents. Often late Republican writers claimed to be the first to transplant Greek forms into Italian soil. When predecessors existed they were often presented as coarse and unrefined, as Horace did Lucilius. Mid-republican writers could have made the same claim (Hinds 1998). Latin literature was created by appropriating and modifying Greek models in the late third century B.C. The precise reasons are much disputed (e.g., Gruen 1992; Habinek 1998) but there is broad agreement that two important contexts are Rome's emergence as an imperial power and a broad fascination with Greek culture among the élites and communities of central Italy (Zanker 1976; Dench 1995).

Broadly similar phenomena accompany the history of other art forms in Rome. Marble statuary was imported as booty from the late third century B.C.: the sack of Syracuse in 211 seemed a key moment to some ancient writers, who contrasted it with the decision by the Roman conqueror of Tarentum in 209 to leave the city "its angry gods." The first major marble monument assembled by a Roman general was probably the portico of Metellus, built in 146 B.C. Individual structures grew grander and grander culminating in Pompey's theatre and Caesar's assembly hall for the Roman voters, the Saepta Iulia (see Fig. 45.A and 47.9). By this time individual marble statues thronged the villas of great Roman generals like Lucullus. It is against this background we have to read Augustus' claim to have transformed Rome from a city of mud brick into a city of marble, and also the preference he seems to have had for some Greek models over others (Zanker 1988).

Each new generation of Roman leaders, from the third century on, refined the public culture of the city, just as the poets redefined Roman literature. All these cultures were 'imperial cultures'. If historians wished, they could write of "Roman cultural revolutions" in the late-third century B.C., in Scipionic Rome, and in the age of Varro and Cicero with equal justification as they can in relation to the lifetime of Augustus. The great change we do see occurring in the lifetime of Augustus is the solidification of the canon, the end of cultural revolutions. Under the principate, cultural change progressed at a more gradual pace. The will to revise the canon persisted. Juvenalian satire is hardly reverential of Horace. Tacitus has never been accused of undue meekness to his predecessors. His *Dialogue on Orators* includes a defence of the new against traditionalists. Second century A.D. scholars like Aulus Gellius still had access to much more Roman literature than has survived today. A few did express preferences for non-canonical works. Cato's speeches could be preferred to Cicero's, the history of Claudius Quadrigarius to that of Livy, Ennius' epic to Virgil's and so on. It is less clear how far works composed after Virgil and Horace wrote ever came close to becoming canonical, but some of Ovid's writings seem to have been widely read, and Statius strove to boost the image of Lucan who had constructed himself as an heir to Virgil.

Yet Virgil, Horace, and Cicero were the victors, even when their politics – Republican and expansionist in places – was "off-message." The reason, I suggest, lies in the provinces. As long as the game of intertextual canon-formation was played within the limits of the city of

Rome, essentially by a handful of aristocratic families and their clients, it was an easy matter to promote or denigrate Ennius, to raise up Accius or put down Cato. Once the canon was established in a wider world – the vast dispersed world of expatriate colonists and wannabe Roman élites in the provinces – it became less easy to demote the classics. Imagine, as a thought experiment, how one would set about decanonising Shakespeare and replacing him with Marlowe or John Grisham. The English reading world is vast, the modern canon is preserved by hundreds of independent institutions, some governmental, some educational, some cultural. Local divergence is a possibility, and in many spheres of Roman culture local divergence is indeed the main story of the second and third centuries A.D., but the canon will never be revised in a coordinated fashion again.

Roman civilization, put simply, having been taken on by the provinces, no longer belonged to the City of Rome. Empire acted as a brake, a vast inertial drag. This, then, is an explanation for the extraordinarily conservative nature of the intellectual life of the principate compared to the innovative dynamism of the Republic. Creativity was perfectly possible for Spanish Seneca and African Apuleius, but it was creativity within a system with an Augustan canon. Just as the monuments of Augustan Rome obscure the city of the Scipios, and as Augustus' imperialism outshines that of Pompey and Caesar, so Augustus' poets persisted as classics. But not thanks to his patronage alone. By good fortune, Virgil was in the right place when the music stopped, and Ennius and Statius were not.

AUGUSTUS IN PROVINCIAL PERSPECTIVE

All human agency is constrained by circumstance. It is no insult to Augustus to see the events of his lifetime as driven more by other forces than by his own policy, will, or genius. There were major changes in his lifetime, right across the Mediterranean world, but with the exception of the end of expansion that followed on the shift to autocracy, he seems to have made little difference to most. He was successful because he did not try to swim against the tide, as his own goals cohered well with processes already underway. Perhaps a different *princeps* would have slowed or accelerated the working out of some processes. Doing without an individual was probably never a very realistic option: concord between the struggling orders and a consensus among all men of influence would have been necessary, and Cicero could not achieve either of those. The

Res Gestae was for public consumption. Privately Augustus probably had a more realistic assessment of what he had achieved. Suetonius tells another story – maybe a true one – of Augustus on his deathbed (cf. Eder, p. 13):

> when the friends he had summoned were present he inquired of them whether they thought he had played his role well in the comedy of life, adding the concluding lines: "Since the play has been so good, clap your hands | and all of you dismiss us with applause."
>
> Suetonius, *Augustus* 99 (transl. Edwards)

We do not need to applaud Augustus, but it is worth following his prompt to thinking about the stage on which he performed (cf. Beacham, this volume) and the script that he did not entirely write himself.

SUGGESTIONS FOR FURTHER READING

Alcock (1993) is not focused exclusively on the Augustan period but is one of the most original approaches to the impact of Rome on the provinces and one of the few to begin from the archaeology. P. A. Brunt, *Roman Imperial Themes* (Oxford 1990) collects a number of fundamental papers on Rome and the provinces. *Cambridge Ancient History²*. Volume X: *The Augustan Empire 43 BC–AD 69* (Cambridge 1996) includes excellent analyses of the institutions of the empire and an invaluable series of provincial surveys. Fentress (2000) collects historical and archaeological analyses of the Roman urban boom from all over the empire. Keay and Terrenato (2001) provide a collection of regional syntheses that show some of the ways in which provincial archaeologists treat these issues at present. MacMullen (2000) is, remarkably, the only book-length study of cultural change across the entire Empire in this period. Woolf (1998) is an attempt to examine the changes often termed Romanization through a case study of one region of the empire.

NOTES

1   I am grateful to my colleague Jill Harries for discussion of these issues. All errors and misconceptions remain my own.
2   For the relation between the concepts of *urbs* and *orbis* see also Chapter 10 by D. Favro in this volume.

3   Perhaps it was most successful in the Augustan age. Much recent literature has dealt with the emergence of Greek centres as rival capitals. On Augustus' relations with eastern communities cf. Bowersock (1965) and Levick (1996).

4   Cf. Scheid in this volume on the continuity of 'Augustan' programs between the Octavianic and Augustan periods of his reign.

5   The potential bibliography is enormous. See most recently Millett (1990), Cherry (1998), Woolf (1998), Keay and Terrenato (2001), MacMullen (2000). Many historians and archaeologists have preferred to deal with these changes in other terms; cf. Alcock (1993), Ando (2000).

6   Many histories of modern imperialism fall into the same trap, representing the victims of European empire as passive and static societies transformed by energetic external ones. For an attempt to evade this see Wolf (1982).

7   Cannadine (2001) offers another modern parallel, showing the closeness of fit between ideals of social hierarchy prevalent in Imperial Britain, and the kinds of social hierarchy with which the British allied themselves in their empire.

8   See the chapter by Karl Galinsky in this volume on the negotiation of this world view in the poetry of Vergil and Ovid.

9   Cf. Erich Gruen's Chapter 15 in this volume on the realities of the succession, and Diana Kleiner's on their embroidering in art.

6: WOMEN IN THE TIME OF AUGUSTUS

Susan Treggiari

THEMES

In the style of Hercules, o *plebs*, Caesar, who was just now said to have sought the bay-branch that can be purchased at the price of death, – Caesar is on his way back to his household gods, a victor from the shore of Spain.

Let his wife, rejoicing in the matchless husband who is all to her, come out sacrificing to the just gods, and the sister of our beloved leader, and, adorned with the ribbon of suppliants, mothers of girls (*virgines*) and of young men lately safe; you, o boys and girls who have now known a husband, refrain from ill-omened words.

(Horace *Odes* 3.14: my translation is indebted to G. Williams, R. G. M. Nisbet and D. West)

Horace in 24 B.C. calls on the Roman *plebs* (the common people) to welcome Augustus who has crushed its enemies in Spain, thus emulating the monster-slaying half-divine hero Hercules, who later became a god. Augustus had been ill and forced to stay at Tarragona the previous year, when his nephew Marcellus had come home to marry the emperor's daughter, his cousin Julia (born 39), and other young officers had been demobilised. The *princeps'* wife, Livia, and sister, Octavia (who, in accordance with republican convention in public speeches, are not named) will go out in procession to meet him. Then elements of the *Plebs* are listed: the mothers of girls (who can now hope to marry) and of young men who have survived the campaigns or will now not be called up; young boys, and girls who have recently married. The summons to the mothers suggests the virgins and men of military and marriageable age (*iuvenes*); the young married women and adolescent boys follow: an elegant variation (I venture to dissent from Nisbet here) on a prosaic listing of adults and adolescents of each sex (wives and men who serve the state; virgins and boys who will soon become grown citizens [cf. *Odes* 1.21.1–2, 3.1.4, *Secular Hymn* 6]). I want to underline two points: the prominent position given in the second stanza to Augustus' closest women associates, and the selection of mothers and the young to represent the population of Rome on this occasion, as those who have most cause for joy, and especially joy in the giver of peace and of the enjoyment of marriage and children. Horace could describe the whole Roman People by sociopolitical class (e.g., senators and the rest, *Odes* 4.5.3–4,7; 4.14.1). But here he prefers to emphasise families and to include women, who did not vote. The imperial family itself is represented by two senior women, both mothers (since the late 40s: Octavia [Fig. 3] had been born in 68, Livia [Fig. 4] in 58); Julia, who was expected to give her father a male heir, is not here.

The upper-class group evoked by Horace here may remind us of the portrayal of a much larger group of men, women, and children of Augustus' extended family which was to appear on the Altar of Augustan Peace a decade later (Fig. 22). How new was this emphasis? I shall argue that the representation and reality of women's role were rooted in Roman tradition, but that the time of Augustus was one of marked development.

Roman citizen women had no right to vote in the assemblies, nor could they stand for office. One of the assemblies evolved from men drawn up for battle; office-holders might lead troops. Women had no share in war. What was their role in the commonwealth of the Roman People (the *Res publica*)? The answer was obvious: they were to breed citizen-soldiers and mothers of soldiers in legitimate Roman marriage. Horace's contemporary, the historian Livy, retelling the legend of the abduction of unmarried Sabine women by Romulus and his gang of bachelor settlers (who saw that Rome would only last a generation without women and who had failed to obtain brides from their neighbours by diplomatic means), insists that the women were given marriage and partnership in fortunes, citizenship, and children (1.9) and became loyal Romans.

As to their rights in the community of citizens, it is clear that women were citizens (*cives Romanae*). This status was relevant to their ability to contract a marriage valid in Roman law with a male

FIGURE 3. Octavia. *Aureus* of Mark Antony, 40–39 B.C. Octavia's portrait appears on coins of both Antony and Augustus while Livia does not figure on Augustan coinage. Photo: Hirmer Archive 2000.187R.

Roman citizen. Such a marriage (when the couple met certain other qualifications such as not being close blood-relations and being of age) produced Roman citizen children. A Roman woman could transmit citizenship to her illegitimate children and to slaves whom she freed formally: if males, they could vote once adult. She lived under Roman law and had its protection.

When he mentions 'fortunes', Livy may be thinking of the chance of the future prosperity of Rome, but also of the 'lot', circumstances and property, of the husbands. If he imagines that the Sabines entered the control of their husbands, their property would merge with that of the husbands, but the women would have claim to maintenance and to a share of the husband's fortune on his death. Control by the husband

FIGURE 4. Portrait of the young Livia, late 30s B.C. She is already represented in the same ageless classicizing style as Augustus. National Museums and Galleries on Merseyside, Liverpool. Museum photograph.

of a wife and her property (*manus*) was uncommon by Augustus' time, but sometimes still used as a legal expedient.

Children were the reason for the institution of marriage, as Livy's whole story makes clear. The state took an interest in the continuance of citizens through breeding (as in the expansion of the citizen-body through enfranchisement of aliens and manumission of slaves). *Matrimonium* means an institution for making mothers (*matres*). The usual phrase describing the act of getting married was 'for the sake of procreating children' or an equivalent. (The word for 'children' includes grandchildren through sons). Men wanted heirs. There was also, Livy underlines, an emotional reason for both sexes: children are the dearest thing there is to the human race (1.9, a frequent formulation).

THE LATE-REPUBLICAN STATUS QUO:
CIRCA 100–38 B.C.

Legal and economic institutions are not to be divorced from the people who created them and from the ideas and emotions that give them meaning. But, for the sake of clarity, the legal and economic framework in which citizen women lived in the first century B.C. before Augustus came to power may be briefly sketched. Women, by ancient custom, could be legal owners of all kinds of property, could inherit and bequeath it. The salient and peculiar institution of paternal power shaped the life of the family. A male who had no living male direct ascendant was the head of a household (*familia*). As *paterfamilias*, he had in his paternal power (*patria potestas*) his children and remoter descendants in the male line (grandchildren by sons, great-grandchildren by grandsons, but not his daughter's children and so on). His death freed all those who were in his power: both sons and daughters became independent; each son became *paterfamilias*. If he had made no will, each child had an equal claim to a share of the family property. (For the small print, see more detailed accounts, such as Crook [1967] 107–13, and Saller [1994] 102–32). Children might be emancipated from paternal power by the *paterfamilias* in his lifetime, daughters could be transferred to a husband's control. While he held this power, the children in power had no property of their own, even what they inherited or earned (though he might let them administer some, e.g., a farm). This restriction was counterbalanced by their rights on intestacy and by their moral right to fair shares (often affected by what the daughters had received from their birth-family in dowry or inherited from their husband's family or by what sons had acquired by their work or from their mothers, and so on). The father's "right of life and death" applied mainly to his prerogative to decide whether a new-born baby should be raised. When he acknowledged a baby daughter, the father accepted a duty to nurture her and (if possible) to arrange her marriage and give her a dowry.

A *paterfamilias* could originally betroth his daughter without her formal consent; by the end of the Republic that consent was probably required. Conversely, his consent was needed as well as hers. Girls would be relatively young at first engagement: later jurists express some shock at the idea that a daughter might not accept her father's candidate. In any case, engagements were not enforceable and were easily broken. A girl might legally marry on or after her twelfth birthday. But the normal age seems to have been in the late teens, though aristocrats frequently married younger. Men of all classes, as far as we know, seem to have married typically in their late twenties, so that an age difference of about a decade was usual at first marriage. Both the bride and her *paterfamilias*, if she had one, had to consent, as did the bridegroom and his. We may conjecture that, since girls were brought up in the expectation that they would marry, they would usually acquiesce in the family's choice, but the possibility of greater freedom of action increased for older brides and second and subsequent marriages (when, besides, it was even likelier than before that the father might already have died). A married man was expected to notify the censors of his married state and children, but public authority was not needed for the formation of a marriage. Religious rituals might occur at a wedding. Bilateral consent by the parties suffices to make a marriage.

Families of all classes seem to have tried to give a dowry. This was primarily the *paterfamilias'* responsibility, and he could get the dowry back if his daughter predeceased him. But others, or the woman herself, might also give all or part. Dowry became the husband's for the duration of the marriage and was seen as a contribution to the wife's keep and that of any children; at the end of a marriage (through divorce or the wife's death) it might be seen as a source of endowment of her children. If the husband died, the wife would need to get her dowry back if she was to remarry. A great deal of (mostly later) juristic scholarship was devoted to dowry, especially its reclamation. For the upper classes, dowry was substantial (in cash, land, slaves and livestock, valuables), but the wife would often have her own property as well, especially once she had begun to inherit from her kin. The Voconian Law of 169 B.C. had limited the right of those in the top property class to make a woman sole heir, but this offended fathers of only daughters and before Augustus they often circumvented the law by asking the heir/executor to pass on property to the daughter. This property was carefully separated from dowry or any joint property of husband and wife.

'Rules' about marriage arose originally from custom. Praetors and other officials refined legal procedures and ideas about what was equitable in case of divorce or difficulties about property. In accordance with the practice 'of all peoples', Romans might not marry ascendants or descendants; Roman law also ruled out siblings. Marriage with first cousins was allowed by the late Republic.

Low life-expectancy (I follow Saller 1994) meant that fifteen-year-old women had about a 62 percent chance of having a father alive, by 20 fewer than half of them still had a father. The chance of being free of paternal power before or soon after a first marriage was relatively high. The daughter would become independent in law, but was required to have a lifelong guardian to authorise her more important property transactions (such as the constitution of a dowry), but not to look after her (e.g., his consent to marriage was not required). The guardian might be appointed by her *paterfamilias*, or be a male agnate or be chosen, if necessary, by an official. Citizen women freed from slavery had their manumitter as guardian, if male. Upper-class women were often thought to use their guardians as a rubber-stamp.

The demographic pattern and marriage customs allowed a considerable concentration of wealth in women's hands: a family might channel most of its property to an only daughter; a wife might inherit from an older husband and deploy considerable economic power and social influence; serial marriages might allow a woman to inherit from a succession of husbands. Aurelia, mother of Caesar, who lived a widow from 85 or 84 to 54 B.C., and Servilia, mother of Brutus and survivor of two marriages, probably owed some of their influence over their sons to economic clout. Independent women could also run into debt (Sallust, *Catiline* 25.3–5).

Solid wealth in the ancient world meant land. The influx of capital caused by imperial expansion and the agrarian revolution of the second century B.C. allowed landholdings to be increased and greater profit made from a variety of crops and livestock. Exploitation of land included quarrying, production of pottery or bricks and lumber or charcoal. Wealthy women were involved in these, and, no doubt, in the running of shops or shipping through freedmen. Lower in the social hierarchy, the peasant's only daughter might inherit the family farm and look for a husband to work it or the craftsman's wife might work alongside him and the marketwoman run a business. (Republican inscriptions rarely attest working women, but we have a freedwoman purple-seller who commemorates her patron, fellow-freedman/husband, and freedman, *ILLRP* 809, and a couple who sell incense, 818).

Divorce could be brought about unilaterally, without recourse to any public authority, by a married person or that person's *paterfamilias*: unilateral withdrawal of consent sufficed. It had presumably always been possible for a husband to divorce an adulterous wife. From the late third century, he could divorce her for sterility without penalty. If he divorced her for other reasons (e.g., incompatibility), he might suffer financial penalty. By the first century B.C. it was legally possible for the wife to divorce the husband. It was also morally acceptable if the husband had committed a grave fault. For instance, Cicero sympathises in court with Cluentia, who was under the painful necessity of divorcing her husband for adultery with her mother (*Defence of Cluentius* 14). He also considered this a possibility for his own daughter when Dolabella's infidelities were flagrant (though he might have taken the legal initiative himself, if she had instructed him. Dolabella's previous wife may have divorced him too (Cicero, *Letters to friends* 8.6.1). Less respectably, we hear of Paulla Valeria divorcing in order to remarry (Cicero, *Letters to friends* 8.7.2). The young Aemilia was manipulated into a divorce and remarriage to Pompey by her mother, for political reasons (Plutarch, *Pompey* 9.2–3). Divorce might be by mutual consent. We cannot assess how common divorce was, even in the senatorial aristocracy. There are only three to five examples where women were or might have been legally responsible, out of a total of 32 attested divorces from circa 100–38 B.C., that is, down to Livia's probably consensual divorce from her first husband.

Legal freedom to divorce and a perceived increase in the number of divorces have been associated with a perceived rise in individualism in the first century B.C., reflected in the introduction to Latin of personal love poetry and the ruthlessly selfish ambition of politicians such as Pompey, Caesar – or Augustus. This picture may be exaggerated by the availability of different types of writing (correspondence from and to Cicero; extensive forensic and political speeches, though all from Cicero, instead of the fragments we have from the second century or from other first-century orators; Sallust's historical monographs, again instead of mere fragments). But it is unlikely to be entirely false. Wealth, a more luxurious lifestyle (*luxuria*, chief target of the moralists, along with disreputable greed for money, *avaritia*) affected upper-class women as well as men. Although historians such as Livy can portray individual women of the legendary period as tragic heroines and we have again non-contemporary writers who make us seem to see second-century women such as Cornelia, mother of the Gracchi, as individuals, in the first century we feel some sense of the personality of individual women, though usually through male writers' perceptions. Who can forget Quintus Cicero's wife Pomponia throwing a tantrum or Brutus' mother, with his wife and one of his sisters present, in family council arranging the administration of the empire (Cicero, *Letters to Atticus* 5.1.3–4, 15.11.1–2)?

WOMEN HAD A SHARE IN DOMESTIC AND PUBLIC RELIGION

The famous Vestal Virgins, six at any one time, recruited before puberty from top families, allowed to retire (and marry) after thirty years' service, had a leading role in cult. They kept alight the fire of Vesta in her round temple in the heart of Rome and prepared the salted grain for public sacrifices. Alone among women, their names are listed by Broughton in *Magistrates of the Roman Republic*. The priest of Jupiter had to be sacramentally married: his wife, who shared some of his tasks, was the *flaminica Dialis*. The wife of the 'king of sacrifices', *rex sacrorum*, was the 'queen'. Certain native rituals were carried out by married women, for instance, the annual December rites in honour of the Good Goddess, performed in the house of a leading official (often a consul or praetor) by the Vestals and women of the upper class, including the ladies of the house, but excluding men. When the Senate decreed public rituals of expiation or thanksgiving to the gods, *supplicationes*, the presence of women is sometimes explicitly mentioned (Livy 10.23.1–3; 22.10.8: town and country men with their wives and children). Livy portrays the celebration of the great victory over Hannibal's brother in 207 B.C. as shared by men and women: 'All the temples for the whole three days had an equal crowd, as married women in their best clothes with their children, freed from all fear just as if the war were over, gave thanks to the immortal gods' (27.51.8). That victory had been won by two remote kinsmen of Livia and her sons (cf. Vergil, *Aeneid* 6.824; Suetonius, *Tiberius* 2): did Livy think of the celebration of 24 B.C.? Cicero, too, writing of contemporary thanksgivings, regards the participation of wives and children as important (*Against Catiline* 3.22) particularly when they could be regarded as having been rescued from danger (*Against Catiline* 4.1). Similarly, when crowds turned out to welcome him on his return from exile in 57 B.C., they consisted of *patresfamilias* with their wives and children and the event was much like a religious festival (*Against Piso* 51). When he reached Rome, he saw the Senate come out to meet him 'and the whole Roman People . . . all men and women of all types, ages and ranks, of every fortune and position' (*Against Piso* 52). Horace's ode is in this tradition of civic occasions where the presence of women is vital if the whole People is to be represented.

Imported cults often involved women, as priestesses or other officials. At certain sacrifices women were excluded. This proves that they might normally be present. They also seem to have officiated at sacrifices, including blood sacrifices. At sacrifices on behalf of the People, the task of slaughtering the animal was carried out by a professional: we need not imagine a woman using an axe on a bull. Women, individually or acting as a group, dedicated objects such as statues to the gods, gave money for repairs of temples. Part of the old rituals of acceptance of a bride into her new family involved cult acts: she was to anoint and adorn the doorposts of her new home and take fire and water from the bridegroom; the next day, at a reception, she made her first offerings to the household gods. From then on, the *materfamilias* and her husband led family worship, making offerings of food and flowers to the *Lares*, *Penates*, and the hearth.

Aristocratic women were not included in all their husbands' social activities, but they might accompany them to public entertainments or dinner-parties, might dine out in the houses of kin or other women, and might entertain at home. What education they got (with rare exceptions) lacked the training for public life that their brothers needed, but they might read lighter types of literature, sing, and dance. They went to stay with friends and travelled to meet husbands or fathers. They could extend protection to social inferiors (e.g., Cicero, *Defence of Sex. Roscius* 27). Within the constraints of class, they had some choice of lifestyles, even, perhaps, sexual liberation. Or so it is alleged of the married Sempronia (Sallust, *Catiline* 25) and the widowed Clodia (Treggiari, 1996, 123).

The troubles of the late Republic affected women directly. The chance of losing male kin in civil war or proscription was added to the normal risk of foreign wars. Increased power and wealth fell to fatherless daughters or to widows. The pain of Sulla's despotism in the late 80s was 'branded on the community of citizens' (Cicero, *Against Catiline* 2.20; the metaphor recurs of other periods of strife: *On the response of the haruspices* 55, *Philippics* 2.117). It was followed by the civil wars of 49–45 B.C. and of the triumviral period (43–30, including proscriptions). Battle and proscription divided families. How could you remain loyal or look after children? Servilia's three daughters were married to Isauricus, Cassius, and Lepidus. Whatever the outcome between Caesarians and tyrannicides, the women would suffer. The proscriptions invited or compelled betrayal, but Velleius claims wives showed more loyalty than sons (2.67) and there is supporting evidence for wives' courage and self-sacrifice. In the civil war to avenge Caesar, the young Livia lost her father (who killed himself when the tyrannicides went down at Philippi in 42 B.C.) and later was forced to flee with her husband Tiberius Claudius Nero and her little son (Velleius 2.75). Another survivor, Horace, who fought at Philippi, speaks repeatedly of the guilt of fratricide and links a breakdown of family morality with civil war (e.g., *Odes* 1.2.21–4, 35.33–40; 3.6.17–48).

Augustus' contemporaries (of whom Horace is most relevant to our purposes) might see the Republic in being, the upheavals of 60–30 B.C. and the comparative tranquillity of his Principate. Some of older generations (e.g., Varro and Nepos) saw the transition. Younger witnesses include Ovid (born 43 B.C.) who came of age about the time Augustus regularised his position. Few of Augustus' own age lived to A.D. 14. Individual lives do not coincide with 'our period'. Women are the great survivors: Livia (58 B.C.–A.D. 29) bridges the late Republic and her son's principate. Junia Tertia, the niece of Cato, sister of Brutus and widow of Cassius, lived until A.D. 22, 63 years after her husband and brother died at Philippi (Tacitus, *Annals* 3.76).

WHAT DIFFERENCE DOES AUGUSTUS MAKE?

The question is short-hand. Augustus was not an independent agent: he was shaped and influenced by others (great allies like Agrippa and Maecenas, writers like Horace) and by the circumstances of his life. It matters that he owed his start in politics to the fact that he was the grandson of Caesar's sister and named as Caesar's heir on condition he took the name. Without his maternal lineage, he would not have become a leader in his late teens or supreme in his thirties. His early marriages were dynastic and terminated by divorce when political needs changed: Antony's stepdaughter, the daughter of Clodius and Fulvia (43–41 B.C.); Scribonia, the sister of the father-in-law of Sextus Pompeius (40–39 B.C.). The marriage to Livia, strengthened it seems by initial passion, growing love, and her abilities, lasted, despite their failure to have children, from 38 B.C. until his death. By Scribonia he had his only child Julia. Eventually, it would become clear that he had to find an heir to his sole power through Julia: her first husband Marcellus, his nephew (died 23 B.C.) or her sons by Agrippa, whom he adopted, Gaius and Lucius Caesar. But back in 40 B.C., he and Antony cemented their renewed alliance by the marriage of Antony and Augustus' full sister, Octavia, who achieved greater prominence than Livia in the 30s and was associated with her in an unprecedented grant of honours in 35 B.C. Her son Marcellus' death caused her virtual retirement from public life. Although Julia was prominent from her first marriage until her disgrace in 2 B.C., Livia's importance was heightened from 23 B.C. by her sons' (Tiberius and Drusus) succeeding to a place very like that apparently designed for Marcellus, as junior magistrates and generals. In the end, her elder son, who survived his brother and Gaius and Lucius, was adopted by his stepfather and succeeded him as *princeps*. Augustus' chief allies in the family were consistently women or connections through women (cf. Diana Kleiner's Chapter 9 in this volume).

Special honours were (though rarely) authorised by Augustus, a mix of public and private: in 35 B.C., sacrosanctity (physical inviolability) like that of the tribunes (Dio 49.38.1; the lone precedents here are Caesar in 44 B.C. and Augustus in 36 [*RG* 10.1, Dio 44.5.3, 49.15.5–6]) and freedom from guardianship for his wife and sister; in 9 B.C., for Livia, to console her for the death of her younger son, the 'right of three children', and in A.D. 9 exemption from the Voconian law. On his death and deification she became his priestess and was attended by a lictor, like a magistrate. Such honours and privileges are unprecedented for women.

Octavia received a state funeral (11 B.C.), with eulogies from her brother and son-in-law (Dio 54.35.4–5). The different elements must be disentangled. The traditional funeral of an upper-class man was led by his kin, began at the house, and ended at the family tomb. It was also a spectacle which demanded an audience and included a speech from the speakers' platform in the Forum. Q. Lutatius Catulus had been the first to give a woman (his mother) a procession and public speech (if we trust Cicero, *On the orator* 2.44). Caesar eulogised his aunt and (an innovation) his young wife (Suetonius, *Julius* 6.1, Plutarch, *Caesar* 5.1–2). Next, the crowd might highjack a funeral: Julia, Caesar's daughter, had been cremated by the People on the Campus Martius and her ashes buried there (Plutarch, *Caesar* 33.4, *Pompey* 53) in 54 B.C. Julia, the link between two powerful leaders, had won the affection of the populace: her funeral is a precedent for that of Clodius. Caesar later held games at the tomb in 46 B.C. Thirdly, the Senate might take official action. Funerals, tombs, statues at public expense were decreed to benefactors of the state (Cicero, *Philippics* 9.15–17). Augustus fixed a state-funded funeral for his mother Atia in 43 B.C. (Suetonius, *Augustus* 61; Dio 47.17). That he could do the same for his ex-childminder and freedman (Dio 48.33, 40 B.C.) shows that a close tie with him could qualify as a public benefaction. The funeral of Octavia establishes a pattern for women of the emperor's family, combining state funding, aristocratic laudation, and the People's grief.

The grants of 35 B.C., the posthumous honours to Octavia and those of A.D. 9 to Livia included the erection of statues. Again, we must distinguish statues which might be put in a house or garden, funerary statues on tombs (both of these might be put up by anyone who could afford it) and those erected by decree in a public space. Apart from three allegedly erected to benefactresses in the legendary period (Taracia Gaia, Cloelia, Claudia Quinta; see especially Flory 1993), the only other attested republican example is a seated statue of Cornelia, mother of the Gracchi, put up by popular decree, clearly as a political statement, in the portico of Metellus (Hemelrijk, 1999, 66–7). It was later moved to the portico of Octavia (Pliny, *Natural History* 34.31). So the grant to Livia and Octavia in 35 B.C. is a special honour. But Roman commanders' female connections had long been honoured with public statues by Greek cities. Soon after living men's heads featured on coins, Antony put the heads of his wives Fulvia and Octavia (Fig. 3) on some issues. The association of important women with deities also began in the triumviral period. Greek cities might identify the two (e.g., Julia as Venus Genetrix: Ehrenberg-Jones 63).

Once Augustus was in control, publicly voted statues were chiefly to members of his family. Being a mother was a particular service. The sudden appearance of portraits of women in public spaces in the city, as role models as well as objects of veneration, showed that all citizen women had a role to play. The members of Augustus' family were on display in the flesh at public occasions, for instance the games, where the entourages of Livia and Julia drew attention (Macrobius, *Saturnalia* 2.5–6) and where later Augustus might show off the young children of Germanicus (Suetonius, *Augustus* 34.2).

Wealthy women had long been involved in the repair of temples or public buildings. But now new projects might bear their names and even (once decreed by the Senate) be funded and dedicated by them: e.g., the portico of Octavia (dedicated some time after 27 B.C., including two temples and a library) and of Livia (built 15–7 B.C.: Suetonius, *Augustus* 29.4 [not claimed by Augustus among his own works]), Livia's shrine of Concord (Flory 1984) and provision-market; women in Italian towns followed the example. The Altar of Augustan Peace was dedicated by Augustus on Livia's birthday, 30 January 9 B.C. Octavia's portico may have contained a 'gallery' of exemplary women, a forerunner of the men in Augustus' Forum (dedicated 2 B.C.). Livia's restorations show a particular interest in cults in which women were involved and which are related to fertility and faithfulness to husbands (Purcell 1986). She was associated with divinised virtues such as Pudicitia (Valerius Maximus 6.1.1).

Benefaction did not just connote being wife and mother of the great. By virtue of their position, women became founts of patronage (e.g., Velleius 2.130.5; Dio 58.2.3). They might intercede with the emperor for mercy or promotion; they inevitably attracted courtiers and dependants. Octavia and Antonia gave hospitality to foreign princes; Livia fostered senatorial hopefuls. Like Augustus, they received legacies: among Livia's servants are people who had previously been slaves of

FIGURE 5. Sardonyx cameo with portrait of Livia, probably of the 20s to teens B.C. One of Livia's finest extant portraits, it features exceptional details, such as the double braid along the top of her head and the silky texture of her hair. Gems of this type were collector's items rather than mass produced. Leiden, Rijksmuseum. Het Koningklijk Penningkabinet. Museum photograph.

Maecenas, Vergil, and Amyntas of Galatia. Livia's morning receptions were like those of a senator; she and Julia gave a banquet for the women of Rome (Dio 55.2.4, 57.12.2).

Certain themes emerge. Octavia and Livia (Fig. 5) win an official recognition impossible for earlier women and a lasting prominence and influence greater than that of well-born and well-connected women such as Servilia or Fulvia. They operated beyond their homes. Both traveled to the provinces with their husbands; both went out in procession for religious celebration and on public occasions. But at the same time, their role within the house, as wife, mother, and stepmother

(Octavia brought up Antony's children by Fulvia and Cleopatra) was primary. Later, Julia and Antonia began to play a similar part. Julia, successful in breeding five children, unhappily failed as a wife: her father ruthlessly removed her in 2 B.C. alleging promiscuity. Antonia, mother of three and faithful widow, worked in the background. Livia sets the pattern for the ideal imperial woman, loyal to the emperor, a helper and confidante who does not push herself into the spotlight. No Roman woman, except Vestals, is alluded to in the *Res Gestae*. (The hostile tradition which portrays Livia as a ruthless schemer who wants power for her son and poisons everyone who stands in his way may be discarded).

We shall never know the details of the planning in the Palace which led to the deployment of Augustus' kin in marriage. From his own early efforts, it was a short step to the union of his sister and Antony, which cemented their alliance and might have produced a son to inherit the empire. Then come Julia's matches with Octavia's son by her previous marriage, with her father's partner Agrippa, with her father's stepson Tiberius. To achieve male heirs through Julia, others must divorce. Augustus, backed by others, imposed his will on all his kin, not through paternal power.

We have seen that Augustus was quick to manipulate his women and their image for political purposes. They, and all women, have a part to play in the state, especially in one area, where they are indispensable. In 18 B.C., he pushed through unprecedented legislation, updated in A.D. 9. He claimed he revived ancestral practices and introduced new examples for posterity (*RG* 8.5). The law on marriage encouraged marriage and procreation between citizens of all classes (apart from those belonging to disreputable professions, who were to be segregated from the freeborn), except that it introduced a prohibition of marriage between a senator or his descendants in the male line and a freed person. Incentives were civic (seniority for men with children) and economic (freedom from guardianship for mothers, particularly desirable for the freedwoman under her patron's supervision, though it may have been difficult for her to produce the four children required). Unmarried and childless people (women aged 20–50, men 25–60) were penalised by being unable to inherit except from close kin; one child allowed a wife and husband to inherit from each other. These sticks and carrots affected the better-off. It had been very rare for freeborn women not to marry (but now a *paterfamilias* was not to prevent his daughter's marriage or refuse to give her a dowry): the difference made by the law was that upper-class men married earlier, so women's chances of a good match were improved, that successful motherhood brought advantages and that not remarrying quickly after divorce or a husband's death might be penalised. The law advertised marriage and interfered in family life.

Roman statutes, even when they represent social engineering, cannot be categorised as intending solely to favor one natural or legal group against another: to be, for instance, pro- and anti-women. The Romans had long ago invented the idea of checks and balances. This law overtly encouraged those citizens who were prepared to marry and, if necessary, remarry, and reproduce.

A second measure, soon after, introduced a new crime, extramarital sexual intercourse, and seems to have been invoked especially against adulterous wives. Divorce became mandatory if a husband caught his wife in adultery; he might kill a low-status lover, but not his wife. In similar circumstances, a *paterfamilias* might kill both. The rules on justifiable homicide were perhaps rooted in folk ideas. The penalties the courts imposed on convicted adulterers were new and severe.

Several other measures had an impact on women. In regulating the age at which an owner might free and a slave be freed, Augustus privileged a slavewoman whom her owner wished to marry (in line with the encouragement of marriage between freed and freeborn people, outside the senatorial class), a nurse or a blood-relation. On the other hand, soldiers were forbidden to be married during their service: this meant that if a man joined up, his marriage became invalid. A husband was not to alienate land that formed part of his wife's dowry without permission.

Laws have an impact on practice, though, as Horace had warned, a revolution in behaviour is not brought about by statutes by themselves (*Odes* 3.24.35–6). Literature may be more effective in shaping and reflecting attitudes. The late Republic showed that women could be attacked in forensic speeches (more guardedly in political speeches) for their conduct, or described erotically by poets. Citizen women continued to figure in love poetry, though more discretion was needed after Augustus prohibited extramarital sex for all but prostitutes and slaves. I highlight here a newly apparent interest in women as individuals. The anonymous woman who rescued her proscribed husband may embody traditional virtues, but she is also a distinctive person, whose courage and sagacity were revealed by unusual trials (*Eulogy of 'Turia'*, esp. 1.30–36). Horace's Cleopatra begins as a foreign monster, but ends as a Roman heroine. (It is hard to believe he had not met her daughter, Cleopatra Selene, raised in the house of Octavia, and the learned Juba, another royal protégé of Augustus, whom she married in the late 20s, about the time he went to be king of Mauretania, 'dry nurse of lions' [*Odes* 1.22.15–6]). Vergil's Dido exemplifies the hard work and courage of a Roman leader and fails like a woman of tragedy. Ovid's *Heroines*, a collection of letters from mythological women to their men, explores a man's idea of what keeping faith was like for women. In his verse letters from exile he empathises with his wife, for the edification and manipulation of a wider audience.

A powerful theme is that women, barred from the dizzy heights of office, conquest, and triumphs open to upper-class men, could still achieve distinction as wives and mothers. Propertius makes the dead Cornelia (step-sister of Augustus' daughter through the possibly strait-laced Scribonia [Suet., *Augustus* 62.2, 69.1; cf. Propertius 4.11.55]) balance the triumphs of her ancestors against her earned (the word is also used of honourably discharged soldiers) status as virtuous once-married wife and mother of three. She reflected credit on her ancestors and left an example to her descendants (Propertius 4.11.27–72; Fantham, 1994, 276–7). She deserved praise: "This is the final reward of a woman's triumph" (Propertius 4.11.71). Later in the first century A.D., Seneca compared men's consulships, military success, fame as orators, and triumphs with the fame derived from the special feminine virtue of *pudicitia* (chaste devotion to a husband), which made Cornelia daughter of Scipio the equal of her husband Gracchus (Treggiari, 1991, 219). Virtues based in the household, in relations with parents, husbands, and children (cf. the eulogy for Murdia by her son; Horsfall 1982) may force a woman to involve herself in action in male-dominated public areas (as when the anonyma defended her family's financial interests or her husband's citizen rights) and may bring her fame, even a eulogy before the People (e.g., Octavia; the anonyma) as an example to other women. Domestic virtues can spill into the public sphere, in counsel to kin and in kindness to non-kin. The virtues applauded in Livia by the favourable literary tradition (and twisted into vices by the hostile) were given canonical form in A.D. 19 in a senatorial decree:

> Julia Augusta, who had served the commonwealth superlatively not only in giving birth to our Princeps but also through her many great favours towards men of every rank, and who rightly and deservedly could have supreme influence in what she asked from the senate, but who used that influence sparingly . . .
>
> (Senatorial decree on Cn. Piso the elder 115, transl. M. Griffin, *JRS* 87 [1997] 252)

Along with the other women of the imperial family (whose marriages and motherhood are where possible singled out), she is praised for her self-restraint in grief for the death of her grandson, by implication setting a good example to all ranks (130–50). Like her kin and other women in their various stations, she had achieved more visibility and power than women had in earlier times, despite restraint and emphasis on family values.

SUGGESTIONS FOR FURTHER READING

On the legal position, see especially Gardner (1996); for paternal power, guardianship of minors and the demographic facts, Saller (1994). Brief discussions of legal technicalities in *OCD* (e.g., 'guardianship: Rome'). On motherhood see Dixon (1988). For Livia, Purcell (1986). This chapter was written without the benefit of Barrett (2002).

My description of cult is heavily indebted to Celia E. Schultz, *Women in Roman republican religion* (Bryn Mawr dissertation, 1999).

PART III

THE EMPEROR'S IMPACT

7: THE EMPEROR AS IMPRESARIO: PRODUCING THE PAGEANTRY OF POWER

Richard Beacham

"For you will live as in a theater in which the spectators are the whole world" (Dio 52.34.2). Dio's citing of an insight he imagines Maecenas having offered to Octavian more than two centuries earlier employs the truth of hindsight. Dio's Maecenas also counseled the young master of the Roman empire on how he might "enjoy fully the reality of monarchy without the odium attached to the name of 'King'" (52.40.2), and that he should "adorn this City with utter disregard for expense and make it magnificent with festivals of every kind" (52.30.1). Dio knew just how well Octavian and his successors had taken such advice to heart. Inside Rome's imperial theaters the spectators were presented with dazzling entertainments calculated to impress them with the glory of their patron, the *princeps*, whose performative presence added to the excitement and splendor of the occasion. The formal public spectacles – pervasive, massive, and influential as they were – demand our attention. But such performances are only the most obvious example of how the spectacular and the theatrical became progressively embedded in every aspect of public life during Augustus' reign. Indeed, the very city itself, according to Strabo (5.3.8), became a vast *mise-en-scène* "presenting to the eye the appearance of a stage-painting, offering a spectacle one can hardly draw away from." Its inhabitants too, ruler and ruled alike, were exhorted by the symbols, mythology, poetry, art, and architecture of the age to conceive themselves as actors in a great historical pageant: the expansion, perfection, and celebration of Roman power and Roman achievement. This theatricalization of perception and experience was a major defining element of the language, style, ceremony, and metaphors through which the Augustan principate imagined and presented itself at every level and on every occasion.

When Caesar's will was read in the Forum on 19 March 44 B.C., it named Octavian, his eighteen-year-old nephew, as heir. Over the next few years as he moved to consolidate that legacy, his behavior was widely condemned as ruthless, unprincipled, and tyrannical – he even condoned the murder of Cicero, who earlier had given him invaluable support, and been viewed as a "father" by Octavian – and yet, long before the end of his life he was universally admired (and widely worshipped) as a benevolent patron of all that was best in Roman culture; and Father and Savior of the Country (see the chapter by Walter Eder in this volume). By ingenious sleight of hand, he even plausibly styled himself as the defender of the old system to which his protection was indispensable, while undertaking its "reform." The process through which this remarkable transformation was achieved owed much to his sure grasp of dramatic art and formidable skill in producing potent acts of theater.

In the immediate sparring for position that followed Caesar's death, Octavian demonstrated his incipient talent as a theatrical master of ceremonies at such events as the *ludi Ceriales* in April and the *ludi Victoriae Caesaris* in July of 44, first to evoke the public's imagination, and then win its approval. Twice blocked by Antony from putting into effect the Senate decree stipulating that Caesar's throne and crown be displayed in the theater amongst those of the gods, he nevertheless secured popular sympathy and esteem by selling his own property to finance (over Antony's attempts at obstruction) the games commemorating Caesar. A further reward – literally heaven-sent – was the appearance of a comet during these games. As Octavian himself recorded, "the people thought it indicated that Caesar's soul had been received amongst the immortal gods" (Pliny, *Nat. Hist.* 2.93–94). A star was born, and with it one of the most powerful and enduring ideas and images of the coming principate (Fig. 6).

DUEL OF THE TITANS: OCTAVIAN "APOLLO" CAESAR VS. MARK "DIONYSUS" ANTONY

Thus, from the start, the stage was set for comprehensive myth-management, and it soon ensued in the struggle with Sextus Pompey. While harassing Roman shipping and disrupting the grain supply from his naval power base in Sicily, Sextus built upon the lingering status

FIGURE 6. *Denarius* of L. Lentulus, Rome, 12 B.C. Augustus places a star on a statue of Julius Caesar, in commemoration of the appearance of the comet (*sidus Iulium*) in 44 B.C. Augustus holds the golden shield (**Clipeus Virtutis**) presented to him by the Senate in 27 B.C. Caesar is shown with the emblems of victory and power: a small statue of the goddess Victoria and a spear. Katalog Niggeler, 2. Teil, Nr. 1055 (Bank Leu/Münzen und Medaillen AG, Oktober 1966). Photo: Fotoarchiv am Seminar für Griech. und Röm. Geschichte der Universität Frankfurt am Main.

of his father Pompey the Great, and the affection widely felt for him amongst the Roman people (who had before them always the provocative memorial of his greatest benefaction, the enormous theater that bore his name), by "representing himself as the adopted son of Neptune, since his father had once ruled the whole sea" (Dio 48.19.2.). Thus as a sort of epilogue, a curious replay of the long-running conflict between Caesar and Pompey was reenacted at the hands of their heirs, each claiming to be the adopted offspring of a god. For almost a

FIGURE 7. *Denarius* with Octavian as Neptune, with his foot on a globe. Mint of Rome, 31–29 B.C. The image appropriates an earlier issue of Sextus Pompey. Katalog Niggeler, 2. Teil, Nr. 1010 (Bank Leu/Münzen und Medaillen AG, Oktober 1966). Photo: Fotoarchiv am Seminar für Griech. und Röm. Geschichte der Universität Frankfurt am Main.

decade, until Sextus' final defeat in 36, Sextus and Octavian waged intermittently both a real and a propaganda war in which each sought to exploit the value of role-playing to secure victory over the other. Their struggle also figured as a curtain raiser to the epic one which ensued between Octavian and Antony; Octavian, in one of his many appropriations from former enemies, would represent himself later as Neptune (Fig. 7).

Octavian could claim association both with the deified Caesar and through him to such suggestive antecedents as Aeneas, and, ultimately, the goddess Venus. Antony countered with a less-impressive claim to

FIGURE 8. Mark Antony with ivy crown of Dionysus. Silver tetradrachm, minted in the Roman East, 42 B.C. BMC Roman Republic East no. 133. Photo: Copyright The British Museum.

descent from Hercules, with whose appearance he liked to be compared; he encouraged the comparison by imitating the demi-god in his attire (Plutarch, *Antony* 4). But following the battle of Philippi and his first sojourn in Asia, he began to reinvent himself as Dionysus (Dio 48.39), and a little later, issued coins in the East depicting his image with a Dionysian crown of ivy (Fig. 8). Making a triumphal progress through the Hellenistic cities, he was hailed as divine, while, as Plutarch (quoting *Oedipus Rex*) asserts, all Asia was filled "with offerings of incense, paeans, and the sound of deep groaning." Moreover,

> as Antony entered Ephesus, women dressed as maenads, men and youths as satyrs and Pans all led the way before him, and the city was filled with ivy and thyrsus wands, with the music

of the flute, pipes and lyre. All welcomed him as Dionysus bringer of joy, gentle and kind.

(*Antony* 24)

In 39 B.C., following his marriage to Octavia, the couple went to Athens, and there Antony pursued a highly theatrical lifestyle, donning Greek attire, giving elaborate festivals, and staging revels in the theater of Dionysus where he constructed a setting designed to resemble a Bacchic cave to hold his banquets. The unctuous Athenians, anxious to please, set up inscriptions hailing him as the "New Dionysus." After 37 B.C., when he had abandoned Octavia and settled permanently in the East, he increasingly embraced this role, which in its embodiment as the Egyptian god Osiris complemented and added mythical luster to his alliance with Cleopatra. She was accordingly represented as Venus, or Isis, come "to revel with Dionysus for the good of Asia," and she accompanied him with a retinue of pages and handmaidens costumed as Cupids, Nereids and Graces (*Antony* 26). In fact, it seems likely that the public presentation of their relationship was deliberately "stage-managed" to enhance the prestige and aura of each. Cleopatra could extend her power over the new dominions presented to her by Antony. He, in turn, by allying with the queen who had borne Caesar's son, Caesarion (a potential rival to Octavian), could lay claim to a share of Caesar's heritage. The twins born from their own liaison were given the names Alexander Helios and Cleopatra Selene, which by their evocation of the sun and moon suggested a divine destiny to rule the world.

Such appeals to popular imagination in the East were, however, vulnerable to counterpropaganda, especially in Italy. Antony had long been accused of debauchery and self-indulgence – indeed Cicero savaged him repeatedly for drunkenness, consorting scandalously with mime actresses, and leading a generally depraved life (e.g., *Philippics* 2.2.ff; 2.24ff; 2.28ff). Now his conduct laid him open to the assertion that he was guilty not just of thoroughly un-Roman indulgence in oriental decadence at Cleopatra's sumptuous court, but of behaving like some contemptible god-king in his administration of the East. In 34 B.C. a minor victory over the Armenians provided the excuse for a grand display when he returned to Alexandria. It closely imitated the traditional form of the triumph at Rome, with the usual panoply of soldiers, booty, and royal captives. Antony followed behind in the customary chariot but then grossly violated sacred precedent by presenting all the spoils of Roman arms not to Capitoline Jupiter, to whom they were due, but to Cleopatra who was seated on a golden throne.

Further outrage followed. As "a theatrical piece of insolence and contempt for his country" (Plutarch, *Antony* 54), Antony appeared at a magnificent pageant together with Cleopatra (costumed as Isis), on golden thrones on a raised silver dais. He then proceeded to confer a vast dominion and exalted titles upon their children. When Octavian reported these things to the Senate, they aroused immense indignation. A sharp rebuke and warning were sent to Antony, who responded by preparing for war with Rome. His forces and those of Cleopatra assembled at Samos, where, as Plutarch records, together with the gathering of

> all munitions necessary for war, it was also proclaimed that all stage-players should appear, so that, while virtually the entire world was filled with groans and lamentations, this one island resounded for days with the sound of the lyre and pipe, full theaters, and the sounds of choruses. . . . Then Antony gave the city of Priene to his actors to inhabit and set sail for Athens where fresh sports and play-acting employed him.
>
> (*Antony* 56–57)

While Antony had been playing the actor-king in the East, Octavian had himself displayed an effective talent for manipulating public opinion through political adroitness, benefaction, and carefully crafted imagery. He did this by taking pains to appear to adhere to traditional Roman practices wherever possible while subtly shaping these both to enhance his own *auctoritas* and secure his political program. His effort to highlight the clearest possible contrast between his own espousal of traditional Roman values and Antony's indulgence in oriental decadence did not prevent him from using mythological imagery to promote himself and communicate the developing ideology of his emergent principate to the Roman audience.

Earlier, in 40 B.C., Octavian was said to have appeared costumed as Apollo at a banquet representing the twelve Olympian deities. According to Suetonius it caused a scandal (*Augustus* 70), and Antony later publicized the occasion to counter criticisms directed at his own unseemly amateur theatrics. Octavian evidently learned from the experience, because thereafter he seems consciously to have shunned excessive personal display or provocative claims to divine status (cf. Pollini 1990). However, the carefully nurtured notion that Octavian enjoyed the particular favor of Apollo was an important element in how the public was encouraged to regard him (cf. Scheid, this volume). In contrast to the sensual self-indulgence and licentious Dionysianism so thoroughly embodied by Antony's antics under what was alleged to be the "spell" of Cleopatra, Apollo stood for discipline, morality, and moderation. These traditional Roman virtues now were urgently demanded for the vital mission of creating a new order, worthy of Rome's past.

In essence, the effect of these rival performances by Antony and Octavian, which in the end caused the Roman audience to favor the latter (perhaps because he proved the more persuasive actor), was to cast an obscuring veil of theatricalized images and metaphors over what in reality was the latest in a series of civil wars waged between rivals for political preeminence. And it helped to establish precedents for a type of dramaturgically determined politics that subsequently characterized to a very significant extent the "public relations" of the Augustan era.

The aedileship of Octavian's friend and ally Marcus Agrippa in 33 B.C. (during Octavian's second consulship) on the eve of the final conflict with Antony, amply demonstrates how Octavian used the time-tested methods of political persuasion to enhance his *dignitas* and authority, and, in particular, to reinforce support amongst the urban masses. Agrippa (who had already served as consul in 37) assumed the relatively junior office of aedile. The post traditionally had been an important means for aspiring politicians to win advancement but – perhaps because of that – had been left vacant for several years. This unprecedented move might have been seen as an extraordinary diminution of status. In fact, however, Agrippa (and Octavian) deliberately used the opportunity to dramatize that, in the absence of any genuinely contested or popularly determined political life, the ruler was concerned not just with the interests of an élite, but also sought to uphold the customs and values of the Republic, and in particular, to safeguard the welfare and happiness of the common people.

Agrippa, moreover, was far from disdaining the more glamorous pursuits formerly associated with his office. He gave extraordinarily lavish and prolonged games, complemented with extensive free allocations of money, oil, and salt. Free year-long admission was provided to the public baths for both men and women, and free access to barbers, while at the theater he literally "rained upon the heads of the people tokens that were good for money in one case, in another clothes, or yet again for something else, while displaying vast qualities of goods for all and letting the people scramble for them" (Dio 49.43.2–4). The custom by which a patron offered small gifts to the clients attending upon him to acknowledge and validate reciprocal responsibilities was thereby extended and *performed* in the most public venue of all. The relationship was consolidated and formalized in 32 B.C. when, as Octavian recorded "all Italy of its own accord swore an oath of allegiance to me and chose me as its leader in the war which I won at Actium" (*RG* 25).

Recognizing the valuable role that buildings for public entertainment could play, Octavian allowed Statilius Taurus in 34 B.C. to construct Rome's first permanent amphitheater, to be used for gladiatorial displays and hunts (Dio 51.23.1), while in 32 he restored, at his own considerable personal expense, the theater of Pompey (*RG* 20). Close to it he is said to have constructed a portico with images representing different nations, possibly incorporating the fourteen such statues placed by Pompey adjacent to the theater (Servius, *Ad Aen.* 8.721.; cf. Pliny, *Nat. Hist.* 36.41; Suet., *Nero* 46). Modestly refraining from adding his name to the dedicatory inscription of the theater itself (or effacing that of Pompey), Octavian took advantage of the refurbishment to move the statue of Pompey from the Senate house, the Curia (subsequently sealed up), where Caesar had died, to a place directly adjacent to the theater where its thought-provoking presence was prominently visible (Suet., *Augustus* 31.5; cf. Dio 47.19.1).

The war against the forces of Antony and Cleopatra was carefully "spun," scripted to encourage its perception by Romans not as a continuation of civil strife, but rather as the decisive event marking their liberation from the crimes of the past, and from those alien impediments to securing a lasting peace and the triumph of Roman values: "a war to end wars." Octavian portrayed Antony as a man who had taken leave of his senses; the true object of the war was Cleopatra and her eunuchs, serving women, and chamberlains (Dio 50.5.1–4; 6.1). Antony was thus in effect "written out" of the script by Octavian, yet stubbornly refused to relinquish his part; celebrating the outbreak of hostilities with sumptuous costumed feasts, and setting the stage for going into battle metaphorically in the guise of Dionysus leading the sacred band (*thiasos*) of his followers.

Cleopatra, too, disdained to play the role assigned her and took her life rather than perform as the chief ornament of Octavian's triumph. It duly took place with a "stand-in" in August of 29 B.C., when "an effigy of the dead Cleopatra upon a couch was carried by, so that in a way she, too . . . was a part of the spectacle and a trophy in the procession" (Dio 51.21.8). There was a further act of suggestive staging. Octavian broke with precedent to arrange for the public magistrates who traditionally came out to meet the victorious general and then preceded him into the city. Instead, they now marched *behind* him, thereby graphically demonstrating his position as leading citizen (*princeps*) of the State.

THEATRUM POPULUSQUE ROMANUS

Apollo, functioning as a surrogate for his favored mortal, soon figured prominently in the ideology and imagery of the new regime.[1] In 28 B.C. a magnificent temple dedicated to the god was erected on the Palatine directly adjacent to Octavian's house, its own association with the god signified by the two laurel trees which the Senate ordered placed by its door (Dio 53.16.4), while inside the walls of the house were richly decorated with Apollonian and theatrical imagery (Plate III). Octavian underscored the association further by holding a festival during the same period (paid for from his private resources) commemorating the victory at Actium that had been secured by Apollo's intervention. This festival and its games were thereafter repeated every four years, with the consuls and priestly *collegia* organizing it in turn. This helped to establish a pattern that continued during Octavian's long reign. "As a showman, none could compete with Augustus in material resources, skill of organization and sense of the dramatic. . . . Each and every festival was an occasion for sharpening the loyalty of the people and inculcating a suitable lesson" (Syme, 1939, 468–9).

In addition to the numerous traditional public *ludi* held annually (including now the *ludi Victoriae Caesaris*), and those commemorating his Actium victory every fourth year (*Actia*), Octavian also later celebrated each year the date when he first was granted *imperium* (7 January, 43 B.C.), as well as commemorating each September 3rd the victory at Naulochus in Sicily over Sextus Pompey (Dio 49.15.1; Appian, *Civil Wars* 5.130). Another festival marked each occasion that his *imperium* had been renewed for further periods of ten or five years beginning in 27 B.C., a practice which Dio notes was followed thereafter by subsequent emperors up to his own day (53.16.2–3). Eventually there was yet another periodic festival, the *Augustalia* (12 October), marking Augustus' safe return from Syria in 19 B.C., which became annual as the *ludi Augustales* after his death in A.D. 14. (Dio 54.10.3; 54.34.1–2; 56.46.4; Augustus, *RG* 11; Tacitus, *Annals* 1.15). After the dedication of his temple in 2 B.C., annual games (*ludi Martiales*) were held on May 12 honoring Mars *Ultor*. Finally, games were given from time to time to enhance the public celebration (*ludi Natalicii*) marking Augustus' birthday (23 September). They were first decreed in 30 B.C. and became annual in 8 B.C.[2] The places and ever more numerous occasions of public performance at Rome symbolized Roman prestige and imperial glory and were an important expression of the official ideology that justified, gave meaning to, and secured public support for the operation of the principate. The emperor was himself the star of the shows, which began with ritual homage to him, and all that followed was expected to be worthy of his magnificence.

In 22 B.C., Augustus prudently transferred responsibility for those State festivals traditionally managed by the aediles to the praetors, at the same time "commanding that an appropriation be given from the treasury, and forbidding any of them to spend more than another from his own resources, or for a gladiatorial combat to be given except by Senate decree, or with more than one hundred and twenty men" (Dio 54.2.4). This effectively curtailed two major sources of public contention and discord – the provision of official *ludi* and of private *munera* (a term originally meaning "service" and then becoming synonymous with spectacles) – while ensuring that the splendor of allowable entertainments offered by others did not outshine his own.[3]

In the light of the novel relationship with the people that Augustus had fostered, it is hardly surprising that thereafter "he surpassed all his predecessors in the number, variety and splendor of his games" (Suet., *Augustus* 43). In a society as self-consciously theatrical as Rome, both the occasions and the venues for performance were not merely opportunities for conspicuous display: they also enabled both patrons and spectators to express, comment upon, and redefine the role of performance itself, including Roman society's relationship to Hellenistic theatrical practice, and the nature and limits of its cultural assimilation. Theatrical performances sent messages of patronage, wealth, popularity, power, piety, and military prowess to their audiences.

During the late Republic, the theaters had increasingly become venues for overt political expression by the audience, and in the case of Caesar been employed in turn to communicate to the spectators the power and glory of the leader as he literally became part of the show. In contrast, Augustus did not exploit such occasions primarily to enjoy popular adulation or promulgate a cult of personality; indeed he actively discouraged such use:

> On one occasion when he was watching a comedy, one of the players spoke the line "O just and generous Master [*Dominus*]', whereupon the whole audience rose to their feet and applauded, as if the phrase referred to Augustus.

An angry look and a peremptory gesture soon quelled this gross flattery, and the next day he issued an edict of stern reprimand.

(Suet., *Augustus* 53)

Instead he fashioned the occasion of the games more subtly to convey an ideological message, and thereby strengthen the political basis for the principate. As part of his thoroughgoing revival of religious practice Augustus sought to link worship and devout feeling to his own program of comprehensive renewal and reform. In the case of the theater, at moments of high pageantry, reverence was focused upon the person of Augustus, and *through* him to the State and its gods. Augustus and the imperial family functioned not simply as revered leaders (their popularity waxing and waning according to changing circumstances), but had become instead dynamic emblems both attracting and inspiring deep and abiding patriotic and religious sentiment.

The great Secular Games (*ludi Saeculares;* so named after ushering in a new *saeculum* or century) of 17 B.C. gave the religious and patriotic themes of the principate their most visible and memorable expression. They were carefully coordinated as an act of myth-making designed to provide a visually impressive and emotionally engaging manifestation of the achievements and ideology of the Augustan regime, and its role in ushering in a new epoch of peace, prosperity, and happiness. After participating in private rites of expiation, the public attended, over the course of a week, a series of formal sacrifices, ceremonies, torchlight entertainments, ritual banquets, performances in both the permanent and temporary theaters, and chariot races. The festivities culminated in the performance of Horace's *Carmen Saeculare* (Hymn for the New Century) whose imagery, themes, and the evocation of particular gods and goddesses closely followed that of the festival itself. Then there was another week of plays in Latin in a wooden theater by the Tiber, Greek musical shows in the theater of Pompey, Greek plays in another theater, and finally, hunts and presentations in the circus.

The *ludi Saeculares* were the most detailed and carefully crafted example of a synthesis of Augustan propaganda and pageantry known to us, but on a great many other occasions similar messages and images were reiterated, as the developing political and ideological concepts informing the regime's policies and programs were both fashioned and communicated through all the artistic media. This "aestheticization of politics" ultimately came first to condition and then to determine how the Roman people thought of, perceived, and *imagined* their rulers and form of government (cf. Diana Kleiner's Chapter 9 in this volume).

The aesthetic of the principate – apart from the intellectual or emotional appeal of the ideas and ideals it espoused – also drew heavily upon the innate and unreflective sensual satisfaction provided by the grandeur, opulence, and scale of its various public manifestations. In his *Letter to Augustus*, Horace provides direct evidence that the "vain delights" of such spectacles in the theater were well-established. All the while, he laments the fickleness of fashion, and how readily the more cultured sections of the audience, whom he identifies as the equestrian order (in the front rows of the auditorium), could be overwhelmed by the "stupid and ill-educated" – the urban plebs – that greatly outnumbered them (*Epistles* 2.1.189–207). Similar sentiment was expressed in the same period by Livy (7.2.13) who condemned the gross lavishness of theatrical art, "the insanity of which is now almost beyond the means of wealthy kingdoms."

Theater's primary purpose was to support an elaborate charade – in which it both participated directly and lent its conventions to the supporting roles of other spectacles and ceremonies – masking the process by which an autocracy displaced a city-state constitution that over the past century had been unable to encompass Rome's situation as a world power, and unworkable, had proven intolerably dangerous and destructive. In effect what Syme termed this "necessary and salutary fraud" of the principate, demanded a "willing suspension of disbelief" or at the least, acquiescence on the part of all concerned (1939, 516).

THE AUGUSTAN REPERTOIRE

To complement Pompey's monument and the occasional provision of temporary theaters, Augustus acquired two more splendid and permanent edifices: the theater of Balbus in 13 B.C., and two years later that of Marcellus (Fig. 9). By the time they were built, extensive regulations were in place (the *Lex Iulia Theatralis*) detailing the disposition of the various sections of the audience.[4] These carefully controlled the allocation of seats, and even the appearance of the crowd, which was thereby transformed into a congregation. They signified, too, that those attending were to be part of a meticulously managed *mise-en-scène*, and help substantiate Horace's assertion that whatever the object of the crowd's attention, a critical observer would "gaze more intently on the audience itself than on the performance, since it provided by far the better spectacle" (*Epistles* 2.1.197–98). The sight of so many thousands of spectators, color-coded and coordinated to resemble a microcosm of society, like so many other expressions of Augustan art and architecture, was simultaneously awe-inspiring and instructive. Here *princeps* and populace reified their political relationship and publicly ratified the legitimacy of their transactions, and indeed of the cultural framework simultaneously bodied forth and celebrated in the theater. Horace refers to the great patron Maecenas being acclaimed by the audience, even detailing that on one occasion "*thrice* the thronging people broke into happy applause in the theater" on his behalf (*Odes* 1.20.3; 2.17.25–26). Tacitus records that once, upon hearing a quotation from Vergil, the theater audience spontaneously rose *en masse* to pay homage to the poet in their midst "just as they would have done to the emperor himself" (*Dialogus* 13). Indeed, according to Macrobius, Vergil's account of Dido and Aeneas was adapted for the stage (5.17.4), and Servius asserts that the same was true of his sixth *Eclogue* (*ad Ecl.* 6.11).

The evidence for the extent and variety of Augustus' showmanship and the responsiveness of the audience is overwhelming. What is far less clear, however, is the actual nature of the subject matter presented in the three theaters eventually at his disposal, accommodating altogether perhaps as many as fifty thousand spectators. Horace writes that the works of earlier Roman playwrights including Ennius, Naevius, Pacuvius, Accius, Afranius, Plautus, Caecilius, and Terence continued to be performed. Their works, he claims, "mighty Rome memorizes, and these she views packed into her crowded theater" (*Epistles* 2.1.60–1). Yet elsewhere he complains the audience is obsessed with spectacle and so noisy and boisterous that the actors can barely be heard. This suggests that, apart from the revival of "tried and true" staples from the repertoire, serious drama did not flourish in performance. Horace laments the tendency of even the more attentive element of the public to resist good, new writing in preference to old favorites. "I am impatient that any work is censured, not because it is thought coarse or inelegant, but simply because it is not old." He condemns the reluctance to admit that much earlier Roman work is second-rate (*Epistles* 2.1.76–8ff.).

As far as comedy is concerned, Horace thinks the audience is too indulgent towards such earlier writers as Caecilius and Plautus, and often too ready to condone shoddy artistry in contemporary poets (*Art of Poetry* 54; 264ff.; *Epistles* 2.1.168–76). He suggests that would-be playwrights should study and learn from the great writers of Greek drama. Horace wanted an "Art of Poetry" that would engender a new repertoire and texts of excellence, modeled on the masterworks of the Greek

FIGURE 9. Theater of Marcellus, Rome. Begun by Julius Caesar, it was finished in either 13 or 11 B.C. Seating 20,500 spectators by social rank, it became the model for the theater boom in Italy and the western provinces. Photo: Hugh Denard.

playwrights, while encouraging contemporary authors to innovate in their artistic expression of Roman values and genius.

A poet for whom he had the highest admiration was Asinius Pollio (born 76 B.C.), who after a political career culminating in the consulship in 40 and a triumph in 39, had retired while still young to pursue learning and the arts, including the composition of tragedies.[5] Horace praised the mastery of rhythmic beat displayed in his dramatic works "singing of kings' exploits" (*Satires* 1.10.43). Vergil too, whom Pollio had befriended, had the highest regard for his qualities as a tragic playwright, considering his verses "alone worthy of Sophocles" (*Ecl.* 8.10). However, he abandoned drama to write a history of the civil wars, a task Horace characterized as "full of dangerous hazard, walking, as it were over fires hidden beneath treacherous ashes," although Pollio prudently stopped with Philippi, avoiding the more topical – and controversial – events leading to Octavian's rule.[6] Horace further expressed (in vain) the hope that Pollio would soon "renew your high calling" and that "your stern tragic muse will be only briefly absent from the theater" (*Odes* 2.1.6–10). Horace was, however, unwilling to subject his own work to public criticism by letting it "return again and again to be looked at on the stage" (*Satires* 1.10.39). While therefore bidding "farewell to show business" (*valeat res ludicra*) himself, he pointed out that "I do not begrudge praise when others handle well what I decline to try myself" (*Epistles* 2.1.180; 208–9).

Two other major Augustan poets are known to have written tragedies, with results that were highly praised, although not apparently, repeated. Lucius Varius Rufus was commissioned to write an original tragedy, *Thyestes*, which was presented in 29 B.C. at the great triumphal games celebrating the victory at Actium. For this Augustus awarded him the enormous sum of a million sesterces, probably in public as a gesture of conspicuous munificence. The work survived to be read by Tacitus, who greatly admired it, and by Quintilian, who deemed it the equal of any Greek tragedy. Both had similar praise for the *Medea* of Ovid, which was probably written about a decade later (Tacitus, *Dialogus* 12; Quintilian 3.8.45; 10.1.98). But, like Rufus, who, following the success of *Thyestes*, devoted himself principally to the composition of epic poetry and editing the *Aeneid* which Augustus had entrusted to him after Vergil's death, Ovid's muse (as he put it) having briefly allowed him to don the tragic buskins and scepter, did not thereafter let him seek applause in the theater (*Amores* 2.18.13–16; 3.1.67–70; *Tristia* 5.7.27–28).

Ovid points out that despite the high moral tone he sought always to encourage, Augustus had a fondness for the low and bawdy farce of the mimes. He condoned the considerable expense of producing them that was incurred both by the praetors sponsoring the official *ludi* – "the stage is profitable for the poet, and the praetor purchases such immoralities at no small price" – and by the *princeps* himself for his own benefactions. Not only the Senate and the Roman people – men, maidens, wives, and children – attended such "obscene mimes, which always contain crimes of forbidden love," but moreover, "these you have yourself often viewed and displayed to others (so gracious is your glory everywhere) and with your own eyes, by which the whole world benefits, serenely watched staged adulteries" (*Tristia* 2.497ff.; cf. 2.513–14). Augustus also appreciated Greek drama. He particularly relished the works of Old Comedy, and had them staged (Suet., *Augustus* 89); he awarded prizes at Greek play competitions (*Augustus* 45); and himself composed a tragedy *Ajax*, which may have been influenced by Sophocles (*Augustus* 85). He undoubtedly encouraged his poets (in Horace's words) to "work with Greek models by day; and work with them by night!" (*Art of Poetry*. 268–9).

In order to lend authority, legitimacy, and stability to the ideological foundations of the new political order, the principate constantly sought to ground these wherever possible in established belief and tradition. This encouraged the use (and frequently the revival or adaptation) of earlier rites, imagery, and forms of artistic expression. The theater, of course, as an ancient and quintessentially Greek art form, provided a major focal point for these impulses. However, its ever-increasing function within Roman society as a medium of political display and as a venue for the celebration of popular enthusiasms, meant that those controlling it (and therefore, ultimately, Augustus himself) could not risk "losing their audience" through any miscalculated exercise in aesthetic fashion. As the evidence of Horace suggests, traditional tragedy – except when "hyped" with such production values as outlandish costumes and gaudy scenic extravagance – struggled to hold a popular audience. In an age when even traditional comedy appears to have been increasingly displaced by the anarchic pleasures of the mime, tragedy with its sometimes obscure language and turgid dramaturgy risked being hooted off the stage, or watched in pious boredom.[7]

This was not what Augustus wanted. If the occasion were to contribute to the greater glory of the regime, the audience so assiduously organized as a microcosm of the Roman people must not be divided against itself between sophisticates and *vulgus* by the elitist fare offered by the house: they must all *enjoy* themselves. Early in Augustus' reign, a new type of "hybrid" theatrical entertainment, pantomime, arose and flourished. It drew on the same mythological sources as tragedy (and may well have appealed to similar emotions), but embodied these in an altogether different and more accessible mode of performance. Just as "classical" forms and motifs were widely used by Augustan artists and architects synthetically, so too in the theater old wine found its way into new skins. Pantomime had its roots in the venerable tradition of mimetic dance from which the earliest dramatic forms of tragedy and comedy had probably evolved, and which continued to hold a central place in Greek education, religion, and modes of artistic expression. It sought to present characterization, emotion, and narrative entirely through the movements and gestures of the body, or parts of the body, of an individual performer who neither sang nor spoke. Thus it could draw on, shape, and interpret well-loved and suggestive myths, which the audience could appreciate on a purely sensual level, while also directly responding intellectually and emotionally to the content of the story or situation, without having to follow a complicated verbal "text."

Its first appearance in Italy took place (according to later tradition) in 22 B.C., although a more likely date would be the previous year at the games celebrated by Marcellus during his aedileship (Athenaeus, *Deipnosophistae* 1.20D; cf. Jory, 1981, 148). It was said to have been fashioned by Pylades from Cilicia, and Bathyllus from Alexandria, each of whom was a superb dancer as well as, apparently, a theoretician of considerable force and sensitivity (Leppin, 1992, 217–19; 284–5). Although it was traditionally asserted that the elements of their art developed and were perfected in the East, more recent analysis has suggested an Italian origin, possibly arising from the venerable and versatile mimes (Jory, 1996, 26–7). In any case – and the synthesis of Greek and Roman elements is a hallmark of Augustan culture – Pylades and Bathyllus evidently established it at Rome by virtue of their own particular skills and personality, through the assistance of fortunate contacts, and because the conditions were right. Both achieved enormous personal renown and success, which enabled them to found schools that preserved their name and art long after their deaths.

Bathyllus was the freedman and beloved companion of Maecenas, close friend of Augustus and patron of legendary wealth (Tacitus, *Annals* 1.54; Horace, *Epodes* 14). He is credited with developing the comic pantomime, which was fairly simple in composition, often lascivious and droll, and evolved its subject matter as witty travesties of the more salacious Greek myths, or burlesques of well-known ancient tragedies. Such contemporary works as Ovid's *Metamorphoses* and *Ars Amatoria* could also, apparently, be adapted for pantomimic performance (Ovid, *Tristia* 5.7.25–30). Bathyllus was remembered for playing such roles as Echo and Pan or an Eros and satyr, presenting these *dramatis personae* simultaneously.

The comic pantomime was much in vogue during Bathyllus' lifetime but appears later to have faded away, displaced perhaps by the mime, whose broad and easily understood humor was able to hold the attention of a heterogeneous theater audience. But the much more extravagant tragic pantomime, first practiced by Pylades, a freedman of Augustus, endured for centuries. It was evidently fashioned from sensational moments from Greek mythology generally, and from the great tragedies in particular; the scenes linked as lyrical solos, and all performed, usually by a single male artist.[8] Lucian, writing a critical account of pantomime in the second century A.D., lists its extensive subject-matter, including a vast range of Greek mythology together with a few subjects drawn from Roman, Egyptian, and Syrian myth. He concludes, "To sum it up, [the pantomime] will not be ignorant of anything that is told by Homer and Hesiod and the best poets, and above all by tragedy" (*On Dance* 37–71). This individual silent performer was backed by musicians playing such instruments as the *tibia* (flute), cymbals, drums, cithara and *scabellum* (a clapper operated by the foot), and further supported by either a single speaking actor or a chorus that sang the part and provided the narrative continuity. The task of the solo pantomime impersonating in the course of his dance all the characters was to give an impression of the whole ensemble and the relationship of one character to another while preserving the sense of the plot, and creating graceful and expressive movements and gestures.

Clearly, this was a formidable challenge demanding enormous skill and imagination from the principal artist, who underwent extensive training to depict both the actions as well as, simultaneously, the emotional state of the several characters. He was aided in this daunting task by appropriate masks and often elaborate costumes (Fig. 10) – which he would change in the course of performance and use to help express his character (cf. Jory, 1996, 11–12) – and by the conventional nature of the most prominent of the many roles he was expected to learn: the movements of which (a sort of gestic vocabulary) were "set" by firm tradition from which the actor strayed at his peril. The most important element was the complex and subtle movement of the hands and arms, which one observer, Athenaeus, likened to the creation of pictures as though using the letters of the alphabet (*Deipnosophistae* 20CD).

Lucian's account (*On Dance* 67; 81) suggests why the versatility of the performer attracted such interest and admiration from the audience:

> In general, the dancer undertakes to present and enact characters and emotions, introducing now a lover and now an angry person, one man afflicted with madness, another with grief, and all this within fixed bounds . . . within the selfsame day at one moment we are shown Athamas in a frenzy, and at another Ino in terror; presently the same person is Atreus, and after a little, Thyestes; then Aegisthus, or Aerope; yet they all are but a single man. . . . The dancer should be perfect in every point, so as to be wholly rhythmical, graceful, symmetrical, consistent, unexceptionable, impeccable, not wanting in any way, composed of the highest qualities, keen in his ideas, profound in his culture, and above all, human in his sentiments.

He records how one pantomimic actor in presenting the madness of Ajax became so overwrought in the role that he snatched the *tibia* from one of the musicians and gave such a blow to the dancer portraying Odysseus that only his helmet saved him. The account provides an intriguing glimpse of the Roman audience (*On Dance* 83):

> The auditorium, however, all went mad with Ajax, leaping and shouting and flinging up their garments; for the riff-raff, the absolutely unenlightened, took no thought for propriety and could not perceive what was good or what was bad... while the politer sort understood, to be sure, and were ashamed of what was going on, but instead of censuring the thing by silence, they applauded to cover the absurdity of the dancing.

This suggestion that the audience was composed of spectators of diverse taste and refinement agrees with the evidence cited earlier. One segment (probably a minority) was keenly sensitive to the subtleties and nuance of the performance, responsive to the profounder ideas and emotions informing the story, and most significantly perhaps, could follow the libretto (often in Greek) which was sung while the dancer rendered his interpretation. Nevertheless, the nature of the performance ensured that there was plenty for less sophisticated spectators to enjoy as well, and this undoubtedly helped to secure it official support and patronage. It was of course open to abuse, and could lapse into bad taste. It was often lascivious and sensual. Juvenal notes the effect of this upon susceptible members of the audience:

> When the soft Bathyllus[9] dances the role of the gesticulating Leda, Tuccia cannot constrain herself; your Apulian maiden raises a sudden and longing cry of ecstasy, as though embraced by a man; the rustic Thymele is rapt: now is the time that she learns her lessons.
>
> (*Satires* 6.6.6)

Ovid had warned of the same effects in the Augustan theater, advising the lovelorn not to

> indulge in theaters until love has quite deserted your empty heart; zithers, flutes and lyres weaken the resolve, and voices and arms swaying in rhythm. Fictive lovers are constantly

FIGURE 10. Fragment from the lid of an ivory casket, sixth century, representing a pantomime actor. This identification is suggested by the three masks he holds in his right hand: in contrast to other theatrical masks, they have closed mouths and natural features. From Trier, now in the Antikensammlung, Staatliche Museen, Berlin, Germany. Photo: Bildarchiv Preussischer Kulturbesitz/Art Resource NY.

> danced: the actor by his craft teaches you what to avoid and
> what pleases you.
>
> (*Rem. Amor.* 751–6)

It was probably the potential for sensationalism together with the extraordinary notoriety of some "stars" that accounted for the pantomime's enormous popularity with the masses. The less restrained element in the audience was at times highly volatile and quick to voice its criticism or approval, and if provoked, to riot. Indeed, five centuries later, the historian Zosimus judged the introduction of pantomime to have been one of the most damaging legacies of Augustus' rule (cf. Jory,

1984). On one occasion Pylades' depiction of the god Dionysus was said to have "filled the entire City with that deity's unrestrained fury" (*Anthologia Palatina* 290). Evidently highly strung himself, once "when a spectator began to hiss, he pointed him out to the entire audience with an obscene gesture of his middle finger" (Suet., *Augustus* 45).

Augustus exiled Pylades from Italy for this offense in 18 B.C., but soon summoned him back, possibly as one of a number of measures taken to appease popular opposition to the moral legislation of the same year.[10] In general, however, he supported and enjoyed the new art form, and considered his patronage of the people's pastime a democratic gesture (Tacitus, *Annals* 1.54). Nevertheless, only a few years after its introduction, he felt constrained to curb the "pantomania" rampant in the Roman audience. Rivalries between Bathyllus and Pylades (or Pylades' former student, Hylas) led to outbreaks of violence among their supporters. Augustus rebuked Pylades, but was in turn admonished by him "you are ungrateful, Master. Let the people kill their time with us!" (Dio 54.17.4). This suggests "that Augustus should be grateful that the people were concentrating on pantomimes rather than on more important matters, a story which if true suggests that the performer was both politically aware and on close terms with the Emperor" (Jory, 1984, 58).

Nevertheless, (reflecting the important role assigned them in the promotion of the principate) Augustus was meticulous in curbing actors' licentious behavior (Suet., *Augustus* 45.4). Together with other stage performers, the actors of pantomimes were subject to severe restrictions. They were denied Roman citizenship. Their descendants were banned through the fourth generation from marrying into the senatorial class, and if caught in adultery, they could be killed with impunity. Augustus was determined that however useful the theater, neither its partisans nor practitioners should be allowed to undermine public decorum or morality. Nevertheless, he indicated his favor and fairness by amending the law that had allowed public officials to beat performers on mere whim: henceforth they could do so only for offenses committed during the games or other public performances (Suet., *Augustus* 45). From time to time as a popular gesture, a performer who had won the crowd's support might be freed, and a successful pantomimic actor could earn substantial sums of money. By the end of his life, Pylades was sufficiently wealthy to give private games at his own expense in 2 B.C., and suitably respectable to present both equestrians and women on stage without incurring Augustus' censure (Dio 55.10.11).

Both as imaginative concepts and as cultural phenomena the theater and theatricalism greatly help to illuminate the persona of Augustus and inform our understanding of his epoch. As metaphor and medium theater permeated and helped to define the social, political and aesthetic expressions of the principate: itself in essence an elaborate act of "make believe."

At the games in A.D. 13 marking Augustus' birthday (23 September), during the Circus races "a madman seated himself in the chair dedicated to Julius Caesar, and taking his crown, put it on. This incident disturbed everybody, since it seemed to have some bearing on Augustus, as indeed, proved true" (Dio 56.29.1–2). The following August, the *princeps* attended the musical and gymnastic events marking the fourth celebration of the *Sebasta* (the Greek equivalent to "Augustan") festival. Modeled on the Olympic games, it had been established in A.D. 2, and was given in his honor at Naples (Suet., *Augustus* 98). Two weeks later, on the 19th of August (the anniversary of his first consulate fifty-seven years earlier), he died aged seventy-six, at Nola south of Rome. After gazing at his image in a mirror, he had inquired if he had played the mime of life well; then answering the question himself, he added: "Since well I've played my part, all clap your hands and from the stage dismiss me with applause" (*Augustus* 99.1). As Dio so perceptively observed, Augustus had consciously fashioned himself as an actor in the greatest show on earth in what, even now, we can admire as one of the most skillfully crafted dramas of antiquity. And indeed, it had been a virtuoso performance.

SUGGESTIONS FOR FURTHER READING

For a discussion of the role of theater in the late Republic and Early Empire, see Beacham (1992). A useful account of performances of Greek drama, and in particular of tragedy in the early imperial age, is found in Jones (1993). For the continuation of tragic performances in the later imperial period, see Kelly (1979). Details of evidence for early pantomime at Rome and its social importance are provided by Jory (1981 and 1984). Jory (1996) offers a useful analysis of the visual evidence for the costumes and masks of pantomimes. For a comprehensive collection of references to individual actors, including mimes and pantomimes, see Leppin (1992). For a discussion of Apollonian imagery in the principate, see Zanker (1988), and Galinsky (1996).

NOTES

1   For a discussion of Apollonian imagery in the Principate, see Zanker (1988) 49–53; 62ff; 84–89; and Galinsky (1996) 188–9; 215–19; and 297–9.

2   They are recorded by Dio as having been first decreed in 30 B.C. (51.19.2); later taking place in 20 (54.8.5); 13 (54.26.2); 11 (54.34.1); becoming annual in 8 (55.6.6), and held for the last time during Augustus' life, in A.D. 13 (56.29.2).

3   According to Dio, from 18 B.C. Augustus "allowed the praetors who so desired to spend on the public festivals three times the amount granted them from the treasury" (54.17.4). He further reports that later, in A.D. 7, under financial pressure, Augustus "ordered that the money which was regularly paid from the treasury to the praetors who gave gladiatorial combats should no longer be expended" (55.31.4). It was probably also in 22 B.C. that Augustus stipulated that an annual gladiatorial display be provided by two praetors, chosen by lot. For the negative effects of competitive *munera* in the last years of the Republic, see Ville (1981) 57–88.

4   For details of the regulations, see Beacham (1999) 122–6.

5   See Bosworth (1972) for an analysis of his career and relationship to Augustus.

6   Titus Labienus, an orator and historian who wrote about the period of the triumvirate, was evidently less discreet. He gave public readings at which he passed quickly over the more controversial passages, with the remark that they should be read after his death. Instead, his books were ordered collected and publicly burned by Senate decree in A.D. 6. (Seneca the Elder, *Contr.* 10 *Praef.* 4–8). While Augustus was unlikely to disapprove, evidence is lacking "that it was primarily Augustus who wished Labienus' history burned" (Raaflaub and Samons, 1990, 441).

7   For a discussion of the continuing staging possibilities for tragedy in the imperial era see Kelly (1979), and Jones (1993).

8   H. A. Kelly (1979) 21–4 discusses the relationship between pantomime and traditional tragedy. Jory (1996) provides a very useful analysis of the surviving visual evidence for the costume and masks of pantomimes, and notes that "while there is considerable variation of dress among the full-length pantomime monuments, as would be expected given the 'tragic' roles portrayed, a long tunic reaching to the ankles features on almost all of them" (19). Galinsky (1996, 265) compares pantomime to the works of Ovid, and particularly his *Metamorphoses*. "The emphasis on single scenes . . . the narrator's bravura performance, his sophistication, the constant shifts and changes, and the graphic, visual appeal of many scenes all have their counterpart in the pantomime . . . [which] required, on the actor's part, a good knowledge of mythology and a superior education. . . . The tragic pantomime became the rage and its stars, the darlings of the higher classes. This is precisely the public for which Ovid wrote."

9   Not the founder of comic pantomime, but a later dancer of the same name, famous during the reign of Domitian.

10   For opposition (particularly from the Senate) to the moral legislation, see the literature cited in Kienast (1999) 167, 284; Syme (1939) 444; and Raaflaub and Samons (1990) 433–5.

8: AUGUSTUS AND ROMAN RELIGION: CONTINUITY, CONSERVATISM, AND INNOVATION

John Scheid

I n his *Life of Augustus*, Suetonius stops at chapter 61 for a prelimi-
nary assessment. He reminds the reader that up to this point he has
given an account of Augustus' conduct in the various offices he
held and in the administration of public affairs (*in imperiis ac magistratibus*) throughout the entire world. Now, Suetonius says, he will go on
to describe his private and domestic life. In the following chapters we
glimpse a few facts about his religious behavior, that is mostly his private
superstitions, and his family life and physical appearance. We are told,
for instance, that he was very afraid of thunderstorms (Suet., *Aug.* 90),
and respected as very significant "the auspices and certain portents"
(*auspicia et omina quaedam*; 92.1). Suetonius here refers to rather trivial
reactions, which would be classified by any educated Roman as common superstitions, such as the right sequence of putting on his shoes,
or the bad significance of certain days (92). We also learn that he often
slept close to the place where he had to celebrate or attend a sacrifice,
because he usually found it hard to get up in the morning (78.2); we
should bear in mind that a sacrificial rite started closely after sunrise.
As for foreign cults, he respected those of old, such as the Eleusinian
mysteries, but not the temple in Jerusalem or the Egyptian Apis (93).
Significantly, Suetonius mentions Augustus' relations with the cults of
foreign cities in this part of the biography: they are not part of his
official conduct in the area of religion, but a private matter. Suetonius
notes, in fact, that Augustus had no private fascination for new and
exotic cults or gods. In short, what we can read in these chapters is very
trivial and does not allow us to reconstruct any religious addiction that

would be strong enough to influence Augustus' policy or would at least explain it.

In contrast, Suetonius, like the other historians of the Augustan period, understands Augustus' religious devotion, *pietas*, in a very different sense. His statement in chapter 61 allows us to infer that all mentions of *pietas* and cultic behavior of Augustus in the preceding chapters belong to the *pietas* in the domain of *imperiis et magistratibus*, and not to some private expression of faith. The mentions of Augustus' piety deal only with his way of conducting public religious business; Augustus and religion means "how Augustus dealt with his official religious duties." All Roman historians writing on Augustus report some lapses – in his youth, for instance, he came to a sumptuous dinner party where the participants were dressed as Olympian gods while the populace was starving – but mainly they highlight his exemplary piety. We may ask whether this conduct has anything to do with religion. Does religion consist merely in maintaining cults and priests, in reconstructing and repairing temples, and in celebrating festivals and pompous rituals? In short, was Augustus' piety defined primarily by administrative acts, combined with heavy political pursuits and cynical self-celebration?

Until recently, modern historians indeed tended to present Augustus as a hypocrite; moreover, in his times Roman religion was supposed to be in total decay. This kind of assertion, mainly due to the very nature of Roman ritualism, was repeated again and again by scholars such as Franz Cumont, Kurt Latte, and Jean Bayet, despite some reservations expressed by William Warde Fowler, Arthur Darby Nock, Ronald Syme, and Pierre Boyancé, to cite only a few influential scholars on either side. The latter group took into account evidence other than Hegelian dialectics or Christian definitions of religion, and emphasized that Augustus actually did what people expected from him. Further, his religious reforms were successful in the sense that they led to three more centuries of polytheistic ritualism.

Today, this perspective, which was outlined with some important nuances already by Georg Wissowa, is shared by most specialists. Wissowa shared the assumption of the decline of Roman religion but went on to assert that Augustus had succeeded in restoring ritual practice. In his opinion, this did not amount to the revival of traditional religion. Rather, he suggested, Augustus' reforms were a new construction and not a reconstruction – "mehr ein Neubau als eine Wiederherstellung" (1912, 72). And the *Neubau* aimed at serving as the foundation for imperial cult. Wissowa's concept, combined with the tradition of undervaluing ritualism, still has a strong influence on the approach to post-Augustan religion. The imperial cult, therefore, is often separated from religion or considered a special part of religion. It is then presented as the only aspect of civic religion that is understandable to the modern mind. Its political aims can be easily detected and deconstructed: the cult of the emperor is a perfectly rational scheme and, accordingly, is grouped with politics and not religion (see Price 1984).

In my view, however, the evidence clearly indicates that Augustus' religious activities amounted to a very real reform of Roman ritual tradition. Augustus' restoration had nothing to do with a change of religion or a deepening of faith. It was merely a reaction against the neglect of public ritual duties and of temples, due to the disorders of the civil wars. And these restorations were part of his political goals. Restoring the *res publica* automatically meant restoring its religious institutions and cult places, especially when they had been neglected or even forgotten. At the same time, there is a political angle: these traditions had to be presented as forgotten and neglected. The best way to legitimate your own power was restoring what your enemies had neglected and violated during the civil wars. Augustus may have been a very traditional character, who longed for an ancestral way of life, at home and in public (Suet., *Aug.* 64), but his restorations were a political necessity. His foes had neglected, confiscated and nearly ruined the *res publica*, he claimed, and now he was handing it back to the people, with all institutions working again, just like before. We may question the reality of this political theme and doubt Augustus' sincerity, but one fact remains: Augustus did it, people mainly accepted it, and the Augustan settlement lasted for three centuries.

The reason for this success is understandable. Augustus restored what was supposed to be the ancestral form of the *res publica*, and in this political construction, *pietas* toward the gods was restored along with *pietas* among citizens. In a ritualistic religion like the Roman religion, *pietas* has nothing to do with faith, eternal life and salvation of the soul. *Pietas* was a correct social relation with the gods; it meant giving them the honors due to their rank and associating them with the government of the *res publica*, as fellow citizens, or rather as good *patroni* of the city. The only faith present in Roman religion actually resided in the firm belief that cultic obligations had to be performed and that the gods did not ask for more than that.

A Deliberate Religious Policy, Forged in the Pre-"Augustan" Years (44–28 B.C.)

Augustus' regime is generally presented as a long evolution and a progressive adaptation that lasted for almost fifty years. If we accept this fact, his religious activities as a whole could be interpreted as empirical opportunism, and not as a long-lasting and deliberate policy. Such a view would be misleading because there was, I would argue, something like a religious program. How can we discover indications of such a policy? I am relying on two facts. First, what could be defined as Augustus' religious policy already was entirely enacted between 43 and 28 B.C. (when he was still Octavian). Second, his reforms took a new, spectacular start and a different orientation after Lepidus' death in 12 B.C. Lepidus had been *pontifex maximus* and Augustus assumed the office in that year.

As Fergus Millar has stressed, the thirties B.C. were a very productive period for the young Caesar, who accomplished his most important innovations during these years (Millar 2000). The years following 28 only hardened and systematized the measures previously taken, but did no longer see much innovation. Here an investigation of Augustus' religious initiatives taken between 44 and 28 B.C. can be very illuminating. During this specific period, we can retrace a good part of his initiatives which he signaled himself and which are also mentioned by all historians of the period.

A first set of such initiatives concerns the attribution of divine honors to Julius Caesar. They were voted in 45 and in 44 B.C., before the dictator's death (Weinstock, 1971, 281–6). After the Ides of March, Octavian immediately fostered all elements of the cult of the Divine Caesar, Divus Iulius. His stubborn initiatives, opposed by Antony, had a great influence on the development of this cult, and outlined the pattern for the imperial cult to come. When the temple of Divus Iulius was begun in 42 B.C., and when Antony was eventually inaugurated as its priest (*flamen*) in 40 B.C., we can conclude that it partly was Octavian's work. He was in Italy and in Rome, and he certainly made the decision about the location and architectural program of this temple, which gave a new axiality and meaning to the old Forum (see Chapter 10 by Favro in this volume, Fig. 37.2). All this was finished by 28 B.C.

The same year saw the completion of the Apollo temple on the Palatine, which was vowed shortly after the battle at Naulochus in 36 B.C. This initiative started with a *prodigium*. Octavian had bought houses and space on this part of the Palatine hill in order to build a residence for himself. Then a thunderbolt struck the place. Octavian solicited the advice of the proper seers, the *haruspices*, and they informed him that Apollo desired the area. Octavian made the entire place a public property and dedicated it to Apollo, but the people resolved that the house should be presented to their ruler at public expense (Dio 49.15.5). Accordingly, a temple was built there, and it was linked to his house. After the victory at Actium, Apollo, whose patronage of Octavian had been suggested by the *prodigium* of 36 B.C. and its aftermath, assumed the role of a mighty protector and war god. Apollo Palatinus now became Apollo Actiacus, and the prodigy of 36 B.C. was in retrospect revealed to be an announcement of victory and *imperium*. With its splendor, its porticoes, and libraries, the temple of Apollo was a symbol of the new imperial regime. For the present purpose it is important to stress that all this was carried out in eight years, before Octavian even took the name of Augustus.

Another initiative was clearly related to the young Imperator Caesar, who was said to be *Divi filius*, "son of the Divine" (Julius) after 40 B.C. (cf. Beacham, this volume). When Octavian was offered a triumph in 35 B.C., he refused it, but he accepted a certain number of privileges for his wife Livia and his sister Octavia (Dio 49.38.1). These privileges were partly religious or had a religious background. His wife and sister were granted sacrosanctity, emancipation from *tutela* (legal guardianship), and statues (a privilege no living women had previously enjoyed; cf. Treggiari and Kleiner, this volume). The grant of sacrosanctity can be interpreted as a way of protecting Livia and Octavia in a period of civil disorders, but there was more. The core of these measures was that two women related to Octavian the triumphator were given male privileges, or rather privileges of magistrates or priests. The sacrosanctity of tribunician inviolability served as a model or, rather, the Senate in 35 B.C. extended to Livia and Octavia the tribunician inviolability granted to Octavian one year earlier. For their emancipation, the model was the Vestal virgins. The scope of the whole construction was to invent a public role for female members of his family. The young Caesar followed the only model available in Roman tradition: the model of the Vestals. Livia and Octavia were granted part of the privileges of the Vestals; in addition, they were given sacrosanctity because they were not protected by their priestly status.

This way of promoting female members of the imperial house to a public position never changed afterwards. In 35 B.C. the Senate, clearly at Octavian's prodding, laid the foundations for the honors and privileges of the Augustan women. The solution of 35 was repeated afterwards, for example when Tiberius celebrated his first *ovatio* and triumph, in 9 and 7 B.C. In 9, Livia was granted a statue and the *ius trium liberorum*, a privilege normally reserved for mothers of three or more children (Dio 55.2; 56.10). And she received a further privilege of the Vestal virgins. In 7 B.C., she and Tiberius' wife Julia sponsored a meal for the *matronae* while their son and husband, Tiberius, hosted the usual triumphal meal on the Capitol. In A.D. 14, after Augustus' death and divinization, the Senate granted new honors to Livia, who had now become Julia Augusta by adoption. Among them was the priesthood of *sacerdos* (i.e., *flaminica*) *divi Augusti*, and as such she was to be accorded the right of having a lictor, again like the Vestal virgins (Vell. Pat. 2.75.3; Dio 56.46.1; Tacitus, *Ann.* 1.14.3). Tiberius opposed some of these honors, on the grounds that one should not give too many honors to women, and refused to let her be preceded by a lictor (Tac., *Ann.* 1.14.3; Dio 56.46.2). A few years later (in A.D. 23), however, Livia was granted the right to be seated with the Vestal virgins in the theater (Tac., *Ann.* 4.16.5). In other words, Tiberius continued the tradition founded by Augustus in 35, and repeated in 9 or 7 B.C.: some, but by no means all, privileges on the model of the Vestals for the female members of his family.

A check of the relevant list of individuals shows that from 40 B.C. on, Octavian systematically controlled the election of *pontifices*. He succeeded in having all descendants of former *pontifices* elected to other priesthoods and in filling the college with his own supporters (evidence in Scheid, 1978, 633–5). The reason is obvious. He had to isolate Lepidus and to neutralize Lepidus' power as *pontifex maximus*. This initiative also shows that Octavian controlled the other priestly colleges, because he had the less reliable candidates elected to be augurs or *quindecimviri* (a board of 15 priests). In 29 B.C. he was granted the right to present candidates for all priesthoods even in excess of the legal number (Dio 51.20.3). Obviously, this privilege along with his membership in all public priesthoods facilitated his interventions.

He also showed interest in the revival of old religious functions and rituals. In 32 B.C., he declared war on Cleopatra according to the rituals of the *fetiales* (Dio 50.4.5); the restoration of this forgotten priesthood must be dated to these years. Similarly, the restoration of the temple of Jupiter Feretrius, whose cult was connected to treaties (the name may be derived from the striking, *ferire*, of a treaty) and to the *fetiales* dates from the same period (Livy 4.20; Cornelius Nepos 20.1.2–3). And we may wonder if the *Caeninenses*, a priesthood which ranked among the highest equestrian priesthoods of the empire, were not also restored or created on this occasion. Obviously linked to Caenina, an ancient town in Latium, and to the Romulean period of Rome, their relation with Jupiter Feretrius might be dependent on the tradition according to which Romulus brought (*ferre*) the spoils of a slain enemy commander (*spolia opima*) to that shrine (cf. Dion. Hal., *Roman Antiquities* 2.34). The *spolia opima* became an important issue in 28 B.C. (cf. Syme, 1986, 274), and we can, therefore, conclude that in 32 Octavian restored the archaic way of declaring war and maybe planned to take *spolia opima* from his enemies. We need to recall that, in 44 B.C., a decree of the senate already had given Caesar the right to put the *spolia opima* in the Jupiter Feretrius temple (Dio 44.4.3). At least Octavian reaffirmed this old tradition by restoring the Feretrius temple, the *fetiales,* and the *Caeninenses.*

Some four years later, approximately in 29 B.C., Octavian re-formed the fraternity of the arvals. Or rather, he gave the *fratres arvales* a public grant and elevated them to a senatorial level. We do not know if there still were *fratres arvales* during the first century B.C. The only argument is the use of the present tense in Varro's explanation of their ritual (*On the Latin Language* 5.85). Anyway, after 29/28 B.C., when their calendar was inscribed on marble, the existence of the *fratres arvales* is documented. From the two surviving Augustan sources for them it is evident that the twelve members of this brotherhood were of the highest social level.

During the same period Octavian created, restored, or transformed the *sodales Titii*. Who were they? According to Varro, they had something to do with the *auspicia* (*Ling. Lat.* 5.85). In the *Annals,* Tacitus explains the name as referring to the purpose of keeping up the Sabine rituals (1.54) – Titus Tatius was Romulus' legendary co-ruler – which might allude to the divinatory rites mentioned by Varro. But this kind of interpretation clearly was not used by the reformer. In the *Res Gestae* (7.3), the title was translated into Greek as *hetairos Titios* ("Fellow of Titius"), and a recently published inscription of the third century A.D. (*Année Épigraphique* 1997, 1425) refers to *hiereus sakerdotiou Titou Tatiou* ("priest of the priesthood of Tatus Tatius"). Accordingly, Tacitus (*Hist.* 2.95) writes that this *sodalitas* had been dedicated to the cult of Titus Tatius by Romulus, and that in A.D. 14, the *sodales Augustales* were created for care of the Julian family just as the *sodales Titii* had been dedicated to king Titus Tatius. It seems, then, that Octavian invented a new function for these priests, and clearly connected them with Romulus. That allows us to date this restoration to the years prior to 27 B.C., which is the end of the period when he considered Romulus as a possible model.

The restoration of the *arvales* and of the *sodales Titii* presumably was part of the granting of new privileges to all public priesthoods (Suet., *Aug.* 31.3), probably when Augustus was censor in 28 B.C. He increased the membership of the most prestigious priesthoods (*amplissima collegia*) and divided all public priesthoods into equestrian and senatorial *collegia*. During the same censorship, he claimed to have restored or rebuilt 82 temples, which were partly or entirely ruined (*RG* 20.4). His own activity, however, as a restorer of temples and his inducement to do so had begun well before 28 B.C. In order to show that Italy, too, benefited from his restorations he paid attention to old and important Italic sanctuaries. For instance, he transformed the grove of Feronia (Lucus Feroniae, Southern Etruria) and a sanctuary of Fortune (Fanum Fortunae, Umbria) into Roman colonies; he confirmed the privileges and the autonomy of the sanctuary of Diana Tifatina (Campania); and finally he founded a colony at Hispellum (Umbria), possibly an old Umbrian federal sanctuary, and gave it the responsibility over the famous sanctuary of Clitumnus. By awarding these places the highest possible legal status, he recuperated for Rome – and for himself – the importance of old Italic cult places, and proved his deep *pietas*. In his *Res Gestae* (24.1), he also insisted on the restitution of sacred belongings, confiscated by Antony, to the temples of all cities of Asia. Most of these measures were taken before 27 B.C. In 29 B.C., he had also celebrated the old ceremony of the *augurium salutis* ("the augury by which the safety of the Roman people is sought") and he closed the doors of the so-called Janus shrine in the Forum Romanum (Fig. 11), an action that signified the end of wars (cf. Vergil, *Aen.* 1.293f., 7.607ff.).

Finally, in 30 B.C., he reacted firmly against any attempt to worship him as a god (Dio 51.19–20). He thereby established the general pattern of imperial cult: no public divine honors for himself in Rome, but, in Italy, in the provinces and according to the Greek tradition, some honors equal to those given to the gods, and cults of Rome and Caesar. Further, since 42 B.C., temporary holidays (*feriae*) were dedicated to all possible gods for his victories.

In short, nearly all of the important religious initiatives taken by Augustus fall into the period between 44 and 28 B.C. when he was still Octavian. There were only a few new additions after that time, and they were always linked to specific events. The general framework of what can be called his religious policy was created during the years of the triumvirate. Or, in other words, the spirit of his initiatives at this early stage of his career already was very similar to what would be his conduct during his long principate.

FIGURE 11. Shrine of Janus in the Roman Forum. The closure of its twin doors betokened the cessation of hostilities throughout the empire, as proclaimed on this sestertius of Nero, issued by the mint of Lugdunum (Lyon) in A.D. 66: "With peace having been achieved on land and sea he closed Janus." Photo: Hirmer 2005.062R.

As early as 44 and 43 B.C., two principal components can be discerned: the enforcement of the laws granting divine honors to Julius Caesar, and a reference to the model of archaic Rome.

First, the enforcement of the decisions about Caesar (cf. Weinstock, 1971, 367–84). According to all the available evidence, Antony behaved in a rather conciliatory and conservative manner after the Ides of March. He delayed Caesar's divinization, and he did not put into effect the honors that had been voted to Caesar recently. As Cicero points out in his second *Philippic*, Antony had been appointed *flamen* of Divus Julius, but he still had not been inaugurated. He had added by law one supplementary day to the races of the Great Games (*Ludi magni*) in honor of Caesar, but according to Cicero this day was not celebrated in September of 44 B.C., and consequently the chariot with the ivory statue of Caesar and the setting up of his gilded chair with a crown were not tolerated either (Nicol. Dam. 28.108; Plut., *Antony* 16.5; Dio 45.6.5). As we will see, Antony also had not allowed the presence of this gilded chair during other public games during the summer. On the other hand, he had a bronze statue of Caesar placed on the Forum Romanum with the inscription *parenti optime merito* ("to the parent who deserved best") and on September 1, enforcing a senate decree of 45 B.C., he had the Senate add one day of *supplicationes* to the gods in the name of Caesar when such supplications were celebrated for Munatius Plancus. As Jean-Louis Ferrary (1999) has pointed out, Antony had a coherent and conservative policy during the first months after Caesar's assassination: he enforced honors and commemorations that were anything but revolutionary, trying to reconcile his Caesarian followers and the so-called liberators.

The young Octavian did exactly the contrary. Obviously, nothing had happened during the *Ludi* celebrated before his arrival at Rome. He tried to impose the setting up of the chair with the crown on the very first occasion, maybe during the *Ludi Florales* of 28 April to 3 May 44, but was opposed by the aedile Critonius, who was in charge of the games and backed by the consul Antony (Appian, *BC* 3.28.105 ff.). For the *Ludi Apollinares* of July 6 to 13 (according to J.-L. Ferrary), Octavian did not dare to set up the gilded chair with the crown, and when he tried to do so on the occasion of the *Ludi Victoriae Caesaris* (Games of the Victory of Caesar), he once more encountered Antony's refusal. But the appearance of the comet pushed him to take courage, and he set up a statue of Caesar in the temple of Venus with a star affixed to his head (Dio 45.6.5–7.1; cf. Chapter 7 by Beacham in this volume, Fig. 6). In 42 B.C., this goal was finally achieved: Caesar was officially deified and his temple was founded in the Forum Romanum; two years later, Antony was officially inaugurated as *flamen divi Juli*. Without any doubt, Octavian played a central role in bringing about of the foundation of the cult, but the final measures were taken with the approval of the other triumvirs.

To turn to the other principal element of his religious policy: Octavian clearly made references to Romulus and tradition when he was elected consul in 43 B.C. We have two accounts of these events, one by Suetonius and the other by Appian. Suetonius (*Aug.* 95) reports them in the context of a set of *omina imperii* (portents of his rule). The first omen – a halo and lightning – appears when Octavian enters

Rome in 44 B.C. Then, after his election in 43 B.C., he took the auspices and twelve vultures materialized for him as they had for Romulus (Dio 46.46.2). This is very peculiar because at this time, according to Cicero (*On Divination* 2.33.71), the *auspicia* were no longer taken by observing the flight of birds. Rather, they now involved the observation of the behavior of caged chickens or the observation of lightning.

A second very favorable *omen* occurred when Octavian afterwards offered sacrifices: the livers of all victims presented the same particulars, a fact which was interpreted by the haruspices as an announcement of greatness and prosperity. This sequence of rituals must be explained. The taking of *auspicia* corresponds to the ritual of the investiture of a consul elect. A newly elected consul first was formally authorized by a special legal action, the *lex curiata de imperio*, to hold the powers of that office. After that, the new magistrate consulted Jupiter about his legitimacy by taking the *auspicia*. It was only after a positive answer of the *auspicia* – of course they always were positive – that he was formally installed. The first act of the new consuls was the fulfilment of the public vows made by their predecessors. It involved the fulfilment of vows to the Capitoline triad (Jupiter, Juno, and Minerva) and to Salus Publica Populi Romani (the personification of the public welfare of the Roman people) and consisted of four sacrifices (an ox for Jupiter Optimus Maximus, and a cow each for Juno, Minerva, and Salus). Appian (*Civil Wars* 3.94.388), who also tells the story, mixes up the facts but gives the same information. The fact that both he and Suetonius mention several sacrifices confirms my interpretation of these rituals as being part of the investiture, because the relevant votive sacrifices actually were four in number. A second fact also speaks in favor of this interpretation: Octavian used the meeting of the most ancient assembly in Rome, the *comitia curiata*, to ratify his adoption by Caesar. Here again he had recourse to the oldest procedure of adoption instead of the contemporary, less solemn, adoption by testament.

We obviously do not know if the *auspicia* of investiture actually were answered by a flight of twelve vultures. It may be only a legend, transmitted by the Augustan hagiographical tradition. The flight of birds may also have been a fortuitous omen while Octavian was taking the *auspicia* in the usual manner, that is, by observing the chickens with the help of their keeper, the *pullarius*. Possibly. But we may harbor some doubt about the accidental nature of the event and ask ourselves if it may not have been entirely planned and staged by Octavian. We have seen that he revived, on the very same day, the old comitial procedure of adoption and that until 27 B.C. he did not stop connecting himself to Romulus. Even if we do not have any explicit evidence, we may suppose that Octavian had organized this Romulean show by releasing some vultures and rapidly rumor made twelve out of them. We actually know nothing about *auspicia* by means of observing flying birds. Were they released by the observer, or did he just sit and wait for birds to fly by? The very formal procedure of the *auspicia* by observing the chickens or "the heaven" at least makes it believable that birds could be released.

Anyway, the legend made it a consultation by birds in flight, on the model of Romulus who became the founder of Rome after seeing twelve vultures. If the story is to be believed, it could be the first demonstrable religious initiative of Octavian, in addition to his support of thoroughly enforcing the decisions concerning the divinity of Julius Caesar. Just as important, the archaic touch, whose first manifestation may have been the installation ceremony of 43 B.C., remained for nearly fifteen years an important element in Octavian's policy. Why did he opt for it?

The reason is to be found in the political context. In March 44 B.C., Octavian was caught by surprise. He wanted to accept Caesar's heritage, and there were only certain possibilities open to him for defining his political existence (cf. Walter Eder's Chapter 1, this volume). As the son and heir of Julius Caesar, he could only make a claim for revenge and for the enforcement to enact his father's honors. It would have been harder for him to do so if Antony had followed a more radical Caesarian line. If we are to believe Cicero, Octavian in 44 B.C. even laid claim to the same divine honors that his father had received (*Att.* 16.15.3). Being a youngster without any *auctoritas*, the only way to differentiate himself from the powerful of the day was to do something special and act in the style of Caesar. He therefore cultivated references to the Roman kings, as his adoptive father had done during the last months of his life.

The same rationale affected his religious policy. All the evidence suggests that Octavian, due to the precariousness of his situation, was constrained to take up the guiding themes of Caesar's rule. Antony's religious policy makes it clear that such constraints did not apply to him. The consul Antony could reasonably hope to prevail on both Caesar's followers and "liberators" in spite, or because, of a policy of compromise. This option did not exist for Octavian: he needed the support of the radical Caesarians. His religious policy, therefore, could not be but Caesar's.

A PARADOX: AUGUSTUS' MANEUVERINGS BETWEEN 28 AND 12 B.C.

With some justification, therefore, it could be said that the two main elements of his religious policy already existed in 43 B.C.: divine honors for the ruler and restoration of the so-called oldest tradition. As we just saw, they initially were due to circumstance. He nevertheless continued developing all his religious initiatives on the basis of these two themes and they turned out to be very successful. As we might expect, their development was accompanied by considerable transformation (cf. the principal theme of Andrew Wallace-Hadrill's Chapter 3, this volume). Once the cult and temple of Divus Iulius had been established, Augustus moderated the desires of his fans and set limits for the imperial cult in Rome and in Italy, as well as in the former Hellenistic countries. But he never considered the possibility of putting an end to the ruler cult. Over the years, he progressively appreciated the risks of a radical ruler cult, at least in Italy and in Rome. Therefore he slowly built a Roman form of the ruler cult, with its *divi*, and its cult of the *genius* and the *numen* of the living *princeps*. As for the archaic trend, it was politically effective for the triumvir who ruled over Italy and Rome. Archaism meant tradition, *mos maiorum* ("custom of the ancestors," a key concept of the Roman mentality), piety, Rome – all themes that Antony, entangled as he was in the East, could hardly use. And after the final victory, traditional piety was meant to legitimate the triumviral, and then the imperial, power.

So the spirit of Octavian's religious initiatives between 44 and 28 clearly was a concomitant part of this policy. Being pious meant to restore tradition, institutions and buildings, in short, to respect the gods just as he declared to respect his fellow-citizens and the allies of the Roman people.

This brings us to the Augustan period proper and to some paradoxes in Augustus' religious policy. How, for instance, could he wait until 12 B.C. before appointing a new priest of Jupiter, the *flamen Dialis*? There also was a problem with recruiting Vestal virgins, and the calendar again was drifting away. It seems surprising that Augustus did not act in such instances and others. Yet this paradox turns out to be very important for the understanding of Augustus' religious policy. It actually offers a clear proof of the existence of a political will, of a religious policy. And it also helps us with defining the nature of this policy.

There is a difference in Augustus' religious activity before and after 12 B.C., when he was elected *pontifex maximus*. Lepidus the triumvir had been elected in 44 B.C., either in a regular way or by an irregular election that had been regularized afterwards. Despite Augustus' critical appraisal of this election (*RG* 10.2), and despite popular pressure to replace Lepidus, he waited until Lepidus' death to do so. Again, he played the part of the restorer of tradition and therefore decided neither to eliminate Lepidus nor to deprive him of his priestly office that had been granted for life. What he could not foresee was that Lepidus would live until 13 B.C. The result was that Augustus had to neutralize the *pontifex maximus* in public religious life, which is what he did until Lepidus died. He avoided all decisions or reforms that would necessitate the consultation or the personal intervention of the *pontifex maximus*. For example, only the *pontifex maximus* could appoint the *flamen Dialis*, but only from a list of three candidates given to him by the *pontifices* or the Senate. It was enough, then, for Augustus to avoid bringing up the matter and to wait.

But the situation was more complicated. Lepidus, while living in confinement, was unable to have such matters brought up in the Senate. This particular fact also explains why Augustus was eager to have Lepidus expunged from the list of the senators, and why, when Lepidus was nonetheless co-opted at the reconstruction of an expurgated Senate, Augustus humiliated him by asking his advice in last place (Dio 54.15.5–6). As a senator, Lepidus always had the right to ask for an interrogation of the *pontifices* about problems of religion and religious reform. In this capacity he could force Augustus either to refuse the consultation of the *pontifices*, which certainly would have been contrary to his praised piety, or to accept the risk that Lepidus would give his advice as a *pontifex maximus* through the pontifical channel. Even if it is not certain that he would have succeeded in influencing any decision by the *pontifices*, his attempt would have disturbed the celebrated consensus of the Romans about Augustus' pious reforms.

To understand this particular point one must consider that a Roman priest – and that includes the *pontifex maximus* – could not act before being asked to do so by the Senate or a magistrate. The *pontifices* had to be consulted before they could intervene in a discussion or a reform. Consequently, if you controlled the *collegium* of the pontiffs from the inside, as Augustus did, it would never protest the neutralization. The *pontifex maximus* could not act alone in a legitimate way: every decision had to be backed by at least three *pontifices*. On the other hand, there was no need to consult the *pontifex maximus* or the college of *pontifices* about getting the assistance of a *pontifex* for the pronouncement of vows or for a dedication. So religious life could go on, if you avoided bringing up matters on which the *collegium* traditionally was expected to be asked for its advice, or in cases where the *pontifex maximus* could act by himself.

That is exactly what Augustus did. Very significantly, the last known decrees of the *pontifices* date from 38 and 37 B.C. (Dio 48 44.2; Tacitus, *Ann.* 1.10.4; Dio 48.53.4–6), and after that, despite the good condition of our sources, we no longer hear of the consultation of the *pontifices*. Anyway, from 36 B.C. on, when Lepidus was arrested and exiled to Terracina, Octavian avoided every situation where Lepidus or the *pontifices* could play a public role that went beyond daily routine. For instance, the restoration of the old priesthoods of the *fetiales*, the arvals, the sodales Titii or the Caeninenses did not necessarily imply a consultation of the *pontifices*. It could be done without it, by a decision of the Senate, a grant by Octavian, and maybe an internal transformation of half-forgotten *sodalitates* to a prestigious priesthood by way of the co-optation of Octavian, of senators and patricians, or of *equites*. The closing of the gates of the Janus shrine and the taking of the *augurium salutis* in 29 B.C. (Dio 51.20.4) did not concern the *pontifices*. Instead, they were ordered by a decree of the Senate. And if a sacerdotal consultation had to be done in the case of the *augurium salutis*, which was a consultation of Jupiter about the welfare of the Roman people at a time when no Roman army was sustaining a war, only the augurs who performed the ritual were concerned. Even the new privileges granted to the public priests did not require the formal advice of the *pontifices*. Augustus made that decision himself during his census in 28 B.C. By special legislation, Augustus was given the right to nominate candidates for the priesthoods even beyond their regular number. As for the building of temples, it had nothing to do with the *pontifices*, as long as there was no dispute about the dedication or a conflict between the anniversary of the dedication and an old festival. Usually, it was only a question for the dedicant and the Senate. Besides, any *pontifex* could assist the dedicant. The festivals in honor of Octavian's victories were voted by the Senate, according to tradition. Again no further consultation of the *pontifices* was necessary, so long as there was no conflict with regular festivals. The Senate and the magistrates could always ask the priests for advice, but they also could do without it, especially when the *collegium* of the *pontifices* did not protest or lobby against any impending action.

Another way of making significant decisions without the *pontifex maximus* was to act in the area of other priesthoods that were not under his purview. The Secular Games of 17 B.C. were organized and cele-brated by the consuls, the Senate and the *quindecemviri sacris faciundis*, the priesthood of fifteen mentioned earlier. In the rich evidence about this festival there is no mention at all of the *pontifices* and the *pontifex maximus*. An earlier event also shows how Augustus acted. When he returned to Rome on 12 August 19 B.C., the Senate tried to give a triumphal character to the occasion and to heap new honors upon him. Augustus refused most of these honors, but accepted the construction of an arch in the Roman Forum, and the foundation of an altar and a sacrifice to Fortuna Redux (the goddess of safe return) as well as the institution of a regular holiday (*feriae*). According to the *Res Gestae* (11–12), however, the Senate decree gave the *feriae* the name of Augustalia, as if the god of the day was Augustus, and not Fortuna Redux. That was extraordinary, and possibly dangerous. A step of this magnitude had to be taken with precaution and required substantial support. Here the advice of the *pon-tifices* and of the *pontifex maximus* would have been of great help against possible opponents of the "imperial cult." According to the known cal-endars in stone of that period, where the word Augustalia never appears, Augustus did not allow the day to be called Augustalia. It was only after his death that the day took this name. Before A.D. 14, the *feriae* con-sisted of a sacrifice to Fortuna Redux, but in 11 B.C., *ludi* began to be celebrated irregularly by magistrates (Dio 54.34.2). In the same way, in 30 B.C., a decree of the Senate had given the birthday of Augustus the status of *feria publica*, but it was never recorded on the calendars before 8 B.C., despite the fact that from 20 B.C. on, the aediles celebrated *ludi* on that occasion (Dio 54.8.5). The subject was touchy; Augustus totally agreed with the project, but again avoided bringing up the matter for formal ratification before he became *pontifex maximus*.

As soon as he was elected in 12 B.C., he could have taken initiatives which were very important for his image (Fig. 12). He did not, however, take them, or at least not right away, for the reason we have just seen. He immediately appointed a *flamen Dialis*, and after making an inquiry about his duties he reformed some of them (Dio 54.36.1; Tac., *Ann.* 4.16.4). Maybe he appointed also a *flamen Martialis*, but we do not know if this priesthood also had been vacant for years. Between 5 B.C. and A.D. 5 he dealt with the recruitment of the Vestal Virgins (Dio 55.22.5), maybe after the failure of his first measures, taken in 11 B.C. or so, to have this priesthood working again (Suet., *Aug.* 31, 3). Another question was the calendar. Until 12 B.C. it remained in a state of disorder because of a wrong insertion of the leap year. So it had to wait until 12 B.C., and eventually, in 8 B.C., it was put in order. At the same opportunity, the

FIGURE 12. Marble statue, probably late Augustan, of Augustus celebrating a sacrifice. His veiled head indicates that the emperor is engaged in a solemn religious rite in the 'Roman' manner. By contrast, sacrificants at a 'Greek rite' were bareheaded. Rome, Palazzo Massimo alle Terme. Photo: DAIR 65.1111.

month Sextilis was called Augustus, by enforcement of a decision taken in 27 B.C. (Macrobius, *Sat.* 1.14.13ff.; Censorinus, *De die nat.* 22.6). Again Augustus had delayed the enforcement of this decision because of Lepidus. In 12 B.C. (Suet., *Aug.* 31.1), he took control of the prophetic Sibylline Books. He had them edited and transferred from the temple of Jupiter on the Capitoline to the Palatine Apollo temple (which, as we saw earlier, was linked to his residence). The transfer involved a change in the organization and function of the Capitoline temple, and it is more than likely that the *pontifices* had to be consulted. And finally, according to Augusto Fraschetti (1990, 204ff.), Augustus authorized in 12 B.C. the celebration of the *Ludi compitales*. The measure concerned a festival that had been restricted since the fifties B.C. to the celebration of the traditional sacrifices of the crossroads (*compitalia*) in the city. It obviously was very popular, and Augustus' action again shows that he refrained from doing what he wanted as long as Lepidus was alive and in charge.

We do not know when, and on the basis of what initiatives, it was obligatory for the magistrates or the Senate to consult the college of the *pontifices* and the *pontifex maximus*. Part of Augustus' conduct, therefore, still cannot be entirely explained. But as a whole, his paradoxical behavior very well fits in the pattern sketched. These delays clearly show that Augustus had a religious policy. For once the impediment was removed by nature, he immediately resumed his reforms. The earlier steps he took, his holding off on some important initiatives, and his vigorous implementation of them after Lepidus' death, combine to provide strong support for this conclusion. His actions in the area of religion amount to more than casual propaganda. They reveal long-range planning along with some nerve, because as a Roman one had to be careful not to overestimate one's longevity. From 44 B.C. on, as we have seen, this planning moved along two major lines. One was the building of what we call the imperial cult, and the other was the strong references to tradition. And even if Octavian soon parted with the radical concept of Caesar's political initiatives, he nevertheless had a very clear idea of his own aims. His conduct in the matter of the *Augustalia* plainly proves his awareness of how things would turn out in the end, while also showing his caution regarding the endurance of his initiatives. The other component of his policy also changed from harking back to the oldest, regal tradition, to a politically more neutral traditionalism. But once more, while strict respect for the republican tradition entailed fewer honors for him as a person it did provide a political benefit that was clear to Augustus. The civil wars had been overcome, and the excesses of Caesarism had been mitigated. Traditional ritualism was piety, and piety was legitimacy.

The reasons for the success of Augustus' policy are, therefore, not hard to understand. His cautious innovations were successful because the Romans, and most of all the Roman élite, were open to innovation but nevertheless remained very conservative.

SUGGESTIONS FOR FURTHER READING

The most informative recent work in English on Roman religion in general is *Religions of Rome*, edited by M. Beard, J. North, and S. Price (Cambridge 1998). Volume 1 provides a chronological and thematic history; volume 2 is a sourcebook, bringing together evidence from literature, inscriptions, archaeology, coins, and art. The traditional handbooks, still invaluable for the collection of literary sources, are Wissowa (1912) and K. Latte, *Römische Religionsgeschichte* (Munich 1960). R. Ogilvie, *The Romans and their Gods at the Time of Augustus* (London 1969) provides an introductory survey, which is dated in some ways. See now J. Scheid, *An Introduction to Roman Religion* (Bloomington 2003).

PART IV

ART AND THE CITY

9: SEMBLANCE AND STORYTELLING IN AUGUSTAN ROME

Diana E. E. Kleiner

PAST AS PROLOGUE

Art in the age of Augustus was such a sophisticated blend of monument and national identity that it is hard to believe that it did not emerge full blown like Minerva from the head of Jupiter. In truth, Augustan art was inspired by such diverse civilizations as Ptolemaic Egypt, Classical and Hellenistic Greece, and Republican Rome, yet what it derived from these was merged into an entirely new creation. Almost as if by magic, a city of brick became one of marble, legendary founders and contemporary dynasts coalesced, and Rome took on the eminence of Alexandria and Athens.

This stunning and nearly flawless result owes a great deal to one man – Octavian Augustus and to his alliance with one woman – Livia Drusilla. The union of Augustus and Livia started out conventionally enough – ambitious man on the rise, disappointed that his wife has not given him a male heir, decides to divorce her in order to marry a beautiful aristocrat with a son and another child on the way. He envisions the new bride's personal and financial assets as a perfect complement to his own soaring aspirations, and he is not disappointed. In fact, it soon becomes clear that her intellect and vision match his own and that they are the perfect power couple.

The pair expanded their exceptional circle by partnering with other talented men and women, among them clever family members, perspicacious military strategists, prolific writers, and astounding architects, who helped them form their dynasty, conquer their world, mythologize their exploits, and construct their empire. They also benefited from one of the darker decisions of the day, the enslavement of vast numbers of captives brought to Rome as a result of many successful wars abroad. Since élite Roman men limited their vocations to politics, the military, and the running of estates, they needed a highly educated but subservient population to do everything else. What this meant was that all of Rome's professional people – its doctors, lawyers, and businessmen – were slaves or former slaves, who hailed from as numerous a variety of ethnic backgrounds as the number of civilizations Rome conquered.

In these capacities, Roman slaves and freedmen frequently interacted with the aristocracy. Physicians, hairstylists, gardeners, and wet nurses alike were in the imperial employ. Foreign architects and artists, both freeborn and of slave extraction, were assigned the awesome responsibility of transforming the emperor's political and social agenda into art. Other professionals headed the architectural firms and art ateliers that catered to other élite as well as non-elite patrons. While there is disagreement over whether these slaves were mistreated or led relatively fulfilling lives, it is certain that many encountered Rome's nobility and were swept into a top-down culture of semblance.

The quality of life for Roman women is also difficult to assess. Even patrician Roman matrons were denied the right to vote and hold public office, which significantly limited their capacity to influence public policy. Nonetheless, a small number circumvented the prevailing culture and shaped the system to match their goals. As Susan Treggiari details in this volume, Livia was first among such women, by dint of her status as empress, but also because of her strong will. Livia was liberated from guardianship, marshaled significant family resources in the service of great public works and benefactions, and was influential in conversations about imperial succession. Her success was, however, something of an aberration because it was accompanied by Augustus' determined drive to suppress the rights of élite Roman women and subject them to strict behavioral codes.

Art commissioned by Augustus and his privileged coterie was, of course, predicated on contemporary realities, some inherited from the Republic and others that were novel – the grimness of civil war, a quest for a national identity, creation of an international empire, the establishment of a new governmental system that would restore the ideals of the Republic while introducing hereditary dynasty, and a conflicted view of the role of women and foreigners in the new world order. These truths were sometimes presented unadulterated, but often they were veiled behind myths and legends, in some instances adapted from those of earlier civilizations. In the latter form, they were reassuringly familiar. These recognizable narratives were, however, amalgamated with a unique invention that can only have been Augustus' – the use of physical semblance to create a dynasty and an empire and storytelling to interweave that dynasty's history and prospect with the saga of Rome.

AUGUSTAN REALITIES AND FOUR EXCEPTIONAL WOMEN

Octavian burst on the Roman scene when he was a mere youth and his rise to prominence is all the more impressive because contemporary competition for the world's attention was intense. Grandnephew of the renowned dictator Julius Caesar, Octavian was not modest in his choice of adversaries, targeting his popular countryman Mark Antony and the incomparable Queen Cleopatra of Egypt, a goddess in her own lifetime. Yet he did not have much choice because well before Octavian fought the celebrated couple on the high seas off the western coast of Greece, Caesar had fathered Cleopatra's son Caesarion. Since Octavian was now Caesar's adoptive son, he feared the potential rivalry of Caesar's biological heir. Caesarion was not just some foreign pharaoh but a real presence in Rome. He had stayed in Caesar's villa with his mother and was proudly featured by his father in a gilded statue of Cleopatra with Caesarion on her shoulder. Even more worrisome was that the statuary group was audaciously paired with that of the Julian family's patron deity Venus in her temple in Caesar's forum in Rome. Octavian's daring paid off because his victory over his formidable rivals at Actium in 31 B.C. and the murder of Caesarion made him the undisputed ruler of the ancient world.

Augustus appears to have been an historical figure larger than life, dominating an era in a masterful and profound way. If behind every great man, there is a great woman, Augustus had four – Cleopatra, Livia, his sister Octavia, and his daughter Julia, a formidable foursome who exerted a greater impact on Rome than Augustus would have ever imagined possible. Even though Augustus enacted some of the most repressive laws for women in Rome's history and excluded his own women from his *Res Gestae Divi Augusti*, he was conflicted about this quartet and the part they played in his life and that of Rome and its empire.

Augustus and his propagandists positioned Cleopatra as Rome's greatest enemy and the Augustan poets slandered her with wilting invective, Horace's *Ode* 1.37 being a notable exception. Yet as the bewitching magnet for vulnerable élite Roman men, Egypt's queen had won Caesar from Calpurnia and Antony from Octavia. Even Octavian professed love to her (supposedly as a political ploy) and hoped to display her alive in his triumphal procession. When she got the best of him and he had to settle for parading her effigy, he made the decision to allow her gilded statue with Caesarion to remain in Caesar's Temple to Venus Genetrix. Since Antony's portraits were destroyed, Augustus' decision to retain Cleopatra's is tantalizing for its implications. Was he under her spell, too? Or did he want to remind the Romans, as he did so often, of what the alternative to his principate might have been? It is unlikely we shall ever know.

Livia was the wealthy patrician and pregnant ingénue who became as much a partner to Augustus as any woman could have. Intelligent enough to have likely contributed in significant ways to the imperial agenda, she unquestionably also set her own. Livia probably encouraged her husband to grant her sacrosanctity, along with Octavia, to give her the right of statuary, and to authorize her to use her substantial financial resources for the public good and to the acclaim of the Augustan dynasty – the construction of temples, a market, and an art museum. Yet, even though Augustus humored his wife, when all was said and done, he did not honor her or her contribution in the way that he should have, denying her such privileges as having her portrait on the official coinage in Rome.

Octavia was the beloved sister. Augustus doted on her son Marcellus and chose him first as his successor, marrying him to his only child, Julia. There was a fine line between Augustus' devotion to his sister and his support of her personal fulfillment and the necessity of using her to further his own political goals. When Augustus gave Octavia's hand in marriage to Mark Antony, he did not do so because he viewed it as a wondrous love match (in fact, he knew well that Antony was already captivated by Cleopatra) but because it was advantageous for him to strengthen his public ties with Antony. When Augustus granted Octavia sacrosanctity, his main motive was not to provide her with greater privileges or to commemorate her in honorific public statuary. Instead, he was coolly calculating: any affront to her sacredness by Antony or others provided Augustus with the pretext to wage war.

Augustus' relationship with his only child Julia may have been the most complex. Like Octavia, Julia became a kind of pawn as Augustus traded her off to a series of men – Marcellus, Marcus Agrippa, and Tiberius – for their loyalty and with the hope that these unions would produce male heirs. When Julia rebelled against her role as producer

FIGURE 13. *Denarius* with portraits of Julia with Gaius and Lucius Caesar. Rome mint, 13 B.C. New York, American Numismatic Society, ex Richard Hoe Lawrence Collection. Photo: American Numismatic Society, NY, 1937.158.390.

of children and embarked on a series of adulterous and very public love affairs, Augustus showed no compassion. Quite to the contrary, he made an example out of her and banished her to a remote island. From Augustus' standpoint, Julia was at her most valuable after the births of Gaius and Lucius. Her production of these boys was so significant in his mind that Augustus granted Julia what he denied Livia – her portrait on the official coinage of Rome (Fig. 13). Her portrayal with Gaius and Lucius is telling because it signaled that her importance lay in her role as first mother of Rome. Yet when that moment passed and what he viewed as Julia's disgraceful behavior forced him to act, Augustus did not prevent the mass destruction of Julia's sculptured portraits in Rome.

Even though Augustus defeated Cleopatra, affianced Octavia to Mark Antony for personal political gain, denied Livia the right of coinage, and banished Julia to a remote island, these remarkable women miraculously found their way into Augustan art and made a striking and indelible mark. Octavia, Julia, and Livia were inextricably bound to Augustus through the emperor's use of semblance in portraiture and emerged as key players on the Altar of Augustan Peace, the Ara Pacis Augustae – the greatest story Augustus ever told. The emergence of female members of the imperial family in Augustan state art was entirely new for Rome, as they took their place beside the key men in Augustus' life – his childhood friend and closest colleague Marcus Agrippa, his grandsons and heirs Gaius and Lucius Caesar, and his adoptive son and successor, Tiberius.

THE ARTS

The realities of Augustus' interaction with these four extraordinary women had an impact on the emperor's concept of city and empire, self- and familial representation, and on the integration of those realities with myth and legend. Augustus' chief contribution to the arts was his ability to think in broad strokes and to create both a partisan and also a multinational vision for city and empire (cf. Chapters 4 and 5 by Purcell and Woolf, this volume). He was resolutely proud of Rome's history and presented the Romans as a kind of chosen people who had both come from Troy to Italy and who had also seemed to have emerged naturally from the rock of the Palatine hill. He wove a mythology that featured the departure of Aeneas and his son from burning Troy and their arrival in Latium, a story that lay behind all of his own goings and comings. He also capitalized on the dramatic and unforgettable story of Romulus and Remus, two infants who were miraculously drawn from the Tiber and nurtured by a motherly she-wolf. The father and mother imagery was transferred to Augustus and Livia and there was no more powerful icon in Augustan Rome than that of the favorite son, in whose person the destiny of Rome resided. That pivotal position was first occupied by the young Octavian and then by a succession of youthful heirs.

Augustan art was born from the clever coalescence of myth, legend, and the personal history of a family dynasty. That family's saga was intensely ideological and Augustus was determined to intertwine his vision for Rome and the empire with his family narrative. He played overarching but contrasting concepts against one another with impressive aplomb – war and peace, nationalism and internationalism, the autonomy and repression of women, with his closest relatives playing starring roles. Nephews and adoptive sons dressed up like Trojans and waged war and founded colonies. Sons-in-law constructed aqueducts, temples, and baths in Rome and elsewhere. Sisters and wives were sanctified and became the subjects of honorific statuary. Daughters sinned and were exiled to distant islands. Men were like Mars, women like Venus.

As actors in a national as well as family narrative, these imperial protagonists played defined roles that required appropriate appearance and dress and were staged in suitable milieux (cf. Richard Beacham's Chapter 7, this volume). Augustus' house was painted with theatrical stage sets decorated with tragic and comic masks (see Plate III), the perfect setting for a man who self-consciously fashioned a family legacy as compelling as Jackie Kennedy's Camelot. Even on his deathbed, Augustus worried about his looks. On the day he died, Augustus called for a mirror so that he could have his hair combed just right and he asked the close friends gathered around him: "Have I played my part in the farce of life creditably enough?" (Suet., *Aug.* 99).

Octavian's immediate predecessor, in terms of such concern for looks as in so many other ways, was the aging and epileptic Caesar, who, like other eminent military tacticians and savvy politicians of the Republic, was imaged in realistic portraits that deliberately featured the highly prized lines that accompanied a lifetime of achievements. Elderly and wizened senators or generals were depicted in portraits that sometimes wondrously emerged from firm muscled and youthful bodies inspired by heroic Hellenistic precedents. A statue of a general, from the temple of Hercules at Tivoli (75–50 B.C.), for example, presents a man who has a deeply lined face with sagging jowls but a perfect physique (Fig. 14). This incongruity was further accentuated by providing the portraits of these distinguished old Romans with dramatic flourishes derived from the portraiture of Hellenistic Greek dynasts and especially Alexander the Great (Fig. 53 on p. 342) – the arrogant toss of a neck or the insouciant wave of a pompadour. In this way, Pompey the Great made himself the ultimate Alexander, with his portrait exhibiting such audacious affectations (Fig. 15). The result was jarring but effective, positioning aged generals and statesmen as commanding heroes in their prime.

Caesar was not above capitalizing on the same techniques, although a full-length statue of the dictator has not survived to confirm

FIGURE 14. Statue of a general, from the Temple of Hercules at Tivoli, ca. 75–50 B.C. Rome, Palazzo Massimo alle Terme. Photo: Alinari/Art Resource, NY.

FIGURE 15. Portrait of Pompey the Great, from the Licinian Tomb on the via Salaria, Rome. Claudian copy of a portrait of 50 B.C. Copenhagen, Ny Carlsberg Glyptotek. Photo: Ny Carlsberg Glyptotek, Copenhagen.

FIGURE 16. Portrait of Julius Caesar, from Tusculum, ca. 44 B.C. Turin, Castello di Aglie. Photo: DAIR 74.1565.

FIGURE 17. *Denarius* of M. Mettius with portrait of Julius Caesar, 44 B.C. Yale University Art Gallery, 2001.87.III, University Purchase. Photo: Yale University Art Gallery.

this. What is supportable is that Caesar proudly wore every feature of his aging face as a badge of an accomplished and well-lived life. A portrait (ca. 44 B.C.) from Tusculum, now in Turin, harmoniously presents every facial crinkle and fold (Fig. 16). Caesar wears the concentric circles of wrinkles around his neck like a shimmering silver torque and his baldness like a princely crown. That is not to say that Caesar was above vanity. Caesar's enemies poked fun at his baldness and used it against him, causing him to find ways to conceal it (Suet., *Caesar* 45). When the Senate and People of Rome voted him the privilege of wearing a laurel wreath, Caesar immediately embraced it, positioning it low on his forehead to mask his receding hairline. Masterful coin portraits, struck in 44 B.C. by Marcus Mettius, depict Caesar with this very laurel crown, cleverly conceived as if it grew naturally from his own locks (Fig. 17).

SEMBLANCE

Caesar's grandnephew Octavian began his remarkable rise to power when just a teenager. In a sea of weary balding elders, he stood out as an energetic tousled-haired golden boy. Octavian's ascendancy was a dramatic breath of fresh air comparable to the election of Jack Kennedy after the post-war weary presidency of Dwight Eisenhower. At his inauguration on a wintry January day in 1960, Kennedy appeared to take the oath without the traditional top hat, enabling his full head of hair to take on mystical power as a kind of talisman of his spanking new presidency.

Octavian was just as sophisticated as Kennedy, turning Roman society upside down by boldly signaling that effective leadership was not the sole province of old men.

Octavian chose not to emphasize long experience by affecting the requisite Republican crow's feet, but instead celebrated a refreshing youthfulness. Eschewing the pragmatic portraits of senatorial compatriots, Octavian modeled himself on a triumvirate of archetypes – the charismatic Alexander, the radiantly divine Apollo, and strapping Greek athletes of the fifth century B.C. The athletic statues provided an encyclopedia of body types with classically posed stances and rippling musculature that served as the armatures for the costumes that Octavian needed to put on as he became in turn world-conquering general, emperor, chief priest, and divinity.

Right after Actium, Alexander was his main man and the energy flowing from the Hellenistic icon invigorated Octavian's locks with a hyperbolic vitality that infused every strand of hair with the magic power of kingship (a title he could not hold in Rome). In a portrait in the Capitoline Museum (circa 30 B.C.), the locks of hair shift every which way, reflecting the liveliness of Octavian's intellect, further accentuated by the contemplative furrow between his brows (Fig. 18). Octavian was the thinking man's Alexander!

When Octavian took on the title Augustus, which bestowed on him an aura of augustness, he self-consciously affected the otherworldly radiance of his patron god Apollo. The result so effectively presented the essence of benevolent authority that it rapidly became the canonical Augustus, replicated in countless copies and disseminated to every corner of the empire. The portrait, called the Primaporta type after an example from Livia's villa at Primaporta, portrays a youthful man with a resolute but compassionate command that inspired calm and confidence in all of those who beheld it (Fig. 19). Augustus recognized that this image, which he took on in his forties, encapsulated his philosophy and eminence. Therefore, he devotedly maintained it for most of the rest of his 76 years.

Once Augustus decided he would stay forever young, that choice not only shaped him as a leader but also became the cornerstone for configuring a dynasty. Livia immediately became Augustus' eternally youthful partner. In Egypt, now Augustus' personal possession, she was quick to become the new queen to replace Cleopatra. Although Augustus was in no rush to strike coins in Rome with Livia's portrait and, in fact, never did so in the capital, he ordered them manufactured in Egypt and, in Rome, gave Livia and Octavia the right of statuary.

FIGURE 18. Portrait of Octavian, ca. 30 B.C., Rome, Museo Capitolino. Photo: Gisela Fittschen–Badura.

Portraits of the empress appeared in Rome and others with her husband and sons were displayed in prominent public spaces in Egypt and other provincial locales. A good example is the portraits of Livia, Augustus, and Tiberius, from Arsinoe in the Fayum and now in Copenhagen, which were set up just after Augustus' death (Fig. 20).

While still alive, Augustus, already attuned to the power of hair, may have encouraged his wife to work with her Rome hairstylists to create a coiffure that would appropriate Cleopatra's but also establish a strikingly new image of the ideal Roman woman, modest and in possession of the requisite female virtues. Together the matron and her maids came up with an ingenious solution, binding Livia's virtues into a tight roll or *nodus* over her forehead and an equally taut bun at the nape of her neck (Fig. 4 on p. 133). Yet the empress did not allow herself

FIGURE 19. Portrait of Augustus, from a statue of Augustus as *imperator*, from the Villa of Livia at Primaporta. Tiberian copy of A.D. 15 of an Augustan original of 20 B.C. Rome, Vatican Museums. Photo: Alinari/Art Resource, NY.

to be drained of all femininity or individuality. It is also likely to have been Livia who instructed her portraitist to permit a few temperamental tendrils to emerge from the otherwise severe coiffure. Livia's hair became just as much a Roman amulet as Augustus' and her portraits became commanding emblems of Roman womanhood at home and abroad.

FIGURE 20. Portrait of Livia. from the Fayum, after A.D. 4. Copenhagen, Ny Carlsberg Glyptotek. Photo: Ny Carlsberg Glyptotek, Copenhagen.

As important as Livia was as first lady, Augustus's stewardship of Rome would persist only if he groomed worthy successors (cf. the chapter by Erich Gruen). While he had a daughter Julia by his former wife Scribonia, Livia had as yet to provide him with heirs, even though her two sons with her first husband suggested she had that capability. Augustus was frantic for heirs and set his sights on Octavia's young son, his nephew Marcellus, to whom he offered Julia in marriage. After Marcellus' heart-wrenching demise in 23 B.C. and burial in the family mausoleum, Augustus rapidly affianced Julia to his oldest friend and right-hand man, Agrippa, and encouraged them to be fruitful and multiply. Julia did not disappoint her father, producing three sons and a daughter in rapid succession. While these multiple pregnancies cramped Julia's yearning for a more liberated and glamorous lifestyle, they achieved Augustus' key objective.

Recognizing the vagaries of existence in ancient times, when death at an early age was a fact of life, Augustus left nothing to chance. He ingeniously conceived of expanding and coalescing the imperial family through a carefully crafted program of synchronized semblance. While Augustus had a biological link to Julia's sons, Gaius and Lucius Caesar, many of Augustus' other family members were connected only by marriage and did not resemble the emperor. Augustus yearned for greater symbiosis and skillfully fabricated a fictional family.

Just as in the Kennedys' Camelot, youth and comeliness were de rigueur for Augustus' family and all members were depicted as if interchangeable. Although not related by blood, Livia, Octavia, and Julia were clones of one another, and Gaius and Lucius Caesar looked as if they could be sons of Marcellus as readily as the offspring of Marcus Agrippa. Countless portraits of Gaius and Lucius, resembling miniature Augustuses and wearing versions of his Actium and Primaporta hairstyles, were distributed around the empire and publicly exhibited. Sometimes, they were paired and sometimes accompanied by Augustus as in a group from the Julian Basilica at Corinth (after A.D. 4; Fig. 21). While the semblance of these boys to their grandfather may have been real, that of other members of the imperial family was intentionally imagined.

The Ara Pacis Augustae, erected in Rome between 13 and 9 B.C., to commemorate Augustus' return from Spain and Gaul after pacifying the region, depicts the entire imperial family on its north and south sides. Formally dressed in proper togas and pallas (the upper garment of Roman ladies), these men and women solemnly process, but do so in

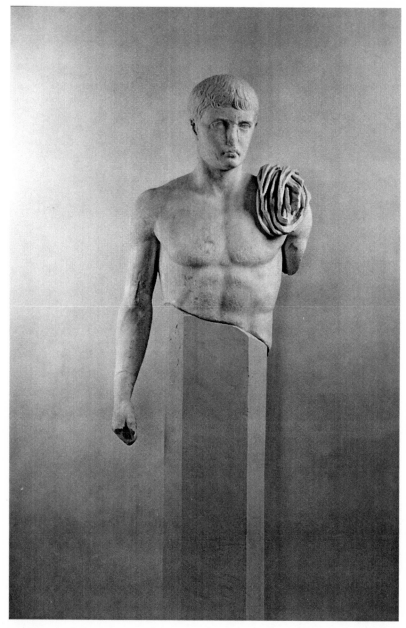

FIGURE 21a. Statuary group of Augustus (b) with Lucius (a) and Gaius (c) Caesar, from the Julian Basilica, Corinth. After A.D. 4. Corinth, Archaeological Museum. Photos by I. Ioannidou and L. Bartziotou, courtesy of the American School of Classical Studies, Corinth Excavations.

FIGURE 21b.

FIGURE 21C.

FIGURE 22. Ara Pacis Augustae, Rome, south frieze, 13–9 B.C. On the left, Agrippa and Livia, followed by Tiberius. The boy in Trojan costume between Livia and Agrippa may be Gaius Caesar. Photo: DAIR 72.2403.

a lively and familiar way (Fig. 22). They converse animatedly along the route and attend to their restless children, who are boisterous enough to be silenced by a woman with her finger to her lips (Fig. 23). Most significant is that members of the family's Julian and Claudian branches resemble one another not because of common genes but as the result of a clever fiction. Real and imagined semblance is the goal, melding the imperial family into a unified ruling élite that, in its indivisible concord, ensures the stability and flourishing of Rome. The portraits of Augustus and Livia serve as prototypes and all members of the procession are potential surrogates for one another. The message of the nearly identical companions is that they are all for one and one for all.

This Augustan semblance, with its youth and near perfect beauty, had roots in a Greek classicism that eschewed individuality in favor of a communal ideal. Every woman on the Ara Pacis has an exquisite oval face and an ample body, sensuously draped, and every man has a muscular build and Augustan cap of hair. Many of the faces are interchangeable and mapped with the emperor's political ideology and

FIGURE 23. Ara Pacis Augustae, Rome, south frieze, detail of Fig. 22.

social mores. While the faces of some of the main protagonists were
restored in the late 18th century by Francesco Carradori, 16th- and
17th-century sketches of the reliefs and surviving ancient portraits of
the same individuals confirm that idealizing visages (there may be
some exceptions, for example, Marcus Agrippa) were the norm in
Augustan times. For the most part, portraiture was not used in the
age of Augustus, as it was in the Republic, as a record of the idio-
syncrasies of the individual face, but as a means by which all members of the imperial family were coalesced into a unified image of
Empire.

STORYTELLING

This coalescence had youthful leadership at its core – a young man with the charisma and restless locks of the great Alexander who, like the legendary Aeneas and divine Apollo, created a dynasty out of the mythology of sons. Ascanius, Romulus, and Caesarion were all conjured up in the persons of Gaius and Lucius. These boys would not have been conceived without the lush fecundity of élite Roman women like Livia, and Octavia and Julia, whose fertility matched that of Cleopatra's productivity.

Augustus' immediate predecessors had waged horrific civil wars that tore at the very fabric of Roman civilization. Augustus engaged in the same internecine warfare as his predecessors, but he recognized the danger in so doing and deliberately redirected the story. He recast his confrontation with his countryman Antony as a battle with a foreign power and a female sovereign Cleopatra and countered them not only through conventional combat but also through matching each of their narrative episodes with one of his own. Yet it was not the obvious waging of war that he featured in his storytelling (there are no soldiers or battles on the Ara Pacis) but the paradise of peace as the result of war, emanating from female fertility and the bounty of Mother Nature.

Even though Mars helped Augustus avenge the death of his divine adoptive father Caesar, it was not the war-like Mars but the patriarchal Mars who guarded his offspring, Romulus and Remus, on the northwest side of the Ara Pacis (Figs. 24, 27). While it was war that made Augustus Rome's first *princeps*, he banished battle from his visual culture, favoring instead the tranquil harmony of the circle of life rejoicing in rebirth and regeneration. Just as Cleopatra's gods, Hathor and Horus, were annually rejuvenated, so too did Rome flower and proliferate. Acanthus plants wound their way endlessly along the surfaces of Augustan relief sculpture, and the fruitfulness of aristocratic Roman women was duly celebrated.

Augustus' story emphasized the peace he brought to Rome after the divisiveness of civil war. Death was replaced by regeneration; plants flourished with abandon, and women were exceptionally prolific and produced children at a rapid pace. Augustus was himself young and charismatic with an attractive and rich trophy wife who was already the mother of two sons. It was a reasonable expectation that the new empress would give birth to other boys and, by so doing, provide Augustus and Rome with their desired future.

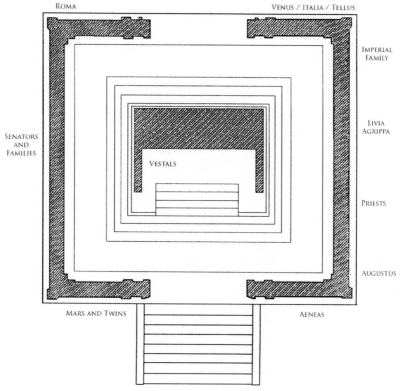

FIGURE 24. Ara Pacis Augustae, Rome, diagram. The reliefs on the outside of the enclosure were designed to encourage multiple associations and connections with one another. The two children, for instance, on the lap of the female figure (Fig. 29; variously identified as Tellus, Italia, Venus, Pax, or Ceres) relate to Romulus and Remus in the Mars relief and to the children in the imperial family (Figs. 22 and 23). Drawing by Chris Williams.

Storytelling in the age of Augustus, like Augustan semblance, was a clever amalgam of truth and fiction. Augustus was not just the leading protagonist in the play of Augustan life, but the author of his dynasty's history and legacy. Just as he freely mixed Alexander, Apollo, and assorted athletes with Augustus, Rome's first emperor did not hesitate to weave myth, legend, and current events into a dramatic narrative of Rome's illustrious past, promising present, and visionary destiny. These elements were so seamlessly bound that it was nearly impossible to disentangle them. And who would want to? What could be more enchanting than being descended from gods and heroes and leading life under their tutelage and with their blessing? Augustus wove a magical

FIGURE 25. Terracotta plaque with Apollo and Hercules, from the Temple of Apollo on the Palatine, circa 28 B.C. Rome, Antiquario Palatino. Photo: Soprintendenza Archeologica di Roma.

tapestry and also displayed an uncanny ability to invest the major themes of his principate with multiple meanings so that everyone could find some significance in them.

This intentioned multiplicity makes some Augustan monuments difficult to decipher today and has led to alternative interpretations. In the terracotta plaques of the temple of Augustus' patron god Apollo (circa 28 B.C.), Apollo is portrayed battling his archenemy Hercules for the Delphic tripod (Fig. 25). Representation of that mythical contest may be all that was intended, but some scholars suggest that the fabled

FIGURE 26. Frieze with the Rape of the Sabine Women. From the Basilica Aemilia in the Roman Forum, circa 14 B.C. Rome, Forum Antiquarium. Photo: Darius Arya.

rivals also exemplified Octavian and Antony and their larger-than-life contest for world supremacy.

Such manifold readings also lead to controversies around the dating of Augustan monuments. Carved scenes of Rome's legendary past in the Basilica Aemilia are attributed by some to renovations of the building in the late Republic, but the alignment of their subject matter with Augustus' marriage and moral legislation also makes 14 B.C. an attractive chronological option. If manufactured then, the scenes provided not only a lively recitation of such oft-told sagas as the rape of the Sabine women (Fig. 26) and the punishment of the Roman maiden Tarpeia, but also served as moralizing lessons for Roman women. Those who paid heed might escape the harsh punishment legislated by Augustus for what he defined as unethical female conduct.

These and other experimental forays into Augustan storytelling culminated in the sculptured masterpiece of the age of Augustus – the Ara Pacis Augustae (Figs. 24, 27). It is in this monument that Augustan storytelling crystallized and reached its apogee. Already a locus for imperial semblance, the altar became the vehicle by which the emperor and his advisers and designers chronicled the history of Rome and the related story of a youthful dynasty that leveraged a promising past into a vital present that presaged a visionary future.

Augustan storytelling left no stone unturned, exploring every overarching human theme: love of family, country, and nature, the necessity for war, the quest for spirituality, the fascination of travel, and enduring loyalty to family, country, and the divine. Heavenly protagonists appear human and humans seem celestial. Augustus' family narrative is

FIGURE 27. Ara Pacis Augustae, Rome, general view from west. The actual altar is visible at the top of the steps. The lower part of the outside of the enclosure consists of an expansive floral frieze. The upper left panel (fragmentary) depicts Mars with Romulus and Remus. On the upper right, Aeneas' sacrifice after his arrival in Italy (Fig. 30). Around the corner from Aeneas is the sacrificing Augustus (Fig. 28) – the connection could not be missed. Photo: Fototeca Unione-AAR 1038.

strikingly similar to the eternal saga of the gods and to the legendary history of the city's founders. The semblance among Augustus' family members is extended to gods and heroes and they are merged into a synchronism of storytelling.

The altar's mythological and legendary protagonists are confined to panels on the east and west sides, none of which incorporate historical Romans. Yet around each corner is the consecration ceremony of 13 B.C. where Augustus and his retinue saunter seamlessly into Rome's fabled past (Fig. 28). They are swept along on the swirling acanthus plants that encircle the monument and miraculously transport imperial and divine participants back and forth through time and fluently weave them in and out with one another.

Circulation around the altar was ritually prescribed with the visitor retracing the steps of the emperor himself. After securing peace in Spain and Gaul through skillful diplomacy, Augustus returned along

FIGURE 28. Ara Pacis Augustae, Rome, south frieze. Augustus and attendants. On the far right, Agrippa (followed by Livia and others: Fig. 22). Photo: DAIR 72.2400.

the Via Flaminia to Rome. That same thoroughfare served as the portal to the Ara Pacis leading to the monument's east side with impressive seated figures of Rome's *grandes dames* – the proud city goddess Roma and a statuesque manifestation of every goddess and every woman (Fig. 29). Around the corner is the imperial family, led by Livia and Julia (Fig. 22). Livia and the composite goddess possess equivalent virtues – beauty, modesty, fertility, and peacefulness – and empress and deity closely resemble one another in face, comportment, and dress.

It is noteworthy that Augustus was willing to begin the story of his dynasty with its women – its goddesses and personifications and the most prominent female members of the imperial family. His so doing brings us back full circle. While the latter were the same women the emperor shunned two decades later when he compiled a list of his greatest accomplishments, they were also among the four exceptional women who stood behind this great man. Above all, the preeminence of women on the Ara Pacis may be seen as a tribute to Livia on whose birthday (January 30, 9 B.C.) the altar was dedicated. Nothing was more important to Augustus in the last two decades of the first century B.C. than the creation of a dynasty and Livia was

FIGURE 29. Ara Pacis Augustae, Rome, southeast panel. Composite goddess or personification, variously identified as Italia, Tellus, Venus, Pax, or Ceres. Photo: DAIR 86.1448.

at the core of that particular enterprise. Augustus, leaving nothing to chance, used semblance to create a family and storytelling to provide its pedigree.

The narrative that was spun established a lineage for these women and for the sons whom they provided their husbands, male heirs who ensured the continuity of dynasty and Rome. As the procession moves from east to west and along the north and south sides of the altar, it passes from the maternal world of women to the paternity of men. Livia, Julia and their children are encountered first with Gaius and Lucius closest to Augustus, himself accompanied by a phalanx of male senators, magistrates, priests, and bodyguards (Fig. 28). Around the corner from Augustus are Aeneas (Fig. 30) and Mars. Gaius and Lucius Caesar, as Augustus' adoptive sons are to the emperor what Ascanius (also known as Julus) was to Aeneas, and Romulus to Mars. These boys are subtly assimilated to one another. Gaius and Lucius wear the costumes of Ascanius' Troy and, like Romulus, they were raised with an eye to

FIGURE 30. Ara Pacis Augustae, Rome, southwest panel, Aeneas sacrificing in Italy. Photo: Alinari/Art Resource, NY.

destiny. Livia's son, Tiberius, is also present, and follows in procession just behind his mother (Fig. 22).

The Ara Pacis experience is mythic, intoxicating, and engaging. The visitor walks alongside the imperial women and their children as they lead the way to Rome's men. Only Mars wears his battle dress; Aeneas and Augustus are in religious garments with veiled heads, as they sacrifice to the state and household gods. They are confident that their sons will carry on their mission. That Gaius and Lucius will succeed Augustus is as certain as Aeneas' journey to Italy and Romulus' founding of Rome. That Livia's beauty matches Venus' is also assured, as is her possession of all the virtues of Rome's foremost female divinities and personifications.

SEMBLANCE AND STORYTELLING AS COLLECTIVE IDENTITY

Augustan semblance and storytelling were not confined to imperial portraiture and relief sculpture in Rome. Augustus' fierce nationalism was matched by an international focus, which gained force as the emperor and other triumphant Roman generals founded cities in conquered lands. These new urban centers were not only provided with Roman amenities and edifices but also endowed with foundation legends starring Roman gods and heroes. Rome's dynamic thrust into regions as diverse as Gaul, North Africa, and Asia Minor and the concomitant appropriation of people were morally questionable. Local residents did find that quality of life improved in their newly renovated cities, but many others were transported back to Rome where they relinquished their freedom for servitude to an unfamiliar state-sponsored ideal. While it is difficult to assess the true impact of this upheaval on its victims, their ethnic and social diversity contributed to a vibrant new multiculturalism in Rome. A rich and varied tapestry of assorted languages, religions, and customs reshaped Roman life in the capital. The resultant cacophony of cultures must have been strikingly apparent in Rome's forums and shops, but, in this instance, art did not imitate life. The striking individuality of Rome's reluctant émigrés was swiftly subsumed in the potent Augustan philosophy of semblance.

Nomenclature preserved in inscriptions on public buildings and sepulchral epitaphs in Rome reveals the range of backgrounds of some of these patrons. They were provincials, freedmen, and slaves – bakers from Greece, merchants from North Africa, seamstresses from Egypt – and yet when these people imaged themselves in tomb portraits or recorded their professional achievements for posterity, they looked uncannily like Romans.

The paired portraits of the baker Eurysaces and his wife Atistia, fashioned for the façade of Atistia's tomb in Rome (late-first century B.C.), show the loving couple as so regal in bearing and so up-to-date in fashion that they could have blended into the Ara Pacis consecration procession unawares (Fig. 31). The pair wears their toga and palla with stately mien and Atistia's hair is piled majestically atop her head as if she were a contemporary aristocrat. It is certain that the couple was wealthy; Eurysaces had made a significant fortune selling bread to a very busy Roman army. Yet he and Atistia were of servile background. Upward mobility in Rome allowed the couple to take on airs and their accumulated riches provided them with the wherewithal to commission a special portrait artist to carve their likenesses. Although the double portrait is severely weathered, it is clear that the sculptor took pains to evoke the finest aristocratic imagery. The body of Atistia is modeled closely on that of Livia and other imperial women on the Ara Pacis. Her garment

FIGURE 31. Portrait relief of Eurysaces and his wife Atistia, from the Tomb of Eurysaces, Rome, late first century B.C. Rome, Museo del Palazzo dei Conservatori. Photo: DAIR 33.749.

alternately flows or is pulled taut to follow the undulations of her curvaceous form and the envelopment of her right hand beneath a tight drapery fold is a motif directly adopted from Livia's Ara Pacis portrait.

Also basking in their *Romanitas* are Lucius Vibius, his wife Vecilia Hila, and their son Lucus Vibius Felicius Felix (Fig. 32). The boy's nickname Felix underscores that he was a happy-go-lucky lad, not surprising since he resembled a Julio-Claudian prince. Felix wears his hair as if he were a grandson of Augustus. His elderly father resembles Julius Caesar with a balding pate, sunken cheeks, and neck, and his mother, who was a slave freed by a woman patron, is portrayed with Livia's *nodus* coiffure.

While Augustus exerted strong control over Rome and its territories, the emperor is unlikely to have dictated portrait style for an Augustan gardener or hairdresser. These patrons chose their own monuments and their own artists. Their personal predilections did come to the fore in the choice of what were sometimes idiosyncratic shapes for their tombs. No Roman aristocrat would have wanted to be buried in a tomb that approximated a bakery, as Atistia's may have, or one that was covered with gladiatorial scenes. Former slaves luxuriated in such ostentatious displays, especially those that revealed their vocations.

Yet when it came to fashioning their faces, these expatriates seemed to want to blend in. The reason for that is hard to know. While slaves brought to Rome from the Republic on often retained their real names as *cognomina* or nicknames, their *praenomina* (first names) and *nomina* (family names) were those of their Roman owners. What's in a name? A great deal. It may be that these individuals thought that taking on a Roman name meant assuming a new identity, one that carried with it an entirely original self. And yet in the age of Augustus that new guise was a conventional one, established by Augustus, Livia, and other members of the Roman élite and shaped by the emperor's quest for semblance. Furthermore, since former slaves could earn their freedom through hard work and loyalty, they rejoiced in what accompanied manumission. Roman society was flexible enough that the offspring of slaves could become citizens, serve in the military or run for office. That potentiality made being Roman more desirable and adopting a Roman countenance was therefore like assuming a badge of citizenship.

What is most impressive is that through the earnest striving of this burgeoning middle class, Augustan semblance, invented to create a privileged ruling élite, served to formulate an indivisible empire. Internationalism became nationalism as colorful difference was subsumed in a collective Roman identity. This appears to have been an organic development even though the fortunate beneficiary Augustus was brilliant and calculating enough to have conceived of it himself (cf. Chapters 4 and 5 by Nicholas Purcell and Greg Woolf, this volume).

FIGURE 32. Funerary relief with portraits of Lucius Vibius and his wife and son. Circa 13 B.C.–A.D. 5, Rome. Vatican Museums, Museo Chiaramonti. Photo: Alinari/Art Resource, NY.

Storytelling among these immigrants was a somewhat different situation. While they liked the idea of possessing Augustus' youthful glow and coiffing themselves like Livia, cavorting among gods and goddesses and imaginary heroes seemed pretentious and even delusional. The subject matter of their sagas was unashamedly Roman. These expatriates did not describe life in the old country or relatives left behind but rather featured their involvement in Roman professions and religious rituals. They described their daily lives as doctors, midwives, lawyers, architects, artists, shopkeepers, bakers, and potters, and the cult practices they shared with their families.

Contemporary aristocrats were also depicted participating in professional activities, but these were limited to battle and politics that often portrayed them enveloped in the mist of myth and legend. In fact, some élite protagonists were so effectively assimilated to divine or heroic counterparts that it is difficult today to disentangle them. The Roman élite thought of themselves on a par with gods and goddesses and as participants in their glorious activities. They could not conceive of preserving for posterity their activity in anything less than noble deeds. A shopping trip to the local linen factory was not the stuff that myths were made of. If the élite were strong, they were as potent as Hercules and, if sensual, as exciting as Venus.

In addition, the stories of the Roman élite were told in a visual language that suited their subject manner. The imperial family on the Ara Pacis glides rather than marches, engaged in nothing more taxing than quiet conversation. Children don't do anything more rambunctious than tug at their parent's garments and even that draws a signal for silence. The quietude of the Ara Pacis is in keeping with the theme of peace that emanates from every square inch of the altar, but it also became the favored mode for storytelling among the élite in the age of Augustus.

In contrast, slaves and freedmen had their feet on the ground and narrated their activities in a more straightforward way. Gods and goddesses did not frequent poultry shops or pharmacies. Their presence in such venues would have been a distraction from work. While in their portraits Eurysaces and Atistia would have liked to be mistaken for Augustus and Livia, the tomb's narrative scenes are a far cry from the Ara Pacis processions. The frieze encircling three sides of the sepulcher depicts the successive stages of the baking of bread – Eurysaces' profession and the source of the family's wealth. Every step – from the grinding of the grain to the formation of the loaves, to the placement of the loaves in the oven, to the weighing of the bread – is presented in consecutive order and in great detail. The relative stillness of the Ara Pacis is replaced by perpetual motion. Workers, in comfortable short tunics, scurry about, mixing batter, prodding recalcitrant mules, and placing loaves in baskets. Their faces are intense rather than serene, and their gestures more erratic than graceful (Fig. 33).

Even with comparable subject matter, slave and freedman narratives were different than their élite counterparts. A limestone relief, from Amiternum, which decorated an Augustan tomb near Rome, displays a freedman version of the Ara Pacis procession, although the ceremony is funerary and private, not a public occasion of state (Fig. 34).

The Amiternum artist's overriding aim was to tell the full story and to give all participants their rightful place in the observance. The panel is filled from bottom to top with a profusion of figures on different turf segments. The deceased is there, as are eight pallbearers, seven musicians,

FIGURE 33. Relief with bakery activities, from the Tomb of Eurysaces. Rome, late first century B.C. Photo: D. and F. Kleiner 73.12.13A.

the grieving family, professional mourners, and the household staff. Unlike the Ara Pacis, where each person flows effortlessly into the next, every figure in the Amiternum relief is distinct. In addition, the procession seems as raucous as the Ara Pacis is peaceable. The flute

FIGURE 34. Funerary procession. From the Amiternum relief, Augustan. L'Aquila, Archaeological Museum. Photo: Alinari/Art Resource, NY, 36101.

players and trumpeters hold their instruments to their lips, the widow and her daughters openly express their profound grief, and professional female mourners noisily beat their breasts and dramatically tear out their hair. The din is so great that even the deceased is as yet unable to rest. Although he reclines on his bier and is already crowned by a celestial canopy of moon and stars, he props up his head in order to take in the entire scene and to sample the many sights and sounds.

The dead man's family had become so thoroughly acclimated to life in Rome that it unsurprisingly honored its *paterfamilias* with a thoroughly Roman funerary ceremony. Yet when the commission was arranged, foremost in the relatives' minds was the importance of recording the entire ritual in a matter-of-fact manner that was grounded in everyday reality. This approach is in striking variance with that of Augustus and other élite storytellers who shamelessly equated themselves with deities and parsed the truth when so doing enabled them to spin a better yarn and facilitate an explicit political agenda.

That said, élite and non-élite Roman storytellers shared one primary objective – preserving for posterity a personalized account of their lives, albeit one defined by a pervasive Roman identity. While aristocrats were born with that identity, Augustus homogenized it into a semblance that was worn by patricians in their portraiture like a second skin. Encouraging those who were in Rome by coercion to employ the same portrait style was much more challenging. Those who did so willingly were probably freedmen who accumulated substantial wealth, an accomplishment that likely made them more positive about their fate. The record of their compliance is the hundreds of surviving marble faces that portray them as bona fide Romans. Their resemblance to élite Romans became an emblem of their assimilation to the Roman ideal. Slaves who could not afford portraits had their identity defined by their masters, witnessed by the even larger number of extant faceless epitaphs preserved in the vast communal burial grounds of the Augustan ruling class.

The Augustan portrait thus became a national and international insignia of Rome. Faces assimilating this portrait atop a wide variety of bodies that typified different Roman roles, turned up in every conceivable public and private architectural context in Rome and in narrative scenes carved on blocks that were part of impressive marble monuments. In this way, storytelling was another dimension of semblance, making semblance and storytelling in Augustan Rome two sides of the same coin.

SUGGESTIONS FOR FURTHER READING

Semblance

For the portraiture of Augustus and the Julio-Claudian dynasty, see Pollini (1987), Zanker (1988), Kleiner (1992), and Rose (1997). Portraits of Livia and other élite Roman women in the age of Augustus are treated in detail in Bartman (1999) and Wood (1999). For extensive discussions of the portraiture of Rome's freedmen and freedwomen, see Kleiner (1977). Studies on Roman coins by Sutherland (1974) and Kent (1978) provide extensive photographic documentation for the official Roman coinage and numismatic portraiture in the age of Augustus. For the impact and imagery of Queen Cleopatra of Egypt, see Walker and Higgs (2001) and Kleiner (2005). Kleiner and Matheson (1996) and (2000) should be consulted for the overall contributions of women to Roman society.

Storytelling

Fuller discussions of the Ara Pacis can be found in Zanker (1988), Kleiner (1992), and Galinsky (1996); Conlin (1997) discusses the monument with particular emphasis on stonecutting technique and restorations. For the narrative reliefs of Rome's freedmen and freedwomen, see Kleiner (1992). For the Tomb of Eurysaces, see Kleiner (1992) and most recently Petersen (2003).

10: MAKING ROME A WORLD CITY

Diane Favro

> *He who takes it upon himself to look after his fellow citizens and the city, the empire and Italy and the temples of the gods, compels all the world to take an interest.*
>
> Horace, *Satire* 1.6.34–37

Today, globalization takes command. Tokyo, New York, Istanbul, and other cosmopolitan centers are dubbed "world cities," generating activities enacted and visible around the globe (Clark 1996). The classical world centering on the Mediterranean basin was more circumscribed, but no less "global" in mentality. During the Hellenistic period, eastern cities such as Antioch, Alexandria, and Pergamon gained world-class status based upon both their importance in politics and commerce, and their urban environments. All had memorable monuments, majestic public spaces, and attractive amenities. As trade, politics, and military campaigns brought the Romans into direct contact with eastern cosmopolitan centers, they grudgingly admitted that the Greeks aimed at beauty in urban design (Strabo 5.3.8). Their own capital, Rome, by contrast was parochial in appearance, characterized by winding, unpaved roads, and uninspiring architecture (Cicero, *Laws* 2.35.95–96). Livy records that Macedonian courtiers openly jeered at both the Romans' limited achievements and "at the appearance of the city itself, which was not yet beautified in either its public places or its private districts" (40.5).

Such foreign criticism was reinforced by internal thinking about Rome. During the second and first centuries B.C., the Romans made a conscious effort to justify their hard-earned stature in the world by confirming a venerable past centered on their premier city. Literature exalted Rome as conqueror of the world; artwork juxtaposed the personified image of the goddess Roma and the world, exploiting the pun of *urbis* (genitive of *urbs*, city) and *orbis* (world), a pairing (cf. Ovid, *Fasti* 2.684) continued in the annual Easter blessing of the Pope. Praising the antiquarian writings of Varro, Cicero noted, "we used to wander as strangers in our own city until your books effectively led us home, so that we could at last recognize who and where we were" (*Academica* 1.9). The Romans came to envision Rome not as the seat of a city-state, but more formidably as the wellspring of Roman culture and power. A city of such significance deserved an impressive and focused urban image which would inspire positive external recognition.

Initial efforts to aggrandize Rome were episodic. During the second and early first centuries B.C., powerful men erected numerous monuments in the city on the Tiber. Victorious generals, in particular, were expected to spend a portion of their booty on magnificent architectural works in the capital. The collective impact of such interventions was limited. In a sprawling city with almost one million occupants, individual works could not easily change the city unless they worked together collectively. Erected by donors seeking to impress a domestic audience, the public projects of this period failed to transform Rome. Only once power became concentrated under one man did concern for Rome's overall urban image begin to be addressed. Julius Caesar was among the first to think globally about Rome. Acquiring dictatorial powers he began several large projects including a voting enclosure (Saepta Julia) with porticos totalling more than one mile in length; a new Senate house (Curia Julia); and an addition to the Forum Romanum (Forum Julium). His oversized ambition is evident in the naming of these projects and in his interest in a broad audience. Caesar's proposed schemes included a Temple of Mars "greater than any in existence," world-class public libraries (Suet., *Julius* 44), and, most startling of all, a reordering of the entire city based on the designs of a foreign planner (Cicero, *Letters to Atticus* 13.33a). These projects lay on the drafting board on the Ides of March, 44 B.C., when Caesar was brutally murdered. The transformation of Rome into a world capital was left to his heir, Octavian Augustus (Fig. 35).

JUSTIFYING URBAN CHANGE

In 44 B.C., Octavian rushed to Rome where he was adopted by Caesar in his will. He found a city demoralized by years of civil conflict, and shabby from neglect. Unemployed people from throughout the

FIGURE 35. Plan showing Augustan projects in Rome, circa A.D. 14. **New Projects:** 1. Pyramid Tomb of C. Cestius; 2. Arch of Drusus; 3. Altar of Fortuna Redux; 4. Arch of Dolabella and Caelian Gate; 5. Temple of Apollo Palatinus; 6. Arch of Octavius; 7. Portico of Livia; 8. Esquiline Gate; 9. Markets of Livia; 10. Aqua Virgo; 11. Mausoleum of Augustus; 12. Horologium (Sundial) of Augustus; 13. Ara Pacis; 14. Pantheon; 15. Basilica of Neptune; 16. Stagnum and Gardens of Agrippa; 17. Baths of Agrippa; 18. Diribitorium; 19. Crypta and Theater of Balbus; 20. Ancient Villa Farnesina; 21. Bridge of Agrippa; 22. Theater of Marcellus; 23. Temple of Jupiter Tonans; 24. Forum of Augustus and Temple of Mars Ultor; 25. Horrea Agrippiana; 26. Arch of Augustus on the Aemilian Bridge; 27. Aqua Alsietina (Aqua Augusta); 28. Naumachia of Augustus; 29. Arch of Lentulus and Crispinus; 30. Forum Romanum. **Restorations:** A. Temple of Diana; B. Temple of Minerva; C. Circus Maximus; D. House of Augustus; E. Temple of Magna Mater; F. Anio Vetus; G. Aqua Julia, Marcia, Tepula; H. Temple of Venus Erucina at Porta Collina; I. Saepta Julia; J. Theater of Pompey; K. Portico of Cn. Octavius; L. Portico of M. Philippus, Temple of Hercules Musarum; M. Portico of Octavia,

236

Mediterranean filled every public space; brace work shoring up totter-
ing structures blocked street traffic. Numerous projects, including those
of Caesar, stood in a mocking, half-finished state. The urban fabric extended haphazardly beyond the early Republican walls to blanket the
hills, valleys, and high plateaus west of the Tiber River. Changing the
image of an entire city is a mammoth undertaking, requiring great resources, panurban power, time, and most importantly, continuous and
focused motivation. The young Octavian may have agreed with Suetonius, "The city was not adorned as the renown of our empire demanded" (*Augustus* 28), yet he initially did not have the resources or
political support to begin clarifying Rome's urban image.

Moreover, continuing conflict restricted opportunities and funds
for extensive urban improvements and other priorities prevailed. One
was Octavian's endeavor to memorialize his military exploits. At Philippi
in 42 B.C. during the heat of battle, he pledged a temple to Mars; he
vowed another to Apollo in 36 B.C. Displayed on coins and promoted
in writings, such architectural vows were good propaganda (Fig. 36).
Actual construction, however, often extended over decades. Octavian
realized his vow to Apollo with a temple dedicated in 28 B.C.; the
Temple of Mars Ultor (Mars the Avenger), dominating his new forum,
was built more slowly (irritating even Augustus, whose motto was to
"make haste slowly") and dedicated in 2 B.C.

In addition, he emulated the architectural works of his father.
Especially notable was the large Forum Augustum adjacent to the Forum
Julium and similar in form with a temple facing a rectangular area
defined by porticos (Figs. 37, 45). Octavian may have initially conceived the entire complex as an homage to Caesar, linking the two both

---

FIGURE 35 (*continued*) temples of Jupiter Stator and Juno Regina; N. Villa Publica;
O. Temple of Apollo Sosianus; P. Temple of Spes; Q. Temple of Jupiter Optimus
Maximus; R. Temple of Jupiter Feretrius; S. Bridge of Fabricius; T. Bridge of
Aemilius; U. Forum Romanum: Basilica Aemilia, Basilica Julia, temples of Vesta,
Divus Julius, Concordia Augusta, Castor and Pollux; V. Lupercal; W. Temple of
Ceres, Liber, and Libera; Campus Martius. **Exact Location Unknown:** Temple
of Neptune; Amphitheater of Statilius Taurus, Campus Martius; Portico of the
Nations; Stadium of Augustus, Campus Martius; Portico of Vipsania, Campus
Agrippae; Altar of Ceres Mater and Ops Augusta, Vicus Iugarius; Temple of Bona
Dea Subsaxana; Temple of Flora; Temple of Juno Regina, Aventine; Temple of
Jupiter Libertas; Temple of Lares; Temple of Penates; Temple of Quirinus; Temple
of Juventas. **Off Map:** Arch at Tiburtine Gate; Arch of Augustus, Milvian Bridge;
Tomb of Eurysaces. Drawing by R. Reif and R. H. Abramson.

FIGURE 36. Coin from Pergamon depicting a projected circular Temple of Mars, 19–18 B.C. Image by D. Favro.

architecturally and iconographically: Mars honored in Augustus' forum was the Romans' ancestor through Romulus and avenger of Caesar's death; Venus revered in Caesar's forum was both the consort of Mars and mother of Aeneas, Rome's Trojan ancestor.

In juxtaposition to the despised orientalism of Antony (cf. Chapters 7 and 9 by Beacham and Kleiner, this volume), Octavian shrewdly championed a Republicanism rooted in the Italian peninsula. He pointed disparagingly to the undisciplined patron gods of Antony; he himself overtly revered Italic deities. Before the battle of Actium, Octavian made special vows to the Capitoline triad of Rome and to all the gods of Italy. He justified his reverence for a Greek god, Apollo, by underscoring the deity's role as savior of Aeneas, Trojan ancestor of all the Romans and, most directly, of the Julian clan. In the thirties B.C.,

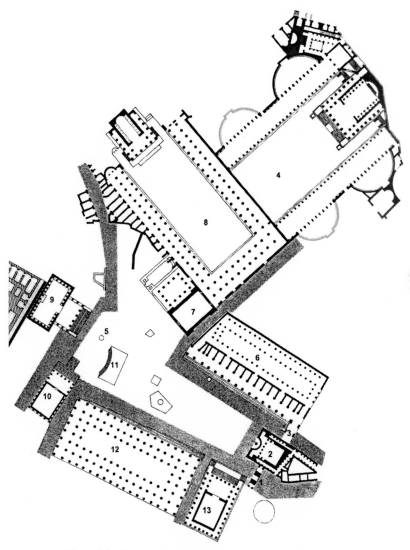

FIGURE 37. Plan of the Forum Romanum, circa A.D. 14. **New Projects:** 1. Arch of Augustus; 2. Temple of Divus Julius; 3. Portico of Gaius and Lucius; 4. Forum of Augustus (gray walls indicate location of exedrae projected from recent excavations); 5. Milliarium Aureum. **Restorations** (completed after 30 B.C.): 6. Basilica Aemilia; 7. Curia Julia; 8. Forum of Caesar with Temple of Venus Genetrix; 9. Temple of Concordia; 10. Temple of Saturn; 11. Rostra Julia; 12. Basilica Julia (Basilica of Gaius and Lucius); 13. Temple of Castor and Pollux. Drawing by R. Reif, R. Vital, and D. Favro.

Octavian purchased a house on the Palatine Hill (Fig. 38). After lightning struck part of the property, he dedicated the spot to Apollo, cleverly using the natural event to justify both a temple site adjacent to his own residence and the worship of a foreign god within the city's sacred boundary. Such a diplomatic and reverential approach was a vast improvement upon Caesar's more cavalier urban interventions, and Antony's foreign favors.

Octavian further underscored his strong ties to the Republic by lavishing attention on the Forum Romanum. Situated in an accessible site between the Capitoline, Palatine, and Esquiline Hills, the Forum was the political heart of the Republican city (Figs. 35, 37). Public assemblies met in the open air Comitium, the Senate convened in the Curia, residents worshiped at numerous shrines and spent many hours socializing and participating in communal events in the Forum. Among various undertakings, Octavian completed the Basilica Julia and in 29 B.C. dedicated the Temple of Divus Julius. At that point, Caesar's heir could stand in the Forum and point in every direction to impressive architectural gifts he had bestowed upon the city and people. There was no place in Rome where Antony, who committed suicide in Alexandria in 30 B.C., could have done the same.

Octavian also demonstrated concern for Rome as a functioning city by encouraging others to undertake necessary, if unglamorous, projects. In 33 B.C., his right-hand man, Marcus Agrippa, assumed the lowly position of aedile, even though he had already held a string of prestigious offices. Aediles had responsibility for the *cura urbis*, or care of the city, though many holders of the office had been remiss in this duty. In contrast, Agrippa repaired public buildings, streets, and sewers, reworked the city's aqueduct system and added two new lines, the Aqua Julia and Aqua Virgo, increasing the volume by approximately 100 percent (Dio 49.43). In addition, Agrippa presented games for 59 days, and gave Rome's residents gifts ranging from rations of olive oil to a year's bathing privileges. As further largess, he embellished the city with sculptures and called for the nationalization of all art. Such efforts simultaneously improved and aggrandized the city, and won popular support for his patron, Octavian.

In the fifteen years after Caesar's murder, numerous buildings had been vowed and begun, yet Rome's urban image had not changed appreciably. Since the predominant impetus for building remained political rivalry between Romans, the recent projects did not attract a broad external audience. However, the east-west juxtaposition embodied in the

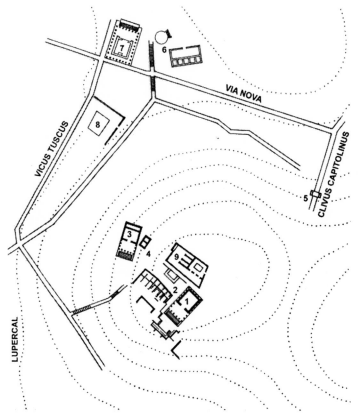

FIGURE 38. Plan of the Palatine Hill, circa 20 B.C.: 1. Temple of Apollo; 2. House of Augustus; 3. Temple of Magna Mater; 4. Temple of Victory; 5. Arch of Octavius; 6. Temple and Atrium of the Vestals; 7. Temple of Castor and Pollux; 8. Horrea Agrippiana. 9. "House of Livia." Drawing by R. H. Abramson.

Antony-Octavian rivalry compelled the Romans to think more globally. Octavian legitimized his architectural projects by adopting a revered, classicizing Greco-Roman style in contrast to overt orientalizing forms. In the early twenties B.C., he limited construction in the Egyptian style by banning worship of Egyptian gods in Rome. At his triple triumph of 29 B.C., Octavian celebrated victories at Dalmatia, Actium, and Egypt, signaling Rome's premier status in the Mediterranean. Writers began to describe Rome as the "head" of a "body" composed of the Empire (Livy 1.16.7; Pliny, *Natural History* 3.38, 28.15). As the acknowledged world leader, awash with the great wealth of Cleopatra, Augustus had an obligation to Rome. Cassius Dio describes advice given Octavian that year:

> Adorn this capital with utter disregard of expense and make it magnificent with festivals of every kind. For it is fitting that we who rule over many people should surpass all men in all things, and brilliance of this sort also tends in a way to inspire our allies with respect for us and our enemies with terror.
>
> (52.30, Loeb transl.)

Caesar's heir stood poised to transform Rome's image.

Foremost among the campaign was a call for reinvigorated piety (cf. John Scheid, this volume). Augustus enhanced the status of various religious groups, promoted the renewal of sacred ceremonies, and instituted other rites. Revitalized religious events affirmed a return to normalcy after the civil wars and simultaneously occupied the urban population. To handle the expanded program of events Augustus improved existing public venues, added new ones, and retrofitted others. He also turned attention to the city's shrines which were in a sorry condition after decades of neglect. In 28 B.C., Augustus ordered temples to be repaired by descendants of the original patrons and personally assumed responsibility for the rest, claiming to have restored 82 temples in a single year (*RG* 20). He completed religious structures pledged earlier (e.g., the temples of Apollo and Divus Julius), as well as those planned by Caesar (e.g., the Curia Julia and Temple of Venus Genetrix). In some cases he modestly maintained the names of the original donors; in others he linked the refurbished shrines with himself. For example, Augustus rededicated several temples on the same date: September 23, his birthday. New religious projects did not as easily fit into the renewal program of the twenties and teens, and were largely relegated to relatives of the *princeps*. The most monumental was the Pantheon, dedicated circa 27 B.C. by Agrippa, who became Augustus' son-in-law not long after (Fig. 39). Initially, Agrippa wished to place a statue of Augustus inside, but the *princeps* wisely refused to be honored as a deity in the conservative capital. Instead, a statue of him was placed in the anteroom (Dio 53.27.3).

As an alternative to new building projects, Augustus encouraged others to follow Agrippa's earlier example and care for Rome's less prestigious works such as sewers and roads. The need was great. With the end of civil conflicts, goods and people flowed into Rome, straining

FIGURE 39. Façade of Pantheon as rebuilt by Hadrian after A.D. 126 with an entablature inscription acknowledging Agrippa as the original donor in 27 B.C. Photo by D. Favro.

the urban infrastructure. Threats from robbers, fires, and floods tarnished the city's image. After experimentation with various solutions, Augustus abandoned the reliance on elected officials, and gradually established permanent boards of appointees to deal with the water system, Tiber River, and roads; he made equally comprehensive provisions for firefighting and policing of the urban environment. He shrewdly provided positions for residents of all classes, giving everyone, from Senator to freedman, a stake in Rome's image (Suet., *Augustus* 27). To provide an effective framework for municipal administration, Augustus reapportioned the city into fourteen new regions in 7 B.C. to include all the built areas (Fig. 40). By emphasizing the urban infrastructure, the *princeps* caused it to be viewed in a new light. Writers celebrated the skill involved in creating and running a large metropolis. Strabo claimed, "The Romans had the best foresight in those matters which the Greeks made but little account of, such as the construction of roads and aqueducts, and of sewers that could wash out the filth of the city into the Tiber" (5.3.8). Contemporaries now equated engineering and management skill, as much as beautiful buildings, with the greatness of a city and boasted that the Romans excelled at both.

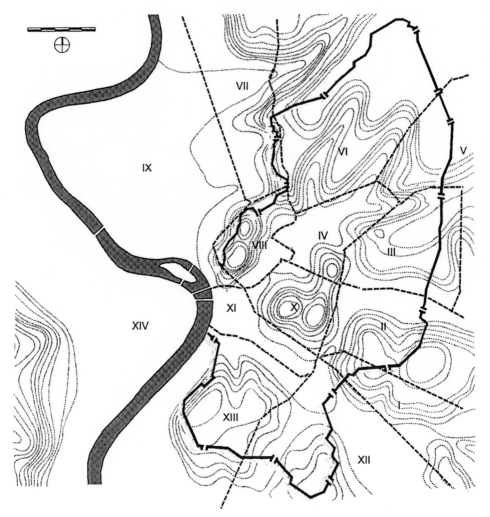

FIGURE 40. XIV new administrative regions established by Augustus in 7 B.C. Drawing by R. Reif.

The audience for architecture in Rome had definitely broadened. Many projects expressly linked the city on the Tiber with the world. In 20 B.C., Augustus placed a bronze-clad marker, the Milliarium Aureum, in the Forum Romanum (Fig. 37) in overt acknowledgment that all roads led to Rome (Plutarch, *Galba* 24). Agrippa clarified the city's position and the State's extent with a giant map of the world displayed in the Porticus Vipsania. Augustus himself created the Porticus ad Nationes

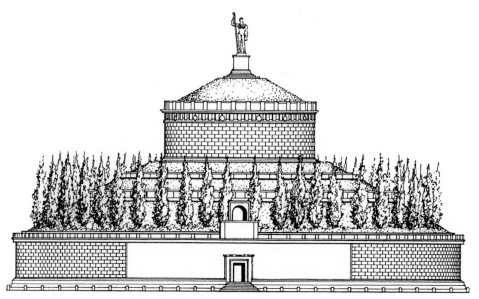

FIGURE 41. Reconstruction of the Mausoleum of Augustus (completed after 23 B.C.). Drawing by R. H. Abramson.

with statues personifying all nations, and included copies of the caryatids from the Erechtheum in Athens in his namesake Forum. Less explicitly, the very type and scale of projects in Augustan Rome addressed a global audience (cf. Purcell and Galinsky, this volume), exploiting multiple readings in the process. For example, the establishment of libraries in Rome emulated competition in library building by Hellenistic kings (Pliny, *Natural History* 35.10). The great Mausoleum of Augustus evoked pan-Mediterranean references to the royal Lydian mounds of Anatolia, the famous circular tomb of Alexander the Great, and the Etruscan tumuli of Italy (Fig. 41). The enormous scale of this one project also spoke volumes. Begun in 28 B.C., the tomb had a marble base over 85 meters in diameter and an earthen mound approximately 45 meters in height crowned with a gilt statue of Augustus. This was a monument for the world, not a city.

To ensure all significant buildings reflected his program, Augustus began to minimize competing messages. Increasingly, he directed the patronage of memorable public projects in Rome, largely ignoring building types of low status. Fortunately, circumstances helped. As peace spread, the number of triumphs declined and with them the number of new triumphal building projects. In addition, Augustus began to restrict the number of those who received triumphs; after 13 B.C. only members of his family were awarded this honor. The *princeps* also revived antisumptuary laws curbing extravagances in private architecture, and placed a limit on building heights along urban street fronts. To justify his dominance over architectural patronage Augustus referenced a well known authority figure, the family head. In Roman households the *paterfamilias* ruled supreme, overseeing the interests of all family members. Similarly, Augustus acted in the best interests of all Romans. Like a *paterfamilias*, he made sure the appearance of his residence, in this case the city of Rome, appropriately reflected the importance of all Romans and himself. Also like a *paterfamilias*, he encouraged worship of his genius and family spirits (*lares*). After officially becoming the head of the state religion (*pontifex maximus*) in 12 B.C., Augustus included the *lares Augusti* in shrines at crossroads throughout the entire city. With his presence permeating Rome, Augustus was naturally compared to the city's original founder; Ovid even called upon Romulus to yield his position to the *princeps* who was recognized by the Romans as the "Father of the World" (*Fasti* 2.130). Augustus' paternal role was formalized in 2 B.C. at the dedication of the Mars temple in his new Forum. With great ceremony, the Senate inscribed a sculpture of Augustus in a chariot, *pater patriae*, "father of his country" (*RG* 35; cf. Eder, this volume). The layout of the new Forum emphasized this association. In the porticoed, colonnaded atrium of his house a *paterfamilias* displayed images of the family's venerated ancestors; in the colonnaded Forum Augustum (Figs. 42, 46) the *pater patriae* displayed statues of illustrious ancestors of the Julii back to Aeneas and the kings of Rome back to Romulus. In effect, the Forum Augustum became the atrium of the State (for a discussion of the Forum Augustum from another perspective, see Barchiesi, pp. 282 and 291).

When proclaimed *pater patriae* in 2 B.C., the *princeps* was in his sixties. As father of his country, he paternally made plans for the future care of Rome and all Romans. For decades Augustus' attempts to identify a specific successor foundered (cf. Chapter 2 by Erich Gruen, this volume). To allay fears he imprinted the cityscape with dynastic monuments. The huge Mausoleum Augustum stood ready to accept many future generations of Julii. After adopting his grandsons Gaius and Lucius at the Secular Games (*Ludi Saeculares*) in 17 B.C., Augustus displayed their names in prominent urban locations. In the Forum Romanum he renamed both the Basilica Julia and the Porticus Julia fronting the Basilica Aemilia after them (Fig. 37). In 9 B.C.,

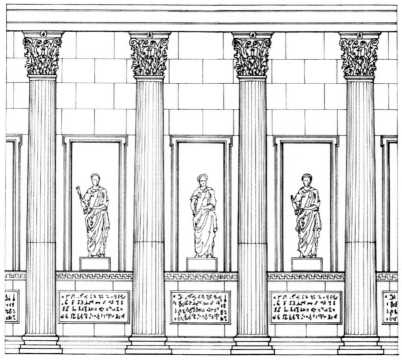

FIGURE 42. Reconstruction of the Forum of Augustus, 2 B.C., showing statues of model Romans with plaques detailing their achievements. Drawing by R. H. Abramson.

Augustus dedicated the jewel-like Ara Pacis in the Campus Martius flanking the Via Flaminia (Figs. 24, 27). On the enclosure wall were carved reliefs of the entire Augustan family, including children of the next generation, marching together in solemnity at a religious event (Figs. 22, 28). Other panels showed the Romans' mythical origins (Figs. 29, 30), tying the past, present, and future of Rome to the fortunes of Augustus and his family. Adjacent to the Ara Pacis, Augustus created a giant sundial with an obelisk as pointer overtly affirming the connection between the conquest of Egypt, peace, Augustus, his heirs, and eternity (Fig. 43).

At Augustus' death in A.D. 14, a list of his deeds accomplished, the *Res Gestae*, was engraved on bronze tablets and placed before the entrance to the Mausoleum Augustum and at sites throughout the Mediterranean. Along with military conquests, offices held, and honors received, the *princeps* proudly included his building projects in Rome.

His justifications for urban intervention had changed over five decades as he evolved from triumphator and humble heir of Julius Caesar to state champion and beneficent father. Yet the sheer number and directed force of his patronage transformed Rome. The process was accretive. Augustus never drew up a master plan. Instead, he redefined Rome's urban image in a piecemeal fashion over decades. In many ways the evolution paralleled Roman expansion in the Republican period, with the formation of an empire resulting from the cumulative effect of individual steps. Throughout, the new urban image was stimulated by consideration of an ever-broadening audience. In the end, as Horace predicted, Augustus compelled all to take an interest in Rome (*Satires* 1.6.34–37).

COMPOSING AN URBAN IMAGE

Augustus shaped his urban image from a familiar kit of parts (Fig. 35). The building types, materials, and ornaments of his numerous projects drew upon the strength of tradition. All were conservative, refined, and unthreatening. In the late-first century B.C., the Greek geographer Strabo described the tangible results of Augustan interventions:

> And again, if, on passing to the old Forum, you saw one forum after another ranged along the old one, and basilicas, and temples, and saw also the Capitolium and the works of art there and those of the Palatine Hill and Livia's Portico, you would easily become oblivious to everything else outside. Such is Rome.

> (5.3.8)

The architectural forms listed – fora, basilicas, temples – were all familiar. What, then, compelled ancient observers to forget all other cities? Or more simply, what composed the Augustan urban image?

Championing a return to an imagined Republican past of harmony and stability, the *princeps* avoided innovative or overtly foreign architectural styles or building types. In contrast to the excessive shapes generated by the building frenzy of competitive patrons in the mid-first century B.C., Augustus gave Rome sedate, conservative architecture suffused with propriety. The form of each project was immediately recognizable and justifiable within the context of late Republican architectural types. Such conservatism was not restrictive; the existing

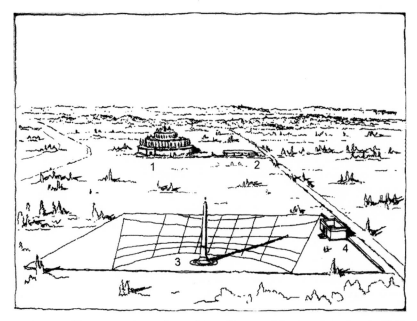

FIGURE 43. Reconstruction of northern Campus Martius, last decade B.C.
1. Mausoleum of Augustus; 2. Ustrinum; 3. Horologium (Sundial) of Augustus;
4. Ara Pacis. Drawing by D. Abernathy and D. Favro.

architectural repertoire that merged Greek and Latin forms offered an impressively wide selection. Vitruvius described the full range of building types in *Ten Books on Architecture* dedicated to Augustus in the late twenties B.C. Often criticized as a paean to conservatism, the text aptly reflects the businesslike atmosphere of construction in Rome at the height of the Augustan age.

The familiar forms of Augustan religious buildings were reassuring to a citizenry buffeted by years of civil conflict. The extensive application of refined, classicizing ornament reminiscent of earlier Attic works placed Augustan projects within an enduring and respected continuum. In virtually every instance, however, the *princeps* and his architects pushed the existing envelope to make each project memorable in the cityscape. The approach might be called "enhanced familiarity." Buildings had traditional forms, but these forms were enlarged and enriched. For example, architects so exaggerated the vertical dimension that Augustan temples towered above others in Rome (Gros 1976). For these important new buildings the *princeps* ignored limitations on building heights, which of course were not meant to curb the architectural ambitions of Rome's "first man among equals," who paternally acted for the common good. In part, Augustan buildings attained greater height by employing the lavish Corinthian order whose attenuated columns had a height nine to ten times the diameter. Those on the temple to Mars Ultor measured well over 17 meters. Excessively tall podia provided further altitude and also served as display spaces and speakers' platforms, as was the case with that of the Temple to Divus Julius (Fig. 37).

Though new governmental and religious functions developed in the Augustan age, the *princeps* conscientiously avoided innovative building forms. Instead, he exploited existing, flexible building types to house the evolving imperial bureaucracy. The Roman basilica is the quintessential multipurpose building, composed of a large colonnaded hall with an undifferentiated interior. In Rome, the largest examples stood in the Forum Romanum. Used by bankers, politicians, lawyers, lovers, businessmen, beggars, and many others, these buildings represented the city to a large audience. Augustus extensively reworked the two basilicas in the Forum Romanum, transforming them into impressive urban monuments (Fig. 37). No wonder Pliny later identified the Basilica Aemilia as one of the most beautiful structures in the entire world (*Natural History* 36.102).

One building form, the honorary arch, increased dramatically in number and urban significance under Augustus. Its attractions were obvious. Arches were excellent billboards for propaganda and useful urban markers, permanently associating particular events or achievements with specific sites. Being bifocal and permeable, arches simultaneously demarcated distinct spaces and acted as urban doorways. Augustus used them with great effect. In 19 B.C., an arch commemorating his Parthian success rose in the Forum Romanum. Flanking the temple to Divus Julius, this elaborate arch linked the achievements of the father and son, and served urbanistically as a formal entry to the central Forum. Inscribed on the sides were the names of all Rome's chief magistrates and triumphators from the beginning of the Republic, underscoring the stability of the Roman state and Augustus as the culmination of its history.

In residential design, the *princeps* urged restraint for the sake of decorum; he himself chose a relatively modest house (Fig. 38). Wealthy house owners followed his example and avoided the external appearance of extravagance in Rome. They instead expended great sums on house interiors or country villas. Observers might remark on the humbleness or uniformity of houses in the cityscape, only to be awed by the luxurious interiors decorated with art from throughout the world.

Augustus' own residence on the Palatine is a case in point, with a modest exterior image, but memorable art and paintings inside (see the following chapter by John Clarke and Plates III and IV, this volume). Anti-sumptuary laws targeting funerary architecture also led to internalization. Patrons began to favor burial precincts with blank walls facing the city rather than ostentatious tombs. Exceptions usually had some positive association with the *princeps*. Thus, anyone seeing the pyramidal tomb of C. Cestius (circa 12 B.C.) immediately thought of Augustus' Egyptian conquest rather than any event in the life of the enshrined (Fig. 44).

Augustus and his architects especially favored quickly-erected, rectangular porticoed enclosures. These complexes presented islands of order within the churning visual confusion of Rome (Fig. 45). Isolating quadriporticos such as the Porticus Philippi, Saepta, Porticus Octaviae, and of course the Forum Augustum, provided ideal stages for their Augustan message. Self-contained and internalized, their design prevented visual and conceptual contamination from adjacent Republican and non-Augustan urban projects. Thus, the towering rear wall of the Forum Augustum not only served as a fire wall, it also blocked views of the shabby neighborhood behind (Fig. 46). Rome's residents flocked to Augustan complexes, attracted by the art and greenery, but equally by the ample open space, a rare commodity in the dense cityscape.

In Republican Rome, sacred groves had provided a few spots of greenery. Under Augustus the city came into full bloom. Hellenistic cities such as Alexandria, which boasted tree-lined streets and impressive urban parks, provided inspiration. In order to be great, Rome, too, needed urban landscaping. Inexpensive in comparison to buildings, gardens dramatically and rapidly transformed the cityscape. Augustus opened the funerary gardens around his Mausoleum to the public and developed parklands on the right bank; Agrippa created a showcase of landscape design in the central Campus Martius fed by the Aqua Virgo. On the Esquiline, Augustus' cultural arbiter Maecenas filled an old fortification ditch, creating a wondrous park complete with warm-water swimming pool and garden auditorium (Horace, *Satires* 1.8). Green space within the city appealed to the eye and provided residents a welcome escape from their crowded living and working conditions. Private gardens also proliferated and enriched the city's appearance, even if not always accessible to the public. Discouraged from erecting showy houses, rich Romans instead created impressive gardens on open land in the suburbs fed by the expanded Augustan aqueduct system. These large, lush estates formed a loose green belt around Rome, signaling a sophisticated city of communal recreation and repose (Fig. 45).

FIGURE 44. Pyramid shaped tomb of C. Cestius, Rome, circa 12 B.C. Photo by F. Yegül.

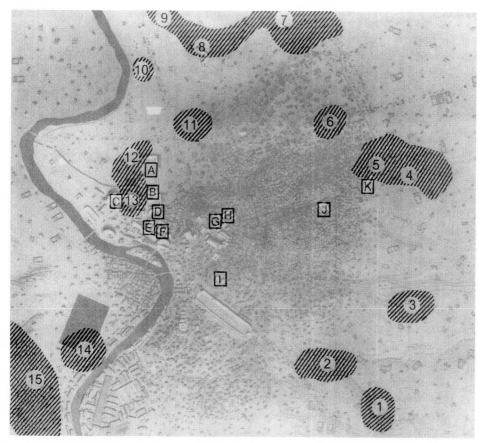

FIGURE 45. Augustan Rome. **Major porticos:** A. Saepta; B. Diribitorium; C. Theater of Pompey; D. Theater of Balbus; E. Portico of Philippus; F. Portico of Octavia; G. Forum of Caesar; H. Forum of Augustus; I. Temple of Apollo complex; J. Portico of Livia; K. Markets of Livia. **Gardens** (*horti*): 1. Horti Asiniani; 2. Nemus Camenae; 3. Horti Vectilii (Imperial period); 4. Horti Maecenati; 5. Horti Lamiani and Maiani; 6. Horti Lolliani; 7. Horti Sallustiani; 8. Horti Luculliani; 9. Horti Aciliorum; 10. Mausoleum Augustum funerary gardens; 11. Campus Agrippae; 12. Stagnum and Horti Agrippae; 13. Horti Pompeiani; 14. Nemus Caesarum; 15. Horti Caesaris. Image by R. H. Abramson and D. Favro.

For the Romans, magnificence and power were outwardly represented by large size and rich materials. As public works representing the state, many Augustan projects reached enormous proportions. Superlatives abound in contemporary descriptions of these atypical structures. Cassius Dio called the Diribitorium for the counting of votes, "the largest building under a single roof ever constructed" (55.8.4). Augustus himself bragged about the size (536 × 357 meters) of the Naumachia Augusti, an artificial pool for spectacles, in the record of his deeds (*RG* 23). On an urban scale, the expansive size of Rome signaled the city's elevated stature. The magnitude of Augustan projects at first seemed to run counter to established traditions, but was readily accepted as an enhancement of familiar forms. Costly materials further signaled superiority. In the Republican city only a few buildings had employed luxurious marbles; with the wealth and peace of the Augustan Age, colorful imported stones poured into Rome. As a result, the *princeps* had the rare opportunity to make a significant change in the materiality of an entire cityscape; he boasted, "I found Rome of mud brick, I leave to you a city of marble" (Dio 56.30.3; Suet., *Augustus* 28). Like physical enlargement, the use of rich materials was another example of "enhanced familiarity," which deftly complemented Augustan adherence to tradition. In addition, marbles offered other distinct advantages. The hard stone could be carved into elaborate, enduring ornament; colorful, shiny stonework immediately attracted attention in a cityscape composed largely of matte stucco and dull tufas. Projects like the Forum Augustum incorporated stones from all over the Mediterranean, underscoring Rome's central importance in the world at large. Extensive use of bronze architectural ornament also conveyed a similar message of wealth and superiority within well-accepted traditions. Throughout the city, sparkling materials physically manifested a new age that was both golden and respectful of the past.

Memorable buildings and materials helped the Romans navigate the complex cityscape of Rome. In general, ancient observers oriented themselves by creating cognitive maps centered on notable urban features, not by referencing a regularized plan. Augustus exploited such experiential way-finding, giving his projects added importance as part of residents' urban ordering system. Of course, the individual interpretation of Rome depended on many factors, from the viewers' education, background, and mood, to the weather and activities on the day of observation. Yet the myriad impressions received while moving through Rome gained clarity and order by reliance on memorable design features such as landmarks, nodes, districts, paths, and edges (Lynch 1960). Augustan public projects stood out amid Rome's nondescript urban infill and drab Republican fabric. All were important in function, large in size, and embellished with eye-catching materials and rich decoration. As a result, many became landmarks used as reference points by Romans navigating through the city. When possible, Augustus ensured

FIGURE 46. View of Forum of Augustus with rear fire wall still standing. Photo by
D. Favro.

landmark status by selecting highly visible sites. The Mausoleum Augustum towering above the flat Campus Martius (Figs. 41, 43) and the
Temple of Apollo atop the Palatine Hill were visible from great distances. Notably, no one Augustan landmark assumed a dominant position. Scattered throughout the city, the new landmarks affirmed the
princeps' paternal benevolence for all.

Augustus also fashioned memorable nodes within the tightly wo-
ven Republican urban fabric. These centers of concentrated attraction
were formed by intersections or interrelated buildings associated with
significant, recurring activities. The *princeps* slowly redesigned and re-
programmed existing nodes and shifted attention to new ones. Above all,
he expended great sums embellishing the venerated Forum Romanum,
and provided additional porticoed open space in the magnificent adjacent fora named after Caesar and himself (Fig. 37). Continuing the
realignment begun by his adoptive father, Augustus brought order to
the Forum's Republican layout. He reinforced the northwest/southwest
axis defined laterally by the two huge basilicas, placing the new Temple of Divus Julius as its southern terminus opposite the great speakers'

platform (Rostra) surmounted with a golden statue of the *princeps*. Although he filled the node with memorials to himself and family, Augustus realized the potency and purity of Republican associations in the Forum Romanum. In response, he wisely transferred many significant activities to new Augustan venues. Increasingly, the Forum Romanum became more of a repository of history than an active governmental center. Nodal attraction shifted to the nearby Forum Augustum where many important events were relocated, including the granting of triumphs, selection of jurors by lot, and significant court cases.

Under the *princeps* a new urban node appeared atop the Palatine (Fig. 38). This hill had been the site of Rome's first settlement, memorialized in a replica of Romulus' thatched hut. Augustus fueled rumors that he had been born on the hill. In addition to buying a house in the Palatine's tony residential district, he erected several monuments. Over the main road up the hill from the Forum he dedicated an arch to his acknowledged human father, and crowned the memorial with a statue of Apollo, the god frequently alluded to as his real, divine father (Pliny, *Natural History* 36.36). Next to his own house, the *princeps* honored Apollo further with a magnificent complex including not only a grand temple, but also impressive porticos, and a dazzling array of artworks. Affirming the enhanced importance of the Palatine, many important activities moved to the hilltop. The growing imperial bureaucracy of state workers unobtrusively occupied houses purchased by Augustus near his own. Anxious to garner favor and ensure the participation of the *princeps* the Senate frequently met in the libraries of the Apollo complex (Dio 53.1.3), and the temple was prominently featured in many events, including the Secular Games that marked a new temporal cycle in 17 B.C. This new center became so powerful that the Palatine Hill threatened to eclipse the Republican religious center on the Capitoline Hill to the north.

The density of the Republican cityscape limited opportunities to establish memorable new districts. Only one distinctly Augustan district appeared: the Campus Martius. During the Republic this flood plain had been largely undeveloped. Improved drainage and flood control, as well as a new aqueduct, improved building conditions, turning the Campus into an urban *tabula rasa* begging for scripting. Augustus and his supporters constructed over twenty permanent structures in the district, restored others, and frequently erected temporary structures for large gatherings. Most projects had a recreational use, ranging from the Thermae Agrippae, great public baths with accompanying

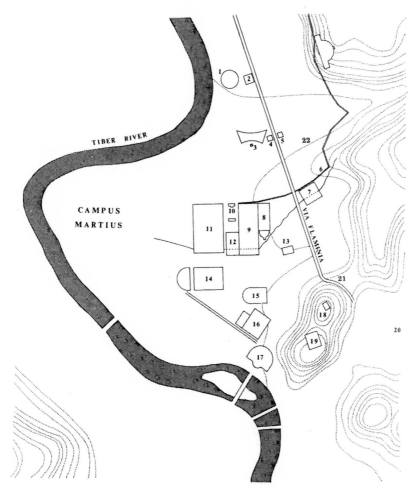

FIGURE 47. Map of Campus Martius, circa A.D. 10. 1. Mausoleum of Augustus; 2. Ustrinum Domus Augustae; 3. Horologium Augusti; 4. Ara Pacis; 5. Julio-Claudian Altar?; 6. Aqua Virgo; 7. Portico of Vipsania; 8. Divorum; 9. Saepta Julia; 10. Agrippan Pantheon; 11. Euripus; 12. Baths of Agrippa; 13. Temple of Mars; 14. Theater of Pompey; 15. Theater of Balbus; 16. Portico of Octavia; 17. Theater of Marcellus; 18. Temple of Juno Moneta; 19. Temple of Jupiter Optimus Maximus; 20. Forum Romanum; 21. Porta Fontinalis; 22. Campus Agrippae. Drawing by R. Reif.

parklands, to the Amphitheater of Statilius Taurus and Theater of Balbus. New additions generally maintained the orientation to the cardinal points established by early Republican temples. The result was a well-ordered district whose orthogonal plan contrasted markedly with the organic layout of the Republican city. Notably, the district addressed a specialized audience: foreign ambassadors and generals seeking permission to enter Rome waited in the sparkling pleasure zone. Looking over the Campus Martius Strabo concluded that its monuments, amenities, and overall cohesiveness gave "the impression that they are trying, as it were, to declare the rest of the city a mere accessory" (5.3.8; Fig. 47).

Carefully choreographed narrative pathways provided another urban ordering device. Ancient observers identified conceptual linkages between urban components encountered while moving through the city. Building upon a shared knowledge base, they wove disparate messages from repeated images, verbal signage, forms, and materials into cohesive narratives. Augustus and his architects scripted narratives by siting buildings along select urban paths. The relentlessly straight Via Flaminia on the eastern edge of the Campus Martius provided an ideal viewing platform and organizational device (Favro 1993). Beginning with a commemorative arch on the Milvian Bridge far to the north, observers encountered a sequence of memorable structures relating to the life and achievements of the *princeps* who appeared throughout in artworks and inscriptions. After following this route, visitors acknowledged Augustus had given Rome enduring stability embodied in the Mausoleum, peace and prosperity shown on the Ara Pacis, military success represented by the Egyptian obelisk, and sophisticated leisure evident in the entire Campus.

In most ancient cities, people oriented themselves in relation to the fortification walls. Augustan Rome had no hard edge. Over the centuries, urban building had extended far beyond the Republican walls. As a result, Rome of the *princeps* had a soft, variable edge, with a green belt of gardens marking the transition to the countryside. Dionysius of Halicarnassus wrote,

> If anyone wishes to estimate the size of Rome...he will necessarily be misled for want of a definite clue by which to determine up to what point it is still the city and where it ceases to be the city...giving the beholder the impression of a city stretching out indefinitely.
>
> (*Ant. Rom.* 4.13.4–5)

The absence of a finite urban edge created legal and jurisdictional problems, but had distinct propaganda advantages. While other cities might fear attack, Rome was capital of an expanding empire that was at peace within. Equating the city with empire, Ovid wrote, "the circuit (*spatium*) of Rome is the circuit of the world" (*Fasti* 2.684).

By the end of the first century B.C., Rome and her first citizen had redefined themselves and their aspirations. Rome's residents no longer wished to reestablish the Republican past. After decades of peace and prosperity and after watching the continuous building construction in their capital, the Romans acknowledged the specialness of their own time. Many agreed with Ovid who, after assessing the transformation to the capital proclaimed, "I congratulate myself that I was not born till now" (*Art of Love* 3.121–2). All wished for the glorious present to continue. The *princeps* himself made provisions for the endurance of his carefully crafted urban image. Vitruvius tells us he fashioned his architectural projects with an eye toward posterity, presenting them as "a memorial to future ages" (*Ten Books on Architecture* 1, pref. 3). The new Augustan structures of marble and other durable materials obviously were built to last. In addition, appointed boards maintained the urban infrastructure; fire and police forces protected people and buildings. Overall, the Augustan projects with their sparkling marble and crisp carvings gave the city a sanitized glow. The positive urban ambience complemented Rome's aggrandized physical extent, and was truly panurban in scope. On a practical level, observers freed from concerns of personal safety were able to relax and read the messages interwoven through the Augustan urban fabric.

Unlike individualistic Republican projects, those of the *princeps* formed a cohesive group in the minds of urban observers. Physical similarities established a linkage between dispersed projects. Partisans self-consciously copied Augustan buildings; other donors appeared to do so simply by following the fashion of the day and using available materials and craftsmen. An umbrella effect resulted. Whenever observers encountered a new structure of shining marble and classicizing ornament in the cityscape they immediately associated the work with the *princeps*, regardless of the actual donor. Thus even buildings erected by Octavian's political rivals in the years immediately after Caesar's death were later placed under the all-encompassing Augustan shadow. Such cumulative associations led to a conceptualization of all Rome as the result of a single man's vision. The message was reinforced by depictions of the man himself. From large sculptural displays to the images on coins jingling in the folds of patrician togas, the visage of Augustus appeared throughout Rome. Confronted over and over with the same face, residents did not have to ask who was *pater urbis* as well as *pater patriae*.

The potency of the Augustan urban image was especially empowered by being part of a comprehensive social, cultural, religious, and political program. Parallel developments in literature, art, and social programming reinforced and enriched the meaning of each urban intervention. For example, Augustan social reforms emphasizing modesty supported decorum in house design, and vice versa. Poetry touting a new golden age found concrete expression in the sparkling materials of the new buildings. Simply, Augustan propaganda was pervasive in the city, and in the lives of all residents. After decades of divisiveness, Rome's residents felt reassured by the unity of thought pervading Rome. Furthermore, they felt personally engaged. All levels of society had opportunities to participate in the care and protection of Rome; all were able to comprehend the Augustan system of ideas and ideals. For example, learned observers interpreted the intricate mythological figures carved on the Ara Pacis, while the uneducated surely appreciated the accessible and universal message of prosperity depicted by the carvings of lush plants (Figs. 22–24, 27–30; cf. Galinsky, 1996, 141–55). Such multivalence helps to explain the vibrancy of Rome for both local observers and those from throughout the Mediterranean.

On many levels, Augustan Rome became the theater of the world (*theatrum mundi*) where all important decisions and events occurred. To promote this image, the *princeps* revived and enhanced communal rituals, giving all a decidedly Augustan slant. In addition to new theaters and amphitheaters, virtually all large urban projects were consciously designed to be stages for public performances (cf. Chapter 7 by Richard Beacham, this volume). The theatricality of Augustan urban interventions led Strabo to choose a stage painting as the most apt metaphor for the newly developed Campus Martius (5.3.8). Communal experiences drew together all participants, and the diverse environments of Rome. Celebrations on the same date associated buildings scattered across the cityscape; parades wending through city streets kinetically linked various projects along selected pathways. People from throughout the world participated. Seneca later wrote, "Come, look at this crowd, which all the buildings of the vast city can scarcely house: the great majority of them have left their birthplaces behind them. From their towns and colonies, indeed from the whole world they have flooded together" (*De tranquillitate animi* 2). Augustus accommodated these diverse peoples by sponsoring performances in all languages (Suet., *Augustus* 43). He himself never stopped playing to the audience; on his deathbed he quoted a line by the playwright

PLATE I. *Aureus* of Octavian, minted in the province of Asia, 28 B.C. The obverse has the typical legend: IMP(ERATOR) CAESAR DIVI F(ILIUS), "son of the Deified" (Julius) and marks the year of his sixth consulship. The reverse (see text on pp. 23–4) refers to Octavian's restitution of laws and rights to the Romans, which may have been announced in a senate decree. The togate figure of Octavian, seated on the official chair of the highest magistrates (*sella curulis*) and holding a scroll in his right, may be based on a lost statue. British Museum, Department of Coins and Medals, CM 1995.4-1.1. Photo: Copyright The British Museum.

Detail of Egyptianizing frieze. North wall of Tablinum 2 of the Villa of Mysteries, Pompeii, circa 20–1 B.C. Photo: Michael Larvey.

The images in this section are available in colour as a download from www.cambridge.org/9780521807968

PLATE II. Cubiculum of the Villa of P. Fannius Synistor at Boscoreale, circa 60–40 B.C. The Metropolitan Museum of Art, NY, Rogers Fund, 1903 (03.14.13a–g). Photograph © 1986, The Metropolitan Museum of Art.

PLATE III. Room of the Masks of the House of Augustus on the Palatine, Rome. South and west walls, circa 40–20 B.C. Photo: Helmut Nils Loose; permission by Soprintendenza Archeologica di Roma.

PLATE IV. Augustus' study, House of Augustus, Rome. Details of the north wall, circa 40–20 B.C. Photos: DAIR F82.427 and F82.423.

PLATE V. Rear wall of the alcove of cubiculum B. Villa under the Farnesina, Rome, circa 20–1 B.C. Photo: Soprintendenza Archeologica di Roma.

PLATE VI. North wall of the "red" cubiculum 16 of the Villa of Agrippa Postumus at Boscotrecase, circa 20–1 B.C. Photo: Michael Larvey.

PLATE VII. Bucolic landscape with statue of a goddess. Detail of Plate VI. Photo: Michael Larvey.

PLATE VIII. Left wall of the alcove of cubiculum B. Villa under the Farnesina, Rome, circa 20–1 B.C. Photo: Soprintendenza Archeologica di Roma.

Menander, "Since well I've played my part, all clap your hands/And from the stage dismiss me with applause" (Suet., *Augustus* 99; cf. Eder, p. 13, and Beacham, p. 173).

Augustus played well the parts of *pater urbis* and *pater patriae*. His impact on Rome was lasting and widespread. Many of his projects remained landmarks in the cityscape for centuries and inspired imitation. The Forum Augustum with its great exedrae served as the model for the adjacent Forum of Trajan (a heritage reinforced by recent excavations revealing the existence of two additional exedrae; see Figs. 37 and 49); the Mausoleum of Augustus inspired the form of Hadrian's tomb, and so on. Although he had not applied a mechanical master plan, in many cases the interventions of the *princeps* established enduring urban patterns. The Augustan alignment of buildings in the Forum Romanum was followed with only slight modifications throughout the imperial period. The new Augustan node created on the Palatine became the eponymous nucleus for Rome's great imperial, "palatial," residences. Extensively exploited by Augustus, the use of multicolored, richly carved marble became a hallmark of Roman imperial construction not only in Rome, but throughout the world. Similarly, the highly decorative Corinthian order became all pervasive. Overall Augustan Rome served as the incubator for "Empire Imagery," establishing the architectural symbols, forms, materials, and configurations which characterized Roman imperial cities for generations (MacDonald 1985).

Looking at the city of Augustus Vitruvius granted that at last, "the majesty of the empire was expressed through the eminent dignity of Rome's buildings" (*Ten Books on Architecture* 1, pref. 2; Fig. 37). The entire Mediterranean basin acknowledged the city as capital of an Empire and of an emperor (MacMullen 2000). Augustus took pains to prevent other cities from rivaling Rome. Municipalities were encouraged to assume honorific family names as "Augusta" or "Caesarea," rather than repeat the sacred name of the capital, thereby honoring him and his family without impinging on the uniqueness of Rome. The *princeps* and ambitious locals filled provincial cities with projects emulating Augustan works in the capital. For example, the citizens of Augusta Emerita (Merida) precisely modeled their new civic center after the Forum Augustum; the client king of Iol Caesarea (Cherchel) imported Italian masons and marble to recreate the column capitals of the Mars Ultor Temple. Such reverential undertakings provided an outlet for allegiance and self-aggrandizement without threatening the central authority. Funding for new colonial cities as well as roads, walls, aqueducts, theaters, and other amenities flowed out from the capital to her dependencies. Two architectural programs stand out in the provincial context. In Rome Augustus had shown no interest in low prestige market buildings, yet he avidly promoted their construction in the provinces in an effort to stimulate trade. In the capital the *princeps* had discouraged constructions of temples in his own honor, yet as early as 29 B.C. he allowed the provinces to follow local traditions and honor him as a god, though insisting his worship always be joined with that to the goddess Roma.

Capital cities are by their very nature containers of collective aspirations. The Republican cityscape of Rome had conveyed the independence and divisiveness of her occupants and government. The urban image became focused only when power coalesced. As Augustus and the state redefined their roles, the cityscape reflected the change. Dressing as the capital of an empire Rome received opulent, large-scale, refined architecture and a structured urban layout that could be appreciated by a global audience. Augustus forged an urban image that was irrevocably Roman, yet just as irrevocably centered upon himself. The achievement was not easily repeated. As soon as physical enhancements to Rome became commonalities, as soon as Rome operated on a global stage, and as soon as other cities copied the capital, the clarity of the Augustan urban image began to fade. Subsequent emperors attempted to impress their own stamp on the city, yet few had the same means, ability, or opportunities, especially since they occupied a capital already transformed. Their additions never had the same dramatic effect as those instituted at the poignant moment when Republican Rome began to dress as an imperial city and stand on a world stage.

SUGGESTIONS FOR FURTHER READING

In *Augustan Rome* (1993), Andrew Wallace-Hadrill succinctly situates the city within its political and cultural context. For walking around Rome, A. Claridge, *Rome. An Oxford Archaeological Guide* (Oxford University Press 1998) is an indispensable and accessible, up-to-date guide. More detailed and comprehensive coverage of buildings from the Augustan Age is found in the detailed catalog and technically advanced maps by L. Haselberger and a team from the University of Pennsylvania, *Mapping Augustan Rome* (2002). In *The Urban Image of*

Augustan Rome (1996), I attempt an experiential and urbanistic analysis of the overall cityscape at the turn of the millennium. The calculated exchange between art and urban environments is explored by S. Walker in "The Moral Museum: Augustus and the city of Rome," in J. Coulston and H. Dodge, eds., *Ancient Rome: The Archaeology of the Eternal City* (Oxbow Books 2000).

11: AUGUSTAN DOMESTIC INTERIORS: PROPAGANDA OR FASHION?

John R. Clarke

We have ample documentation, both from archaeological finds and in ancient texts, for interior decoration in the age of Augustus. In Rome itself we have considerable remains of the wall and ceiling painting from Augustus' own house on the Palatine, as well as the painted and stucco decorations from a villa that may have belonged to Agrippa and Julia. At Boscotrecase, near Pompeii, archaeologists excavated several rooms of a villa that may have belonged to Agrippa's son, Postumus. Vitruvius, an architect who dedicated his treatise to the Emperor around 20 B.C., describes the established style of wall painting and then goes on to complain about a new style coming into vogue at the moment. Pliny the Elder discusses the work of a certain Studius active during the Augustan age, crediting him with inventing a special kind of landscape painting.

Art historians and archaeologists have studied these Augustan monuments and texts with great intensity and considerable imagination. The resulting narratives make a broad range of claims. The earlier accounts focussed on chronology (Mau 1882; Beyen 1938–1960); in Mau's famous dating scheme of the Four Styles of Romano-Campanian painting, the paintings from Augustus' house on the Palatine (circa 30 B.C.) mark the midpoint of the last phase of the Second Style (40–20 B.C.), and those of the villa of Agrippa and Julia (dubbed the Villa under the Farnesina) mark the transition from the Second to the Third Style (about 20 B.C.). The Villa at Boscotrecase then serves as the finest example of early Third Style painting (15–1 B.C.)

More recent studies have analyzed the imagery of these key monuments as reflections of the mentality of the Augustan age. One scholar has proposed that nearly every aspect of the new decorative systems for walls and ceilings – from their representation of thinned-out, miniature architecture to the content of pictures and stuccoes – reflected Augustan cultural propaganda (Zanker 1988). Another scholar has argued that wall painters, like the poets of the period, expressed Augustan ideals through their imagery (Leach 1988). Some have characterized the appearance of Egyptian motifs in the visual arts as an "Egyptomania" inspired by Agrippa's and Augustus' triumph over Egypt (de Vos 1980), and others have expanded Pliny's account of Studius through analysis of the landscape paintings found in excavations in Rome and Campania (Ling 1977).

In what follows, I reassess these and other scholarly narratives by considering Augustan-age decorations in their architectural contexts. If the walls are speaking to the viewer, what are they saying? Are they in fact preaching an Augustan ideology of neoclassicism, piety, and restraint, or do they simply express a new, elegant, and much-copied fashion in interior decoration? In assessing stylistic change in Augustan wall painting, it is necessary to distinguish between art and fashion. The changes in styles of high art are slower, and follow more predictable patterns, than changes in fashion (Kubler 1962). The decoration of the interior surfaces of a house – even the house of the Emperor – could be highly refined, but hardly the stuff of high art. In contrast to works of Greek artists brought to Rome and placed on display, the paintings, stuccoes, and mosaics in the houses and villas of the Augustan age were the work of skilled artisans intent on providing fashionable backgrounds to the business of everyday life.

CHANGES IN DECORATIVE SYSTEMS DURING THE AUGUSTAN AGE

We can get a sense of the magnitude of the changes in decoration during the age of Augustus by examining a room painted in the dominant style of the mid-first century. The trompe l'oeil perspectives of the mature Second Style (60–40 B.C.) transformed the room into a kind of colonnaded pavilion. The painter employed all the techniques of illusionism to create a range of architectural forms that seemed like real architectural features both to project in front of the actual wall plane and to recede behind it. In the well-preserved cubiculum from the Villa at Boscoreale the effects are dazzling (Plate II). The dominant illusion is that the room is a colonnaded pavilion. The artist creates this illusion by representing regularly-spaced supports around the room's perimeter. In the anteroom, red marble columns adorned with gold filigree rest on a podium; in the alcove for the bed, bossed pilasters extend from the floor to the cornice. Complex scenes open up between these columnar supports. On the walls of the anteroom the painter constructed cityscapes behind doors to either side of an elaborate central gate. On the sides of the alcove the painter represented the entrance to a sanctuary, complete with a view of a round temple enclosed in a two-story peristyle that opens up behind the gate. The rear wall takes up a different theme: a rocky landscape tamed by a grotto with spring below and a semicircular arbor above.

Many scholars have seen in each theme – cityscape with doors, entrance to sanctuary, and landscape – the translation into wall painting of the comic, tragic, and satyric sets from the theater (a notion finding some support in the passage from Vitruvius discussed below). Indeed, the Second-Style artist may have learned his craft from theatrical scene-painters. The paintings show that he knew the rules of perspective and commanded the techniques of trompe-l'oeil painting, since in addition to creating architectural vistas he had to be able to produce the effects of light and shadow as they appeared on various objects: colored marbles, gilded tracery, theatrical masks, ritual vessels, and glass bowls of fruit. He probably received his training in Alexandria, Athens, or in one of the important cities of Southern Italy, Magna Graecia.

Recently, scholars have challenged the long-standing notion that the Second Style emerged from stage decoration. Some believe that the Second Style originated in wall painters' imitation of the precious materials and elaborate architectural forms of Hellenistic palaces (Fittschen 1976). Others propose that the paintings from Boscoreale belong to a genre of "porticus" paintings that represent the extravagant architecture of the villas of the very rich. In this scenario, it is possible to link the mature Second Style with a workshop in the region around Pompeii whose prosperous patrons wanted to impress visitors with walls mimicking the flamboyant excesses of plutocrats (Leach 1982). Whatever the precise connections with the theater were, it is clear that wall-painters were creating a kind of stage setting for the owner and his guests. Whether the fictive colonnaded rooms of the Second Style imitated the throne rooms of the Hellenistic dynasts, or whether they symbolized the princely luxury introduced into Italy by Roman generals of the late Republic, this kind of interior decoration clearly had strong associations with grandiose display, bordering on the regal. Personal political clout, accompanied by a regal personal image and sustained by shifting alliances and intrigue, was the order of the day. When the Second Style became simpler and more staid in its last phase, some scholars argue it was a response to the sober code of behavior that Augustus advocated for public figures.

VITRUVIUS AND THE NEW AESTHETICS OF LATE SECOND-STYLE PAINTING, CIRCA 40–20 B.C.

Despite his avowed devotion to Augustus, Vitruvius bristled at the changes in wall painting that he witnessed in the first ten years of Augustus' reign. In *On Architecure* Book 7, Chapter 5, he describes the development of the Second Style: "Then they proceeded to imitate the contours of buildings, the outstanding projections of columns and gables; in open spaces, like exedrae, they designed scenery on a large scale in tragic, comic, or satyric style." As we have seen, the cubiculum from the Villa at Boscoreale illustrates the salient characteristics of the mature Second Style of Vitruvius's description, and could even present the three scenic modes: the side walls of the anteroom could represent the comic setting; the side walls of the alcove the tragic; and the rocky garden and grotto the satyric. Yet by the time Vitruvius was writing, this solid perspective-based fictive architecture was fast disappearing, much to his displeasure:

> But these subjects which were imitations based upon reality are now disdained by the improper taste of the present. Monstrosities rather than definite representations taken from definite things are painted on the plaster. Instead of columns there rise up stalks; instead of pediments, striped panels with curled leaves and volutes. Candelabra sustain representations of shrines and above the summits of these, clusters of thin stalks rise from their roots in tendrils with little figures seated upon them at random, or shoots split in half, some holding little statues with human heads, some with the heads of beasts. Now such things do not exist nor can they exist nor have they ever existed, and thus this new fashion has brought things to such a pass that bad judges have condemned the right practice of the arts as lack of skill.
>
> (*De arch.* 7.5.3–4)

Vitruvius attributes people's acceptance of the new decorative conventions in wall painting to their understanding, so "darkened by imperfect standards of taste," that they accept what cannot exist in reality.

I doubt that Vitruvius represents progressive thinking during the early Augustan period. The discussion following his outburst discloses a possible motive for it: to allow him to plead for representational art against the new abstraction which had taken over interior decoration. Vitruvius advocates a commonsense art that looks "real." In particular, he wants architectural perspectives that convince the viewer of their ability to do what traditional architecture does in reality: support weight in all the variations of post-and-lintel construction. Vitruvius believes that art should conform to nature, and he wants to persuade his readers to abandon the excesses of the new, fanciful representations of architecture. When one realizes that Vitruvius's diatribe arises from his naive conception that the only proper decorative schemes are those that create convincing illusionistic architecture, his reasoning seems reactionary. After all, no one ever believed that mere painted columns actually supported the ceiling or that a windowless wall really opened to the idyllic, sacred, or urban architecture pictured there. Like the decorations of ceilings and floors, even the highly illusionistic perspectives on the walls articulated flat surfaces.

High-quality wall painting from Augustus' own house, and dating to about 30 B.C., illustrates the very changes that Vitruvius decries. The central reception space of a wing of Augustus' house on the Palatine in Rome (called the 'House of Livia' because a water pipe bearing her name was found in the excavations) announces the two most fundamental and long-lasting changes in wall decoration (Fig. 48). The first change is the introduction of the aedicula, a pavilionlike structure with columns supporting a pediment. The aedicula replaces the regularly-spaced columns of the mature Second Style and shifts the viewer's attention to the center of the wall. The second change is the introduction of pictures within the central aedicula.

In effect, these pictures replaced perspectives. They shifted the viewer's attention from the perspective system designed for the whole room to a single axial focus on each wall – the picture in the aedicula – with all perspectives converging on the aedicula. When views of architecture do appear "behind" the wall, the perspectives are shallow and arranged symmetrically in rectangular openings to right and left of the central aedicula. In addition to the big mythological paintings (only two are preserved), the artist has represented little paintings with shutters resting atop ledges in the upper zone to right and left of

FIGURE 48. Rome, 'House of Livia,' Tablinum C. circa 40–20 B.C. Photo: Anderson/Art Resource, NY, 420.

the aediculae. From this point forward in Roman wall decoration, the motif of the central aedicula framing a painting dominates almost every wall-painting scheme.

Two rooms from the south wing of the house illustrate further aspects of the late Second Style. As the plan demonstrates, excavators were unable to determine just how this wing, called the House of Augustus, originally connected with the so-called House of Livia. The Room of the Masks (Plate III) announces its spare aesthetics in a scheme focused on a plain central aedicula on each wall. Each aedicula frames hazy, nearly monochrome landscape paintings. Contemporary viewers accustomed to overloaded mature Second-Style rooms like the Boscoreale cubiculum must have marveled at its plainness – especially the way the decoration simplifies the complicated perspectives characteristic of the earlier style. Although the artist has articulated the flat wall with architectural features that seem to recede and project, this is a far less demanding illusion than that of the Boscoreale cubiculum of twenty years before. What is more, the aedicula on the longer south wall (to the left in the photograph) is less substantial than the one in Room C of the House of Livia; only thin yellow columns support the gabled roof. To right and left of this aedicula are segments of cinnabar-red walls. Two half-aediculae framing doors complete the composition, although they do not reach the corners. This entire construction rests on a white podium that itself rests on a purple-brown platform running around the room's perimeter.

If the south wall's design represents a fairly timid version of the central aedicular composition, that of the west wall attempts grander spatial effects, with heavy columns supporting the aedicula's convex gable, and three yellow piers of rectangular section pushing out to either side. But the artist has radically thinned the piers and compressed their spatial illusion so that they will fit on the same white podium as the more timid columns on the south wall. And – again in contrast to the mature Second Style – the spaces behind this shallow perspective construction are themselves shallow and pale: no cityscapes or temple precincts here. Fantastic creatures balance on the outer edges of the gables, and the theatrical masks that gave the room its name sit on the walls to either side of the aediculae. As in the House of Livia, white-ground paintings in pale shades contrast with the bold colors of the architectural framework. The viewer discovers the greatest depth of perspective in the central pictures.

Scholars have characterized the frescoes of the Room of the Masks as representations of wooden theater sets standing on the podium of a stone theater. In this way they explain the thinness of the columns and piers. The excavator of the Room of the Masks believed that the land-scape paintings represent cloth hangings used to set theatrical scenes (Carettoni 1983). I doubt that painters had such a stock in reproduc-ing theatrical sets literally; the eclectic representations of thinned and flattened architectural elements act as frames for the central pictures. By deemphasizing "real" architecture, the artist draws the viewer to the center pictures and their meanings.

MINIATURISM AND EGYPTIANIZING ORNAMENT

Some scholars believe that the small but finely-painted room at the southeast corner of the House of Augustus was the "Syracuse" or *techno-phyon* ("little workshop") mentioned by Suetonius (*Augustus* 72.2), an elevated room where the emperor retired when he wanted to work in private or without interruption (Plate IV). Whether it is the Syracuse or not, Room 15 demonstrates two other themes that begin in the late Second Style and develop markedly in the Third: miniaturism and Egyptianizing ornament. Miniature friezes, vegetal ornaments, and fantastic creatures encouraged the observer to move close to the wall to examine the precise and inventive details; this closeup viewing contrasted sharply with the distant viewing position needed to understand the perspectives of the mature Second Style. These fantastic miniatures are, of course, the very innovations that incited Vitruvius' disapproval.

At close range, the viewer marvels at the delicacy of the ornament. A frieze of stylized lotuses on a black background defines an upper zone just below the aedicula's architrave. The frieze runs "behind" a column *en ressaut*, that is, a column holding a section of architrave that seems to project from the wall surface. On the ledge defined by the black frieze sits a fantastic metal vessel composed of lotus petals and supported improbably on a tiny base (Plate IV). Monochrome panels, probably representing marble bas-reliefs, decorate the wall (Plate IV). In them we see stylized flowers, more vessels, and, at the top of the wall, a black-ground frieze with facing swans holding up swagged garlands. In another place, the painter introduced the more properly "Egyptian" motif of cranes poised on cobras (*uraei*).

One painted room, called the Aula Isiaca because of its Egyptian ornament and first recorded by F. Bartoli in 1721, may have been part of Augustus' house (Ling 1991). Decorative motifs in its frieze includes atef crowns, uraei, heraldic ibises, and panels with Egyptianizing figures, including one with a priestess of Isis. The mythological landscapes, now for the most part lost, included non-Egyptian themes taken from classical mythology (Iacopi 1997).

With the wall decorations from the Villa under the Farnesina in Rome (dated to 19 B.C. by scholars who wish its owners to be Agrippa and Julia), we arrive at the end of the Second Style. The architecture thins dramatically, perspectives become simpler and shallower, and new elements appear. Egyptianizing ornament, already present in the House of Augustus, seems to take precedence over the architecture. Carefully painted lotus-bud capitals and friezes, palmettes, rosettes, and symbols of the cult of Isis appear everywhere. A detail of the decoration of cubiculum B illustrates the changes (Plate V). Although the aedicula framing the center picture is relatively substantial, the proportions of the columns are quite tall. Ornate easels hold up pictures on either side of the aedicula. Everywhere the artist emphasizes linear ornament, and there are no views into architecture "behind" the wall plane. As in the House of Augustus, the painting in the aedicula now provides the spatial depth once achieved by architectural perspectives in the mature Second Style. Most characteristics of the Third Style are present in one form or other: central aediculae, attenuated architecture, avoidance of perspectives that pierce the wall, monochrome rooms, love of miniaturistic details, Egyptianizing motifs, and the proliferation of painted representation of pictures.

If the transition is clear, the precise beginning of the Third Style is a matter of controversy. One firm date seems to be the paintings of the tomb chamber of the Pyramid of Cestius in Rome, completed in 15 B.C. Unfortunately, the paintings are fragmentary. Wall paintings from the villa of Agrippa Postumus at Boscotrecase, near Pompeii, are of the highest quality but of uncertain date.

Analysis of the red cubiculum from Boscotrecase (Plate VI) shows how the tendency to flatten the wall went to the extreme. The viewer has to search for an indication of foreshortened architectural members because every element of the scheme – base, aedicula in the middle zone, and architectural members in the upper zone – has become a preciously detailed miniature. There is no illusion of architectural members projecting forward or receding behind the actual wall plane. If this Third-Style scheme restores the wall to its actuality as a flat surface, it is because it has systematically eliminated illusionistic perspectives. Only in the central picture does illusionism reign, in a miniature pastoral landscape floating on a white ground (Plate VII).

THE "INVENTION" OF THE THIRD STYLE: THE BOSCOTRECASE WORKSHOP AND STUDIUS

This survey of the fairly rapid and seemingly dramatic changes in styles of interior decoration during the age of Augustus suggests a purpose that goes beyond the merely formal concerns of the decorator or architect. Were patrons tired of the theatrics of Second-Style schemes, so that painters invented simpler, flatter, and more restful compositions, or did the new style emanate from the court of Augustus himself? Who was the first artist to flatten the wall radically and to make pictures the object of the viewer's attention? If the Villa under the Farnesina belonged to Agrippa and Julia, it is possible to link this villa in Rome with the one at Boscotrecase, which Agrippa would have willed to his posthumously-born son. The Farnesina would have been decorated on Agrippa's return to Rome in 19 B.C. Here is one proposed scenario:

The atelier must have been the outstanding one of its time; it could boast of work "by appointment of the court." Here were the best and the most advanced painters leading the way towards a new form of decoration in spite of Vitruvius' and perhaps other conservatives' denunciation. Protected and perhaps encouraged by the Emperor's daughter and her husband, the most progressive and talented among these painters became the founders of what we call the Third Style. One of these, probably the finest, was again commissioned to work for the Imperial family, this time as a leading painter in the Campanian villa near Boscotrecase belonging to the just deceased Agrippa.

> (Blanckenhagen and Alexander 1990, 47f.)

The passage continues, characterizing this unknown artist through analysis of individual paintings, noting that because he was a painter to the imperial court, he was widely copied in Pompeii: "A painter of the most elegant and sophisticated set at the Imperial court where Ovid and his taste ruled supreme." In this way the authors chart the transmission of the Third Style to Pompeii and identify two artistic personalities: the Farnesina painter and the Boscotrecase painter.

Not everyone accepts this explanation. Some would date the Villa at Boscotrecase to A.D. 1–25 – too late to fit this "court painter" hypothesis. The definitive publication of the Villa under the Farnesina also takes a conservative approach, even though the authors claim that the artist in the workshop consciously used the Egyptianizing elements in its decoration to allude to the triumph of Augustus and Agrippa over Egypt, celebrated in 29 B.C. In their scheme, artists copying this Roman workshop's innovations brought the Third Style to Pompeii and its surrounding area (Bragantini and de Vos 1982).

It is also possible to take a literary approach to find the author of the Third Style. One scholar explores Pliny the Elder's account of Studius, a painter of the Augustan period who was the first major figure in a new genre of landscape painting (Ling 1977). It is worth quoting Pliny's passage:

> Nor must Studius, active during the time of the Divine Augustus, be cheated of the praise he deserves. It was he who first instituted that most delightful technique of painting walls with representations of villas, porticoes and landscape gardens, woods, groves, hills, pools, channels, rivers,

coastline – in fact, every sort of thing which one might want, and also various representations of people within them walking or sailing, or, back on land, arriving at villas on ass-back or in carriages, and also fishing, flowing, or hunting or even harvesting the wine-grapes. There are also specimens among his pictures of notable villas which are accessible only through marshy ground, and of women who, as the result of an agreement, are carried along on the shoulders of men who totter along beneath the restless burdens which are being carried, and many other lively subjects of this sort indicative of a sharp wit. This artist also began the practice of painting representations of seaside towns on the walls of open galleries, thus producing a charming view with minimal expense.

(Pliny, *Natural History* 35.37.116–117)

After linking Pliny's account with a similar one from Vitruvius, our modern author characterizes this artist's contribution: his role was "the bringing to perfection of a whole genre of peopled architectural landscape in wall painting." He also suggests that Studius may have been the founder of one of the leading ateliers which decorated the three houses thought to be connected with the imperial family (the House of Livia, the Farnesina, and Boscotrecase).

However, analysis of the landscape paintings from the sites mentioned reveals more variety than unity in style. For example, the size of the figures in relation to the landscape varies greatly. In the mythological painting of Io and Argus from the House of Livia (see Fig. 48), the figures are quite large, yet in the central paintings from the Villa at Boscotrecase they are tiny, and the landscape itself is an isolated floating triangle within the pictorial space (Plate VII). Whether Studius was also responsible for the fantastic thinned-out architecture that so annoyed Vitruvius, or whether he only painted landscape pictures in a variety of formats, we will never know.

We do know that the reduction of trompe l'oeil architecture called for new skills that focused on miniatures and on the central picture. If the complex perspectives of the mature Second Style called for artists who could imitate regal architecture, the styles of decoration during the Augustan age required artists who could invent fantastic architectural miniatures and those able to paint convincing center pictures. Nearly-exact replicas of pictures in different houses at Pompeii and its surrounding area suggest that these picture-painters used model-books. Patrons could choose the pictures they wanted from the model-books. Unfinished wall decorations show that the ordinary wall painters would do their work first, leaving the rectangle of unfinished plaster for the picture-painter, who painted guidelines on the penultimate layer of plaster to aid him in achieving his composition (Moormann 1995).

THE PINACOTHECA AND THE CULTURE OF CONNOISSEURSHIP AND COLLECTING

It is in the analysis of these center pictures and their place in wall-decorative schemes that we get the most convincing evidence for the changed aesthetics and perhaps the new ideology of the period between 30 B.C. and A.D. 14. For one thing, although it is true that the miniature friezes filled with fantastic creatures, and sometimes with Egyptian motifs, encouraged the viewer to come close to the wall, the central picture takes up much more of the wall area (Plate I). For another, on the basis of our knowledge of ancient Roman viewers, analysis of paintings centers on ekphrasis, the fanciful explanation of mythological pictures. Ekphrasis was a common after-dinner exercise, when guests would vie with each other in extracting meanings from pictures in galleries called pinacothecae, or picture galleries (Bartsch 1989). Such picture-collections must have included paintings in a variety of styles, to judge from painted representations of pinacothecae like the Farnesina cubiculum (Plate V). Whether the pinacotheca was a real picture-gallery or a painted representation of a picture gallery, it encouraged the viewer and the owner to wax eloquent about the meanings of the paintings. In this way the pinacotheca encoded social roles quite different from those appropriate in earlier decorative schemes.

If the First Style's seemingly substantial marbles and moldings attempted to transform the house into the image of great public buildings, and the Second Style's grandiose, lavishly ornamented colonnades and sanctuaries depicted spaces fit for a king, the Third Style's picture galleries presented the owner as a person of culture, connoisseur of the great Greek masterpieces. It may be that the new civic-minded sobriety promulgated by Augustus also encouraged the development of the Third-Style picture gallery. Augustus encouraged individuals to give up their private collections of great pictures and sculptures for public display (Leach 1982; Wallace-Hadrill 1988). The Roman citizen was to keep a quiet private profile, in sharp contrast to the lavish personal display and bombast of the Late Republic (Leach 1982). Both the artist and patron must have conceived schemes like that of the tablinum in the House of Livia and cubiculum B of the Farnesina as imitation pinacothecae.

The designers of Third-Style imitation pinacothecae followed the conventions of the real-life model. Elaborate aediculae frame the paintings at the centers of each wall. Display of the smaller pictures is equally elaborate. In the Farnesina cubiculum, ornate easels in the form of sirens hold up archaizing pictures to either side of the central aedicula. Along the side walls of the same cubiculum round-headed aedicula frame the central pictures, and small erotic pictures with shutters resting on a ledge (the one on the right has been stolen), with black-ground painting in octagonal frames between them (Plate VIII). The fact that these representations of paintings each call up a different identifiable style from the past suggests that the ancient viewer was to see them with a connoisseur's eye: here a drawing on marble in the Greek archaic style, here a copy of the full-blown illusionistic paintings of the fourth century B.C., and so on. Even the erotic paintings spoke to the Augustan-age connoisseur, if Ovid's letter to Augustus, written around A.D. 10, is any gauge:

> Even in your house, just as figures of great men of old shine
> painted by some-artist's hand, so somewhere a small picture
> depicts the various forms of copulation and the sexual posi-
> tions. Telamonian Ajax sulks in rage, barbarian Medea glares
> infanticide, but there's Venus as well, wringing her dripping
> hair dry with her hands and barely covered by the waters
> that bore her.
>
> (*Tristia* 2.521–28)

In describing the picture gallery, Ovid mentions mythological paintings of Ajax and Medea, but also reminds the emperor that his picture collection, if it was a worthy one, included paintings that represented various sexual positions, and at least one painting of Venus, the goddess of love, beautiful – and stark naked, albeit covered by water.

PROPAGANDA, IDEOLOGY, OR DECORATION?

Anyone who delves into the rich contemporary literature on the role of the visual arts in the age of Augustus will find claims that particular center pictures, decorative details, or even complex decorative ensembles including painting, stuccoes, and mosaics, expressed aspects of "propaganda" promulgated by Augustus and his circle. More even-handed accounts make the modest claim that these forms of interior decoration partake in the renewal of old-fashioned religious ritual that Augustus sponsored. Rather than claiming any self-conscious attempt on the part of Augustus or other patrons to express a new ideology in their domestic decorations, I would argue that fashion – whether in dress, grooming, speech, or interior decoration – is part of a larger discourse and therefore the modern interpreter runs the risk of overde-termining individual details of any specific part of that discourse. In short, to understand the dominant ideology of the Augustan age, the historian must assess the weight of all its signs. Despite our luck of hav-ing so many examples, in the form of preserved decorated rooms and textual testimony, of one sign of Augustan visual culture, I believe that interior decor, and even that of Augustus' own house, was at best a mi-nor part of the dominant discourse. We should extrapolate larger claims about the spirit of the age from more important signs, such as imperial portraiture in sculpture and on coins, expensive building programs in Rome and throughout the empire, and major literary texts.

Seen in the context of the hugely expensive projects that Augustus and his allies patronized, the relatively inexpensive decoration of his house was in keeping with the *princeps'* refusal to surround himself with luxury: no marble columns, old master paintings, or famous statues. Even the highly-competent imitation picture-galleries in the Villa under the Farnesina were, after all, carried out by skilled wall-decorators and constituted inexpensive and durable substitutes for the real thing. The new conception of interior decoration that arose during the reign of Augustus might have upset Vitruvius, but probably caused no more of a stir among élite Romans than the reinstatement of toga wearing.

What is more, current scholarship suggests that the seemingly rapid diffusion of the new style to the area around the Bay of Naples may not have been so rapid after all. In my study of the painting and mosaic decoration of the huge and opulent Villa of Oplontis, built around 40 B.C., I found that the Third Style did appear, but only when, after about forty years' worth of wear, a group of rooms had to be replastered, and an addition to the villa got new pavements and wall paintings in the new style. Significantly, the owner opted to keep five of the Second-Style rooms just as they were: as "period" rooms (Clarke 1987).

The new fashions in interior decoration – sober, elegant, attentive to detail – were just that: expressions of a changed aesthetic promoted by decorators. The miraculously-preserved paintings, stuccoes, and mosaics from Augustus' house, along with the other interior decorations datable to the age of Augustus, allow us to imagine the setting for the rituals of daily, domestic life. These were not "talking walls," their imagery preaching religious or moral lessons to the men, women, and children who looked at them. Rather, their allusions to the sacred grove, the Roman landscape, and the picture gallery, if anything, reminded their viewers of themes from high art that clever wall painters had learned to integrate into the new taste for moderation in interior design.

SUGGESTIONS FOR FURTHER READING

For an overview of the painting and mosaics in Roman Italy, see Clarke (1991). See Ling (1991) for painting throughout the empire. Leach (1988) is especially useful for questions of patronage and ideology. For the Villa under the Farnesina, see Bragantini and de Vos (1982); for the House of Augustus, Carettoni (1983); for the Villa of Agrippa Postumus, von Blanckenhagen and Alexander (1990). Zanker (1988) and Galinsky (1996) are especially useful in framing the cultural context of artistic production under Augustus.

PART V

AUGUSTAN LITERATURE

12: LEARNED EYES: POETS, VIEWERS, IMAGE MAKERS

Alessandro Barchiesi

Periodizations are tools that very few trust but everybody uses. Some periodizations become more popular than others: the Augustan Age, as this volume will no doubt confirm, has achieved unparalleled stability among the many constructs of historicism. This result has many authors, but what is really striking is that the process of stabilization is initiated by poets contemporary with Augustus, people who pioneer the claim (Horace, *Odes* 4.15.4: *tua, Caesar, aetas*; Ovid, *Tristia* 2.560: *tua tempora, Caesar*) that a new age and a different age has come, perhaps a definitive new age for Rome. Our acceptance of the Augustan age as a well-defined period of history is deeply collusive with strategies of self-representation in Rome during the watch of Octavian-Augustus. The other obvious example that comes to mind, the periodization of the Great Century (or Generation) in 17th century France under Le Roi Soleil, is not an independent term of reference, but the result of conscious appropriation of Augustan models at the court of Louis XIV.

True, the Augustan age has consolidated under the influence of many factors, most of them political, but I would say that the crucial factor for modern scholars (and readers) has been the possibility of making multiple connections between political change, material culture, ideology, literature, and the visual arts.

This chapter offers readings of Augustan poetry in its relationship to the poetics and politics of visual representation: poetry will be viewed neither as independent nor as passive in its relationship to political art, but more like participating in a complex interaction.

HOW TO IMAGINE LOST MONUMENTS

Some links are evident to modern observers. Aeneas approaches the Cumaean Sibyl in the guise of a Greek settler looking for a colonization oracle, and promises in return, in his future kingdom, a marble temple for Apollo and Diana, accompanied by festivals and consultations of Sibylline books (*Aen.* 6.69–74): Aeneas is anticipating the entire Roman tradition of Apolline and Sibylline authority, a long tradition connecting various moments in Roman history, but the marble temple cannot help but be only a specific hint toward the dedication of the Apollo Palatinus sanctuary by Octavian, rather than by King Aeneas, in Rome rather than in the Latin city settled by Aeneas, and as late as 28 BCE. The poem functions as a prophecy after the event of both the building and its program of renewal and control over Sibylline oracles. On the other hand, art can not only validate sham prophecies, but also turn literature into a real prophecy: it is hard to react to the figurative program of the Forum Augustum (Fig. 49; cf. Fig. 37), inaugurated in 2 BCE, almost a generation after the publication of the *Aeneid*, without thinking of Virgilian approaches to history and dynasty. The twin galleries with statues of the Julian family and of the great Roman leaders (Fig. 42) have been compared countless times to the *Aeneid*: it is unlikely that most of the late first century visitors had actually read much of the poem, or read any literature at all, but the work was already influential in the late Augustan age, and the receptions of the text and the monument will have begun to complicate each other quite early (for Ovid's reaction to this link see pp. 285–8).

Sometimes we even feel that a passage in poetry incorporates re-actions to a lost artifact. On the Shield of Aeneas, in the final panel (*Aen.* 8.720–28), we 'see' Augustus reviewing the foreign populations in their variety of languages, arms, and clothing: the *gentes* and *populi* are Berber nomads, Asian and northern barbarians, with their mighty rivers. Augustus is imagined in front of the temple of Palatine Apollo, next to his own residence; yet we know about a monument in Augustan Rome that displayed a gallery of frontier populations in their picturesque diver-sity, the so-called *Porticus ad Nationes* (Servius on *Aen.* 8.721). We can access a spin-off of this figurative tradition at Aphrodisias, and locate a predecessor in the testimonies about the Portico of Pompey. In spite of the complexity of the literary text, which is not even an ecphrasis of some material artifact, but a narrative about Aeneas watching the image of a historical event within the prophetic 'pre-creation' of Rome on a divine-made shield, we can suggest a relationship between word

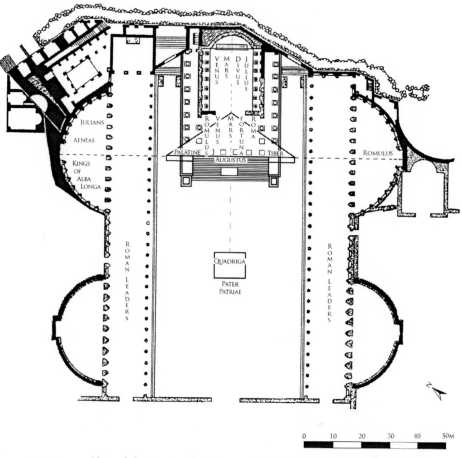

FIGURE 49. Plan of the Forum Augustum, 2 B.C. The central area was framed by porticos with statue galleries of Roman leaders and, in the exedrae flanking the temple of Mars, the statues of regal and Trojan ancestors. Together with relief panels in the upper part of the galleries that evoked Athens and Alexander, the quadriga of Augustus in the center, and the figures in the Temple's pediment, they coalesced into a comprehensive pictorial program. Remains of the exedrae at the lower end of the Forum (cf. Fig. 37) have recently been excavated; we have as yet no evidence of possible sculptural decoration. Drawing by Chris Williams.

and image that requires, as a supplement, the influence of a specific monument.

Even more obviously, some poetic texts are strategic for art historians because they are able to contribute fresh evidence for archaeological sites. Both the temple of Palatine Apollo and the Forum Augustum are understood only partially through the physical remains. There is, therefore, the option of using literary texts as testimonies for lost art and architecture. Different interpreters of poetry will press the details to a different degree. We use Propertius 2.31, a rare case of a poem completely dedicated to an Augustan building, as a witness for the reconstruction of Apollo Palatinus. We combine this testimony with the later comments on the same temple in Ovid's *Amores*, *Art of Love*, and *Tristia*. Propertius visits the brand new temple and admires 'the female throng of old Danaus' (2.31.4); Ovid after Propertius watches the same portico of the Danaids and speaks about *Danai agmen* (*Am.* 2.2.4): *agmen* means both 'row' and 'military column' so it sounds slightly more aggressive than Propertius' *femina turba*. Propertius must be teasing Cynthia, since he is late on a date: where have you been? Look, the Princeps is displaying fifty new girls in public – a.k.a. the stern, hieratic Danaides. But Ovid is looking for a girl under the portico and feels threatened by protectors and regulations: in this new atmosphere, the *agmen* reminds viewers that the Danaides were women who slashed their bedmates in order to protect their virginity and comply with their father's murderous assignment. We have to wait until the *Ars Amatoria* to learn that Danaos, the father who instigated the family murders, was also represented: at *Art of Love* 1.74 his statue is under the spotlight, "the fierce father stands there with his drawn sword" (*stricto stat ferus ense pater*). A cruel father is now in sight: from his exile, years later, Ovid sends his book of *Tristia I* to Rome, and there he is again, Father Danaos, unsheathed blade and family war again, and a barbarian now, *stricto barbarus ense pater* (*Trist.* 3.1.62: a barbaric counterpart capping traditional images of Brutus the founder of the Republic?). Ovid's downfall as a love poet is all in the trajectory from *Danai agmen* to *ferus pater* to *barbarus pater*: the monument is still the same, but readers are being taught different approaches.

Danaos had no importance to Propertius, but in 2.31 there is a subtle interest in the images of Apollo. This is, of course, a crucial issue for reconstructions of Apollo Palatinus: how many images of Apollo, and where? It must be important that Propertius actually mentions *two* images of Apollo, almost like two distinct epiphanies: both of them are lyre-playing Apollos, one with Latona and Diana, one a single image that looks 'more beautiful than Phoebus himself.' This is intriguing, because the iconography of Apollo had been converging with the official image of Octavian long before 28 BCE. Perhaps this Apollo is 'more beautiful than himself' because it brings into play resemblance with the princeps, while that other Apollo is a cultic image by an ancient master. Alexandrian poets had taught Propertius how to express this kind of flattering hesitation – 'this is an image of Aphrodite but, look, could it be Berenike? I am uncertain how to tell apart the goddess and the queen.' So when we use Propertius to reconstruct the figurative program we should also pay attention to allusion and intertextuality. Those processes of literary signification of course cut both ways: Propertius admires the silent melody of the marble Apollo (*marmoreus tacita carmen hiare lyra*; 2.31.6) and Stephen Heyworth has pointed out that the line imitates a line from Callimachus' *Hymn to Apollo*.[1] It seems like a very appropriate model for the ecphrasis of an Apollo statue, except that the line was about the unspeakable torture of Niobe, a victim of Apollo, and associated with the idea that even Niobe has to stop her lament when the festival of Apollo comes (Call., *Hymn*. 2.24; cf. Propertius 3.10.8). Niobe was of course represented on one of the temple doors, Propertius attests (according to him the frieze on the door 'mourns' the suffering of Niobe). So the allusion to the Greek model in literature complicates the reading of the Greek art in the temple: one quickly learns how to read Apollo the killer in Apollo the musician, how to listen to imaginary music but also to echoes of suffering and repression.

The Forum Augustum emerges in modern discussions as the true culmination of Augustan political art, although the monument is only fragmentarily reconstructed. Ovid's poetic tour of the Forum in *Fasti* 5.545–98 has a fundamental role in archaeological debates:

> **hinc videt** Aenean oneratum pondere caro
> et tot Iuleae nobilitatis avos;
> **hinc videt** Iliaden umeris ducis arma ferentem.

> [On this side he sees Aeneas weighed down by a dear burden,
> and so many forebears of Julian nobility; on the other side
> he sees the son of Ilia carrying the (vanquished) leader's arms
> on his shoulders; 5.563–65].

Paul Zanker has observed[2] that the symmetry at the level of language "on the one side he sees / on the other side he sees" can be used to fill in the outline of the two matching galleries: the two symmetric exedrae (Fig. 49), he proposes, had an Aeneas and a Romulus (Figs. 50 and 51), united by a sightline intersecting the main axis that ran between the pediment of the Mars Ultor temple and the central quadriga of the emperor. The poet and his visual competence are thus honored by a conspicuous responsibility in the process of architectural

FIGURE 50. Aeneas fleeing from Troy, carrying his father Anchises (who carries the box with the household gods) and guiding his son Ascanius/Iulus (the ancestor of the Julian family). The image attained iconic status especially after the publication of Vergil's *Aeneid* and became ubiquitous in sculpture (Fig. 52) and painting and on everyday utensils such as lamps. Here, as in the Forum Augustum, it is the companion to that of Romulus (Fig. 51). Mural from a shop in Pompeii. Photo: After Spinazzola (1953) fig. 183.

reconstruction, and beyond: Ovid is clearly interested in what the symmetry of Romulus and Aeneas can tell about the ideology of the complex. The poet does even more than this: he supplies a micro-narrative explaining how the Mars Ultor complex was vowed by the princeps so long ago, on the battlefield at Philippi. This is again a crucial service for viewers and visual historians: at least we know that one Roman author wanted the Forum to be read directly against the memory of the civil wars.

FIGURE 51. Romulus with the armor of a slain enemy leader (*spolia opima*). From the same shop in Pompeii, first century A.D. Photo: After Spinazzola (1953) fig. 184.

Ovid, a master of intertextuality, goes even further: the prayer he attributes to Octavian at Philippi – "Mars, be present and satiate my sword with the blood of criminals" (*Mars, ades et satia scelerato sanguine ferrum*; 5.575) reminds us of the slaughtering of Remus by Romulus and of Turnus by Aeneas in their respective master-narratives, the *Annals* of Ennius and the *Aeneid* of Virgil. The intertextuality connecting Octavian to Aeneas and Romulus is a very precise equivalent of the visual symmetry enacted by the sightlines of the Forum: Ovid is providing the instructions in three steps. (A) explore the link between Augustus and the temple of Mars, then (B) glance sideways, Romulus on one side, Aeneas on the other. You end up by learning a lot about the ideology of the principate – but unless you control the poetic intertextuality very firmly, you also end up asking yourself in what ways Augustus needs to be compared to the symmetric lateral exempla of Aeneas and Romulus, and so (C) you will be using the civil wars as a shared area of reference. Is it most of all about the need of killing suppliants and relatives in order to re-found Rome? A possible reading of the Principate, but perhaps too blunt for many art historians looking for a shared ideology and Augustan propaganda. Yet Ovid's contribution cannot be limited to filling in material gaps in the evidence: he also has things to say about how to read violence in the stately architecture of the Forum, and this reading cannot be dismissed as irrelevant. As in the case of Propertius' Apollo, once the poet is allowed to play a part in the reconstruction, he also deserves a hearing on how people were participating in the game of interpretation. Danaos and Apollo, Aeneas and Romulus are scrutinized and interrogated by viewers who are trying to learn how to live with the Principate and make sense of it.

However, the range of connections to be traced between visual and literary modes of representation is much broader. Some links are easily made, when we are dealing with shared subject matter: e.g., the decorative flora of the Ara Pacis and typologies of nature in poetry; the basis for critical guesswork on, for example, the 'healing' function of those motifs in a post-civil war society; or with similarities of style, and attitudes to the Greek tradition (see subsequent section).

PUBLIC AND PRIVATE, ART AND TEXT

Some analogies are tantalizing, and even more interesting, but harder to pin down, and it is best to dismiss the pressure to find a relationship of cause and effect. In the *Aeneid*, for instance, one notices a sequence of verbal similarities organized, across a vast narrative space, around the concept of *longo ordine* 'in a long row': the tag applies to, respectively, Trojan captives deported by the Greeks from a burning Troy, a silent chorus of Trojan spirits in the underworld, Roman descendants of Troy in the heroic parade in the underworld, exotic subjects of Augustus' Empire, and a funeral procession in which ritual and sorrow unites the Trojans and the Greek settlers of the future Rome. Those categories of people are all visualized as moving in a long orderly procession toward some shared, collective goal (2.766: *pueri et pauidae longo ordine matres*; 6.482: *Dardanidae, quos ille omnis longo ordine cernens / ingemuit*; 6.754: *et tumulum capit unde omnis longo ordine posset . . . legere et . . . discere*; 8.722: *incedunt uictae longo ordine gentes*; 11.143: *lucet uia longo / ordine flammarum*).[3] A fitting analogy in the natural world is the long orderly column (1.395 *ordine longo*) of migrating swans, a reassuring omen whose import for the Trojans goes beyond face value and promises a successful goal in history instead of a diaspora. This approach to movement across space puts together notions of place, time, end-oriented action, and solidarity, often within a ritual frame of reference. Is it far-fetched to think that the motif of procession in Augustan art is a related phenomenon?[4] The problem is what to make of the analogy; it is difficult to make it work as analogy without importing issues of ideology into the discussion. The resulting vision will be hazy, but it is important to try to go beyond relationships that are simply decorative and superficial – the *Aeneid* providing captions for the monuments, Aeneas on the Ara Pacis as an illustration for the *Aeneid*, which had been completed a few years earlier.

On the private side, again we have suggestive analogies. The boom in late Hellenistic art, soon to be appreciated by Roman customers, had been desire and lust in mythological settings. Images of a Faun, Pan, or satyr create grotesque contortions of desire and rape, ugly males intertwined with nymphs. This is the tradition we sometimes call *symplegmata*, 'embraces' (but the word evokes also 'fornication' and 'rhetorical combination'). Greek originals are replicated in copies to be located in Roman gardens: on the ground we assume, without a pedestal, slightly smaller than life, allowing multiple viewpoints and teasing perspectives. This tradition requires sexual poses with intertwining of satyrs and girls, open-ended situations of quasi-rape, female nudity, male desire exposed, satisfaction uncertain or delayed. Set in the Roman landscape of *otium* (leisure), the garden, those images provide sexual stimulation combined with cultural self-positioning: it becomes distinctive of the Roman élite to be able to watch Greek eroticism from a distance, as an alternative to the orderly processions of official art. Again we can look for analogies in literature. Ovid has a double series of episodes of sexual predation in his major works: the sequence in the *Metamorphoses* is mostly dark and violent, and mobilizes power fantasies and fright of superhuman powers (often major Olympic gods) in a scenario of wild nature. There are grotesque elements, in spite of the epic mode, but no sense of a comic complicity between author and readers. In the *Fasti*, by contrast, there is a string of sexual episodes that has all the features of the *symplegmata* tradition: comic situations, arousal, frustration, presence of satyrs and other Dionysiac and stagey characters. Here it is easier to feel that the poet is catering to the *symplegmata* taste, and it is impressive how archly the format of elegiac-antiquarian aetiology has to be reshaped in order to fit the satyresque vignettes into the poem.

The master of love elegy in the previous generation, Propertius, competes with more austere genres of mythological painting. Not that he depends upon the typical scenes of painting – although he can capitalize on them: he seems more interested in competing and showing that poetry can reveal more surprising angles and experimental approaches. His mythological exempla and micronarratives often dwell on the pathetic and the deviant, and there is very little sexual exposure.

The decisive factor in Propertius is the self-conscious asceticism of his love poetry – the elitist aversion for the body, the construction of love as a never-ending trial, what Joy Connolly[5] calls the "asymptotes" of pleasure in Roman elegy: he defers or recreates bodily presence and constructs analogies in absentia; readers are referred to Greek models of myth and there, via figurative art, they can find a paradoxical plenitude of physical presence: the sleeping Cynthia is, moment by moment, like Ariadne or Andromeda or a Maenad on their respective rocks (1.3.1ff.). When she cries rivers she cries more than Briseis or Andromache (2.2.1–2); to love her is like feeling the adulterous desire of Paris watching Helen step naked out of Menelaos' bed (2.15.14–15). Greek territories are a patchwork of names, myths, and recognizable images (3.22) while Rome is more of an abstraction, a land of honor family and morals, no 'marvels'. The visionary spectacle of Spartan girls of myth evokes the regular entertaining of more decently clad Laconian ballerinas (3.14), a visual presence both live and in figurative art. In short, visual art supplies the physical plenitude, the shapes and images that elegiac courtship withholds, defers, mystifies, and obfuscates through its rhetoric of life choices and perennial service.

Even this brief panorama suggests that all the major genres of Augustan poetry have interfaces with the world of visual art. The problem is how to select the points of contact, how to make those interfaces relevant. Often in the past we have tried to interweave rough data with rough data – but at the price of extracting rough data from complex systems that deserve to be compared with complex systems. The result of the comparison depends on how we read images and how we read texts, and the question was delicate for the Romans too, for they had no automatic access to real, authentic meaning.

We tend to take for granted a separation between public and private, and to extol the public impact of Augustan art vis-à-vis the more private space of literary communication. It is crucial to understand that there was a transfusion between the fields of private and public, and indeed the distinction is not hard-and-fast and may be excessively modern. For example, the access and openness of some Augustan monuments may have been exaggerated. If we compare the Forum Augustum with the Republican Forum, we find that the new Forum had, by comparison, limited dimensions, less traffic, less openness, a sense of rigid architectural separation, a strong propaganda value, precious art on public display, and that only a limited and symbolic selection of public activities was admitted (the military and the judicial). Should we accept a museal vision of the monument, one that is even too easily supported by imaginations of Rome in historical movies? There is some evidence of spectacles in the Forum, when other venues were flooded; on the other hand, less clear testimonies of people casually strolling in the new Forum – no love poets around any more. Even if our sources do not mention this, it is legitimate to ask whether admission and circulation of visitors was restricted and controlled: that question should make some difference for modern imaginations of Augustan 'communal' atmospheres and 'integrative' strategies. The tones and moods that we perceive in some of the poetic texts may be indeed only a symptom of élite communication, but there is no way to exclude that the impact of the monuments was not always easy to absorb for some groups of Roman society.

THE USES OF GREEK TRADITION: ROME AS A HOTHOUSE OF MEANING

Both literature and visual culture in this period are based on Greek imports. A comparative approach, therefore, readily suggests itself.

The title for this essay, *Learned Eyes*, is based on a Ciceronian expression. Cicero is addressing the limits of the ideal autonomy of Roman individuals, i.e. élite Roman males. Even those ideally 'free' citizens, he argues, can become enslaved; they are slaves to their eyes, for example, when they capitulate to the magnetism of visual pleasure in art – yet, he concedes, it is not easy to dissociate oneself "for even we have learned eyes" (*nam nos quoque oculos eruditos habemus*; *Paradoxa Stoicorum* 5.38.2). The important thing, for Cicero, is that Greek sculpture and painting should remain forms of entertaining, but not achieve mastery over the senses. Otherwise, he argues, we (Roman élite slave-owners as well as art viewers) are slaves to our own possessions. The context is of course very particular, but this angle of reference to Greek art is useful for our discussion, especially when we compare Cicero's situation with the Augustan sequel. In fact one of the core ideas of Zanker's influential book is that the power of art over the viewer, and especially the dangerous power of Greek art, is being used in the Augustan regime as a way of producing consensus and control. The innovation is this: the content that is being expressed is not the enslavement of Roman culture to Greek aesthetics (as Cicero might want to put it), nor appropriation of/by an alien culture, but the political message of Augustan control – the first two messages are typically Republican, the third typically imperial. In this context Zanker has made the crucial observation[6] that one of the greatest innovations of Augustan visual culture is that Greek works of art – looted, copied, relocated, displaced, or whatever – are now invested with a political meaning that does not require one-on-one correspondence or direct motivation. The underlying symbolic meaning can be operative without being constrained by the specific iconography, and the metaphors and metonymies generated by the process intensify the effect of aura and authority. So the Venus Anadyomene of Apelles is now an acceptable stand-in for the moralized Venus Genetrix of the Iulii; the lyre-playing Apollo by Skopas can serve as a cult image related to the fighting Apollo of Actium. Zanker stresses consensus and control, and this is necessary, otherwise one can imagine that the process of turning images into meanings could be disturbed by interferences, precisely because it is about re-use and transference, troping and displacing.

Here the comparison with literature is significant, because allusion and intertextuality in Augustan poetry are often means to express tensions and repressions that are not acceptable as surface meaning. We may start from a preoccupation that has been expressed about Zanker's methodology:

> The other characteristic of Augustan Rome is that it was filled with stolen Greek art – in private contexts, in temples, but also in the open air. While Greek art cannot be said to embody 'opposition', it would certainly have represented a disturbance to the 'coolness' of the visual field. How should we conceive of the relationship, for the contemporary viewer, of Greek art and the art of the regime? Were they distinct – to put it crudely, 'art' on the one hand and 'propaganda' or 'decoration' on the other? Or were they more juncted?[7]

It is not difficult to retort that this view is basically unhistorical. There was no 'art' in the modern bourgeois sense. We have no clue as to whether Roman viewers would perceive the reuse of Greek art as dissonant in the context of official propaganda. Yet some of the intertextual energy of Augustan poetry is precisely about hammering together unbearable contradictions: you cannot really 'say' that Augustus is at the same time destroyer and protector, monarch and restorer of the Republic, but you can use traditional models to express this idea through allusion and recycling, and learn how to view the monuments through this aura of ambiguity and polysemy. If we focus on the 'thick' semiotics available to Hellenized Romans, the preoccupation begins to look less unhistorical.

STORYWORLDS AND IMPLICATIONS

One could argue that the spectrum remained very broad. Even victory monuments need control and interpretation. After the sack of Carthage, we know the story of the embarrassing L. Hostilius Mancinus: he would hang out near the painting illustrating his deeds (Pliny, *N.H.* 35.23) and volunteer explanations. But what about, for example, the painting of Marsyas in chains imported to Rome and set in the new precinct of Concordia Augusta (35.66)? It was clearly more difficult to provide guidelines for interpretation. Different perspectives were doubtless available to many viewers. Provenience: was it brought to Rome from Athens, hence implications about its status in Athenian culture? New context: to what extent is the location in the Concordia Temple important? Iconology: the iconography of Marsyas has the clear implication that Apollo is going to administer his punishment. The relationship to political institutions: the painting was replicated in cities endowed with *ius Italicum*, the highest legal privilege available to provincial towns. The statue of Marsyas in the Roman Forum was a rallying point for the Roman plebs, a celebration (perhaps) of the end of debt-bondage, reinterpreted by some in later generations as a symbol of élite dominance, of the victory of the aristocratic Apollo over the upstart satyr. Octavian-as-Apollo was not far from the image of this new Marsyas.

The meaning of the Greek art is also the meaning of the act of transference and recontextualization: this is interesting for our topic when we consider that similar constraints and polysemous implications are also typical of Roman intertextuality with Greek literary models. Intertextuality is a process, not a state; an operation, not a result. Just like individual acts of literary imitation, the relocation and display of Greek art could not be considered – at least for the cognoscenti – in isolation from a web of stories and connotations. We know that Livia dedicated the ring of Polycrates, set in a golden horn, in the Temple of Concordia (Pliny, *N.H.* 37.4). The golden horn suggests Fortune, the dedication suggests disavowal of private wealth, the setting implicates political harmony. So the object was appreciated for its face value but also for its storyworld (cf. Diana Kleiner's Chapter 9 in this volume for a similar perspective): viewers who were also readers were in a position to understand that Livia was dedicating the material object, the ring, plus its importance as a subject of history and epigram. Epigram had celebrated the ring for its association with power and supremacy – as we now know from the new Posidippus poem (II 3–6 Bastianini-Gallazzi), where the ring appears in a frame of allusions to Alexander and to the Ptolemaic world empire as seen in the feminine world of gem cabinets. Herodotus, in one of his most widely read stories (3.40ff.), associates the ring with the rise and fall of an ambitious tyrant and his thalassocracy, and he concentrates on the idea that material possessions are easier to control than power and chance. Anacreon, the poet who had made a name for himself and also for Polycrates through songs of pleasure and civilization, had famously said that he would not like the horn of Amaltheia (17 Page) – for the many Roman admirers of Anacreon, the ring of Polycrates is now monumentalized by a royal (Alexandrian?) cornucopia.

The dedication by Livia thus combines ideas of stabilization and restraint with a display of luxury – different viewers could of course recombine in various ways this set of values and impressions, and the object of their deciphering was not just the ring, but the process of its displacement and recontextualization. The idea of a public semiotics that operates with previously owned artifacts – paintings and rings, poems and ideologies – invites us to compare and contrast the strategies of poetry and the visual arts. The question remains of course of whether readers and viewers were aware of the origins of these artistic and architectural objects, and cared about them. In my view scholars who, for example, identify 'allusions to the Acropolis' of Athens in Augustan architecture (Galinsky 1996, 203) are on safe ground. Even if periodization and historicization of another culture were not the Romans' forte, perhaps space and dislocation (sometimes even time) were available to many people as categories of interpretation. Not every viewer would know and care, but in private art we do know that the relocation of artworks was a serious pursuit. So we can imagine viewers reacting not just to the new function of the art object but also to the operative, transactional meaning of its being translated from somewhere else: and that allows us to put viewers and readers in some sort of dialogue, because readers had to cope with appropriation and transference all the time.

VIRGIL: THE MAKING OF VIRTUAL MONUMENTS

Before Ovid invents the poetics of the *flaneur*, the two main poets of Octavian's generation take a completely different but related approach to the visual impact of monuments. Horace (as Philip Hardie[8] has pointed out) develops a competitive approach in which poetry rivals, not complements, the power of art. No ecphrasis, no reference to Augustan buildings, but private focus, inwardness and country *buen retiro*, the villa as the 'other Rome' versus the growing importance of public architecture.

In discussing Virgil, it is easy to start from the sheer abundance of visual material in his poetry.[9] The three great monuments of the *Aeneid* – the temple of Juno in Carthage, the temple of Apollo in Cumae, the shield of Aeneas (the last-named is a portable object, but its vertiginous richness of images clearly evokes a whole complex of representations) – and the great monument of the *Georgics*, the Caesareum in Mantua, clearly offer a visual culture that goes way beyond known precedents in Greek epic.

According to the famous distinction drawn in *Aeneid* 6 (847–53), visual art is the province of Others, who will some day make 'breathing statues' and 'living faces' out of bronze and marble. In the world of the poem, these Others must be already active in Dido's Carthage (1.455–65: who else could have brought the Trojan cycle to Africa?), and certainly the archetypal artist Daedalus has landed in Cumae, anticipating the Trojans by an aerial route. Thanks to his technology, Greek Daedalus escapes his own labyrinth (6.29–33) and brings Greek art, golden images on temple doors, to Italy: Aeneas, for his part, is a viewer of art in Carthage and Cumae, but has less time for art as the action progresses, and ends up in Latium, a territory that looks significantly lower in art. In fact, the Latins and Italians too have art, but when we seem to glimpse (*Aen.* 7.177–91) the public art of the Latins, there will be no praise of art in terms of visual illusion and precious material. What we see is statues of ancestors and gods, made of *cedrus* (cedar or juniper: Ovid will pointedly substitute marble for wood when he recuperates one of those images in his poem: *Met.* 14.313). According to Virgil, early Latin culture focuses on *imagines*, a visual apparatus to identify and celebrate ancestors and rulers, and then of course there are spoils: *spolia* are real objects on doorposts, *postes* (7.183, the starting point for objects 'designed' as decorations, a Roman obsession: shields incorporated in stone, Parthian spoils as architectural decorations. There will be foreign trophies on *postes* in Rome too, when Augustus will become the world ruler: 8.720–22). The final image is Picus the augur-king, sitting, traditional in his official garb. Initially we are told that this is Picus himself (7.187: *ipse*), yet it turns out the memorial image is all that is left after shape-shifting, not death: the body had been turned by Circe into a multicolored bird. Circe reminds us of the power of Greek myth and iconography, almost as a prophecy of what Ovid will accomplish by invading the memories of Latin culture with a new apparatus of Greek images and miracles of mutability.

One may wonder what the role of Trojan art is in this Graeco-Roman picture. The Trojans are clearly not viewed as bringers of art to Italy, since this is the traditional role of Greek influence. Viewing the Trojans as essentially Oriental would produce an image of artistic luxury: Phoenician possessions are already wonderful in the *Odyssey*, to be sure. But Virgil has Dido's Carthage (e.g., 1.637–42, 723–41) representing the lavish decorations of Homeric Phoenician culture (and its reflections in the middle ground between Greece and Orientalizing cultures, Phaeacia), while his Trojans are in a process of purification from excesses of material art: Priam's palace falls down with its trophies and barbarian gold (2.503–4), the Greeks greedily amass gold and Asian textiles (2.763 *gaza*, itself an exotic word), other possessions will be swept away in the storm (1.119 *gaza* together with the austere, epic *arma virum*), or distributed as guest gifts and prizes, often with monarchical suggestions.[10] True, in Italy at least two warriors, Turnus and Pallas, are wearing complicated mythological figures of metallurgy, but in both cases the iconography is Greek and there is a suggestion of a Greek heirloom (Turnus is related to the royal house of Argos, Pallas is an Arcadian with links to Herakles). Camilla will die because of her naive fascination for gold and fancy clothing (Phrygian luxury: 11.768–82).

Some of the *narrative* images in the Italic section of the poem are anticipations of public artwork, famous through serial reproduction. For example, the Lavinian sow, fundamental for Latin cities, is briefly glimpsed as a miracle – and promptly sacrificed by Aeneas (8.81–85); the poem offers us a transient vision of the living model of so many replicas. The she-wolf of Rome is of course waiting to happen in the future, but she has been prophetically turned into a work of art: not of course the historical statue of the she-wolf that graced the Lupercal

FIGURE 52. Aeneas with Anchises and Ascanius. Statue group from Pompeii, first century A.D. Similar groups were set up throughout Italy and the provinces. As in Pompeii, they were often part of the sculptural décor of a forum; the ultimate model was the Forum of Augustus. Photo: After Galinsky (1969) fig. 6.

(as in Livy 10.23.12), but an image of the real she-wolf suckling the twins in the green Lupercal, so on the shield of Aeneas (8.630–34). This anticipates the interplay of art and landscape that was so typical of memories in the city of Rome: are we being offered an image of the 'real' cave in the age of Romulus, or an image of the memorial? Virgil inserts his text into the process of communal appropriation of images and wants the *Aeneid* to participate in the exchange: before watching the Lupercal in art, Aeneas had been shown the pre-Roman, Arcadian cave that no historical Roman will ever contemplate (8.343–44). Everybody, in the Augustan age, had some familiarity with the family group of Aeneas, Anchises, the Penates, and Iulus (Fig. 52), but there was not yet any official standard for the image. Virgil pointedly avoids a regular description of the group through his narrative: what we get is a first-person account by Aeneas, where the iconography is being revisited from within, and readers are invited not to scan the picture again, but to feel what it was like to be the powerful, but anguished, family leader in a night of horror (2.721–24). Even better, we get a speech by Aeneas explaining how the choices he made – father on the shoulders, Penates held by the father, son being led by the hand, wife out of sight: all the familiar details that make his own image recognizable in coins, friezes, statues, and paintings (Galinsky 1969) – are the results of dramatic decisions made under pressure in a time of genocide. Of course we possess only a fraction of the visual capital of Augustan Rome, so we are able to catch a small part of the interactions going on between the literary text and the shared resources of figurative traditions.

As a text, the poem has the ambition of being really imperial and universal, and Virgil is clearly aware that visual strategies are at work in the same direction: he is interested not only in (anachronistic) public monuments, but also in the fact of their reproduction and diffusion *through other monuments and other images* – it is more Roman and, in fact, typically Augustan to have temples accessible through mobile images on coins, and altar-bases in distant lands preserving glimpses of Rome. Illustrations include Aeneas witnessing an image of fallen Troy in a temple at Punic Carthage, and a colonial attempt to create a Trojan 'memorial park' in Greek Buthrotum. The Daedalean temple of Apollo in Graeco-Italic Cumae has miniature images of the harbor of Athens and the Labyrinth of Crete. Aeneas does not participate directly in the game of visual links: his powerful secret, never on display in the story, is the domestic talisman of the Penates and Trojan 'Vesta.' His promise of a temple to Apollo is not related to actual foundation by himself. Yet he lives in a world where religious images already transmit visions of distant places and twinned cults, and build unity in diversity: Venus in Sicilian Eryx, matching Paphos in Cyprus; Apollo in Delos, Cumae, and Soracte, waiting for the Palatine; Juno in Samos, Argos, Carthage, and the Latin cities; Athena in Ilion and in the city of Latinus. Religion tends to emerge in well-organized clusters of monuments, even when the Homeric background would suggest dim and solitary images of heroic cults: Venus already has a hundred altars in Paphos, the ambitious barbarian sheikh Jarbas promotes a hundred shrines for Jupiter, and finally Augustus will rule over three hundred holy places in Rome (all visible in miniature on Aeneas' shield).

The Shield of Aeneas itself is a multiple, a super-monument made of several monuments and imaginations of monuments. There are five or six Romes on the Shield, different in time, outlook, and topographical foci: historical evolution emerges from the shift in focalization, first the primitive Palatine before the foundation, then some core areas for Republican identity (Circus, Tiber bridge, Capitoline, but no Forum), and finally the Palatine again, in the monumental Augustan version. The two anonymous cities on the Shield of Achilles, the City in Peace and the City at War, had sometimes been interpreted as a double allegory of Athens. The new shield is a portable and fragmented vision of Rome.

The importance of ecphrasis is more understandable if we assume that this is an age of intervisual appropriation: monuments replicating monuments, *mise en abyme*, multimedia reproduction with change of size, witty visual puns, private encapsulating public, public absorbing private. So it is not just about texts reproducing or inventing monuments, it is about visual art reproducing or reinventing other visual art. The difference with innovation in artifacts is not very sharp here. What kind of real object, for example, is the cuirass of the Prima Porta Augustus? It commands attention for what it is not: it is definitely not a replica of a real piece of armor. The monument is intertextual with armored statues, with real cuirasses, with cuirasses in stone, and with literature: Virgil is educating its viewers through his representations of art-viewing.

The crucial text for this poetic program is the prooemium to the third book of the *Georgics*. Virgil declares that, in his own Mantua, he will found a sanctuary in honor of Octavian Caesar, complete with visual celebrations of victories. In spite of the metapoetic value of the metaphor, the project of a literary monument, one should recognize a precise social and political model. In those years, it was up to individual 'big men' of the provinces to help spread the cult of the new regime outside Rome. Small and conspicuous centers of the Italic territory are sprouting monuments dedicated by local dignitaries, and in the visual programs the divine honors for Octavian, then Augustus, are particularly explicit. Those people are taking care of the building activity but also of the rituals, they organize games, sacrifices, shows, every kind of public and religious happening: we can compare Virgil's activity (at *Geo.* 3.21–25) with what is known of, for example, early Augustan Pompeii. So we observe not only a shared Zeitgeist, but a precise, deliberate politicization of literature in response to important steps taken in the direction of a Romanized and Augustan Italy:[11] the parallel between text and architecture is crucial to this link. The poet is sponsor, ringmaster, director, sacrificer, and architect: the precedents of Classical and Hellenistic poetry are important but they are invested with a new function.

The Pindaric metaphor (temple) and the Pindaric practice (agonistic celebration) are recognizable, but their strategic value is sometimes unappreciated. The poet is now addressing someone with much more power to get things done, more than any of Pindar's patrons had. New temples and new *ludi* are available to the princeps as strategies of self-representation – except that he would assert his *auctoritas* in enlisting *others* to do the monuments. Viewed this way the poet is one of the makers of Augustanism in monuments. His patron is more like the Ptolemies in the texts of Callimachus or Posidippus than like the average patron of epinikian songs, but there is one important difference. The poet also accepts a diminished status versus the Hellenistic poets: the idea of monumentalizing one's birthplace is found in Hellenistic culture not only about rulers but about authors who are monumentalized in statues and even receive heroic cults in their homeland. Virgil steps down from this pedestal precisely when he competes with Ptolemaic poetry. Yet the poet also expresses his special – perhaps greater – power of, for example, narrative and time, *condere nomen*. The epic author is now the maker of monuments, while elegiac poets (Propertius, Ovid) will have to invent the new poetics of the *flaneur*, the roving male viewer who approaches official monuments at an oblique angle.

THE QUESTION OF STYLE

The really hard question to ask, in literature as in art, is how far the difference of styles in the reuse of Greek models was perceived as significant. Both in literature and in art, we are not sure whether the Romans would conceptualize categories or periods like Hellenistic versus Classical in anything like the way that we do. In literature, we have a few more indications, but not enough to imagine a kind of "emic" literary history (except for Cicero with his influential, but special agenda). In art, some approaches place a great emphasis on style, especially Zanker's idea of a movement from Hellenistic (luxury, pathos, emotion, private grandeur) toward Classical (restrained gravity, communal values). Others, as in Hölscher's functionalist idea,[12] claim that style choices are fully controlled by a system of social performance: for example, Hellenistic was good for battle representations, Classicistic for rituals and civic actions. Both approaches seem simplistic, especially if we think of, again, our privileged elitist group of readers and viewers. If their eyes were trained and 'learned,' they may have been looking for links between traditional stylemes and contemporary intentions, the way they would while reading Horace or Ovid. So they would presumably identify different styles as coexisting in a pick-and-mix situation, as in Hölscher's model of synchronic alternatives, but also care about the relationship to Greek prototypes, as in Zanker's model.

Let me end by positing a couple of aesthetic questions based on the example the Forum Augustum. We have seen how important it was to Ovid that Aeneas and Romulus stood out (above, pp. 285–8) in the two matching galleries of statues. But what can we say about the *visual style* of the statues? Based on reconstructions and analogies, I would expect a series of Republican great men characterized by traditional qualities – whether *togati* or in military garb, they would present the viewer with a subtly revised continuation of the most distinctive form of Roman public art, the standing honorific portrait. Could it be significant, then, that precisely when it comes to Romulus and Aeneas we seem to have evidence of a different style of representation? Neither fully Romanized nor alien in their attire, Romulus and Aeneas are represented as *dynamic* figures, striding toward the future and carrying something with them. Some kind of 'swoosh' style, more dynamic and (we are tempted to say) 'modern' or 'recent' would seem to go with that kind of pattern. The difference with the historical Roman heroes surely had some edge. Here is precisely my point. Was the diversity perceived as standard classicistic eclecticism, or was the different representational idiom carrying a baggage of ideology? If the result was that Romulus and Aeneas appeared stylistically more modern, there is an analogy with the *Aeneid*. In the poem, the distant, heroic past is more present (and Augustan) than the recent past: the gallery of descendants / ancestors in Book 6 has an Ennian feel to it, a traditional, communal past distinct from the 'new', dramatic past that is being reinvented by Virgil.

The other anomaly is about little Iulus in the Aeneas group. The boy was represented as Oriental. The decision was taken to introduce little Ascanius in the traditional iconography of Aeneas and Anchises but "he was dressed like an easterner, with trousers and a Phrygian cap. The group was therefore an intriguing mix of east and west, with the costume of the father representing the future, and the costume of the son signifying the past."[13] How striking was this? Iulus was presumably

the only child in the entire Forum, and also the only Oriental, unless there was some visual reminder of Parthian and Persian victory.
In the visual repertory of Augustan Rome, there was a whole series
of good-looking Oriental boys suggesting either pleasure, luxury, and
sexuality, or Asian cults, or both – Attis, Paris the shepherd, Ganymede,
the cupbearers; and there was the exotic, monarchic show of Parthian
children as hostages. We don't know how viewers marked the difference between those models. But we can look at the *Aeneid* and see one
interesting analogy. As in the Forum Augustum, in the *Aeneid* Iulus is
the individual on whom history depends. In the Forum, the little prince
was also exceptional in being present twice, in the escape image, and in
the Julian gallery, as the grown-up first king of Alba Longa, predecessor
of Romulus and Augustus. In the *Aeneid*, he is the anointed: the plot
of the poem enacts a series of tragic losses, and by the end of the action
Aeneas is *the only character* who has a still-living male offspring.

Yet Iulus is enigmatic, surely because he is too young: he never
takes the initiative to speak when his father is present, except for the
miracle of the edible tables (7.12–17). He is normally not described, certainly not in Oriental terms, yet he tends to be focalized from the outside, even objectified, sometimes in aestheticized and hedonistic terms.
As beautiful as Cupid, kidnapped to Venus' botanic gardens of Cyprus;
even in the thick of battle, as beautiful as a cameo or an Orientalizing
jewel: "The Dardan boy himself, the favored one of Venus, handsome
head uncovered, glitters just as a jewel set in tawny gold as an adorn-
ment for the neck or head, or gleaming ivory inlaid with skill in box-
wood or Orician terebinth' (10.133–38, transl. Mandelbaum). So the
one on whom everything depends is also strikingly un-Roman, stylistically quite Other. The real question here is not whether the *Aeneid*
had an influence on the images of the Forum. It is more interesting to
ask what was so special about Iulus in words and images, and how texts
and images cooperated in a Roman discourse about the paradoxes of
the new state of things. In the *Aeneid*, at the climax of the story, Juno's
agenda is simply that the Latins should not be Trojanized by adopting
Oriental garb, *vertere vestem* (12.825).

The approach I have used is open to objections on several counts.
The main problem is that, while I aim to combine visual arts and literary
texts in the hope to recreate implications and differences, I am in fact
subscribing to two dangerous contemporary illusions: the reification
of ideology in art, and an implicit 'liberal' view of literary production. The first illusion suggests that it is legitimate to mine artifacts in
order to recreate a unified, centralized political meaning; the second

entails a suspicious identification between Roman poets and the typical subject of academic performances, a liberal 'free' subject working in the European tradition. The context of this book will certainly show that there are alternative approaches, perhaps more holistic, yet I hope that my comments can be useful in suggesting, as a corrective, a vision of the Augustan age from the margins – the margins, admittedly, not of society at large, but of the Augustan élite, the margins of the center.

SUGGESTIONS FOR FURTHER READING

The relevant bibliography until the mid-nineties is incorporated and discussed in Galinsky (1996). I add a few items, mostly more recent, arranged in the sequential order of my paragraphs. For a recent discussion of the methodology of studying verbal expressions of visual messages see Herbert Golder's article on "Visual Meaning in Greek Drama," in Fernando Poyatos, ed., *Advances in Nonverbal Communication: Sociocultural, Clinical, Esthetic and Literary Perspectives* (Amsterdam and Philadelphia, 1992) 323–60.

On the Porticus ad Nationes: R. R. R. Smith, *JRS* 78 (1988) 71–7. Propertius 2.31: A. Laird, "*Ut figura poesis*: writing art and the art of writing in Augustan poetry," in J. Elsner, ed., *Art and Text in Roman Culture* (Cambridge 1996) 75–102 (important also for my topic as a whole); S. Heyworth, "Some allusions to Callimachus in Latin poetry," *MD* 33 (1994) 51–79. Ovid's *Fasti* on the Forum Augustum: A. Barchiesi in G. Herbert-Brown, ed., *Ovid's Fasti. Historical Readings at its Bimillennium* (Oxford 2002) 1–22.

Art and sexuality: P. Zanker in S. Settis, ed., *I Greci*, II 3 (Torino 1999) 572. Images of rape in Ovid's landscapes: C. Segal, *Landscape in Ovid's Metamorphoses* (Wiesbaden 1969); S. Hinds in P. Hardie, ed., *The Cambridge Companion to Ovid* (Cambridge 2002) 122–49. The body in Roman love elegy: J. Connolly, "Asymptotes of pleasure: thoughts on the nature of Roman erotic elegy," *Arethusa* 33 (2000) 71–98. Access and the ideology of the Forum Augustum: E. La Rocca, "La nuova immagine dei Fori Imperiali," *MDAI(R)* 108 (2001) 171–213, esp. 210–11.

For general ideas on the semiotics of Greek art in private and public contexts, P. Zanker, "Zur Funktion und Bedeutung griechischer Skulptur in der Römerzeit," in H. Flashar, ed., *Le classicisme à Rome aux*

Iers siècles avant et après J.-C. Entretiens Hardt 25 (Vandoeuvres-Geneva 1979) 283–314.

The story of the Ring of Polycrates, Hellenistic gems and gem literature: A. Kuttner in K. Gutzwiller, ed., *The New Poseidippos: A Hellenistic Poetry Book* (Oxford), 2005. Objections to the 'intertextual' model of visual appropriation: T. Hölscher in J. Porter, ed., *Classical Pasts* (Princeton), forthcoming.

Horace and resistance to the power of images: P. Hardie, in N. Rudd, ed., *Horace 2000: A Celebration* (London 1993) 120–39. Virgil and images of metamorphosis: P. Hardie in A. Powell, ed., *Roman Poetry and Propaganda in the Age of Augustus* (Bristol 1992) 59–82. My reading of visual culture in the *Aeneid* should be seen in connection with the discussions of Romanization and diaspora in Chapters 4 and 5 by Purcell and Woolf in the present volume.

Importance of cultural packages in accounts of Romanization: Woolf (1998). Provincial image-making and Augustan ideology: case study of Pompeii in P. Zanker, *Pompeii* (Cambridge, Mass. 1998) 95–112. Virgil and ecphrasis: A. Barchiesi in C. Martindale, ed., *The Cambridge Companion to Virgil* (Cambridge 1997) 271–81 (with bibliography).

Problem of how Roman observers would conceptualize distinctions such as Hellenistic/Classical: the question is asked in the review of Zanker's *Power of Images* by A. Wallace-Hadrill in *JRS* 79 (1989) 157–64. Redefinition of classicism and eclecticism: J. Elsner in Porter (see above).

On the two traditions, pathetic-battles and suffering, classicistic rituals and civil power, see T. Hölscher, *Römische Bildersprache als semantisches System* (Heidelberg 1987). Thorough study of the Forum Augustum: M. Spannagel, *Exemplaria Principis.* Archäologie und Geschichte 9 (Heidelberg 1999).

Trojan boys and Imperial apotheosis: P. Hardie, "Another look at Vergil's Ganymede," in T. P. Wiseman, ed., *Classics in Progress* (Oxford 2002) 333–61. Oriental boys, Trojan princes in art: C. Brian Rose, "Bilingual Trojan iconography," in R. Aslan *et al.*, eds., *Mauerschau. Festschrift für Manfred Korfmann* (Remshalden 2002) 329–50; see also R. M. Schneider, "Die Faszination des Feindes," in J. Wiesehöfer, ed., *Das Partherreich und seine Zeugnisse − The Arsacid Empire: Sources and Documentation. Beiträge des Internationalen Colloquiums,* Eutin (27.–30. Juni 1996). Historia-Einzelschriften 122 (Stuttgart 1998) 95–146.

The *Aeneid* as a poem about monarchy: F. Cairns, *Virgil's Augustan Epic* (Cambridge 1989). Convincing in demonstrating the importance of this political model, Cairns underrates the tensions and difficulties, mediations and repressions generated by the recuperation of kingship as a driving force in Roman history. Cf. now J. Fish in D. Armstrong *et al.*, eds., *Vergil, Philodemus, and the Augustans* (Austin 2004) 111–13.

NOTES

1   Heyworth (1994).
2   Zanker (1968) 16f.
3   2.766: "Boys and frightened mothers stood in a long line"; 6.482: "The (fallen) Trojans, whom Aeneas bemoaned when he saw them in a long file"; 6.754: "And (Aeneas) took a stand on a mound from which he could see and pick out all of the souls in their long procession"; 8.722: "The defeated tribes march along in procession"; 11.143: "The road shone with a long line of torch lights."
4   However, it can be argued that the 'long order' surrounding the sacrificing emperor of the Ara Pacis is in fact a circular one: K. Hanell, *Opuscula Romana* 2 (1960) 33–123.
5   Connolly (2000).
6   Zanker (1979).
7   The question reproduced in the text was posed by Greg Rowe (followed by T. Hölscher's response paraphrased in my text) in Giovannini (2000) 277.
8   Hardie (1993).
9   See now A. Smith (2005).
10   1.648–55: for Dido, Helen's mantle, Ilione's *sceptrum*, pearls, and crown; 5.250–57: for a winner in a contest, an embroidered purple chlamys with the story of Ganymede; 7.245–52: for Latinus, the *sceptrum* and diadem of Priam, textiles, and Anchises' ritual *patera* (a saucer or bowl); in book 11.72–75, Aeneas is giving away Dido's precious gift, a Punic gold and purple textile, for the funeral of his beloved Pallas.
11   Cf. John Scheid's Chapter 8 in this volume on Augustus' religious program being shaped greatly already during his Octavianic period.
12   Hölscher (1987).
13   Rose (2002) 339.

13: Augustan Poetry and Augustanism

Jasper Griffin

ugustus, like Queen Victoria, belongs to that special group
of rulers who have given their name to a great period of art
and literature. What we are happy to call "Augustan literature"
was to be no less epoch-making for the later literature of Rome than
Augustus himself proved to be for later Roman history. Such, in fact,
was the continuing impact of both on the mind of posterity that it
seems quite natural to speak of an "Augustan" period of English literature, too: that from John Dryden, greatest English translator of Virgil,
to Alexander Pope and Jonathan Swift, both of whom in their own
verse constantly echoed and imitated Virgil and Horace. Pope indeed
addressed to King George II, that eminently unpoetical monarch, an
"imitation" of Horace's *Epistle to Augustus* which turned it into a suavely
sarcastic poem of feline satire.[1]

There is an element of luck in the universal acceptance of the
term. Most of the poets whom we think of as Augustan had grown
up and made their name before Caesar's heir reached the position of
being, in his own phrase, "by universal consent in complete control of
affairs" (*per consensum universorum potitus rerum omnium*; *RG* 33). Yet the
only great poet actually produced in the reign was the recalcitrant and
irritating Ovid, never really on message, who eventually provoked the
Princeps, normally ostentatious in his 'clemency' – *clementia* was one
of the virtues commemorated on the shield of virtues voted to him by
Senate and People (*RG* 34) – into banishing him forever to the end of
the earth.

The poets had other patrons, too, in those early days, beside the
future Princeps. In his *Eclogues*, Virgil addresses poems to Asinius Pollio
and even to the second-rate figure of Alfenus Varus; he is impressed

with Cornelius Gallus, both as poet and as man of action. There is in the *Eclogues* no Maecenas, and – for that reason? – no Octavian. In the *Eclogues* he is not named and appears only obscurely and ambiguously. The reader is surely to identify him as the wonderful "young man" (*iuvenis*) of Eclogue 1.42ff.; perhaps he is the carefully unnamed general and Sophoclean tragedian of 8.6ff. (Octavian did write a tragedy, the *Ajax*). Some readers have found him in the apocalyptic fantasies of *Eclogue* 4, later known as the "Messianic" *Eclogue*.

The plurality of patrons, and the addresses to friends, are features which remind us that this period is the direct inheritor of that of Catullus and his friends, rivals, and enemies.[2] Horace addresses poems to a range of men of high position: Agrippa, Pollio, Sallustius Crispus, etc. Augustus, even by the end, never achieved a complete monopoly of the best work produced in his time. Virgil was impressed by Lucretius, whose characteristic rhythms and subject matter are echoed in *Eclogue* 6.31ff. He studied Catullus 64, Peleus and Thetis, which would echo in his mind in connection with his own Dido, and (doubtless) Catullus 66, a scrupulously close translation of a recherché poem by Callimachus, which combined mythological fantasy with courtly flattery of Ptolemy III and his young queen.[3] Its arch allusions to the sexual relations of the royal couple could not, of course, be imitated in connection with the Princeps and Livia.

The friends of Catullus and Calvus ostentatiously turned away from politics, except for short squibs, and burned the midnight oil to versify abstruse Greek myths in a style at once emotional, erudite, and cool. The poems in vogue were Catullus' own *Peleus and Thetis* and *Attis* (64, 63), and such other hothouse blooms as Caecilius' *Magna Mater* (Cat. 35), or the *Zmyrna* of Cinna, that short and highly wrought treatment of incest in the mythical period: destined, Catullus wrongly thought, for immortality (95). No sophisticated person would be seen writing full-length historical epic, like the ghastly Volusius with his shitty (so Catullus, rather directly, in poems 36 and 95) *Annales*.

Neither these remote and exquisite creations nor the personal squibs – Julius Caesar himself was not spared[4] – offered a way forward to poets pondering the possibility of producing encomiastic verse on the latest dynast, Octavian. In the stormy 40s and 30s there had been poets at work, glorifying Caesar's deeds (*res gestae*). But the panegyrists of the Dictator lost the battle for the respect of their generation and of the next. The future lay with those who could combine the technical refinement and emotional intensity of Catullus and his friends with a closer relationship, somehow, with life and reality.

The first great attempt was Virgil's shimmering and complex *Eclogues*. We see at once that the poet has no intention of making matters simple. His Muses are Sicilian; Theocritean, we infer (4.1); he is writing in the bucolic convention established by that Hellenistic master and followed by later Greeks. Exquisite passages of melodious verse, in which the Latin language sang as never before, spoke for the excellence of the poet's ear, and for his study of the most refined models. His first readers needed to look no further than 1.1–5, an eye- and ear-catching start. Many other passages rival it. He had of course learnt from Catullus, as well as from the Greeks. But references to Rome, to Italy, and to events and persons of Virgil's own time, show unmistakably that this poetry is complex. These rustics know their Lucretius, their Callimachus, their Euphorion; they are *au fait* with Roman politics and the most fashionable Latin poetry (see, e.g., 6.1ff., 6.72).

Nor is this merely the glittering surface. The attitudes expressed are often not those which the Princeps wanted his citizens to imbibe. We have not read twenty lines of the First *Eclogue* before a rustic speaker disavows knowledge or interest in Rome; he has had to go there only because the military are bringing misery on the country people, confiscating their land to reward the soldiers of civil war:

> en quo discordia civis
> produxit miseros: his nos consevimus agros!
> (*Ecl.* 1.70f.)

"See where civil war has brought the unhappy citizens! It was for them that we sowed our fields!"

The Ninth *Eclogue* returns to the same bitter grievance.[5] But Virgil does not, cannot, name the Triumvirs: Octavian was one of them.

The *Eclogues* are not a promising start for an Augustan classic; Syme (1939, 253) referred to their "mannered frivolity and imitated graces." There are indeed traces of more positive attitudes. But a promise to praise a Roman grandee is either cleverly evaded as it is made, as at 6.6ff., where Varus is fobbed off with a couple of fulsome lines and the assertion that "others" (not me!) will be keen to versify at full length his dour campaigns, his *tristia bella*; or projected into the uncertain future, as at 8.7ff., where Virgil enquires, rhetorically, whether the day will ever come when he can extol his (unnamed) patron's achievements (*en erit umquam/ ille dies, mihi cum liceat tua dicere facta?*); the sceptic might wonder what was stopping Virgil from writing the encomium now. Or it is wrapped in such oracular matter and style, as in the most famous poem of the collection, *Eclogue* 4 (the "Messianic *Eclogue*"), that left contemporaries no less perplexed than posterity about the exact reference and meaning.

Then there is the song of Silenus in *Eclogue* 6: beautiful, learned, remote from life, wandering without apparent plan through the artificial garden of Alexandrian mythology, and lingering longest on the perverse passion of Pasiphae for the bull (6.51):

> a, virgo infelix, tu nunc in montibus erras. . . .

"Ah me, poor girl, you are now wandering the hills. . . ." We are back in the world of *Zmyrna* and *Io*, from the latter of which that line has been wittily adapted. We glimpse the sort of poet Virgil might have been, had he followed his inclination and the poetic fashion of his youth, deaf to the urgings of Maecenas and Augustus. *Eclogue* 2, the mellifluous lament of a love-lorn shepherd for his inaccessible boyfriend, is another hothouse flower (2.63–5):

> torva leaena lupum sequitur, lupus ipse capellam,
> florentem cytisum sequitur lasciva capella,
> te Corydon, o Alexi; trahit sua quemque voluptas.

"The grim lioness pursues the wolf [a curiously perverse vision], the wolf pursues the she-goat, the playful she-goat pursues the clover, you, Alexis, are pursued by Corydon; their own desire drags each one along."

Even a real and active contemporary is seen in the same perspective of plangent passivity. The collection closes with Cornelius Gallus, part-time poet but active and competent public servant, transfigured into a rustic singer: in Arcadia he languishes for love, pitied by rocks and trees, and surrounded by his pastoral animals. *Stant et oves circum*, his flocks were standing round, Virgil assures his urban reader (10.16). As the cruel Lycoris goes off over the Alps with a rival, he prays that ice and snow may not hurt her tender feet (46–9)! Naturally she is imagined, in this style, walking barefoot – in real life, she would have travelled in a litter.

By an effort of will, Virgil turned away from the artificial paradise. From Gallus in Arcadia, singing of hopeless love and difficult Hellenistic poetry, he advanced to the sturdy and active Italian rustics of the *Georgics*, dedicated to Maecenas and to the Princeps. Men are now a hard race, *durum genus* (*Geo.* 1.63). No Corydons need apply! The key note is *labor*. Hard work conquers all; that, and the harsh pressure of need in poverty:

> labor omnia vicit
> improbus et duris urgens in rebus egestas.
> (*Geo.* 1.145)

And: *in primis venerare deos*! ("Above all, venerate the gods!" 1.338). In the Christian phrase, work and pray, *ora et labora*. Plangent sympathy and obtrusive erudition alike give place to that edifying plan, in which Our Leader, too, will play an important role. The first and the third books open with resounding passages of panegyric. In the first, Caesar is addressed as a god: may he favour the poet in his bold enterprise and pity the poor country people, who do not know the way (*Geo.* 1.40–2)!

What are Virgil's readers to learn from his poem, and why is Caesar to patronise it? Agricultural precepts rub shoulders with moral exhortation and poetical allusion, the whole expressed in ravishingly musical verse. Not enough detailed instruction to enable a gentleman to run an estate; too much high-falutin literary stuff for your working farmer or his steward (*vilicus*). It is notable that that word, like that person, never sullies Virgil's page, in sharp contrast with Cato's *On Agriculture* (sections 2 and 5) or indeed with the *Epistles* of his friend Horace (esp. *Epist.* 1.14). They are closer to the realities of life, in which one's steward was a very important person.

The *Georgics* is not thought of as an Augustan poem for nothing. Virgil indeed reveals uncertainty: how to approach so overwhelming a person as Octavian? The first book opens with a curious exhibition of exaggerated and rather bookish praise. Will Caesar be a god of sea or land? Certainly not a god of the Underworld; although (the poet cannot resist self-indulgently adding) it is true that Proserpina is happy down there. . . . The signs of the Zodiac are at this moment squashing up, to leave him more than his share of the heavens! The book does not end without a solemn prayer that "this young man, at least," should not be prevented from saving a world on the brink of ruin (*Geo.* 1.498ff.).

The Second Book praises Italy, tough yet fertile, a true mother of men; (Octavianus) Caesar gets little mention, but (sure enough) a deft allusion places him, along with such heroes as the Scipios, Camillus and Marius, as paragon of military activity and salvation for Italy (*Geo.* 2.163–76). Italy, as usual in the *Georgics*, rather than Rome. Not an arbitrary preference: "It was not Rome alone but Italy, perhaps more than Rome, that prevailed in the War of Actium" (Syme, 1939, 453).

Embarking on the second half, Virgil evidently felt the need for something more elaborate. Embarrassment is, perhaps, to be detected in the massive structure of praise which he will, if life lasts, lavish on Caesar. A marble temple, statues in the classic taste, games to eclipse Olympia, Caesar in the centre, his exploits depicted on the walls along with his mythical ancestry right back to Troy: no device of panegyric will be absent (*Geo.* 3.10–48). And when will all this happen? Why, soon (*mox*; 46). The passage, at once profuse and evasive, must have suggested to the Princeps that Virgil indeed envisaged an elaborate encomium of himself, the personal epic so often mentioned, asked for, postponed, and evaded.

There are some survivals from earlier styles: Scylla and Nisus (1.404–10), protagonists of a myth of love, betrayal, and metamorphosis, the subjects of the self-consciously decadent *Ciris*; or a passage in Lucretius' highest style, a perspective which makes all politics, even Rome, transient and unimportant (2.475–99); or a surprisingly lengthy excursus, illustrated with myths, on the destructive power of love (3.242–83). But only at the end does the poet allow himself a whole epyllion of tragic love and loss: Orpheus and Eurydice, haunting in its beauty, but an unexpected close to a poem of patriotism and self-help. Finally, Virgil wrenches the rudder abruptly back to an "Augustan" course, with a dutiful reference to the greatness of Caesar, thundering on the distant Euphrates, while he himself has been enjoying himself at Naples in the studies of ignoble ease (4.560–6). The ending looks, in a way, modest; but the shape of the lines puts poet, not dynast, in the position of supremacy, and implicitly Virgil claims parity with the Princeps.

Octavian is not easy to find in the poetry produced before his final victory in 31 B.C.[6] That is a revealing fact. From a time when all was over, when a poet no longer risked lavishing his loyal laudations on the wrong dynast, date the *Sicilian War* of Cornelius Severus and a now anonymous poem on the Actian campaign (*FLP* 334–40). Posterity feels no keen regret for their loss. Never named in the *Eclogues*, never appearing in the mellifluous verses of Tibullus, Caesar's heir is barely traceable in the First Book of Horace's *Satires* and he makes only one appearance, highly invidious in manner and substance, in the First Book of Propertius (1.21, esp. 7–8).

Virgil's *Eclogues*, published (probably) in 38–37 B.C., bore little resemblance to the sort of thing – upbeat, straightforward, edifying, and patriotic – which we might expect the Saviour of his country to expect from his loyal Augustan poets. With Horace and Propertius the case is similar. It was problematic for ambitious young writers to keep their artistic self-respect, if they put their pens to the service of politicians.

Maecenas, absent from the *Eclogues*, is absent, too, from Propertius I. But once a poet had published with success, Maecenas got busy. First Virgil and Varius, then Horace and Propertius, were drawn into his ambit. Horace indeed opened his *Satires* with the name of the patron: *Quo fit, Maecenas?* "How is it, Maecenas, that we are all so foolishly dissatisfied with our lot?" The patron gets prominent mention; he gets nothing else (and dissatisfaction, of course, is not imagined as taking a political form: no more Catilines!). Maecenas is not allowed to answer the question, and passages in the poem phrased in the second person have no connection with the millionaire aesthete who is the nominal addressee. "Your wife wishes you dead, so does your son; all your neighbours and acquaintances loathe you, boys and girls alike. Can you be surprised. . . . ?" (*Sat.* 1.1.83ff.) We are not to think of Maecenas in such a passage, and clearly the opening address is a formal compliment. Horace describes a trip with him to a political meeting of the highest significance, the Pact of Brundisium which averted war with Antony in 40 B.C.: he eschews politics, let alone propaganda, and sticks scrupulously to private matters (*Sat.* 1.6). Niall Rudd (1982, 370) has aptly observed in this context that "it is misleading to classify Horace as an Augustan poet *tout court*. His life was more than half over when the Augustan age began, and the Emperor survived him by more than twenty years. Most of the satires and epodes belong to the period before Actium."

In the first book of *Satires*, then, Horace offers deftly reorchestrated treatments of uncontroversial moral maxims: "Don't be discontented!" (1). "Don't be critical of your friends' weaknesses, you have plenty yourself!" (3). "Noble birth is morally unimportant!" (6). The poems are enlivened by anecdotes and vignettes: from his own life, from gossip, from literature. The morality, like the style, is not of the highest. "Avoid adulterous entanglements with respectable married women, but don't rush to whores either; go for economical arrangements with women of humble position!" (2). "The basis of society is *utilitas*, forget the overstated moral arguments of the Stoics!" (3). "I'd be mad to desire wealth – it would make my life so difficult" (6). The manner of Lucilius is deftly adapted to subject matter which avoids giving real offence; the Catullan bite turns to barking at fictitious or insignificant targets. From that inheritance (Horace speaks of Catullus rarely and without warmth) both personal invective and mythological set-piece have been superseded.

Most of the *Epodes* and of *Satires*, Book 2, must also have been written in the 30s. With the exception of a couple dutifully celebrating Actium (*Epodes* 1 and 9), they are mostly squibs and shadow-boxing with unreal opponents, men of straw who put on objectionable airs (*Epode* 4), or who falsely pretend to be outspoken (6), or who, simply, stink (10). There are women, too: lustful but repulsive (8, 17), or practising black magic (5, 17). Of politics, it seems, the poet despairs. Past, present, and future are alike terrible. Only some inherited collective guilt can explain the headlong rush of Rome to disaster, and all that remains is for us to abandon Italy and settle in some unknown land of the far West (7, 16). Horace saw no need to change that, in a book published after Octavian's victory.

Satires 2 dwells with a drooling show of disapproval on the pleasures of the table (2, 4); convicts all but the [Stoic] sage as madmen (3) and slaves (7); derides doctrinaire Epicureanism (4); pillories fortune-hunters (5). Caesar's name appears rarely. Horace imagines an interlocutor asking why he does not abandon satire and "tell of the achievements of Caesar the Invincible"; the rewards, adds the tempter, would be great:

> aude
> Caesaris invicti res dicere, magna laborum
> praemia laturus
>
> (*Sat.* 2.1.10–12)

But the poet mentions the possibility only to decline it urbanely ("if only I did possess the outsize talent needed! But unfortunately. . . ."). The device is a form of praise, but with the minimum of effort or commitment.

Propertius' first book, the *Monobiblos*, appeared, probably, in 30–29 B.C. Its twenty elegies are set in a world in which Rome, politics, Maecenas, and the Princeps himself do not exist. Interesting alone are poetry, friendship, and, above all, an obsessive love: voluptuous, magical, shameful. Only in the two closing poems, appended like afterthoughts, do we find the name of Caesar: his soldiers menaced the life of Gallus, the poet's friend (1.21.7–8). Out on the Etruscan hills Gallus perished, and there, too, Propertius' own home country around Perusia was ravaged in civil war. Every reader knew that at Perusia Octavian had perpetrated a massacre; rumour whispered of human sacrifice (Dio 48.14). The gentle elegist takes the opportunity to remind us, in the normally innocent context of signing off ("You keep asking me about my origins and my family. . . ."; 1.22). Still in Book 2, Propertius, who

has now been taken up by Maecenas, flattered, and urged to write panegyric, shows recalcitrance: he is, defiantly, a love poet, and a poem on
Octavian's achievements, if he wrote one, might not please – he would
have to tell of the ruin of Etruria. . . . (Prop. 2.1.25ff.).

Even though Maecenas was no great poet himself and his taste was
rather old-fashioned,[7] he had an eye for talent and the supreme gift of
patience. The authors of the *Eclogues*, the *Epodes*, and the *Monobiblos*,
unpromising as they might well have seemed for the purpose, were to
be rewarded, coaxed, flattered, pressured, and guided into serving the
regime (cf., for a somewhat different perspective, Peter White's chapter
in this volume). The task would call for great delicacy of touch, and
the poets could not all be handled in the same way. Horace liked to
be in Rome, he enjoyed a party, he relished being seen in Maecenas'
company (*Sat.* 1.6.47; cf. 1.43ff.; 2.6.29ff., 41–58). Virgil was shy, he
"came to Rome so rarely that, when he was spotted there, he took
refuge in the nearest house from people following him and pointing
him out" (Donatus Vita 11.4). Propertius presented himself as the poet
of private life par excellence, preferring to Rome the delights of Baiae,
and living for Venus and Bacchus. Proper Romans called such a life
by the unflattering name of *nequitia* (worthlessness); Propertius set out
to raise and dignify the life of pleasure with the shimmer of poetic
stylisation, Greek myth, and intense emotion. But he showed no sign
of wanting to praise the Dear Leader.

Altogether, then, a difficult crew. The question for Maecenas and
Augustus was: What can poets do for the regime? Either (a) in the directly "political" sense of bolstering the personal position of Octavian/
Augustus as permanent head of state, or (b) in the more general sense of
enlisting support for the moral and social revival which should distinguish his Rome from the disasters of the late Republic. Rome's future
should be strong enough to endure; it should be Roman in the best
sense, and it should deserve the moral respect of citizen and foreigner
alike.

Augustus was reshaping the city (see Chapter 10 by D. Favro,
this volume). Promoted from brick to marble, no longer inferior to
the cities of the Greek East, it must become the worthy capital of the
world. It must also serve the glory of Augustus and his new order.
The role of the visual arts was carefully planned. The Princeps perhaps
attached less importance to poetry, but excessive scepticism is inept. The
inscription recording the Secular Games of 17 B.C. gives prominent
place to Horace's *Carmen Saeculare*: "Carmen composuit Q. Horatius
Flaccus." His name appears along with those of the imperial family

and the highest grandees of Rome: heady promotion for the freedman's
son! A true laureate work, it prays that the young may be biddable,
the old unharassed, the birth-rate high, Roman arms supreme, and a
pious people rewarded with peace and prosperity.[8] Naturally, in his
last odes, Horace found occasion to refer to the *Carmen* and his own
performance of it (*Odes* 4.3, and especially the last stanzas of 4.6). As
for Virgil, Suetonius preserves some precious scraps of correspondence
between Virgil and Augustus, the master of the world begging and
cajoling the poet for a glimpse of some part, at least, of his forthcoming
Aeneid (Donatus Vita 31).

Clearly, Maecenas played a vital role here. Somehow Augustus
was convinced that poetry could contribute to his serious purposes.
No doubt he was familiar with Cicero's speech for the poet Archias.
A middle-brow Roman jury was expected to accept that poetry contributed importantly to the glory of Rome: there were precedents,
notably Ennius, the poet whom everyone had read at school.

The poets all profess to be under pressure to produce patriotic
and martial epic, to the glory of a dynast.[9] The suggestion is flattering
to both parties, not least in the formulae of refusal of the poisoned
chalice of large scale encomium. There is an element, no doubt, of
the conventional; but real relief breathes in a passage like Propertius
2.34.55ff., where the elegiac poet glories in his own erotic and personal
subject matter and greets with triumphant acclaim the news that the
national epic is actually getting written – not by him, of course, but by
Virgil. It will be greater than Homer! cries Propertius, in his delight:

> Cedite, Romani scriptores, cedite Grai!
> nescioquid maius nascitur Iliade.

> Yield, ye Roman writers, yield ye Greek!
> Something greater – I can't fathom it – than the *Iliad* is taking
> shape.

Augustus, it is reasonable to suppose, wanted and expected panegyric
verse about himself. Father Ennius had praised his patron's campaigns:
the *Annales* were to end triumphantly with Fulvius Nobilior's victories
in Aetolia, though later Ennius added further material. But Ennius
was sadly out of fashion with *les jeunes*. A ruler, newly and controversially established in power by civil war, who would lay out
Rome itself to his own greater glory, complete with a vast Forum
Augusti, naturally expected no less. The Princeps had hopes of L. Varius,
and not he alone: "Varius will write of your triumphs," Horace

obligingly promised Agrippa (*Odes* 1.6), but it seems that Varius, too, never did.

With Actium it became clear which way the wind of power would, from now on, be blowing. Horace in his *Epodes* finds different ways of glorifying that decisive but not wholly satisfactory engagement. He tries exploring the anxious feelings before the crisis (*Epode* 1). He tries, more ambitiously, to combine that anxiety with an account of the progress of battle and a celebration of victory (*Epode* 9); it is no wonder that interpreters have floundered. Finally, in the more classic genre of an ode, he falls back on Alcaeus: Now is the time to get drunk! (as if at the death of a personal enemy); yet the Egyptian queen, though a monster, drunk with success and surrounded with an unsavoury entourage of eunuchs, is allowed a gleam of dignity in death (*Ode* 1.37). Not all readers have been happy with the resulting mixture. It was left to Virgil to glorify the battle by distancing it as the depiction in the heroic past of something looming in the far future, intelligible only to the gods; and also to emulate the humanity of Homer, not withholding from an enemy the tragedy of defeat (*Aen.* 8.671ff., especially 711–13). The Nile, mourning for his children, spreads his mantle to call home the vanquished. No such note, years later, in Augustus' *Res Gestae* (Sections 24 and 25).

Propertius, before his Fourth Book, cannot bring himself to touch the tremendous theme without irreverence. "If all men lived the life of love, like me, the sea at Actium would not be full of Roman dead!" (2.15.41–4). And again: "Sterner men than I have been dominated by a woman, so don't blame me: look at Antony – an unworthy love lost him the Battle of Actium!" (2.16.37–40). And finally, with inexpressible relief: "Let me delight in a life of parties and passion; Actium is a subject for Virgil!" (2.34.59–63). Only in Book Four, as late as 16 B.C., does he attempt the topic in apparent seriousness (4.6). "In various ways peculiar, the poem does not look like a serious effort," comments Syme (1984, 184) and Propertius cannot keep up the pose of seriousness to the end. *Bella satis cecini*, he cries, "Enough of war!" and the poem ends with a party and plenty to drink (4.6.69).

In the end, of course, Augustus had to accept that Maecenas' poets would not produce that panegyric epic. He would have to be content with something else; and that was not so little. He had come to believe, or to say, that the collapse of the Republic was ultimately caused by the citizens' moral failings. These were not unfamiliar thoughts. The historian Sallust, a conventional moralist in literature if not in life, professed emphatic agreement (*Catiline* 2.5, 3.3–5, 5.8, 10–13, etc.). Wherever you looked, the decline of good old *disciplina* and *mores* was apparent, and a range of remedies was called for. Divine service must be revived, temples rebuilt. Young men must be athletic, girls chaste. Citizens must serve: as soldiers, as magistrates, and (where appropriate) as senators. Bachelors must renounce selfish celibacy, marry, and rear children for Rome.

The poets knew their own business better than the great master of propaganda: they declined panegyric verse but acquiesced in moral exhortation. Unmarried Horace, perhaps influenced by his impressive (though celibate) friend Virgil,[10] extolled the old-style Italian mother disciplining her sturdy sons.[11] The hero of a score of erotic odes and epodes urged the authorities to stamp out licence, by moral legislation and a simultaneous clean-up of public attitudes:

> quid tristes querimoniae,
> si non supplicio culpa reciditur:
> quid leges sine moribus
> vanae proficiunt?
> (*Odes* 3.24.34–7)

"Complaint without punishment is vain; laws without morality are useless."

The Epicurean who had lightly boasted that he had "learned that the gods lived undisturbed by human affairs" composed weighty hymns and told the Roman, in lapidary phrase, "You possess your empire because you conduct yourself as subordinate to the gods" (*dis te minorem quod geris, imperas*; *Odes* 3.6.5f.). Even that not inconsiderable claim is not enough. Horace adds that poets are the teachers and guardians of civilisation generally (*Epist.* 2.1.126ff.). So much for the art for art's sake of Catullus and Calvus!

Tibullus never mentions Augustus, but he does rise to a vision of ideal life in the Italian countryside, pastoral and erotic, admittedly, but also industrious and god-fearing, in which he will love to hear of the military triumphs of Messalla and Rome. That in its way endorsed the Augustan programme, in everything but praise of the Princeps himself.

So in the end the great poetry was forthcoming. In his last Book Propertius did what he could for Actium (4.6) but also succeeded much better with some edifying Roman aetiologies (4.1, 2, 4, 9, 10) and with a moving poem in memory of a lady, exemplar and paradigm of the Roman virtues and, by fortunate chance, connected to the imperial house (4.11). Horace buckled down and wrote the Roman Odes

(*Odes* 3.1–6), in which the political and religious side of Alcaeus was married with something of the grand manner of Pindar, to create a lyric capable of doing justice to the moral worth of Italy, the military glory of Rome, and the superhuman merits and historic achievement of the Princeps. In his Fourth Book he praised the young princes Tiberius and Drusus (not, of course, forgetting their father, Augustus) with the skill of a true laureate: their martial prowess and devotion to the country reanimates the Roman past and guarantees a truly Roman future! Even Ovid applied himself in the *Fasti* to the versifying of the Roman calendar and Roman history – not, of course, forgetting the supreme position and merits of Augustus and his family. From exile he pleaded that, were he allowed home, he would complete that unfinished work. The Princeps was unmoved, and the month of August remained unwritten. The memory of the calculated cheekiness of the *Amores* and, still more, the *Art of Love*, with their cool derision of cherished moral exhortation, was not erased by servile insertions into the *Fasti* and the last book of the *Metamorphoses*.[12]

The poets did what they could, more or less, with whatever inconsistency or eccentricity, for the New Age. But above all Virgil produced his *Aeneid*: the closest approach, it turned out, which was possible for a real poet to an epic on Augustus. "Augustus was singularly fortunate in discovering for his epic poet of Italy a man whose verse and sentiments harmonized so easily with his own ideas and policy," comments Syme (1939, 466).

Virgil had put himself through a rigorous training. First he translated a Hellenistic master, absorbing the influence of such Roman predecessors as Catullus, Calvus, and Gallus, whom he would transcend by including weighty matters of politics and the future of Rome. For that he must invent new ways, neither hackneyed nor unsophisticated. Next he challenged Hesiod, an archaic master of very high rank, with a work on a substantial scale. It was to satisfy the most exacting technical and poetic standards, but also to touch real life, both at the level of workaday existence and at that of values, patriotism, and moral regeneration.

The *Aeneid*, finally, required the creation of a new kind of epic. Homeric framework and manner must accommodate very different styles and material. Nothing was to be left out, and an epic on the grandest scale must satisfy the most refined modern poetic taste. Rome's manifest destiny and old-style Olympian power politics; Punic Wars and Platonic philosophy; Lucretius and Apollonius; the tribes and cults of Italy; Ennius and Euripides and Euphorion: all were to play a part in the poem. It should reconcile nostalgia for the Republic with enthusiasm for the Principate. It should endorse imperial claims at their fullest, and yet sympathise with the pathos of defeat and loss. The radiance of its verbal magic should allure the recalcitrant and dazzle the conservative. It should glorify Augustus, without being obviously about him. It should grieve for Dido and yet support the moral revolution.

An epic on Augustus presented insuperable problems. Augustus himself, talented as he was, could hardly be presented as an Achilles, a fearsome single-handed warrior, and Actium was an eminently unpoetical battle. Interaction with the gods of epic Olympian machinery would be a terrible obstacle to a contemporary audience. Not least, Virgil would be unable to deploy some of his greatest poetic strengths, especially his proven talent for ambiguity and for pathos: the defeated would have to deserve their defeat but not be denied sympathy.

It was, in fact, an undertaking so difficult that the poet himself said he must have been mad to attempt it. But attempt it he did; and to such effect that without the *Aeneid*, Augustan poetry, and the world's view of Augustus and his age, would be *Hamlet* without the Prince, or a Rome, not of marble, but of brick.

Suggestions for Further Reading

R. O. A. M. Lyne, *The Latin Love Poets: From Catullus to Horace* (Oxford 1980) presents a sensible and accessible overview of the elegiac and "new" poets in pre-Augustan and Augustan times; cf. his article on "The Neoteric Poets" in *Class. Quarterly* 28 (1978) 167–87. Useful and informative discussions of these poets, and of Virgil and Horace, may also be found in M. von Albrecht, *A History of Roman Literature*, vol. 1 (Leiden and New York 1997) and in the *Cambridge History of Classical Literature*, vol. 2 (Cambridge 1983). I have discussed aspects of the present topic from some other perspectives in Millar and Segal (1984) 189–218.

Notes

1   "Pope's imitation is a satire on George II, the British Augustus, and on the follies and flatteries of the age.... [It] concludes with an ironical panegyric on the king, conceived and expressed in his happiest manner" (Bonamy Dobree, in the Everyman edition of *The Collected Poems of Pope* [London, revised edn. 1956, 292]).

2   So too Propertius I. Horace's late works do tend to concentrate on the imperial family: *Odes* 4.1, 2, 4, 5, 14, 15; *Epistles* 2.1.

3 *Aeneid* 6.460 notoriously echoes Catullus 66.39. There has been much discussion of this apparently surprising fact. See Russell (1979) 13; O. Lyne in *G&R* 41 (1994) 187.

4 Catullus wrote that he had no wish to please Caesar, nor to know even as much of him as his complexion; he did not flinch from woundingly direct attack – though the Dictator accepted the slur with good grace: Catullus 93, 57; Suet., *Julius* 73. Calvus, too, composed scandalous pieces about the Dictator's sex life: Suet., *Julius* 49. That was the way to write about politicians, if one did it at all.

5 Ever since they were written, people have wanted to know exactly how these poems relate to experiences of Virgil's own. Did he lose his family land? Did he get it back? The ancient *Lives* have a lot to say, most of it obviously guesswork. What does appear is that hereafter the poet is to be found, not near Mantua, but near Naples (*Geo.* 4, apart from less reliable snatches in the *Catalepton*). My guess is that he lost his ancestral land and was compensated elsewhere: an unpoetical story, which he could make into poetry only by stylising and darkening it.

6 It is worth remembering that Augustus returned the compliment: none of the poets whose work glorified him and his restoration of Rome was thought by that subtle tyrant (the phrase is Edward Gibbon's) to deserve mention in his own account of his career, the astonishing *Res Gestae*.

7 Cf. the fragments preserved in *FLP* 276–81. They include galliambics, in which he is the only poet to follow Catullus 63, and hendecasyllables: fragment 3, "ni te visceribus meis, Horati/ plus iam diligo. . . ." is closely modelled on Catullus 14, leading Courtney (*ad loc.*) to comment: "One wonders how Horace felt at being addressed in Catullan terms."

8 "The greatest triumph of Horace's achievement as a lyric poet," in the judgment of Fraenkel (1957) 381. Not everyone agrees.

9 Wimmel (1960) assembles the passages: Virgil, *Ecl.* 6.1–12; Horace, *Sat.* 1.10.31ff., 2.1.4ff.; *Odes* 1.6, 2.12, 4.2, 4.3, 4.15; *Epist.* 2.1.250ff.; Propertius. 2.10, 2.34.25ff., 3.1, 3.3, 3.9, 4.1; Ovid, *Amores* 1.1, 1.15, 2.1, 2.18. As we should expect, Virgil sounds the most serious, Ovid the most frankly frivolous, in declining to produce historical epic on request. See my discussion in Millar and Segal (1984) 189–218. The tact of the Princeps is emphasised by A. Wlosok, *RhM* 143 (2000) 83.

10 References on that: V. Buchheit in *RhM* 143 (2000) 139f.

11 *Odes* 3.6.33–44; it is a pleasing touch of cynicism, perhaps, or at least of distance, that only two poems later Horace is writing, on the occasion of the Matronalia festival that was celebrated jointly by wives and husbands, "what shall I do as a single man on the Kalends of March?" (*Martiis caelebs quid agam Kalendis.* . . . ?).

12 For various views of the Augustan nature of the *Fasti* see Barchiesi (1997) and Herbert-Brown (2002).

14: POETS IN THE NEW MILIEU: REALIGNING

Peter White

The two decades of civil war preceding the Augustan Principate did not extinguish poetic activity in the capital. Libretti continued to be produced for scenic festivals each year and verse in other genres was being written in the 40s (notably by Cornelius Gallus, Varius, and Vergil) and in the 30s (when Horace made his debut). But the wars took a toll. The poets Helvius Cinna, Cornificius, Cassius Parmensis, and Ticida met violent deaths, to say nothing of victims like the Ciceros for whom poetry was an avocation. Gallus succumbed to politics in the peace immediately afterwards. Wholesale proscriptions and confiscations caused a transfer of wealth that touched many who did not lose their lives, apparently including Vergil, Horace, Tibullus, and Propertius.[1] And it was not only the effects on poets that depressed literary culture. The wars bled the whole upper class that had consumed and fostered poetry. Twenty years would have sufficed to transform literary society in any case, but there can be no doubt that the wars accelerated the turnover. Of the many personalities celebrated in Catullus' poems, the only one still active when peace returned was Asinius Pollio.

THE POST-WAR LITERARY MILIEU

The 20s both revived a cultural life that had flourished earlier and brought opportunities that were new. In the first place, poets regained the peace and ease they idealized as *otium*. In Roman society, *otium* had long been recognized as the proper domain of literary activity, the time off from serious commitments that could legitimately be reserved to culture. But it was an ideal formulated in opposition to war as well as to public and domestic business. In post-Actian Rome, the operative associations were the cessation of a protracted state of strife, the demobilization of thousands of officers and troops, and the prospect that property arrangements might finally stabilize and that society might again operate by settled norms (compare Velleius Paterculus, 2.89.3–4). *Otium* in this period often connotes feelings of relief, security, and entitlement. Tacitus thought that the mood was deliberately induced as Augustus "seduced all with the sweetness of ease" (*Annals* 1.2.1). One consequence was that Augustan Rome developed its own streak of Restoration license, well expressed by a poet who observed (apropos of Maecenas) that "a new ease softened the old standards. All things befit the victors when war subsides" (*Elegiae in Maecenatem*, 49–50).

Peace carried other consequences as well, the most important of which was improved longevity. The Augustan period acquired a distinctive literary character in part because so many of the leading players were able to sustain their roles. Tibullus died young, but in an era when life expectancy was typically lower, Vergil lived to almost his 51st birthday, Horace to almost his 57th, and Ovid to 58 or 59. Longevity created the possibility that poets could have careers. Vergil, Horace, and Ovid all remained productive over a span of 20 to 30 years or more. The great taste-makers of the age lived even longer than their protégés. Maecenas reached at least the age of 58, Messalla Corvinus 72, Augustus 76, and Pollio 80.

Peace also swelled the public that was prepared to attend to poetry. In the post-war period poets followed the example of rhetoricians and began to seek large, live audiences for their work. Since the Sophists of fifth-century Greece, teachers of rhetoric had trolled for custom by staging public demonstrations of their expertise. At Rome this practice culminated in the declamation, a speech improvised on a theme or situation drawn from a standard scholastic repertory. In the drought of genuine political oratory that set in with the end of the Republic, performances of show oratory began to attract new interest. The declamation moved out of the schools and became a successful form of entertainment, drawing grown-ups as well as students and educated enthusiasts as well as professionals.

The young Ovid became a habitué of the declamation circuit (Seneca, *Controversiae* 2.2.8–12). But a larger consequence was that the declamation model was adapted to performances of poetry. This crossover was a stroke by Pollio, a poet in his own right and an aficionado of declamation, who at some point in the 30s or 20s became "the first of all Romans to recite his works to an invited general audience" (Seneca, *Controversiae* 4 *pr.* 2). The formal poetry recitation differed from the declamation in that a competitive element was absent and poets were not expected to improvise. The venue was also different. Recitations were most often held in the townhouses of the leaders of society, who could guarantee that a throng of their friends and dependents would attend. On such occasions poets played to much larger audiences than the groups of comrades or dinner guests to whom they read their work informally.

Tacitus coupled wealth with *otium* among the instruments of Augustan policy, and for poets the prosperity of the principate had effects as important as the effects of peace. The winner-take-all cycle of the civil wars had concentrated unprecedented riches in the hands of Augustus and his partisans – vastly more than Julius Caesar was able to amass in the early rounds. Poets saw that a boom was on (Propertius 3.9.27–28; Ovid, *Amores* 2.9.17–18, *Art of Love* 3.113–14) and the right use of wealth emerges as a concern in many kinds of verse.

Their concern was not purely abstract. Poets gained opportunities to tap the wealth of the new plutocracy directly if they established personal relationships that bore fruit in the form of benefactions or bequests. I will have more to say about these relationships shortly. But poets also had a stake in the enormous sums that were being expended publicly. Richard Beacham (Chapter 7, pp. 160–73) shows that theatrical performances were multiplied and subsidized more extravagantly than ever as new theaters and new festivals proliferated during Augustus' reign. How poets contributed to the stage is the least documented aspect of their activity in this period, but the fact of their involvement is not in question. Of eight sketches of poets that Suetonius is known to have written for the Augustan portion of his *On Poets* (*De poetis*), one was of the mime writer Philistion. Ovid judged that script writing in his time was uniquely lucrative ("a poet can make money from the stage," *Tristia* 2.507). Varius was paid one million sesterces for a tragedy produced at games celebrating Augustus' Actian victory, and the demand for material was strong enough that even non-dramatic poetry was adapted for theatrical performances.[2]

Apart from shows, other public observances sometimes featured verse and probably verse written for pay. The most famous case is the celebration of the Secular Games in 17 B.C., for which Horace composed the extant hymn. But poets also contributed to less exceptional events, as to dedication ceremonies for temples that were built or rebuilt in this period.[3]

Another area of lavish investment was libraries. Although Rome did not have a single public library before the 30s, in the span of about fifteen years it acquired three (in the Atrium of Liberty off the Forum, in the Temple of Apollo complex on the Palatine, and in the Porticus Octaviae in the southern Campus Martius). Libraries benefited Augustan poets in two ways. Much of Latin poetry (Ovid's *Metamorphoses* or *Fasti* would be good examples) was erudite poetry meant to display the writer's knowledge and transcendence of exemplars both Greek and Latin. Such poets needed books in order to compose and the new libraries offered them a readily accessible stockpile. Less than a decade after Augustus opened the library adjoining the Temple of Apollo, Horace assumed that a young poet friend would be taking advantage – excessive advantage, he feared – of "the writings which Palatine Apollo has gathered" (*Epistles* 1.3.17).

Because libraries established a new avenue of access to the public, the Augustan poets also wanted to make sure that their own works were represented there. Horace pokes fun at the "pride and intensity" of colleagues who "inspect the building space available to Roman bards" (*Epistles* 2.2.92–94). Ovid's works occupied a niche in the public collections before he was exiled in A.D. 8 (*Tristia* 3.1.65) and in one of his exilic poems he envisions that a new manuscript will trudge from library to library seeking entry (*Tristia* 3.1.59–74). The attraction of its library partly explains why the Temple of Apollo is mentioned more often in Augustan poetry than any other contemporary monument (cf. also Barchiesi, this volume).

Poems that readers could consult in libraries they could, of course, purchase in bookshops. Although bookshops were already operating in Rome by the time of Catullus and Cicero, during the Augustan period more is heard about them. They may have been given a boost by the libraries. With booksellers in command of trained copyists, it is hard to imagine them *not* involved in the drive to create three public collections within a decade and a half. In any case, Horace increasingly takes it for granted that new poems including his own will be available in bookstores (*Satires* 1.4.71–72; *Epistles* 1.20.2; *Ars Poetica* 345, 373). The fact that Ovid continued to launch work in Rome for eight years after being disgraced, exiled, and banned from the libraries also suggests the enterprise of booksellers (one of whom is probably to be identified as the recipient of *Tristia* 3.14).

Whether cultural institutions predated the war years, like theaters and bookshops, or sprang up at the end, like formal recitations and libraries, the post-war surplus of wealth and leisure invigorated them all. Poetic vocations multiplied. Vergil's *Eclogues* and Horace's *Satires* show both men engaged with a variety of colleagues and rivals even before the wars ended. Ovid names seven poets in the ascendant when he began in the late 20s (*Tristia* 4.10.41–52) and he lists thirty-one in a retrospect written at the close of his career (*Letters from Pontus* 4.16). We know of still other Latin poets whom he does not mention, as well as of Greek poets active in Rome who do not enter his purview at all.

For a critic seeking to generalize about Augustan poetry, the abundance of poets creates an obvious problem of extrapolating from five who are extant and knowable to some three dozen others who are not. But for the poets themselves, or at least for their poetry, it was probably salutary that there were so many of them. In the generation after the Augustans, Velleius Paterculus observed that Rome's greatest poets clustered in close proximity to one another (1.17.2), and he explained the phenomenon in terms of competition: "Emulation nourishes literary talents, and envy and admiration by turns incite imitation" (1.17.6, compare 2.36). The Augustan poets (to generalize) were competing as intensely with contemporaries as with the literary predecessors of whose influence we are most aware, and the currents of envy and admiration ripple often through their work.

Augustan Rome thus stimulated poetic activity in several ways. That is what can save from triviality even a minimalist definition of Augustan poetry as verse written in Rome between 27 B.C. and A.D. 14. However divergent in theme and politics, all poets of this era shared the advantage of writing in a milieu which was more supportive of poetry than ever before. Not the least important facts about Augustan verse are the quantity in which it was produced and the appetite for it.

SOCIAL ATTACHMENTS

That the Augustan poets enjoyed greater opportunities of cultivating a public than their predecessors comes out in a shift of attitude toward readers. Neither Tibullus nor Propertius nor Ovid echoed Horace's claim to write only for the discerning few (*Satires* 1.10.73–90), and Horace himself moved from decrying vulgar publication (*Satires* 1.4.71–72) to abetting it (*Epistles* 1.20.1–5). Yet it would be a mistake to think that their access to the public was unmediated. From almost the beginning of Roman literary history, poets are regularly associated with more powerful members of society who champion them. Poems in the smaller genres often pay compliments to such persons and sometimes allow glimpses of the relationship. Vergil's *Eclogues*, for example, compliment men who were militarily active in the civil wars and who are said to have protected Vergil at that time and in that capacity (Pollio, Varus, Caesar Octavian, and Cornelius Gallus). Horace's *Odes* and *Epistles* advertise those who flourished in the subsequent peace. At least seventeen of the contemporaries whom he addresses are either senators or eminent knights (Maecenas and Sallustius Crispus), and the poems written for them are often spun out of situations that place poet and addressee in the same company, such as suppers and drinking parties, visits to country estates, and literary pursuits. Propertius addresses about a third of the poems in his first book (1, 5, 6, 10, 13, 14, 20, 22) to two young aristocrats whose pastimes he presents himself as sharing. Even the choice of genres reflects this background. Satire, love elegy, and the verse epistle all celebrate in different ways the intercourse which poets and their friends enjoyed outside the poetry.

The poems intimate that the poets stood on familiar terms with their society friends. Horace asserts as much in his boast that he had "pleased the first men of Rome at home and on campaign" (*Epistles* 1.20.23). This habit of intercourse with the élite draws attention to an important fact about the poets' background. Although poets of the period differ widely in status, ranging from freedmen like Melissus to great senators like Pollio and even to Augustus himself, the five who epitomize Augustan poetry for us all cluster at the threshold of the upper class. They are not outsiders or dependents like many of the early Latin poets. Tibullus and Ovid came from equestrian families (*Vita Tib.* p. 112 Luck; Ovid, *Tristia* 4.10.4–8). Propertius, who describes himself as a scion of "ancient Umbria with its well-known households," says that his family was prosperous up until the expropriations of the civil wars (4.1.121–30). Although Vergil's origins were humbler, he had sufficient resources to devote himself to a career of art and study in north Italy, Rome, Campania, and Sicily (Donatus, *Vita Verg.* 7, 13; Vergil, *Georgics* 4.563–64). Horace insists that despite his freedman parentage, he received the same liberal education in the capital that "any senator or knight would bestow upon his own offspring" (*Satires* 1.6.77–78) and in his early twenties he served as an equestrian officer in a Roman legion (*Satires* 1.6.48). Though none except perhaps Ovid would be counted rich by Roman standards, all five enjoyed the education, leisure, and respectability that fitted them to join in the amusements and cultural pursuits of Roman knights and senators.

In part it was because knights and senators were apt to be writers of verse themselves that they liked to associate with poets. The rise in vocations for poetry among the upper class can be and has been seen as one consequence of the establishment of the Principate. Augustus now directly or indirectly determined the fate of careers in oratory, politics, jurisprudence, and the military. Of the traditional paths to distinction, literature was the one over which he had the least sway, and perhaps for that reason, it became an attractive alternative. Whatever the reason, it lured many. Ovid almost immediately abandoned the quest for a Senate career in favor of poetry, saying that political ambition entailed too much stress (*Tristia* 4.10.37–38). Horace hints at a similar experience in *Satires* 1.6, and the *Ciris* poet confesses that he turned to poetry after failing at politics (1–4). Propertius says he opted for poetry rather than oratory (4.1.133–34). Half of the seventeen grandees to whom Horace addressed his *Odes* and *Epistles* wrote verse, a pursuit which he says had spread through capital society like a craze (*Epistles* 2.1.108–10).

Poetry in this milieu was not merely a common taste but in some degree a communal activity. Its devotees wrote together and read their work to one another, offered suggestions about possible subjects, and exchanged criticism of results.[4] Where the parties diverged – though they remained linked – was over their concern with publicity. Socialites desired to be celebrated in the verse of their more talented poet friends, whereas poets who were not themselves upper-class and not yet well-known counted on the prestige of their connections to help launch them professionally.[5] The practical consideration behind Horace's appeal to the few (*Satires* 1.4.73) was that whatever the leaders of society approved, others would soon embrace.

Poets who were taken up by the great were also in a position to benefit financially. Munificence had an important place in the ethic of friendship, and especially at the top of society. Since poets' relationships are known to us mainly through their poems, however, and since the poems maintain a certain reticence about material benefits, we know few specifics. But Horace assumes in *Epistles* 1.18 that an aspiring poet who establishes a tie with a rich man would normally profit from it, and gifts happen to be recorded for Vergil, Tibullus, Ovid, and Horace himself.[6] The pattern of munificence in Roman society suggests that although the gifts poets received from friends could be large, they would not have amounted to anything so reliable or steady as a pension. The most common form of benefaction was the inheritance or testamentary bequest (which is what inspired Horace to compose a satiric instruction about legacy-hunting in *Satires* 2.5).

MAECENAS, MESSALLA, AND POLLIO

The society projected in Augustan verse is reminiscent in some ways of that seen a generation earlier in the poems of Catullus. Poets associate freely with aristocrats and other notables because they have some footing in the upper class in their own right, personal alignments are manifold and overlapping, and poetry is a widely-shared pursuit. What is different about the Augustan milieu is that three figures appear to play a disproportionate role in organizing it.

Maecenas, Messalla, and Pollio – Augustus will be considered in the next section – undeniably loom large in sources for the period. But the sources suggest that their relationships with poets differed from those of other magnates primarily in being more durable. In Latin sources they are normally characterized in the same way, as "friends" rather than as "patrons," and their demands for the companionship of poets were the most insistent. A fragment from an ancient life of Tibullus says that it was Messalla to whom Tibullus "showed his love ahead of others" (*Vita Tib.* p. 112 Luck). The implication is that Messalla was only one of Tibullus' connections, but the one he cultivated most attentively. The writer of the *Panegyricus Messallae* assured Messalla that he too would attend him faithfully.[7] Ovid's attachment to Messalla lasted for over two decades, from his own youth until Messalla's death. Vergil was associated with Maecenas for almost as long a period, from about 40 to 19 B.C. Horace's relationship continued even longer, from 38 to 8 B.C., and many passages in his work show that it involved him in a steady round of obligations (for example *Satires* 2.6.42–43; 2.7.32–35; and *Epistles* 1.7. 25–28).

Those in society with whom poets developed close ties lasting over many years could be expected to reciprocate with more generous gifts than less intimate acquaintances. As three of the richest men to emerge from the civil wars, Maecenas, Messalla, and Pollio were well able to be generous, and all are in fact said to have made gifts to poets. Maecenas especially was lauded for his generosity in the accolades of poets who hailed him as "my stronghold," the "pillar" or "guardian of my estate," and the "enviable hope of my youth."[8] His liberality was the quality most often recalled by wistful poets of the following era as well.[9]

The after-image of Maecenas raises an incidental point that is relevant to our perceptions of the Augustan milieu. Of the three men who seem to dominate it, he is the only one whose fame as a supporter of poets outlived him. Testimony to Messalla's and Pollio's role is confined mostly to contemporary sources and more particularly to the Tibullan corpus in the one case and the text of Vergil with its scholia in the other. Yet if the totality of Augustan verse were extant, it would surely enlarge and perhaps alter our sense of the social background. When Juvenal reviewed the great models of generosity to poets in times past, he listed Maecenas in first place. Of Messalla and Pollio, however, he made no mention, naming instead four others (Proculeius, Fabius, Cotta, and Lentulus) about whose activities very little happens to be recorded (*Satires* 7.94–95).

Lacunae in the record notwithstanding, the wealth and prestige of Maecenas, Messalla, and Pollio would certainly have put them in a position to outbid most of their peers for the attention of poets. How systematically they attempted to do that we are left to infer from indications which are meager and indirect. But vicarious literary glory does not appear to have been Pollio's ambition. Although he can be linked with Vergil and a couple of other poets down into the 30s, after that the only sign of active ties with anyone is a single poem of Horace (*Odes* 2.1). Pollio made himself a force on the literary scene by organizing the first public library, by pioneering the practice of recitation, and by promoting himself as a writer of both prose and verse and as a critic. But so far from indicating that he acted as a mainstay to other writers, anecdotes about him expose an abrasiveness that led one contemporary to call him "congenitally bloody-minded" (Seneca, *Controversiae* 4. pr. 4). It was his own work, not others', that he is said to have launched at recitations.

The situation is different with Maecenas and Messalla, each of whom cultivated ties with many poets. At least nine can be named who came within Maecenas' orbit: Domitius Marsus, Fundanius, Horace, Melissus, Plotius Tucca, Propertius, Varius, Vergil, and Viscus. As many or more can be associated with Messalla, though not all are identifiable by name: Horace, Ovid, Sextilius Ena, Sulpicia, Tibullus, Valgius, Vergil, and the anonymous authors of the *Panegyricus Messallae, Catalepton 9,* and the *Ciris* (if those poems are authentic products of the Augustan period). These are remarkable numbers, equaled elsewhere in Roman literary history only by Pliny's record of friendships among poets. The number alone would raise the possibility that Maecenas and Messalla set out to gather coteries around them.

Unfortunately, the available data disclose little more than that they had contacts with poets, rarely what the contacts were like. In the case of Messalla, for example, we learn that Horace and the authors of the *Ciris* and of *Catalepton 9* addressed poems to him, that Horace and

Vergil were cast with him as interlocutors in a literary dialogue by
Maecenas, that Sextilius Ena gave a recitation at his house, that Valgius
was acquainted with him and the author of the *Panegyricus* wanted to
be better acquainted, and that his ward Sulpicia found him an obstacle
to visiting her lover. Only Tibullus and Ovid testify to an ongoing
relationship, and not in much detail. The one literary pair who do
emerge in the round are Maecenas and Horace, thanks both to Horace's
poetic focus on the everyday and to a biographical sketch of Horace
that Suetonius composed. But even in this case the evidence is one-
sided. No letters of Maecenas and only fragments of his other writings
survive. The sort of first-person testimony that exists to back up Pliny's
claim to be a friend of letters a century later is wholly unavailable for
the Augustan period.

What sort of influence Maecenas and Messalla exercised over the
work of poets they took up therefore remains a mystery. The people around them may well have formed relatively stable and coherent
groups. Horace once asserts that Maecenas' literary friends were organized in this way (*Satires* 1.9.43–56), and the Tibullan corpus has been
seen as a relic of the coterie that flourished around Messalla. It consists of verse by Tibullus and (seemingly) four other writers, most of
whom obviously do, and all of whom may, have ties to Messalla. It is
the only Latin collection known in which the social affiliation of the
poets appears to have determined the selection.

But for those around Messalla and around Maecenas alike, it is
uncertain whether social coherence also implies ideological coherence.
Sources for all periods describe Latin poets and their society friends as
collaborating in the writing process, and throughout Latin literary history poets alternately make claims to be writing at the behest of friends
and maneuver to evade their impositions. In *Epodes* 14, for example,
Horace claims that he is under pressure from Maecenas to finish his
iambics, and in *Epistles* 1.1 that he is under pressure to produce more
love lyrics. Propertius intimates that Maecenas urged him to compose an
epic (3.9). Vergil says that he wrote his agricultural poem at Maecenas'
bidding (*Georgics* 3.41). It is open to debate, however, how far such
hints of direction make Maecenas' entourage comparable to those literary circles of the Renaissance and afterwards in which the impetus of
a leader or a shared agenda is crucial. Nothing that the poets say about
Maecenas' literary role distinguishes it from the role played by other
Roman magnates before and after him.

Modern readers who have nevertheless suspected that Maecenas
and Messalla did provide ideological leadership point to a difference

in the orientation of their protégés. None of the writers represented in the Tibullan corpus ever mentions Augustus, whereas poets who can be tied to Maecenas – Horace, Vergil, Propertius, and Varius – are responsible for most of the contemporary panegyric on Augustus. That disparity has suggested that Maecenas was recruiting talent for the regime, while Messalla may have been a counter-force toward whom oppositional poets gravitated.

Although neither of these inferences can be confirmed or disproved, the latter has less to commend it than the former. The silence regarding Augustus in the Tibullan corpus is after all a silence. The poets say nothing either negative or positive, and their apparent obliviousness of Augustus can be explained as a consequence of their absorption in concerns of private life. Except for the author of the *Panegyricus*, they all kept to love poetry. Moreover, it is arbitrary to take into account only the evidence of the Tibullan corpus and to disregard Messalla's links with Horace and Vergil. But the most improbable part of this interpretation is its presentation of Messalla as a leader of the opposition. Although he had opposed the future Augustus early in the civil war, he soon rallied to him. He made propaganda against Antony in the 30s, fought for Augustus at Actium, and amassed honors, offices, and riches all through his reign. It was Messalla who in 2 B.C. proclaimed that Augustus merited universal recognition as the "Father of His Country."

Nothing, on the other hand, tells against the possibility that Maecenas might have encouraged verse in praise of Augustus. In the Roman milieu it was not unusual to solicit favors, including literary favors, on behalf of one's friends as well of oneself. For their part, poets were well aware that Maecenas was close to Augustus, and they may indeed have thought to use him as a stepping-stone.[10] But Maecenas made too exuberant a splash to have been acting *simply* as the agent of Augustus. He aspired to celebrity in his own right as a poet and prosateur, and so far as the extant fragments show, his works did not have a political orientation. Though several of his protégés wrote enthusiastically about Augustus, the particular poems which Maecenas is said to have encouraged – Horace's iambics and love lyrics and Vergil's *Georgics* – are not the most fervent portions of their oeuvre. Some members of his group, like the comic playwrights Melissus and Fundanius, may have written nothing political at all.

Maecenas' implication in the panegyrical slant of Augustan poetry is likely. But evidence of it is too scanty to be interpreted except in context of a broader argument about Augustus' own role. In any case, politics would be but one dimension of Maecenas' engagement. It should not prevent us from seeing that he fits the conventional profile of dilettante, impresario, and benefactor as perfectly as anyone in Roman literary history.

AUGUSTUS

Augustus, too, exhibited some of the characteristic behaviors of a friend of letters. According to Suetonius, "he encouraged the literary talents of his day by every means. He generously and patiently listened to recitations, not only of poems and histories but also of speeches and dialogues" (*Augustus* 89.3). But his relationship to poets and poetry is too complex to be understood in those terms alone. And while the very complexity of his relationships resists efforts to analyze them, we cannot get along without recourse to some sorting tools. Here it will be useful to distinguish three contexts in which Augustus could engage with contemporary poets: as a personal friend or acquaintance, as a head of government, and as an emblem of society and nation.

The first relationship is represented in its most intimate form by his ties with Vergil and Horace, which lasted for over two decades. He exchanged letters with them, solicited poems from them, and lavished presents on them.[11] He attended private readings of the *Georgics* and the *Aeneid* and received a presentation copy of the *Odes*.[12] He took Vergil into his entourage during a trip abroad and invited Horace to assume a secretarial position in his household.[13] He was named heir in both their wills and he pressed for publication of the *Aeneid* when it lay unfinished at Vergil's death.[14] Apart from one dubious story that he made Vergil rewrite part of the *Georgics*, we know no more about efforts on his part to prescribe poetic content than we know in the case of Maecenas or anybody else.[15] But his attentions would have established a powerful claim on the poets' good will.

The intimate relationship that Vergil and Horace established with Augustus put them on a different footing from all other poets, with the possible exception of Varius. That it was unique is part of what makes it difficult to interpret, and it was doubly unique. Not only were Vergil and Horace in a privileged position among three dozen or more poets of their own day, but their experience was never repeated afterwards. Although many of Augustus' successors had literary tastes, none formed comparable literary attachments. Augustus himself made no new move in this direction during the two decades following Horace's death.

Even with Vergil and Horace, however, Augustus did not form the same kind of relationship as did other Roman gentlemen. One reason was practical. He was absent from Rome and Italy for more than half of the two decades after the battle of Actium, and with the exception of an invitation to Vergil to join his entourage when they once encountered each other abroad, we never hear that he took poets along on his trips. Even during periods when he was resident in the capital, his responsibilities impeded the sustained contact that was normal in friendships between poets and the great. None of Horace's occasional poems points to dinners or visits with the emperor, and a fragment from one of Augustus' letters confirms that Horace was not a regular at the palace (Suetonius, *Vita Hor.* 297.26 Roth).

But a more fundamental complication of the relationship was that personal acquaintance did not supersede the other two dimensions of Augustus' influence. The great friend of Vergil and Horace was also their de facto ruler – formally at least, Horace's commission to compose the *Carmen Saeculare* emanated from the government rather than the man – and the most conspicuous symbol of Roman sovereignty on their horizon.

Augustus' power as symbol was the most tenuous of his three forms of influence over poets but it was the most pervasive; there was probably no poet of his day on whom he failed to make some impression. The emergence of a paramount *princeps* had completed a teleology at work in Rome since long before the civil wars. The figure who now stood at the apex of society became a model of style and behavior from whom others took their cues, as Tacitus observed (*Annals* 3.55.4). The emperor engrossed the field of politics as well as social performance. Since there was no aspect of political life to which he was irrelevant, he quickly became an emblem of the state. In the perceptive word-play of Ovid, *res est publica Caesar* – "Caesar is public property" and "Caesar is the Commonwealth" (*Tristia* 4.4.15).

Augustus' ascendancy drew a more engaged response from poets than simple acquiescence, and here again their social standing is relevant. The poets of this period were as proud of their place within the bourgeoisie as they were of their consecration by the Muses. Civic and patriotic themes, many related to Augustus, appear in the work of every one of the five who are extant. Horace in several of his pieces goes so far as to claim the role of spokesman for the entire citizen community.[16] Even Tibullus and Ovid, who are not thought to have stood in close proximity to either Augustus or Maecenas, contributed praise of the new imperial Rome then under construction. Though Augustus is not named in Tibullus' long poem on the induction of Messalla's son into the priestly College of Fifteen (2.5), for example, he is an inescapable point of reference for it. Messalinus was a fellow-priest whom Augustus appointed. In that capacity, he was charged with consulting Sibylline prophecies which Augustus had authenticated, in a ritual performed in the Temple of Apollo which Augustus had built. The poem for the occasion hints at Apollo's role in vanquishing Antony at Actium and gives pride of place to a Sibylline prophecy about Aeneas and his son that parallels the plot of Vergil's epic.

Critics have had notable success in examining those themes, traits, and tendencies of Augustan poetry which can be interpreted as collective responses to the new milieu. Galinsky (1996) and Zanker (1988), for example, describe both ideological and formal convergences of artistic production during the period. But if it is true that Augustus' power was at its most diffuse when it was projected as symbol, reactions by individual poets should diverge as much as they overlap. Galinsky stresses that responses to Augustus do vary from poet to poet and even from poem to poem by the same poet, and most critics have acknowledged the distinctive features of Vergil's response. But not all poetry about Augustus has received an equally empathetic reading. When he is the focus, critics have often hesitated to proceed on the normal assumption that a poem is an autonomous exploration of an inviting material, worked out in terms specific to that piece.

Attention to individual poetic responses has been displaced by a preoccupation with the second dimension of Augustus' influence. Augustus could exert effects on poets not as friend and enthusiast or as symbol only, but also as government. In some cases he used governmental power to benefit them, when, for example, he showcased work by his friends Varius and Horace at public festivals. But there were also poets who fared badly under his rule. The elegist Cornelius Gallus found himself with no options but suicide after he gave offense in an office to which Augustus had appointed him (Dio 53.23.5–7; Suetonius, *Augustus* 66.2), and the tragedian Gracchus is probably the Sempronius Gracchus later exiled for an affair with Augustus' daughter (Ovid, *Letters from Pontus* 4.16.31; Tacitus, *Annals* 1.53.3). While Gallus' and Gracchus' downfall would seem unconnected with verse they had written, Ovid maintains that *he* was exiled in part for having written the *Art of Love* (*Tristia* 2.207–12). During Augustus' last decade in power, when another species of verse incurred his ire, he began prosecuting the authors of defamatory lampoons for treason (Suetonius, *Augustus* 55; Tacitus, *Annals* 1.72).

Consideration of Augustus' reach as head of a government has not been limited to these obvious cases. Political motives are widely thought to be the key to his interactions with poets generally, and to interactions via Maecenas as well. The Augustan Principate introduces a new framework for thinking about the relationship of literature to the state. For the first time since the regal period, Rome had a stable, decades-long administration centralized in one man. It was now possible to pursue political programs more systematically than before, and in the particular regime instituted by Augustus, programs were not necessarily overt. The blurring of the distinction between public and private roles is a hallmark of the Principate. It is therefore not unreasonable to suspect that Augustus may have manipulated literary interactions which for other aristocrats would have belonged to the realm of the apolitical.

The problem has been to decide how it could be verified that Augustus made poetry an object of policy and how he went about implementing it if he did. Having nothing comparable to archives for the Principate – or any other period of Roman history – we know relatively few details of his administration. Furthermore, all that we do know suggests that if he had a literary policy, it would have been improvised over the course of his reign and would not have looked the same by the end as at the beginning. Both factors limit the chances of discovering a consistent pattern in his relations with poets.

Interpreters have tried to overcome the dearth of primary evidence by drawing from explanatory models. The suggestion that Augustan po-etry is a kind of court poetry, for example, or that Augustus encouraged some poets to create propaganda for his regime and censored others rests on ideas borrowed consciously or unconsciously from more transparent systems. Yet it is implicit in the term that any model inevitably stands at some remove from the phenomena it is called upon to organize. One reason that Augustan poetry is rarely discussed as court poetry nowadays is that royal courts have become alien to our experience. But even if that were not so, the model would be inadequate because Augustus went out of his way to dissociate his regime from contemporary monarchies and because Roman poets who might have wished to represent him as a monarch lacked an established idiom in which to do so. Another idea whose explanatory value has waned is that Maecenas functioned as Augustus' Minister of Propaganda. Distortions occur at both focal points of this model. For all his influence with Augustus, Maecenas took no actual role in government after the 30s. And as Eich (2000) most recently has insisted, our notions of propaganda are so tied up with political institutions and techniques of the last two centuries that they cannot easily be projected back upon the operations of the Roman state. Eich has criticized the applicability of the concepts "censorship" and "publicity" for similar reasons. But new models for understanding Augustus' influence over poetry continue to be proposed and debated. In the wake of Foucault, critics have begun to study Augustan texts as part of a discourse conditioned by circumambient and saturating power, an approach of which Kennedy (1992) may stand as an articulate early example.

Many of these ideas, including some which have been criticized as inadequate, do serve to clarify aspects of Augustus' role. Although Vergil and Horace may not exactly qualify as court poets, for example, it cannot be fortuitous that for centuries afterwards, their tropes and language were borrowed by poets who did have occasion to address monarchs. Nor is censorship a wholly inappropriate label for Augustus' action in publicly denouncing the *Ars Amatoria* and having it removed from the state libraries. But thinking with models always carries the risks that we may allow the model to distract us from data it is unable to account for, or worse, allow it to mask or substitute for non-existent data. In any case, no model has yet succeeded in becoming standard. Scholars are probably less close to agreement about the proper framework in which to understand Augustus' relationships with poets than at any time since the debate began.

Understanding can still be improved at a lower level of abstraction, however. As noted earlier, many poems of Horace, Propertius, and Ovid that focus on Augustus deserve further scrutiny. By way of closing, let me suggest four other areas that might repay investigation:

(1) Conclusions about poetry under Augustus have been based predominantly on the five canonical Latin poets. But in the flotsam of unattributed, pseudonymous, and minor poems that have come down to us are several which speak about Augustus and which are probably contemporary (epigrams of Domitius Marsus, the *Consolatio ad Liviam*, and the *Elegiae in Maecenatem*, for example). Second-rate productions are apt to be more revealing in proportion as they are less accomplished. The *Consolatio* in particular seems an important witness to the Augustan milieu, regardless of who wrote it.

(2) In addition to Latin verse, there is a not inconsiderable corpus of epigrams by Greek poets (some resident in Rome) who celebrate the imperial house but position themselves differently than Latin poets. These poems, too, need to be integrated into our understanding of the Augustan literary climate.[17]

(3) Any account of the relationship between government and literature under Augustus should prepare us to understand the sequel. In general, the structures that Augustus introduced remained in place and the emperors who followed him also had sophisticated literary interests. If Augustus made poetry a target of policy, what became of that policy under his successors?

(4) Suetonius was uniquely placed to know the role of poetry under the Principate. He served as a palace secretary under Trajan and Hadrian, he wrote sketches of Latin poets, versions of which are extant for Vergil and Horace, and he wrote biographies of emperors in which literature was a regularly featured rubric. Apart from the details for which he is cited, does Suetonius offer us any framework for understanding poetry in relation to the Principate?

Every advance in our understanding of Augustus' interactions with poets is likely to induce some alteration in our understanding of Augustan politics generally. The historical attrition that destroyed most other contemporary writings about the new regime happened to leave much of the testimony by poets intact. Through default they are our primary record of Augustan discourse.

SUGGESTIONS FOR FURTHER READING

Good bibliographies for individual Augustan poets are available in many recent studies devoted to them, especially as the relevant volumes in the *Cambridge* and *Brill's Companion* series become available. In addition to the titles listed throughout this volume, the following are worth consulting for broad perspectives on the Augustan literary environment:

H. Bardon, *La littérature latine inconnue* (Paris 1952). This useful complement to conventional literary histories seeks to recuperate and place in context those Latin authors known only by fragments or as mere names. The first third of volume 2 surveys lost literature of the Augustan period.

E. Fantham, *Roman Literary Culture: From Cicero to Apuleius* (Baltimore and London 1996). Conceived as a social history of Latin literature rather than as a literary history, this study emphasizes institutional elements that conditioned literary production: schooling, libraries, booksellers and book technology, aristocratic patronage and Greek intellectual dominance, and the power of the emperor.

R. Gurval, *Actium and Augustus: The Politics and Emotions of Civil War* (Ann Arbor 1995). Gurval analyzes the ideological meaning of Augustus' victory at Actium, arguing that it was constructed less by the government than by poets, and that the poets took divergent views of it.

Raaflaub and Toher (1990). This volume, comprising almost a score of essays, is dedicated to Ronald Syme and pursues a number of issues that are associated with him. Six papers discuss Augustus' impact on contemporary writers.

P. White, *Promised Verse: Poets in the Society of Augustan Rome* (Cambridge, Mass. 1993). A more detailed argument along the lines of the preceding essay.

T. Woodman and D. West (eds.), *Poetry and Politics in the Age of Augustus* (Cambridge 1984). The eight papers range from close readings to broadly framed essays; they also take an instructive range of positions on the nature of the influence Augustus exerted and on the way poets responded to it.

NOTES

* I am grateful to Robert Kaster and Karl Galinsky for suggesting improvements at several points in this essay.

1 Donatus, *Vita Verg.* 19–20 Hardie; Horace, *Epistles* 2.2.46–51; Tibullus, 1.1.19–20 and 41–43; Propertius, 4.1.128–30. The author of the *Panegyricus Messallae* testifies to a similar reverse in lines 181–90.

2 Varius' honorarium: H. D. Jocelyn, *Classical Quarterly* 30 (1980) 387–400. Adaptations: Donatus, *Vit. Verg.* 26 Hardie (Vergil); Ovid, *Tristia* 2.519–20, 5.7.25–28 (Ovid).

3 Ovid, *Tristia* 2.23–24. Origins in performance have occasionally been hypothesized for other Augustan poems on the basis of internal indications, as for example Horace, *Odes* 1.37 and Propertius, 4.6.

4 Communal reading and writing: Horace, *Odes* 2.9.17–20; Ovid, *Letters from Pontus* 2.4.13–14, 3.5.39–40; *Ciris* 19–20. Suggestions: Vergil, *Eclogues* 6.9, 8.11–12; Horace, *Epistles* 2.2.58–64; the *Ars Poetica* is an extended suggestion to the Pisones. Shared criticism: Ovid, *Letters from Pontus* 2.4.17–18, 4.12.25–26.

5 The poet confers glory on those he names: Vergil, *Eclogues* 6.6–12, Horace, *Odes* 1.26; Ovid, *Tristia* 3.4.67–68; *Letters from Pontus* 4.12.1–3; *Panegyricus Messallae* 1–7, 24–27, 177–211; *Ciris* 35–41. The poet himself derives fame from the prestige of his connections: Vergil, *Georgics* 2.40; Propertius, 2.1.74; *Panegyricus Messallae* 27.

6 Gifts to Vergil: Donatus, *Vita Verg.* 9 and 13 Hardie (from Pollio and unspecified others); to Tibullus: *Vita Tib.* p. 112 Luck (from Messalla); to Ovid: *Letters from Pontus* 4.5.37–38 (from Sextus Pompeius); to Horace: *Odes* 2.18.12–14 with scholia; *Epistles* 1.7.15 and 39 (from Maecenas).

7 Lines 192–9. The application to join a great man's entourage became a literary convention. The *Panegyricus* has an analog in *Catalepton* 4, and Horace produced

a variation on the form at *Satires* 1.6.45–62 – which did not discourage a pseud-epigrapher from concocting a prose letter in which Horace introduces himself to Maecenas (Suetonius, *Vita Hor.* p. 298.25–26 Roth).

8   Horace, *Odes* 1.1.2, 2.17.3–4; *Epistles* 1.1.103; and Propertius, 2.1.73 respectively.

9   *Laus Pisonis* 230–48; Martial, *Epigrams* 1.107, 8.55, 11.3, 12.3; Juvenal, *Satires* 7.94.

10 For poets' awareness of the relationship between Maecenas and Augustus, see for example Horace, *Satires* 2.6.40–56; *Odes* 2.12.9–12; Propertius, 3.9.27–34; *Elegiae in Maecenatem* passim; and Calpurnius, *Eclogues* 4.157–63.

11 Correspondence: Tacitus, *Dialogus* 13.2; Donatus, *Vita Verg.* 31 Hardie; Macrobius, *Saturnalia* 1.24.11; Suetonius, *Vita Hor.* p. 297.24–34 and p. 298.13–19 Roth; requests for poems: Donatus, *Vita Verg.* 31 Hardie; Suetonius, *Vita Hor.* pp. 297.35–298.7 Roth; gifts: Horace, *Epistles* 2.1.245–47; Servius on Vergil, *Aeneid* 6.862; Suetonius, *Vita Hor.* p. 297.34 Roth.

12 Donatus, *Vita Verg.* 27 and 32 Hardie, and Horace, *Epistles* 1.13.

13 Donatus, *Vita Verg.* 35 Hardie, Suetonius, *Vita Hor.* p. 297.17–23 Roth.

14 Donatus, *Vita Verg.* 37 and 41 Hardie, Suetonius, *Vita Hor.* p. 298.31–33 Roth.

15 In his commentary at *Eclogues* 10.1 and *Georgics* 4.1, Servius reports that a tribute to Cornelius Gallus was removed from book 4 after Gallus' disgrace (3: 118.4–9 and 320.6–10 Thilo).

16 Most clearly in *Epodes* 7 and 16, and in *Odes* 1.2, 3.6, and 3.24.

17 One relevant text that has recently received near-monographic attention from Barbantani (1998) is *Supplementum Hellenisticum* 982, celebrating Augustus' triumphant arrival in Egypt in 30.

15: VERGIL'S *AENEID* AND OVID'S *METAMORPHOSES* AS WORLD LITERATURE

Karl Galinsky

A mong the many poetic accomplishments of the Augustan age, two stand out and tower over the rest: Vergil's *Aeneid* (written between 29 and 19 B.C.) and Ovid's *Metamorphoses* (published around A.D. 8). The reason is not just their epic length – 12 books for the *Aeneid*, 15 for the *Metamorphoses* – but their richness and scope of defining the human experience. It is for that reason they have become, deservedly, world literature, a dimension that is fully borne out by their reception in later literature, art, and music, a reception that has lasted to our days in both the old world and the new. The term 'world literature' also characterizes the roots of these poems in the Augustan milieu and their contributions to that milieu. On a very literal level, they encompass a world that was not limited any longer to Rome and Italy but a world that had been opened up into what the Romans called the *orbis terrarum*; Ovid would designate Augustus as *pater orbis* ("father of the world"; *Fasti* 2.130). The special and enduring quality of Vergil's and Ovid's poems is that they extended this universal perspective to their treatment of the human condition.

As all works of world literature, then, the *Aeneid* and the *Metamorphoses* are both products of their own culture-specific time and transcend it. Given the special character of the Augustan age, these two aspects are not dichotomous, but complementary. One further aspect of interplay needs to be stressed before I take up some particulars. Poets like Vergil and Ovid do not simply "reflect" the spirit of their age. Rather, they contributed to shaping it because they saw the creative possibilities.

THE AUGUSTAN OIKUMENĒ AND THE
NEW UNIVERSALISM

Oikumenē literally means "the inhabited world." The concept had been enunciated before Alexander but took on new meaning in the wake of his conquests. They were a watershed: the windows of the Greek world were opened up as never before, and there was no turning back to previous horizons. *Oikumenē* came to denote not only the changed geography, which included the Middle East and parts of Asia, but also its social, political, and ethnic dimensions. A cosmopolitan variety of peoples and cultures lived under the aegis of a ruling power. Even though that power was fragmented soon after Alexander's death into three major Hellenistic successor states, the cultural and physical reality of the *oikumenē* persisted. So did the idea of political reunification. Polybius, the Greek Alexis de Tocqueville, commenced his *Histories* in the second century B.C. by reminding the Romans of this role, and Alexander the Great became the inspirational role model for subsequent Roman leaders. Augustus brought it all to fruition. He entered onto the world stage at the same young age as Alexander; his distinctive hair lock was the stylized version of that of the youthful world conqueror (Figs. 53 and 54), a distinctive emblem, already used by Pompey (Fig. 15), that he retained in his later and never aging portraits (Fig. 19) and even passed on to his grandsons (see Figs. 21a–c); and the Mediterranean *oikumenē* ruled by him was seen as the more perfect successor to Alexander's. Italy and Rome were at the center, but the outlook was universal rather than parochial.

Historiography and the *Geography* of Strabo, Augustus' contemporary, provide ample documentation. Polybius led the way, presenting simultaneous events in various parts of the world: Greece and Macedonia, Italy, Sicily, Asia, Egypt, Spain, and Africa. He explicitly states (2.37) that this new, universal approach to history was occasioned by Rome's entering upon the stage of history. He thereby implicitly differentiated it from the earliest, and strictly diachronic, attempt at universal history, that of Ephorus (fourth century). The massive successor to Polybius' *Histories* was the *Bibliotheca Historica* of the Sicilian Diodorus, which he published in 40 books around 30 B.C., the year Octavian conquered Alexandria. Like Polybius, he was of Greek birth and a long-time resident of Rome. His *Library* began with mythical times and ended with Julius Caesar's foray to Britain in 54 B.C. The perspective is sweeping, not only in terms of the historic continuum and

FIGURE 53. Alexander the Great. Detail from a mosaic in the Casa del Fauno, Pompeii, first century A.D. Photo: DAIR 58.1448.

the geographic areas (specifically denoted as *oikumenē*) and peoples he covered but also for the variety of perspectives and topics: besides political history, they included mythography, ethnography, geography, and religion. Yet closer to Augustus was Nicolaus of Damascus. A protégé of Herod the Great, he wrote a laudatory *Life of Augustus*. His principal work, in 144 books, was his *Histories*, which included the civilizations of both the ancient near east and the Mediterranean, and ended with the death of Herod in 4 B.C. Another contemporary practitioner of the genre was Pompeius Trogus, a Romanized Gaul. While his emphasis, perhaps in response to Livy's completely Rome-centered output (142 books "From the Foundation of City"), was on the Macedonian kingdom (hence the title "Philippic Histories") and its successors, he ended with Augustus' wars in Gaul and Spain. It is fitting, and by no means coincidental, that the very origins of these universal historians reflect

FIGURE 54. Marble head of Octavian, early 30s B.C. From a private collection in La Alcudia, Mallorca. Photo by Peter Witte, D-DAI MAD R-1-71-11.

the Augustan *oikumenē*: the east (Syria), the center (Sicily), and the west (Gaul).

Similarly universal in outlook is the unique *Geographies* of the Greek Strabo. He was born one year before Augustus and managed to outlive him. Ranging over the Augustan world, his *Geographies* (17 books) is a blend of history and geography. The focus is on Rome; conversely, the horizon extends beyond Rome to the breadth and variety of the empire, far from the parochial perspectives of a Livy and that influential critic of the principate, Tacitus, who narrowly concentrated on the imperial court. Another aspect of Strabo's universality is his use of various literary traditions, and not just those of geographical handbooks, for constructing the Roman world (K. Clarke, 1999, 334). The relevance to the *Aeneid* emerges: the author whom Strabo cites most often is Homer and, corresponding to *labor* in the *Aeneid*, effort (*ponos*), and not luck or some other factor, is the basis of Roman success (Engels, 1999, 311).

VERGIL'S *AENEID*

One affinity the *Aeneid* shares with the Augustan reign is that, because of their enduring success and their becoming "classics" in their respective realms, both have often been taken for granted – they had to turn out the way they did; there was no other. That assumption is fundamentally wrong, as there were plenty of alternatives.

The general expectation was that Vergil would write an epic about Augustus, an *Augusteid*, and incorporate the Aeneas story – the Julian family was named after Aeneas' son Julus (cf. figs. 50 and 52) – by flashback. Such praise epics, in honor of a statesman or general, had been the fashion in Rome for decades. Another weighty predecessor was Rome's first hexameter poem, the *Annals* by Ennius (239–169 B.C.), who chronicled the history and, especially, the expansion of Rome from Romulus' time to his own. Geographic sweep was not lacking here, nor would it have been in an epic about Augustus' military campaigns in Illyria, Greece, Egypt, and Spain. To Vergil, however, the unprecedented breadth of Rome's geographic horizons served as an impetus to explore yet wider and more universal horizons of the Roman experience.

One result was the reversal of the time frame. The story is that of Aeneas, the founder, and not of Augustus, the apogee. We are seeing Rome from the perspective of its beginnings: there will be achievements, but they are yet to come and will occupy the course of many centuries. The emphasis is on the journey and not on the destination, and on the underlying ethos and values rather than an enumeration of yearly events and battles. Of course, the perspectives of Aeneas and the Augustan audience coalesce, as they do so often: the Augustan age was notoriously devoid of proclaiming self-satisfaction, and Vergil died only eight years after the initial 'settlement' of the principate; in fact, things were far from settled by 19 B.C. and any stability was precarious. Ongoing effort, therefore, is the motto of the *Aeneid* and of the Roman condition: "So great a task it was to found the Roman nation" (*Aeneid* 1.43).

At the hands of another poet, even this orientation could have been subservient to writing the sort of paean on Rome that we would expect from a national epic. Vergil's vision again was wider. The *Aeneid* is an extended meditation on the Roman experience: it deals with successes and setbacks, sacrifices and achievements, elation and grief, hope and disappointment, human emotions and events beyond human control, and, above all, choices, and tough choices at that. The Roman condition thereby becomes a paradigm of the human condition. In the words of one Vergilian scholar: "The purpose of the *Aeneid* was essentially an exploration of varying and sometimes contrasting aspects of human experience" (Williams, 1990, 36). Enhanced as it is by Vergil's focus on the complexity of both the Roman and human experience, this quality of his work has assured the *Aeneid* its remarkable vitality over time.

The programmatic preface ("proem" in the terminology of classicists) to the *Aeneid* is a good example of how this Roman story immediately broadens out into wider perspectives. The first two words of the epic, "arms and the man" (*arma virumque*) evoke the Homeric epics, which were themselves a source of universal inspiration (more about this shortly). The sentence rolls on over seven lines, summarizing Aeneas' journey and mission, and ending emphatically with "the walls of high Rome" (*altae moenia Romae*). But even here, there is a note of wider relevance. Aeneas is the Roman founder all right, but he is also a refugee (line 2: *profugus*), a fate shared by many in history. Accentuating this aspect, Vergil deliberately couples *profugus* with *fato* – destiny is a universal condition. Further, the poet postpones the traditional invocation to the Muse until verse eight to introduce a central theme of the epic: Aeneas is a good man, "outstanding in responsibility and commitment" (*insignem pietate*), and yet he is relentlessly persecuted by a vengeful higher power. We are confronting the question of Job, which was also a cardinal theme in Greek tragedy.

So much, for the time being, for the big picture. The various strands of the poem's universalism constitute an interconnected whole, and it is worthwhile looking at the major ones in some detail.

The *Aeneid* presents a panorama of the Augustan *oikumenē* in terms of geographic and cultural space. Aeneas comes from Asia. Setting out from Troy, his fleet proceeds to northern Greece and then heads southward through the Aegean Sea, including islands like Delos, to Crete. He continues up the west coast of Greece (and today's Albania) to cross over to southern Italy. A seastorm wrecks the fleet off the coast of Africa; from Carthage it is on to Sicily and, ultimately, Latium and Rome. The catalogue of warriors in Book 7 presents us with the many regions and tribes of Italy, including the Etruscans. Landfall in Spain and Gaul would have been anachronistic, but their presence is evoked by the name of Aeneas' destination: Hesperia, literally meaning "land in the west" (*Aen.* 1.530, 2.730, and elsewhere).

Much more is involved than a mere catalog of sites, although by Vergil's time a welter of traditions had sprung up that connected Aeneas with a myriad of places – George Washington slept here – that were eager to associate themselves with the Roman ancestor. Typically, Vergil streamlined those traditions and placed the quality of the experience ahead of quantity. Aeneas is an updated Odysseus (and I will return to this very important model shortly) whom Homer programmatically introduced as a man who "saw the cities of many men and learned their minds" (*Odyssey* 1.3). The *Aeneid* expands on and deepens this theme. While the story of the epic is set at the time of the fall of Troy, its cultural discourse is that of the Augustan *oikumenē*.

A significant theme, therefore, is the fusion of peoples. Aeneas was a Trojan, and the Trojans could be considered as either Greeks or Asiatics. In the decade before Vergil wrote his epic, Asia had been pilloried by Octavian's propaganda as the pit of debauchery, luxury, and effeminacy for the simple reason that is was the habitat of his rival Mark Antony and his Egyptian consort Cleopatra. It was not enough, therefore, for Vergil to describe the mere genetic fusion of Trojans and Latins into a new race – and the Romans were always aware of being a multicultural people – but Aeneas had to be de-asianized and Romanized in terms of attitudes and values. The poet did so in several ways. For the first time as far as we can ascertain, Aeneas was given an Italian ancestor, Dardanus (3.167, 7.207). Further, Aeneas the oriental prince is divested of most of his riches (*Aen.* 1.119: *Troia gaza* – a Persian word) in the shipwreck and inured to the pristine lifestyle of Italy – by a Greek, king Evander ("Goodman"), who inhabits the site of Rome long before the time of Romulus and Remus (Book 8, esp. 364f.).

To the denizen of the Augustan world, this episode would have been far from surprising. Roman culture had coalesced with Greek for more than two centuries. This synthesis reached new heights at the time of Augustus in arts, letters, architecture, religion, and lifestyle (Galinsky, 1996, 332–63). In the *Aeneid*, we see a process of both conversion and convergence among Greeks and Trojans, pointing to a future Italy and Rome that will unite them and the Latins (and others). True enough, Jupiter issues the nationalistic prophecy that the sons of Troy will conquer Greece (*Aen.* 1.283–5). The complementary dictum, if not riposte, of Horace found greater resonance: "Captured Greece captured the fierce conqueror and brought arts to rustic Latium" (*Letter to Augustus* 156–7). In the *Aeneid*, it is the assimilation of the two nations that becomes a guiding theme. The memory of the bloodthirsty, devious Odysseus who destroyed Troy in Book 2 is soon mitigated in the face of the joint danger the Trojans and Achaemenides, "a companion of unfortunate Ulysses" (3.614, 690), are facing in Sicily. Diomedes, one of the mightiest Greek warriors at Troy, has moved to Italy and explicitly urges the Latins not to revive the Trojan war (11.280: "The bad old days") and to make peace with Aeneas. Evander's Greeks, of course, are Aeneas' staunchest allies in Italy. The outcome, again prophesied by Jupiter, will be a blend of Trojans and Italian natives "that will surpass all men and even gods in devotion" (12.838–9). This in response to Juno's insistence that the Trojan identity be effaced (12.828).

Both the Romans, however, and the *Aeneid* were more ecumenical. The Trojan heritage was kept alive and well as Rome's noblest families laid claim to Trojan descent and their scions participated in the elaborate equestrian Troy game (*lusus Troiae*) at the time of Augustus. Characteristically, Aeneas's first prayer upon arriving in Italy is wholly ecumenical as it is addressed to local deities, Greek deities, Jove from Mt. Ida at Troy and the Phrygian mother goddess (7.135–40). This last divinity was imported by the Romans in 204 B.C., and Roman religion was a well-known amalgam of various traditions from around the Mediterranean. A stellar example of this phenomenon in Augustan architecture is the Temple of Mars the Avenger that dominated his Forum (Figs. 46, 49). Besides commemorating Octavian's revenge on the murderers of Caesar, it was a monument to Augustus' 'victory' over the Parthians, Rome's foremost eastern enemy, in 20 B.C. While the exterior of the temple followed Greek and Roman norms, the interior, and especially the inner sanctum, incorporated elements from oriental temple architecture (Ganzert 2000). The victor took over traditions from the defeated.

We are looking at a typically nuanced mixture of intentions or messages. On the one hand, such a takeover evidenced the Romans' superiority. On the other, it manifested their cosmopolitanism. We find the same mix in the *Aeneid*, and a resulting, central idea is that precisely because Rome is espousing an ecumenical culture is she qualified to be the master of the *oikumenē*. The concept informs Vergil's succinct, and therefore often quoted, formulation of the Roman national character (6.847–53): the Romans are not lacking in, let alone spurning, accomplishments such as sculpture and rhetoric in which other nations excel, but they are complementing them with the arts of good government.

And, as always, Vergil presents counter-examples to such enlightened attitudes. One is the boastful Italian chauvinist Numanus Remulus, who is fixated on the superiority of his native culture. He disparages the Trojans and, not coincidentally, their worship of the Phrygian mother goddess (9.590–620). His fate? He is shot in the head by young Julus, with the approbation of the Greek god Apollo.

After Aeneas, Dido is probably the best known character of the *Aeneid*; in fact, she easily surpassed Aeneas in both the sympathy and frequency accorded to her in the later tradition, whether in music, literature, or art. She exemplifies universal human experiences, notably through her intense, conflicted emotions, and her unhappy love affair. Again, that level of universality is made possible by the phenomenon of Vergil's ecumenical outlook. It would have been easy to represent her quite differently: as The Other, the African Queen, the mother of Rome's Punic archenemy, the avatar of Cleopatra; and so on. Instead, she is a refugee from the east, like Aeneas, with many of his qualities (no wonder they are so attracted to each other) that are core Roman virtues. She is a brave and fearless leader (*virtus*); she is dedicated to the welfare of her people to the point of self-sacrifice and she is a devout worshiper of the gods (*pietas*); she is a fair lawgiver (*iustitia*); she has worked unceasingly for establishing her nation in a hostile land (*industria*). The ideal to which she has tried to live up is that of a Roman *univira*, a woman who would not remarry after the death of her husband (a tradition that was countermanded by Augustus' marriage legislation), and the epitaph she pronounces for herself (4.655–6: "I built a famous city, saw my great walls, avenged a husband, and made my brother pay the price") in its starkness and simplicity is in the tradition of the sepulchral inscriptions of Roman nobles (Clausen, 1987, 58). Another universalizing element of Vergil's characterization of Dido is, as in the case of all major characters of the epic, the intricate web of allusions to previous literary figures, such as Medea and the Homeric trio of Nausicaa, Calypso, and Circe.

Homer, of course, stands out as a model. The *Aeneid*, as ancient commentators recognized immediately, was a combination of the *Iliad* and the *Odyssey*, as we already saw from the phrase *arma virumque*, and Vergil's adaptation of Homeric scenes, characters, and themes is pervasive and has been studied extensively. This makes it all the more important not to lose sight, amid all the details, of the principal reasons for Vergil's choice. Homer was the universal poet of Greece, the Bible so to speak. His epics were not just literature, but they were about life. His work was considered the fountainhead – the "Ocean" in the words of an Alexandrian scholar – from which all later literary traditions flowed: not just epic, but tragedy and comedy, too. Nor was his influence limited to poetry: for Strabo, as we saw earlier, Homer was the founder of geography. He was a towering figure, and no one before Vergil had attempted to write epic not just on a Homeric scale but, more importantly, to offer a similarly comprehensive vision of the human experience. If Vergil wanted to be universal, he had to incorporate Homer.

A significant parallel emerges in this context. Just as Vergil's vision was shaped by the new horizons of the Augustan *oikumenē*, so had Homer's been by the new horizons of the Greek world in the age of colonization (meaning "entrepreneurial expansion" [Redfield 1983] rather than military colonialism). What Susan Treggiari (1996b, 902) said of the Augustan period applies, even if not on the same scale, to the eighth and seventh centuries B.C.: "The world was opened up both physically and mentally." This applies especially to the *Odyssey* which left more of an imprint on the *Aeneid* than did the *Iliad* (cf. Cairns 1989). Odysseus, as Carol Dougherty (2001, 161) has put it, "helps forge a new sense of Greek identity out of his experiences among the peoples and places overseas." He is not the same Odysseus who simply returns after twenty years, and his return to Ithaca is more than a simple return: "In landing on unfamiliar shores, killing the threatening male suitors who occupy his land, and eventually (re)marrying Penelope, the local queen, he essentially re-founds Ithaca.... By drawing so closely from his "colonial" experiences Odysseus transforms mythic prewar Ithaca and resettles it in the New World of archaic Greece" (Dougherty 2001, 162).

Aeneas' actions and role mirror and extend those of Odysseus. Both are culture heroes for a new age and reflect the values of their respective times. Those of the *Aeneid* are more advanced than those of the *Odyssey*. They are the values of Rome in the Augustan age which, in several crucial aspects, are still quite different from those of Christian Europe that embraced Vergil as "a Christian soul by nature" (so Tertullian, a church father of the early 3rd cent.) and the "Father of the West" (the title of a book [1931] by the German essayist Theodor Haecker). This has led to moral colonialism on the part of Vergilian interpreters, especially in regard to Aeneas' actions as a warrior and avenger – by the epic's end, he has not turned into Mother Teresa, a metamorphosis even Ovid would not have attempted – and to excessive de-Homerization of the *Aeneid*. The commonalities are more important: both Homer and Vergil used the expansion of their contemporary worlds for exploring the larger issues of human life.

R. W. B. Lewis articulated this brilliantly more than a half century ago (Lewis, 1950, 52):

> In telling the story of the beginnings of Roman history, Virgil wanted to establish something about the peculiar character of Rome in a way which would explain something about the peculiar character of life itself. He sought to make Rome co-extensive with the world: not merely physically as large as the given cosmos (which Jupiter predicts it will be in the first book), but of the very nature and essence of human experience. If, in so doing, he has seemed instead to reverse his order and make life a reflection of Rome, it may be because the task he set himself was beyond the powers of even Virgil. What else there is which appears inadequate in the conception of empire is not the fault of the poet; it is the inadequacy of experience. Virgil's view of Rome was identical with his view of life.

Another, and related, Vergilian characteristic enhances this universal or cosmopolitan aspect of the *Aeneid*: his tendency to illumine a given situation or issue from a variety of perspectives and points of view. Traditional epic, and especially warrior epic, consists in large part of a number of stock scenes that are regularly repeated: arming of warriors, departures for battle, combats, supplications, boasting over slain enemies, and the like. Befitting his complex times, Vergil excels at varying and contrasting not only such episodes – Turnus' killing of Pallas and Aeneas' slaying of Lausus in Book 10 are a good example – but major themes and ideas of the epic. The themes of *pietas* and anger, for instance, are treated not monolithically, but from different perspectives and in different contexts. Or take Aeneas' self-control and self-discipline. They are totally admirable when he is trying to rebuild the shattered morale of his followers after the shipwreck with an optimistic pep talk, after which the poet explicitly comments (1.208–9):

> So ran the speech. Burdened and sick at heart
> He feigned hope in his look, and inwardly
> Contained his anguish.
>
> (transl. Fitzgerald)

But, as we all know, our greatest strengths can also be our greatest liabilities. The hero's unwavering display of utter self-control in the face of Dido, who cries out for some sign of emotional response (4.368–9), only makes things worse. When he encounters her again in the underworld – ever the poet of the human condition, Vergil knew that running into former lovers can be a special kind of hell – he has learned and tries to soothe her (6.455–76), but it is too late.

It is this "very marked openness to the problematic elements in life, which renders it different from a typical national epic" (Conte, 1994, 284) that has been a vital reason for the timelessness of the *Aeneid*. Vergil, as we have seen, wrote on the human experience within the framework of the Roman experience. There was a natural convergence as "the Roman way of life was one involving constant problems" (Williams, 1990, 28). Yet the result is not diffuse indeterminacy. Vergil's sympathy with different viewpoints and with the major characters of the epic – there are no villains – does not amount to mushiness. Firm convictions are not hard to find, and while Turnus, for instance, may elicit some sympathy, he is wrong and often wrongheaded (cf. Jenkyns, 1998, 418). In its combination of inclusiveness and firm guidance the *Aeneid* once more reflects, and reflects on, the Augustan *oikumenē*.

OVID'S *METAMORPHOSES*

While Horace called Vergil "the other half of my soul" (*Ode* 1.3.8) it is really Ovid who is the true pendant to Vergil. Just as the *Aeneid* was a constant dialogue with Homer's epics, so the *Metamorphoses* is a constant dialogue with Vergil, and with Vergil's epic in particular. Scholars like binary opposites, and the matrix has been conveniently applied to Ovid and Vergil. No doubt, they are very different, but they are also complementary. Their works reflect different aspects of the Augustan age, and our view of that age would be incomplete if we concentrated only on the *Aeneid* and dismissed the *Metamorphoses* as the harbinger of "Silver Age" Latin poetry.

Generational considerations are relevant. Augustus' reign lasted for 45 years and included more than one generation. Vergil was seven years older than Augustus and had lived through the horrors of the civil wars. A principal theme both of the *Georgics* (written in the 30s B.C.) and the *Aeneid* is the conflict between order and disorder, and the longing for stability. In contrast, the *Metamorphoses* celebrates change in its very title. Was this un-Augustan? Far from it: after Augustus had brought back stability, change became a key characteristic of the period wherever one looks. Tradition was paired with innovation, and the one issue contentious Augustan scholars agree on is that the Augustan age was one of transformation. This is the age Ovid knew: by the time he was thirteen, the civil wars were over. Rome was being rebuilt (cf. Diane Favro's Chapter 10, this volume), providing splendid venues for a *jeunesse dorée* and other sophisticates, and horizons were wider and less clouded than ever. Ovid was twenty-five when Vergil died, and there was no need to create another *Aeneid*. Nor was there any need to look at the human experience from the perspective of the Roman experience. Freed from such constraints, Ovid could be yet more universal in the *Metamorphoses* than his epic predecessor Vergil. In several ways, he was, and the confidence in his transcendence resonates in his epilogue to the *Metamorphoses* (15.875–9):

> Yet I'll be borne,
> The finer part of me, above the stars,
> Immortal, and my name shall never die.
> Wherever through the lands beneath her sway
> The might of Rome extends, my words shall be
> Upon the lips of men. If truth at all
> Is stablished by poetic prophecy,
> My fame shall live to all eternity.
>
> (Melville transl.)

It is instructive to note that while Ovid lays claim to transcending time – this may be his appropriation, for himself, of Jupiter's famous prophecy in *Aeneid* 1.278–9 that the Romans and their rule will not be bounded by time – the space for his fame is not unlimited but coincides with the Roman *oikumenē*. It is, of course, the space where most of the myths in the poem are located. They are a yet fuller reflection of the *oikumenē* than was the *Aeneid*. Vergil's epic centered on one myth, that of the Roman ancestor, which he used as a prism for viewing the human condition in general, effacing the boundaries between nationalism and supranationalism. Ovid tells some 250 myths, and what ultimately holds them together is not a greater vision of Rome, but the poet Ovid. Like the *Aeneid*, the *Metamorphoses* was a grand experiment, with numerous innovations, and not simply the accomplished versification of codified material. In a way deliberately different from Vergil's, the *Metamorphoses* is a kaleidoscope of human (and divine) emotions and vicissitudes. That is the central aspect of its universality (again attested by its immense reception in later literature and art), and I will return to it shortly after highlighting some others.

When one divides the number of lines of the *Aeneid* by the number of days Vergil spent writing it, one winds up with less than three verses a day. It is a telling indication of the immense concentration and complexity of the *Aeneid* in all ways. Ovid's narrative is far more exuberant, and he boasted to his friends that "whatever I tried to say forthwith became a verse" (*Trist.* 4.10.26). This should not mislead us for a moment into thinking that he was careless and inattentive, although those who look for a tidily overt structure in the *Metamorphoses* usually wind up imposing it extraneously. Rather, as Ovid himself put it in the Pygmalion story, "art is concealed by its own art" (*Met.* 10.252). His incorporation of a scheme of universal history is a good example.

Appropriate to the fluidity of metamorphosis, it is not a rigid scheme. Ovid, however, is much more explicit than Vergil about the affinity of his epic with universal history and thereby implicitly asserts his claim to greater universality. Like the historians, he clearly defines the starting point and end point of his work in chronological terms in the proem (Wheeler 2001): "From the first beginning of the world to my times" (1.3–4). As in the historians, universality does not simply involve a temporal sequence, but it is spatial as well, representing simultaneous events in different parts of the *oikumenē*. Ovid uses both methods. He implements the chronological framework not pedantically, but, as so much else in the *Metamorphoses*, through suggestion. There are the four ages, then the flood, followed by a line of heroic and regal genealogies. In the last five books, we move from Troy to Rome; Aeneas is part of this process, but by no means the only one. And we end explicitly, and not just by prophecy, with Julius Caesar and Augustus. The synchronic spatial perspective loosens up and complements the suggestion of linear time. In Book 6, for instance, we are looking at simultaneous events in Thebes, Athens, and Thrace. Enhancing this geographic universalism are sweeping surveys. Ovid inserts the most prominent and comprehensive example early into the poem, detailing the conflagration brought about by Phaethon (2.214–59): like Phaethon, we see the world (*orbis*, 227) "from all parts" as Ovid presents a bravura catalog of mountains from east to west and north to south, though not in any geographical order – that again would be too predictable and pedestrian.

We saw earlier that Homer was regarded as the source for all subsequent literary traditions and genres. In the *Aeneid*, Vergil recombined mainly epic and tragedy, which does not mean that his world view is "tragic" in today's routine sense of the word. Rather, like the Greek tragedians, he focused on the problematic aspects of human experience and illuminated it from various perspectives (cf. Galinsky, 2003). Ovid, however, went much further in reuniting the variety of literary genres within a poem of epic length. There is plenty of comedy, much of it centering on the gods as in stories such as Apollo's pursuit of Daphne and Jupiter's of Europa, which Ovid summarizes pithily by saying that "majesty and love don't go together well and share the same abode" (2.846–7). Tragedy is in the eye of the beholder as Ovid never pushes tragic themes to the point of Aristotelian catharsis. Serious-minded readers, however, can involve themselves in tragic love stories, such as Pyramus' and Thisbe's, despite the attendant imagery that includes a comparison of the young lover's blood spurting into the air with water shooting up from a broken lead pipe (4.121–4). And Ovid has a knack for formulating the crux of a tragic situation, such as Medea's: "I see what's better and I approve; I follow what is worse" (7.20–21). But there is much more, including burlesque, pastoral idylls, elegiac laments, and even didactic poetry, such as Pythagoras' rambling discourse about the omnipresence of change (15.75–478).

This universal spectrum of literary forms has its equivalent in the breadth and variety of narrative techniques and devices. The *Metamorphoses* is a poem of many moods, tones, and styles, often within the same story. It is here that the real metamorphosis takes place. Change is a universal principle, but most stories are not centered on transformation as an actual subject. Instead, metamorphosis is more important as a principle for Ovid's way of narrating, ranging from changing and innovating earlier versions of a myth to varying the tempo and tone of a given story; the story of Erysichthon (8.738–878), which is told in many different keys, is an excellent example (Galinsky 1975, 5–14).

The stylistic and tonal variety and variability are the fitting accompaniment of the vast and unceasingly entertaining panorama of human emotions and vicissitudes that are not subordinated to higher visions for a new nation. Ovid's subject is mankind in general, and while gods figure prominently in many of his myths, they are very human and, at times, subhuman. Jupiter leads the way as he is metamorphosing himself into a bull to carry off Europa. Pointedly, Ovid remarks that he, "the father and ruler of the gods," leaves the *gravitas* of his scepter behind (2.847–8). We catch one more glimpse of his mighty divine physique – the right hand that wields lightning and the nod that shakes the world (Ovid uses the term *orbis* with its associations of *oikumenē*; cf. Favro, p. 235) – before being treated to a far longer itemization of his new attributes as an animal (2.850–58). Typical of the variety of the *Metamorphoses*, this is not the only way the gods are portrayed. Besides being benign, they can be capricious, although this aspect of their behavior does not rise to a level of purposefulness that we could identify with Ovid's central perspective on human and divine affairs. As always, there is room for debate: the very first instance of a human transformation is that of Lycaon, who butchers innocent guests for pleasure. Jupiter's lightning strikes his abode and kills everyone in sight – except for Lycaon. He is changed into a wolf, only to keep indulging in his "accustomed lust for slaughter" and he "delights in blood even now" (1.234–5).

Is that divine justice? Unlike Vergil, Ovid does not ask that question. And the one time he raises it explicitly, he diffuses it right away. That is at the end of the story of Actaeon, who by a simple mistake (*error*) and with no intent happened upon a naked Diana in the woods. Enraged, she turns him into a stag and his hounds lacerate him. The reader is distracted from pursuing any tragic implications by Ovid's virtuoso catalogue of Actaeon's thirty-four dogs, all of whom have Greek speaking-names (like Pamphagos, "Eat-all") that are breathtakingly accommodated to meter (3.206–24). Diana's wrathful vengeance on an innocent mortal is more heinous yet than that of Vergil's Juno, leading to Actaeon's grisly death (3.249–52):

> Now they all around him, tearing deep
> Their master's flesh, the stag that is no stag.
> And not until so many countless wounds
> Had drained away his lifeblood, was the wrath,
> It's said, of chaste Diana satisfied.

But instead of triggering a moral outcry, Ovid ends on the sedate note of people's ability to have different opinions on the matter (3.253–55):

> As the tale spread, views varied; some believed
> Diana's violence unjust; some praised it,
> As proper to her chaste virginity.
> Both sides found reason for their point of view.
> (Melville transl.)

Vergil's technique, akin to that of the Greek tragedians (and we know of several tragedies about Actaeon) of actively treating a problematic issue from different perspectives, is genially metamorphosed by Ovid into the bland statement of a non-binding principle: to each their own (cf. 3.141f.). It is in the nature of metamorphosis that it provides a way out of a potentially tragic situation, and Ovid uses it to that literal effect ever so many times: people in a predicament are transformed into birds, stones, or plants. Their problems are not solved; instead, they are permanently retarded or simply go away by virtue of a metamorphosis.

Often, as we saw in the case of Lycaon, the transformed state is a fitting continuation of the earlier one. Or, and this is only one more variation of many, people are transformed at their most poignant moment, which thereby is preserved for posterity. Niobe brags about the superior number of her children, who are then systematically killed off by Apollo and Diana. She begs for the survival of her smallest child, but (6.301–5)

> As she begged
> The one she begged for fell. She sat bereft
> Amid her sons, her daughters and her husband,
> All lifeless corpses, rigid in her ruin.
> Her hair no breeze can stir; her cheeks are drained
> And bloodless; in her doleful face her eyes
> Stare fixed and hard – a likeness without life.
>
> (Melville transl.)

Her emotional petrification leads into her physical one, and she becomes an icon of grief. Ovid could have ended the account right here, but it is ever so characteristic of him that he doesn't – a tendency that earned him both ancient and modern criticism – and exploits the metamorphosis theme some more. In the next few lines, he treats us to a picture of Niobe's innards being changed into stone only to capture, and again this is quite typical, a timeless tension in the concluding image (6.311f.). There is physical closure as she now is a rock on top of a mountain, but the emotional dimension continues as "the marble exudes tears even today." We have come full circle – from the emotional state to the physical and back again to the emotional – and the circle does not end. Metamorphosis results in both fixity and continuum.

It is presentations like these that make the poem universally accessible. Ovid does not burden us with heavy psychology or searching analysis; hence the affinities with the pantomime (see Beacham, pp. 167–72). The story of Narcissus is a good example. It is not about narcissism, but about Narcissus, a boy who is not terribly bright and ultimately falls in love with his own image. Ovid's narration takes up some 170 lines. The first seventy are given to Echo and center on the amusing dialogue she manages to establish, despite her verbal handicap, with Narcissus (3.379–92). The ensuing description of Narcissus' infatuation sparkles with Ovidian play on literary conventions, such as an elegiac lover's lament – Narcissus is both the lover and the loved one – and ends with a series of brief, vivid vignettes. Narcissus beats his breast red and, upon seeing the reflection in the pool, collapses with autoerotic passion. He fades away, but "even after he entered the underworld did he keep gazing at himself in the waters of Styx" (3.504–5).

The reasons for the universal appeal of this kind of storytelling are not hard to discern. First and foremost is the energizing combination of Ovid's lively presentation with the latitude he leaves to the reader for response (the same is true of painters: the different renditions of Narcissus, for one, by Caravaggio, Poussin, and Dali are a good example). Vergil, too, gives the reader room for response, but the issues are always serious in tone and existential in substance. The Ovidian spectrum is far wider: we can read a given story for sheer entertainment or involve ourselves in as many of its possible implications as we like to pursue. The basic form of Ovid's narrative enhances this purpose. As in Augustan art, it is the emphasis on the individual scene. Ovid blended the preference of Hellenistic poets, such as Callimachus (3rd century B.C.), for short, individual episodes with the outward length of the "continuous song" (*Met.* 1.4) of Homeric epic. In contrast to Vergil and Homer, Ovid proceeds from one story to the next and does not center his narrative on the evolving exploration of a grand theme like the wrath of Achilles or Aeneas' mission. Metamorphosis as a theme is handy for the reasons we have seen; they do not include its systematic exploration or evolution. Sure, change is a universal principle as well as being uniquely relevant to the time of Augustus, but there is no heavy-handed message. When Pythagoras in Book 15 tries to come up with one, his hyperdidactic attempt at systematizing only serves as foil to Ovid's own handling of metamorphosis.

As one might expect from Ovid, the master of *The Art of Love* and other erotic poems, love rather than metamorphosis is the real subject of the *Metamorphoses*. We encounter it in all its manifestations – the gamut runs from the selfless to the self-absorbed, from tender innocence to brutal rape, from homoerotic to heterosexual, from marital commitment to incest, from mutual understanding to jealousy, and so on. It is typical of Ovid that he did not base his cosmogony in Book 1 on the principle of Love and Strife that was made popular by the Greek philosopher Empedocles (5th century). That would have been too abstract. Instead, he literally fleshes out the theme of love by presenting a scintillating panorama of all the emotions it engenders. The patroness of love, of course, is none other than Venus, who is a guiding force throughout the poem (Barchiesi 1999); at one point (5.365–79) she specifically appeals to her son, Cupid, to keep conquering the world, divine and human alike. At the same time, she is the ancestress of the Romans and the Julian family, and the poem's final transformation, Julius Caesar's into a star, comes about with her active participation. Venus stands for the universal impulse that that makes the world go around, and she also is the Venus Victrix, the victorious Venus, of Julius Caesar and the Romans who conquered the earthly universe, the *oikumenē*.

We saw that Vergil captured this ecumenical aspect by locating the *Aeneid* not in Italy from the start, but by Aeneas' movement from east to west. Ovid, as always, mimics his predecessor. In the final books, we move toward Rome. Roman myths, such as that of Vertumnus and Pomona, come to the fore, and the theme of transfer is made most palpable by the story of Asclepius (15. 622–744, immediately preceding Caesar's apotheosis and Ovid's epilogue) whose cult was adopted by Rome from Greece in 292 B.C. By the time of Augustus, Rome had become a synthesis of Greek and Roman, and the Roman world was one of many cultures. The *Metamorphoses*, with myths of many different origins, reflects that world and, as Ovid predicted so presciently, thereby ensured its enduring place in world literature.

SUGGESTIONS FOR FURTHER READING

J. Griffin, *Virgil*, 2nd ed. (Bristol 2002) is a good overview of Vergil's oeuvre, with a conciseness uncharacteristic of most Vergilians, while P. Hardie, *Virgil. Greece & Rome. New Surveys in the Classics* No. 28 (Oxford 1998) is the most up-to-date review of recent scholarly and interpretive (and there often is a difference between the two) trends. A lively introduction to Ovid is N. Holzberg, *Ovid. The Poet and his Work* (Ithaca and London 2002). J. Solodow, *The World of Ovid's Metamorphoses* (Chapel Hill 1988) provides a good, extensive treatment of the *Metamorphoses* while E. Fantham, *Ovid's Metamorphoses* (Oxford 2004) is an informative and intelligent overview. Useful also are the *Cambridge Companion* volumes on Vergil (ed. by C. Martindale, 1997) and Ovid (ed. by P. Hardie, 2002). Accessible translations of the *Aeneid* and the *Metamorphoses* are, respectively, by Robert Fitzgerald (first published in 1981) and A. D. Melville (1986). Nicolet (1991) is indispensable for the geographic and geopolitical background. For the cultural impact of the empire on Rome see C. Edwards and G. Woolf, eds., *Rome the Cosmopolis* (Cambridge 2003), esp. these two scholars' chapter on "Cosmopolis: Rome as World City" on pp. 1–20.

PART VI

EPILOGUE AS PROLOGUE

16: EPILOGUE AS PROLOGUE: HEROD AND THE JEWISH EXPERIENCE OF AUGUSTAN RULE

L. Michael White

Despite its small size and inauspicious geography, Judea played a significant role in the Augustan Empire. This, quite apart from the greater limelight still that would be cast upon it as a result of the eventual "triumph" of Christianity both in Roman politics and European culture. Yet long before Judea became synonymous with Jesus or "Holy Land" (Wilken, 1992, 21–45), it had become Augustus' gateway to the East, thanks in large measure to the political fortunes of Herod. Indeed, Augustus' rise to imperial power was very much tied to Herod's career at a number of key points. As client to Rome, and under the patronage of Antony and then Octavian, Herod greatly expanded the Judean kingdom from 40 to 4 BCE. Along the way he was associated with some of the most noted figures of his day, including Pompey, Caesar, Cleopatra, Agrippa, Asinius and Vedius Pollio, and more. On his death, his lands were divided among his surviving sons; however, in 6 CE Judea came under direct Roman provincial administration. This change would also have profound effects on the social and political climate of Judea – and Rome itself – under Augustus' successors and thus set the stage for the emergence of Christianity and Rabbinic Judaism.

AUGUSTUS AND HEROD (40–29 BCE)

Herod, Antony, and Octavian in Rome (40 BCE)

According to the Jewish historian Flavius Josephus, Herod seems to have met Octavian in person for the first time in December of 40 BCE.[1]

The circumstances of this meeting and its results would have long-term implications for the political history of Judea. In the Fall of 40 BCE, Herod fled Judea for Alexandria. With Cleopatra's help he sailed for Rome, but his ship was severely damaged by storms off Rhodes. While staying there Herod enacted civic benefactions and commissioned a new trireme to complete his voyage (*Ant.* 14.376–78).

On reaching Rome in early December, Herod turned to Mark Antony, whom he had known for nearly twenty years. Only a year earlier, Antony had been Herod's guest in Antioch, when Herod helped orchestrate his dramatic and fateful introduction to Cleopatra (*Ant.* 14.324–26; Plutarch, *Antony* 25–27). Now, on hearing of Herod's narrow escape, Antony offered him hospitality and agreed to present his case to the Senate. Apparently Antony enlisted Octavian's help, based on their recent pact and Antony's marriage to Octavia the preceding month. Josephus says:

> Now [Octavian] Caesar was also quite prepared to assist with his claims and with the cooperation that Herod wanted, on the one hand, because of both the military campaigns of Antipater[2] – in which he came to the aid of his father [Julius Caesar] against the Egyptians – and his hospitality and good will in everything, and, on the other hand, as a favor to Antony, who was exceedingly zealous concerning Herod.
>
> (*Ant.* 14.383; cf. *B.J.* 1.283)

When the Senate was convened, Herod's case was presented by M. Valerius Messalla Corvinus and L. Sempronius Atratinus, with Antony stepping forward to lend support.[3] The Senate then voted to proclaim Herod king. Afterwards, the consuls Cn. Domitius Calvinius and C. Asinius Pollio led Herod, flanked by Antony and Octavian, to the Capitolium where they performed the requisite sacrifice and deposited the Senate's decree. That evening Antony gave a banquet in honor of the new king. Within a week of his arrival, Herod was on his way back to Judea to claim his kingdom (*Ant.* 14.381–89; *B.J.* 1.283–85).

A decisive factor in Antony's support and in the Senate's decision seems to be the threat of a Parthian invasion of the East. An alliance between the Parthians and Hasmonean factions was a key factor in the final stages of the Judean civil war which had been brewing since before 63 BCE. Herod's father, Antipater (2) had been entrusted by Pompey in 63 (reaffirmed by Julius Caesar in 48) with supporting the Hasmonean

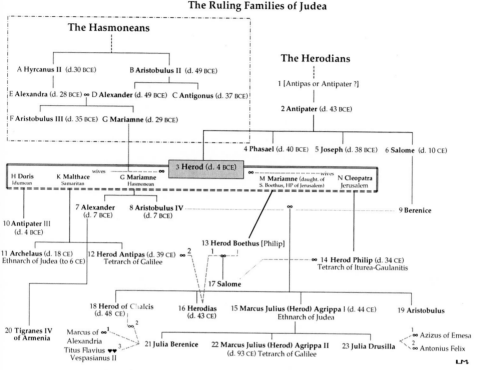

The Ruling Families of Judea

FIGURE 55. The ruling families of Judea (Michael White).

monarch, Hyrcanus II (A) (*Ant.* 14.136–37; 333; cf. *B.J.* 1.248). Parthian intrigues were implicated in Antipater's assassination in 43 and the effort to kill Herod in 40. The Senate was assured that Herod would champion Rome's eastern interests against the Parthians (*Ant.* 14.281–82; 341–73; *B.J.* 1.255–77; cf. Richardson, 1999, 127–9).

The Preparatory Years: Pompey and Caesar (63–40 BCE)

The story goes back a few years earlier. When Pompey arrived in Damascus in 63 BCE, Judea had enjoyed a century of semi-independent statehood under the Hasmonean ruling family, leaders of the Maccabean revolt (167–164 BCE). By 67 BCE, however, the dynasty had devolved into a bitter civil war.[4] Opposing political factions had aligned behind two Hasmonean heirs: Hyrcanus II (A) had taken the title of "King;" his brother Aristobulus II (B), High Priest (see Fig. 55).[5] Several years of political intrigue ensued until Pompey began the annexation of Syria.

Meanwhile, he sent M. Aemilius Scaurus to Jerusalem, where he was met by delegations from both Hyrcanus II and Aristobulus II requesting approbation of their title claims. Pompey finally decided in favor of Hyrcanus. This produced the occasion on which Pompey, to wipe out resistance from Aristobulus' partisans, took Jerusalem and marched into the Temple (*Ant.* 14.69–74; *B.J.* 1.152–54).

Pompey appointed Antipater (2) as governor of Judea to assist Hyrcanus and insure that Rome's interests were protected. The family of Antipater had ascended to a position of trust within Hasmonean circles due in large measure to their status as local chieftains from the southern region of Idumea, specifically the territory of Hebron and Masada. The Idumeans were descendents of the Edomites, an Iron Age Semitic tribe from the Negev.[6] By the Hellenistic period they had largely been subsumed by the Nabataeans, but part of their northern territory had been annexed to the Hasmonean kingdom (Josephus, *Ant.* 13.257–58; cf. Strabo 16.2.34). Many of these Idumeans, including Herod's grandfather, voluntarily converted to Judaism.[7] Antipater had succeeded his father (1) as local governor for the region of Idumea, supporting Hyrcanus II (*Ant.* 14.10; 29–57; 80–84; *B.J.* 1.127–32). Under Pompey, Antipater's position as governor was expanded to encompass virtually the entire Hasmonean kingdom.

It was in the following years that the young Herod (born circa 73 BCE) first met Mark Antony, who was then serving under Gabinius, Pompey's legate in the East (*Ant.* 14.98–104; Richardson, 1999, 101f.). When Crassus became governor of Syria in 55 BCE, Antipater was named *procurator* of Judea, continuing under Cassius (53–51 BCE).

Whereas Antipater naturally supported Pompey, in 48 BCE he went to the side of Julius Caesar who was then marching on Alexandria. For his services, Antipater was reaffirmed as *procurator* and granted Roman citizenship. While Sextus Caesar was serving as governor of Syria (47–46 BCE), Antipater's two sons were appointed local governors: Phasael (4) for Jerusalem and Herod (3) for Galilee and then Coele-Syria (*Ant.* 14.158–60, 273–280). Again as a result of loyalty and support, Julius Caesar accorded the Judeans numerous concessions (*Ant.* 14.185–216). Even so, following on the assassination of Caesar, Antipater himself was poisoned (*Ant.* 14.217; 280–4). Following the defeat of Brutus and Cassius at Philippi in 42 BCE, Herod and Phasael were appointed joint tetrarchs for Judea. By early 40, arrival of new Parthian contingents prompted a revolt in Jerusalem; Antigonus (C), the son of Aristobulus II, was named king. Hyrcanus and Phasael were taken prisoner: Phasael eventually committed suicide, while Hyrcanus was tortured, disfigured, and sent to Parthia (*Ant.* 14.294–301). An attempt was also made to capture Herod, but he escaped to Alexandria by way of Masada, and from there made his fateful bid to reach Rome (as discussed above).

From Rome to Actium (40–29 BCE)

Herod's acclamation by the Senate was an unexpected triumph; however, he would still have to reclaim his kingdom (*Ant.* 14.386–87; cf. Richardson, 1999, 129). In the vacuum created by Herod's flight, Antigonus (C) had taken control of Jerusalem and the whole country as king and high priest. Herod's younger brother Joseph (5) held the ancestral fortress of Masada, but was under siege. Meanwhile, the Parthians had mounted an invasion of Roman Syria. Herod sailed for home. With Roman support units, he began campaigns to take control of the Galilee before moving south into Judea proper (*Ant.* 14.390–98; Dio 48.41; Stern, 1974a, 222).

By 38 Herod had regained control of much of Judea, so he left his brother Joseph (5) in charge of the armies while he himself went with reinforcements to assist Antony at Samosata against the Parthians. Josephus credits Herod with saving Antony from an ambush, for which he was again rewarded (*Ant.* 14.439–47). On his return, however, Herod learned that Joseph had been killed by Antigonus in an engagement at Jericho. Herod marched on Jericho bent on revenge. After first defeating an intercept force in Samaria, Herod routed Antigonus' main force. By spring of 37 Herod had moved on to besiege Jerusalem with the aid of legions under the command of Caius Sosius, governor of Syria. After five months of siege, the city fell. Antigonus was captured and taken to Antioch, as Antony wished to display him in his triumphal procession at Rome. Herod followed and entreated Antony for an immediate execution. Thus, the last reigning Hasmonean dynast was beheaded at Antioch in late 37 BCE. Herod was now master of his kingdom and a client of Antony (*Ant.* 14.439–90; cf. 15.5–10; *B.J.* 1.357).[8]

Herod soon benefited from Antony's policies toward building Rome's power in the East by relying heavily on client kings.[9] Herod's kingdom now included Idumea, Judea, Cuthaea (i.e., southern or ethnic Samaria), Perea, and Galilee (Fig. 56). These were the territories originally considered "Jewish" following the settlement of Pompey in 63 BCE; however, the kingdom was disjointed and landlocked, as Galilee was not contiguous and the coastal cities remained independent.

Apparently Cleopatra took the opportunity to reassert Ptolemaic power over Judea and southern Syria. Antony ceded some of Herod's lands to her in 37. She was able to press further because of intrigues within Herod's family. In late 37, Herod negotiated for the release of Hyrcanus II from Parthia and invited him to return to Judea and reside at court. Herod, however, appointed Hananel of Babylon, a Zadokite, as high priest, the first non-Hasmonean high priest in nearly a century. This move angered Herod's mother-in-law Alexandra (E), the daughter of Hyrcanus II, who wanted her son Aristobulus III (F) to succeed him as High Priest. Herod had married her daughter Mariamne (G) just a few months earlier.[10] Thus, when Herod chose Hananel instead of his wife's own brother, Alexandra (E) wrote Cleopatra to exert pressure through Antony (*Ant.* 15.18–40).

Eventually, Herod conceded, deposed Hananel, and appointed the seventeen-year-old Aristobulus III (F) high priest in 35. Because Aristobulus III claimed descent from both Hyrcanus II and Aristobulus II, he proved popular enough to raise concerns; so, Herod had him killed within the year (*Ant.* 15.50–60; *B.J.* 1.437). Alexandra brought charges through Cleopatra, and Antony summoned Herod to Laodicea. Apparently, Herod admitted to his role in the affair but managed to convince Antony that it was to safeguard Rome's interests against threats of another Hasmonean-Parthian uprising (*Ant.* 15.74–79). In 34 Antony ceded more territories to Cleopatra, including Gaza and the fertile Plain of Jericho; Herod was then forced to lease them back from her by paying tribute (*Ant.* 15.106, 132; *B.J.* 1.362). Similar machinations led to ongoing tensions between Herod and the Nabateans that lasted for years (Stern 1974b, 232–33; Richardson 1999, 165–6).

As the pact between Antony and Octavian began to collapse, Herod clearly supported Antony and was preparing to join him. His own troubles with the Nabatean king Malichus forced him to delay, and Herod thus missed Actium and Antony's stunning defeat. He was now in a precarious position. First, he decided to remove any remaining Hasmonean claimants by orchestrating the trial and execution of Hyrcanus II. Next, Herod sailed to Rhodes to supplicate Octavian and offer his allegiance. Octavian accepted and ratified Herod's position as king of Judea. Octavian then used Judea to pursue Antony and Cleopatra, with Herod as escort and provisioner (*Ant.* 15.161–200; *B.J.* 1.386–94; cf. Plutarch, *Antony* 72–74). In addition to public proclamations of Herod's rule, Octavian transferred most of Cleopatra's lands in the region to Herod (*Ant.* 15.217; *B.J.* 1.396–97). The newly acquired areas included upper, mostly Hellenistic, Samaria and the adjacent coastal region, the coastal

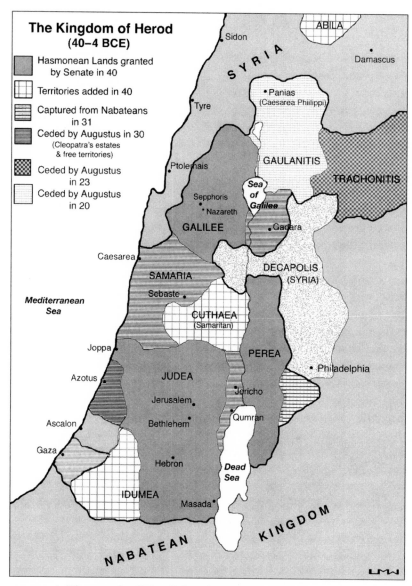

FIGURE 56. The growth of Herod's kingdom (Michael White).

strip from Joppa to Gaza, and the Decapolis cities of Hippos and Gadara (Fig. 56). When both Antony and Cleopatra committed suicide, Herod, as client to Octavian, was left as the most powerful figure in the region. When Octavian assumed his imperial title in 29, Herod's position was set as "friend of the Romans" and "friend of Caesar."[11]

HEROD'S KINGDOM (29–4 BCE)

Herod's remaining career can be broken into two discrete phases. During the "middle period," from 29–13 BCE, he was engaged in massive building programs at home and managing his extensive political connections throughout the Empire. The "final period," from 13 until his death in 4 BCE, was one of severe personal decline (see section on Judea from Client Kingdom to Province, below).

The Kingdom Builder (29–13 BCE)

Herod began extensive building programs in the mid-20s BCE, while also supporting Roman expansion in the East.[12] In 23 Augustus ceded to Herod the regions of Batanea, Trachonitis, and Auranitis that lay to the east of the Sea of Galilee and south of Damascus (Fig. 56). Formerly apportioned to Zenodorus, the chieftain of Gaulanitis, these areas were troubled by local bandits and were viewed as politically unstable; Herod insured better control (*Ant.* 15.344–48). In the winter of 23/22 Herod went to visit Marcus Agrippa, with whom he had already become friendly, while the latter was based on Lesbos as the emperor's "deputy" for the East.[13] The alliance with Agrippa proved to be one of Herod's strongest through his middle years (*Ant.* 15.350, 361; *B.J.* 1.400). Augustus made a state visit to Syria in 20 BCE. On Zenodorus' death that same year, Augustus added his territories (Gaulanitis and Huleh) to Herod's and made Herod *procurator* for areas of southern Syria, including Abila. With these additions, Herod's kingdom reached its maximum extent (see Fig. 56). Herod soon announced plans to build a Temple to Augustus in Panias (later renamed Caesarea Philippi), and Augustus agreed to visit Herod's kingdom as guest of honor. Augustus probably visited two other recent foundations named in his honor: Sebaste (formerly Samaria) and the new harbor of Caesarea (formerly Straton's Tower). In both locations, Herod also announced plans to build temples to Roma and Augustus (*Ant.* 15.356–64; *B.J.* 399; see the next section for more discussion of the building programs).

In 15 BCE Marcus Agrippa also visited Judea as Herod's guest (*Ant.* 16.12–15; cf. Philo, *Embassy to Gaius* 294–97). He apparently toured Caesarea and Jerusalem itself to great popular acclaim.[14] In the following year, Herod then joined Agrippa's official entourage for a state visit through the Aegean, the Bosphorus, and central Anatolia. Among other things Herod brokered concessions and provided public benefactions for local municipalities. As a result of the close friendship with Agrippa, Herod established strong political alliances with other leading Romans of the day, including Caius Petronius, prefect of Egypt (24–21 BCE), M. Titius, governor of Syria (circa 10 BCE), and P. Quintilius Varus, governor of Syria (6–4 BCE; see *Ant.* 15.307; 16.270; and 17.303, respectively).

Herod as Builder and Benefactor

Herod was an energetic builder and benefactor both at home and in other parts of the East. Yet, he seems to have refrained from engaging in such activities farther to the West, perhaps because he did not want to intrude in Augustus' own areas.[15] The most extensive and costly projects were conducted within his own kingdom, and it is clear he thought to make it a showplace as well as a gateway for the eastern empire. In other cases, certain key areas of the country saw little or no improvement from Herod's largess.

Beginning in about 23 BCE Herod inaugurated a full-scale renovation project in Jerusalem, focusing especially on the area of the Temple. Some parts were not completed until 64 CE, only a few years before the Temple was destroyed (70 CE) at the end of the First Revolt. Effectively, Herod enlarged Hasmonean foundations at the base of the Temple complex in order to create a large, elevated rectangular temenos supported by high retaining walls all around (Fig. 57). On top he built forecourts, a basilica and audience halls, bridges, stairs, and ramps for access, decorative gates, and water systems. He paid for renovations and decoration of the sanctuary proper, which were reportedly carried out by priests. He also built extensively around the Temple area and in the larger area of Jerusalem, including the Antonia Fortress, the Hasmonean palace, the fortified towers on the western side of the city, a theater and amphitheater (or hippodrome), and numerous other projects (*Ant.* 15.380–425; 20.219–222; *B.J.* 1.401; Pliny, *N.H.* 5.70). In addition to public works and general improvements, it appears that Herod conceived of these projects as making Jerusalem rival some of the great Hellenistic cities, both in opulence and in design. Athens itself, where he certainly visited and made public benefactions, might well have served as a model.

Herod's second major project was the founding of Caesarea as harbor for his kingdom and gateway to extensive middle-eastern trade routes. Josephus compares it to Piraeus (*B.J.* 1.408–16; *Ant.* 15.331–41; 16.136–41). In 6 CE, when Judea came under direct provincial administration, Caesarea became the capital. The project began in 22 BCE and was completed in 12 BCE. The location was a small Hellenistic coastal

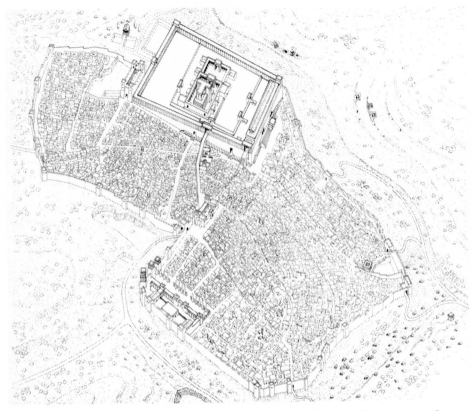

FIGURE 57. Herod's Jerusalem. Reconstruction drawing showing the expansion of the city prior to 70 CE. The elevated Temple platform is at the top. By permission of Dr. Leen Reitmeyer.

installation, previously held by Cleopatra, known as Straton's Tower. Using Roman engineers and construction techniques, they created an artificial mole and breakwater to form an inner harbor with towers, docks, and warehouses (cf. Holum 1988, 55–105; see Fig. 58). The harbor itself was named Sebastos (Greek equivalent of Augustus); the north mole was named after Drusus. On an elevated platform overlooking the harbor, Herod built a temple to Roma and Augustus. Housing colossal statues of both the Emperor and Roma, it reportedly had a golden roof that could be seen for miles by land or sea. The city proper was lavishly furnished in Roman style with a colonnaded thoroughfare, amphitheater, hippodrome, aqueduct, and theater (Fig. 59). Finally, on a southern promontory he built a palace overlooking the ocean. Originally intended to serve court life and entertain dignitaries, like his other

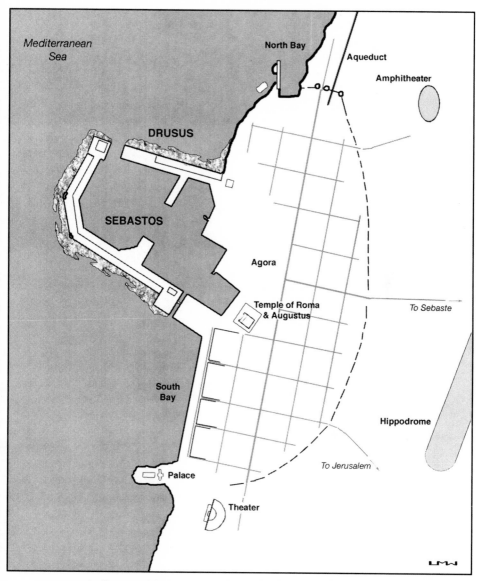

FIGURE 58. Caesarea Maritima. City plan of Herod's harbor in the first century BCE. Drawing by Michael White.

palaces throughout the homeland, the promontory palace later became the praetorium for the Roman procurators and prefects (cf. *Acts* 23:35).

The other major city foundation of Herod was Caesarea Sebaste (ancient Samaria), which lay in the predominantly Hellenistic northern

FIGURE 59. Caesarea Maritima. Aerial view of the Hellenistic Theater, circa 12 BCE. Photo: R. Cleve, ROHR Productions Limited.

region of Samaria. It was made over as a Roman city, with stadium, theater, forum, aqueducts, and colonnaded streets. It too received a Temple to Roma and Augustus (*Ant.* 15.292–98; 16.136–41; cf. Strabo 16.2.34; Fig. 60). Herod built a third temple to Roma and Augustus along with a palace and walls at Panias, a Hellenistic sacred spring dedicated to Pan, later renamed Caesarea Philippi (*Ant.* 15.363–64; cf. Matt 16:13; Mark 8:27; Luke 9:18). The other cities that were either new foundations or refoundations included Phasaelis, Antipatris, Agrippias, and Sepphoris (later renamed Diocaesarea). As with many of his projects they were named to honor either members of his own family or members of the imperial family.

He built numerous palaces on his personal estates throughout the kingdom. The one at Betharamphtha he allowed Agrippa to rename Livias/Julias (*Ant.* 17.277; 18.27; cf. Pliny, *N.H.* 13.44; Ptolemy, *Geog.*

FIGURE 60. Sebaste (Samaria). Aerial view of the Temple of Roma and Augustus, circa 12 BCE. Photo: R. Cleve, ROHR Productions Limited.

5.15.6). The other existing cities of his kingdom to receive substantial buildings and benefactions include Hebron and Mamre, Ascalon, and especially Jericho, where he also had a large estate and two palaces. In addition, Herod built a number of fortresses or fortified palaces. The most famous are Masada (cf. Strabo 16.2.40) and Herodium, where he was thought to be buried (cf. Pliny, *N.H.* 5.70). The others include three in Peraea – Machaerus, Esbus, and another Herodium – and four more in Judea – Cypros, Docus, Alexandreion, and Hyrcania. In each of these he shows considerable interest in Hellenistic style, especially in the use of colonnaded audience halls and dining rooms, heated baths, and lavish decorations (Nielsen 1999).

Herod's public benefactions in the province of Syria were extensive and similarly show his interest in promoting Hellenistic urban style (*B.J.* 1.422). They included gymnasia at Ptolemais, Tripolis, and Damascus;

theaters at Damascus and Sidon; temples, halls, and agora at Tyre and Berytus; amphitheater and baths at Berytus; city walls at Byblus; and an aqueduct at Laodicea. At Antioch, the provincial capital, he paved a broad thoroughfare and provided a colonnade (*B.J.* 1.425; *Ant.* 16.148, 427).

Finally, Herod made substantial civic benefactions to numerous cities in Greece and Asia. Most of these occurred during his travels with Marcus Agrippa in 14 BCE (*Ant.* 16.16–24), but others occurred during his trips to and from Rome. At Rhodes, for example, he rebuilt the temple of Pythian Apollo (*Ant.* 14.378; 15.183; 16.147). On a visit to Greece in either 12 or 8 BCE he presided over the Olympic games and paid for extensive restorations (*B.J.* 1.426–7). He also made extensive "offerings" to Sparta, Athens, and Delos (*Ant.* 1.425). During the tour of 14 BCE he made "gifts" to Lycia, Pergamon, Samos, and Chios. He provided "tax relief" for the city of Phaselis and made gifts to cities in Cilicia, Ionia, and Kos (*B.J.* 1.423, 428). Herod's sons, grandson, and great-grandchildren continued as benefactors to Greek cities (cf. Richardson, 1999, 209–11). In addition, Herod's extensive family network was further strengthened by intermarriage with some of the other leading client kings of the Empire, including Archelaus of Cappadocia, Tigranes of Armenia, and Juba of Mauretania.

Herod's Reputation

Today, most people think that Herod was a paranoid despot and megalomaniac. To some extent the reputation is deserved, as we shall see in the next section, based largely on his later years. On the other hand, some points are exaggerated or due to later legendary fabrications, such as his ordering a mass execution of children at the time of Jesus' birth (see following). Herod's reputation in his own day was that of a capable ruler (Strabo 16.2.46), a shrewd and powerful man with considerable military prowess, especially as a horseman (*B.J.* 1.429–30). That he was at times ruthless is without question, especially when it came to his enemies or to scheming by his wives or children. Augustus reportedly made a pun out of it, in Greek no less: "It is better to be Herod's pig (*hys*) than his son (*hyios*)" (Macrobius, *Saturnalia* 2.4.11). Whether the story is true or not, the implication is clear enough. Even so, Augustus seems to have prized his loyalty and his ability to control his territory and protect Rome's interests. Neither political expediency nor ruthless efficiency was a vice in Augustan Rome, much less in provincial administration.

It has also been suggested that Herod was universally loathed by the Jewish people because of his oppressive tactics and his pagan religious sympathies. Or because he was only "half-Jewish." While he was Idumean by birth, his family had been fully converted to Judaism for three generations. Again, this view seems to come from later sources in light of Judea's troubles after the devastations of two revolts against Rome. By contrast, Herod's reign produced an unprecedented period of building and accompanying economic growth. Many Jews seemed to be very favorable, and we hear at least obliquely of political supporters called "Herodians" (Matthew 22:16; Mark 3:6; 12:13). Religiously, at least, Herod seems to have been quite careful about showing his support for Roman religious practices or the imperial cult in Jerusalem and other predominantly Jewish areas of his kingdom. All three of the temples that he dedicated to Roma and Augustus were in traditionally Hellenistic areas where even ordinary Jewish residents would have been quite accustomed to such religious activities. On the other hand, his veneration of Augustus went far beyond what ordinary Romans would have experienced at Rome itself, at least during Augustus' own lifetime. The growth of the imperial cult was much more typical in the eastern part of the empire than in Rome or the West, and Herod helped lead the way. Herod certainly did foster an even greater degree of "Hellenization" and "Romanization" of Judea at the cultural level through the construction of theaters, baths, gymnasia, and amphitheaters both in "Roman" cities, such as Caesarea and Sebaste, and in Jerusalem itself. His own palaces were lavishly decorated in Hellenistic style and enjoyed the latest in Roman architectural design and techniques.

JUDEA FROM CLIENT KINGDOM TO PROVINCE

Herod's Decline and the Problem of Succession (13–4 BCE)

In Herod's later years succession was to become a sore subject. Having divorced his first wife, Doris (H), to marry the Hasmonean princess Mariamne (G), Herod had two sons, Alexander (7) and Aristobulus IV (8) (Fig. 55). But by 29 Mariamne's scheming with her mother Alexandra (E) angered Herod to the point that he finally had them both executed (*Ant.* 15.185–87; 202–51). In 23/22 Herod sent his sons Alexander (7) and Aristobulus IV (8) to live in Rome. They were hosted by Augustus after staying first in the home of one of the Pollios (either Asinius or Vedius, *Ant.* 15.342–43; Suetonius, *Augustus* 47–8; cf.

Richardson, 1999, 231). At this time Augustus also granted Herod the right to name his own successors (*Ant.* 15.344); the result was messy, with a series of intrigues and altered wills (Richardson, 1999, 33–38).

Herod married five more times during the 20s; twice to relatives in 28. In 27, about the time he began to rebuild Samaria/Sebaste, he married Malthace (K), a Samaritan. In 25 he married Cleopatra (N), from a noble Jerusalem family, and in 24 he married another Mariamne (M), daughter of Simon ben Boethus, whom Herod had named as High Priest (*Ant.* 15.320; 17.19). His younger sons by these later marriages, Archelaus (11) and Antipas (12), both by Malthace, and Philip (14), by Cleopatra, would also travel to Rome for education as guests of Augustus (*Ant.* 17.20). Herod's grandson, Agrippa I (15), son of Aristobulus IV (8), moved to Rome with his mother Berenice (9), shortly after his father was executed in 7 BCE. Enfranchised by Augustus, he was given the name Marcus Julius Agrippa in honor of Herod's friendship. He grew up in the imperial palace in the company of Drusus, Caligula, and Claudius (*Ant.* 18.143–46; cf. 19.292–96).

Herod traveled to Rome in 17 BCE to bring Alexander (7) and Aristobulus IV (8) home (*Ant.* 16.6–7); he named them joint heirs, aping Augustus' announcement of that year regarding Gaius and Lucius. Because of their Hasmonean lineage, however, their presence in Jerusalem soon prompted rumors, and Herod renounced them. In 12 BCE, after prodding by Augustus, Herod publicly announced a new will naming Antipater III (10) as king, with the sons of Mariamne as "subordinates" (*Ant.* 16.90–135; *B.J.* 1.445–66). By 7 BCE, however, the tensions resurfaced and escalated into a reign of terror as Herod went into paranoid seclusion (*Ant.* 16.235–40, 257–60; *B.J.* 1.492–94). Archelaus, client king of Cappadocia and father-in-law to Alexander (7), tried to calm things down; however, Gaius Julius Eurycles, the Spartan dynast, spurred Herod on.[16] Finally, Alexander and Aristobulus IV were placed under house arrest, tried, and executed (*Ant.* 16.320–34, 362–394). Augustus never officially interceded in the matter, although public opinion at Rome held that Herod should merely leave them under house arrest. Eventually, Antipater III suffered a similar fate; he was executed only five days before Herod himself died, in March of 4 BCE (*Ant.* 17.93–167; *B.J.* 2.1–100). These well-publicized executions of his own sons, although all of a mature age, undoubtedly lay behind the later Christian legend that Herod tried to kill Jesus out of fear (so Matthew 2:16–18). In fact, there is no evidence that Herod ever ordered a general slaughter of male infants during the last years of his life (Richardson, 1999, 288, 295–98; Brown, 1977, 226–28).

Administration of Judea in the First Century CE

Augustus ultimately approved of Herod's final will dividing the king-dom among his three surviving sons: Archelaus (11, then age nineteen), Antipas (12, age seventeen), and Philip (14, probably age sixteen). The whole affair convened in Rome with advocates for all sides present. Augustus chose to accept a division of the kingdom, even though it weakened the control that he might have wished by having another strongman, client-king like his "friend" Herod (cf. Richardson, 1999, 21–29; Bowersock, 1983, 45, 54).

Archelaus was given the territories of Judea, Idumea, and Samaria and the title "Ethnarch" (but not "King"; see Fig. 61). Antipas was given the territories of Galilee and Perea, while Philip was given Trachonitis, Gaulanitis, and Aurantis; both were titled "Tetrarch." Antipas and Philip were generally successful rulers, lasting until 38 and 34 CE, respectively. Archelaus, however, was deposed after only ten years. In 6 CE Augustus exiled Archelaus to Gaul, where he died in 18 CE. Next, he reorganized his ethnarchy into the province of Judea with its own procurator, who was in turn answerable to the Legate of Syria. Judea was now a "second-class" administrative district annexed to Syria. It was also at this time (6 CE) that Augustus delegated the new Legate of Syria, P. Sulpicius Quirinius, to conduct a census of Judea (*Ant.* 17.355; 18.1–2, 26; *B.J.* 2.117; cf. Stern, 1974b, 309–312). This change would have profound effects in Judea.

According to the Gospel of Luke (2:1–2), this census was the oc-casion for the birth of Jesus; however, the dates and events are irrecon-cilable with the fact that all accounts place Jesus' birth before the death of Herod in 4 BCE. Josephus clearly places the census under Quirinius but after the removal of Archelaus when Judea was transferred to a procuratorial province:

> Now Quirinius, a man of senatorial rank, when he had pro-gressed through the other magistracies to the consulship, and who was extremely distinguished in other respects, arrived in Syria, dispatched by Caesar to dispense justice to the nation and to make a valuation of their property. And Coponius, a man of equestrian rank, was sent along with him to govern the Jews with all authority. Quirinius also came to Judea, which had been annexed to Syria, to make a census of their property and to liquidate the estate of Archelaus.
>
> (*Ant.* 18.1–2)

The date for Quirinius' governorship is confirmed by both inscriptions and coins, and Dio (55.25, 27) places the removal of Archelaus during the consulship of Aemilius Lepidus and Lucius Arruntius (also in 6 CE).[17] There were two apparent goals or aspects to this census: first, to appraise property and liquidate the estates of Archelaus, which now devolved to the imperial treasury; second, to complete a tax enrollment of Judea under the provisions of Augustus' earlier edicts (28/7 BCE), since as a client kingdom none would have previously been required.

Procuratorial rule of *Provincia Judaea* developed in two major phases. The first phase lasted from 6 to 41 CE; the second, from 44 to 66. The first procurator was Coponius (6–7 CE), but Pontius Pilate (26–36 CE) has long been the best known due to the later traditions about his handling of the execution of Jesus (cf. Tacitus, *Ann.* 15.44). Josephus further specifies that Coponius, an equestrian, had "authority even for capital punishment" (*B.J.* 2.117). The same applies to Pilate. Pilate was appointed under Tiberius, and an inscription from Caesarea mentions his activities in regard to a Tiberieion (or imperial cult sanctuary to Tiberius). The text also gives his correct title as *praefectus* rather than *procurator*.[18] Other than the highly legendary accounts in the Christian gospels, the main sources for this portion of Pilate's career come from Josephus (*Ant.* 18.55–59; *B.J.* 2.169–74) and Philo (*Embassy to Gaius* 18.299–305); both portray him as ruthless and generally unfavorable toward Jewish religious sympathies. The actual date for the death of Jesus is uncertain but must fall in the first few years of Pilate's administration (circa 27–29 CE).[19]

In 37 CE with the accession of Caligula, Judea experienced a brief return to the status of autonomous client kingdom. Following the death of Philip the Tetrarch (14) in 34, Caligula dispatched his childhood friend, Marcus Julius Agrippa – better known as Agrippa I (15) – grandson of Herod, to assume Philip's territory with the title of king.[20] This move prompted protests by the tetrarch Antipas (12), Agrippa's uncle; Antipas' various entanglements finally led to his removal in 38. He died in 39.[21] Caligula then named Agrippa king over all the northern regions.

Josephus then reports that Agrippa I was instrumental in the accession of Claudius after the assassination of Caligula.[22] In 41 Claudius named him king over all of the remaining territories of Herod, including Judea and Samaria. Perhaps because he had reunified the "kingdom" with self-rule and was also of Hasmonean descent, he seems to have been very popular. The detailed and glowing account of Josephus is at odds with the only other mention of him in Jewish or Christian

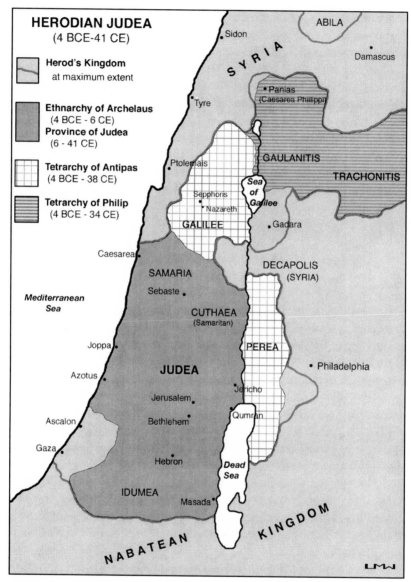

FIGURE 61. The division of Herod's kingdom and the province of Judea (Michael White).

sources, where he is vilified for executing James, the son of Zebedee (*Acts* 12:1–19).[23] When Agrippa I died unexpectedly in 44 CE, the air of optimism soon faded. Claudius determined that his son, Agrippa II (22), at age fifteen, was too young to assume the throne. So, Claudius returned Judea to provincial status, now placing all of the lands of Herod under direct Roman rule. Josephus credits this second phase of procuratorial rule with the escalation of brigandage and revolutionary violence that would result in the outbreak of the First Revolt from 66 to 74 CE (*Ant.* 20.162–172; *B.J.* 2.254–265). Following the Revolt and a period of military occupation under the Tenth Legion Fretensis, the Province of Judea (including all areas but those eventually given to Agrippa II) was reorganized under the name *Provincia Palaestina.* When Agrippa II died (circa 93), some of his territory went to Syria, while the remainder was reabsorbed into the new province, thus establishing the general territorial boundaries that would continue into the later Empire.

ESSENES, JESUS, AND OTHERS: RELIGIOUS & SOCIAL CONDITIONS IN JUDEA

Some areas of Herod's kingdom (Sebaste, Caesarea, Panias) were predominantly pagan; others, predominantly Jewish; and others still (such as the Upper Galilee), quite mixed. Then there were Idumeans and Samaritans, whose religious status was historically tenuous. Moreover, it appears that Herod at times undercut the social and economic powers of the landed aristocracy of Judea, which had ties to the Temple and to the Sadducaic party. Despite the positive economic impact of Herod's building programs, the long-term impact was to weaken the economic infrastructure. It may well have contributed to the growing social and religious tensions in the period leading up to the First Revolt (so Goodman 1987; Horsley and Hanson 1985; cf. Richardson, 1999, 241–2, 252–4). Even so, the problems did not really surface during Herod's lifetime or the Augustan era. Even Herod's rebuilding of the Temple was generally met with favor (Richardson, 1999, 248–9).

More stringent forms of protest were nonetheless present, and they would eventually bubble to the surface in the second phase of procuratorial rule (44–66 CE). For example, of the numerous bandits, false prophets, and extremists mentioned by Josephus in the period before the revolt, the vast majority occurred after 44 CE. One particular family seems to be central, at least according to Josephus. He credits the resurgence of banditry and beginnings of the so-called Zealot movement (also called "the fourth philosophy") to Judas the Galilean. In particular, this Judas led a tax revolt in 6 CE in response to the census of Quirinius (*Ant.* 18.3–25; 20.102; *B.J.* 2.117–18; cf. *Acts* 5:35–37). Two sons of Judas the Galilean, James and Simon, were active in the 40s CE; they were eventually captured and executed by the procurator Tiberius Julius Alexander, Philo's nephew (*Ant.* 20.102). One other son of Judas, Menahem, was active during the early part of the First Revolt (*B.J.* 2.433–44), and another relative, Eleazar son of Jairus, was leader of the rebel group that fled the final siege of Jerusalem and held out at Masada until 74 CE (*B.J.* 7.253ff).

Other groups maintained some degree of both political and religious opposition to Herod while not falling into open rebellion. This seems to be the case for the Pharisees, who were not a major political force during the Herodian period nor in the early first century CE. Pharisees found some support among members of Herod's family, but others were executed by Herod (*Ant.* 17.149–67; *B.J.* 1.648–55; Richardson, 1999, 15–18). Nonetheless, Herod does not seem to have tried to eradicate the Pharisaic movement as such, probably because they had little real power (cf. Richardson, 1999, 254–6). Only in the period after the First Revolt (66–74 CE) did they emerge as the new voice of Jewish piety and evolve into Rabbinic Judaism.

A similar situation obtains with the Essenes, who reflect perhaps the strongest religious opposition to Roman rule in the pre-revolt period. Herod seems to have held them in great respect and awe for their rigorous piety and prophetic powers (*Ant.* 15.372–79). Nor does it appear that the Essenes opposed Herod directly. Instead, the Essenes had originally arisen in direct opposition to Hasmonean "usurpation" of the office of High Priest, because they were not of Zadokite lineage. So, when Herod deposed the last Hasmonean High Priests (Antigonus in 37 and Aristobulus III in 35/4 BCE) and installed a true Zadokite, Hananel (*Ant.* 15.22, 40), it must have pleased the Essenes. In the period after Herod's death, however, the invective of the Dead Sea Scrolls clearly shifts against Roman rule in general (cf. Richardson, 1999, 258f.). Their animosity grew steadily through the period of procuratorial rule and helped fuel the apocalyptic expectations of the First Revolt, as reflected in the *War Scroll* from Qumran.

Jesus was born sometime during the last few years of Herod's life (so Matthew 2:1, 19–22; Luke 1:5). Beyond that there is little certainty or scholarly agreement regarding the actual circumstances, even the birth in Bethlehem (Brown, 1977, 514f.), and there is no evidence of any awareness, much less a reaction, on the part of Herod (Brown,

1977, 226–228). By all accounts, Jesus grew up in Nazareth. Recent archaeological work has shown that Nazareth was a satellite village to the city of Sepphoris, one of Herod's urban foundations. Under Antipas, Sepphoris became the capital of the Galilee and underwent a significant building boom. It has been suggested, therefore, that if Jesus (or his father) were working as carpenters in the building trade, it was likely in Sepphoris. As a social and cultural setting, Sepphoris also has important implications since it seems to have been multilingual and cosmopolitan in nature. It is now regularly suggested, therefore, that Jesus likely knew some Greek, even though his native language was probably Aramaic (Meyers and Strange 1981; Reed 2002). In any case, the Galilee was not typically considered in the mainstream of Jewish religious practice, but neither was it a cultural hinterland.

Jesus came to public prominence in the late 20s CE, during the reign of Tiberius and the procuratorship of Pontius Pilate (26–36 CE). The career of John the Baptist belongs to the same time. In marked contrast to the Gospels, Josephus says that Antipas had John the Baptist killed fearing he would lead a popular uprising. Regarding Jesus, it is difficult to say on what grounds he was actually executed. It probably also stemmed from some fear of insurrection, growing out of apocalyptic rhetoric. The final responsibility fell to Pilate alone, and he was well known to have ordered executions without any sort of trial (so Philo, *Embassy to Gaius* 302). Meanwhile there are numerous historical difficulties with the supposed trial scenes in the Christian Gospels (Brown, 1994, 679–722, 787–820).

Even the initial years of the sect that emerged after Jesus' death are cloaked in remarkable obscurity. It was one among the many Jewish sects of that period. Its followers, like Jesus himself perhaps, may have advocated (or at least appeared to) some sort of political or economic reform couched in apocalyptic rhetoric. While they must have grown and even spread in Judea and Syria in the period prior to the First Revolt, it was primarily in the period of post-war reconstruction that they – now called Christians – and the Rabbinic movement would come to prominence and vie for religious leadership of the Jewish tradition. Even so, it is fair to say that the effects of Augustan rule on Herod and his immediate successors set the course for these momentous events. The real growth of the Christian movement, however, occurred in the Diaspora and moved through the local social networks of Diaspora synagogue communities. *Acts* portrays numerous interactions between Paul and Roman authorities both at Caesarea (*Acts* 24–26) and elsewhere (*Acts* 16–19).

The Situation of Jews in the Diaspora

From Hellenistic times there had been Jewish communities dwelling outside Judea, especially in Egypt, Syria, and Anatolia. By the end of the first century CE Jewish enclaves could be found throughout the Roman Empire with large communities in some of the major cities, including Rome itself. The experience of Jews in the Diaspora was mixed, ranging from pogroms and oppression (albeit sporadically), to general prejudice, to mild curiosity and some cases of localized acceptance. Even so, the legal status and rights of Jews were generally upheld (Goldenberg 1979; Gruen 2002; Kraabel 1979; White 1996–97, 1.60–101). Several Diaspora communities received decrees from Julius Caesar or the Roman Senate (*Ant.* 14.188–216, 228–264; cf. White 1987). It may well be that Caesar's good relations with Antipater and sons influenced his favorable attitudes. Herod interceded concerning the rights of Diaspora Jews in several cities when he traveled with Marcus Agrippa (Ant. 16.27; *B.J.* 1.428).

During the Augustan period it appears that some strong relations existed between these Diaspora communities and Judea. All Jews were expected to contribute annually to the support of the Temple. With Herod's rebuilding, it seems that donations were solicited. For example, Alexander the Alabarch, brother of Philo and titular head of the large Jewish community in Alexandria, donated a set of golden doors for the new Temple.

The Jewish community in Rome was perhaps the second largest outside of the Homeland. Some ten different congregations are known from Jewish inscriptions, although most of these come from later centuries. The names of these congregations, however, suggest that as many as three or four had connections to Herod and other members of the Augustan circle. One was called "synagogue of the Herodians" (*CIJ* 173), while others were named after Augustus himself (*CIJ* 284, 338, 368, 416), as well as Marcus Agrippa (*CIJ* 365, 425, 503), and perhaps the governor of Syria, Volumnius (*CIJ* 343, 402, 417). Such honorifics suggest patronage of the Jews by these aristocratic Romans (cf. Richardson 1998; Leon 1960; Rutgers 1995). On the other hand, Josephus reports that some Jews from Rome joined the Judean delegation in posthumously criticizing Herod before Augustus (cf. *Ant.* 17.300).

While the rights of Jews in the Diaspora were generally acknowledged by Julius Caesar and Augustus, there were several notable incidents after the deaths of Herod and Augustus. According to Josephus, the Jewish community in Rome was "expelled" by Tiberius in 19 CE, after an incident involving the wife of a senator (*Ant.* 18.81–84; cf. Tacitus, *Ann.* 2.85.4; Suet., *Tib.* 36; Dio 57.18.5). Josephus portrays those responsible as renegades, rather than ordinary members of the Jewish community, but the issue seems to have been conversion of Roman citizens. That all the Jews were actually expelled seems unlikely (Grabbe, 1992, 398; Smallwood, 1976, 210–215). In any event, the effects were temporary, since Suetonius (*Claudius* 25; cf. *Acts* 18:2) records a second such "expulsion" of Jews in 49 under Claudius.

Other sporadic outbreaks of anti-Jewish sentiment are known from Antioch and Caesarea later in the first century, but the most infamous incident occurred in Alexandria in 37 during the governorship of Flaccus, when tensions between Jewish and Greek citizens erupted into violence (Grabbe, 1992, 399–401). The results were general rioting and looting in the Jewish quarter; Flaccus blamed the Jews and levied steep fines for the damages. His handling of the affair and his general antagonism toward the Jews led them to send a delegation to appeal directly to the Emperor. The delegation was headed by Philo himself, now quite elderly, who drafted the petition to Caligula (*Embassy to Gaius*). By the time they arrived in Rome, however, Caligula had been assassinated and Claudius installed as the new emperor. The delegation waited for an audience with Claudius and was rewarded with a decision in their favor, as reflected in Claudius' *Rescript to the Alexandrians* (41 CE). In addition to reversing the judgment against them, Claudius' edict reaffirmed both the citizenship rights and the general religious privileges and concessions that had been granted earlier to the Jewish community.

It must be remembered, however, that Claudius had also grown up in Augustus' palace with Agrippa I, whom he named King of Judea in 41. In the same year Agrippa's daughter, Berenice (21), at age thirteen married Philo's nephew Marcus, son of Alexander the Alabarch. In circa 60, Berenice reportedly heard Paul's defense before her brother Agrippa II (22) and the proconsul Porcius Festus (*Acts* 25:23–26:32), while her sister Julia Drusilla (23)[24] had married the preceding procurator Antonius Felix (*Ant.* 20.144; cf. Acts 24:24). This same Berenice eventually became the mistress of the future emperor Titus while he was in command of the Roman armies during the First Revolt. Rumors flew around the affair when she joined him in Rome in the mid-70s (Tacitus, *Hist.* 2.2, 81; Dio 66.15.4–5; 18.1; Suet., *Titus* 7; Quintilian, *Inst.* 4.1.9; cf. Braund 1984b). The phenomenal web of influences of the ruling family of Judea continued to play an important role in imperial politics throughout the first century and beyond.

SUGGESTIONS FOR FURTHER READING

The best overview of Herod's life and career with a balanced treatment of his achievements and his problems is Richardson (1999). For his building program at Caesarea as seen from recent archaeological discoveries, Holum (1988). In general on Jewish history Lester Grabbe's two volumes (1992) provide an excellent overview with considerable nuance on numerous critical issues especially as they relate to biblical history. On the political and religious conditions at the time of Jesus: Goodman (1987) and Horsley and Hanson (1985). More specifically on Jesus, Raymond Brown's *Birth of the Messiah* (1977) and *Death of the Messiah* (1994) are among the most careful treatments of the complex sources and issues, while Reed (2002) is the most up to date on the cultural and social conditions of Jesus' immediate background. For the growth and development of the Jesus movement, with special attention to the historical and social conditions of the Roman world, see White (2004). Finally, Robert Wilken's *The Land Called Holy* (1992) follows the romantic allure of the topic well beyond the scope of this study.

NOTES

1   *B.J.* 1.277–285; *Ant.* 14.379–89. The two historical works of Flavius Josephus are the main sources for Herod's life and career, although they were based on a chronicle by Nicolaus of Damascus, Herod's court historian and Augustus' biographer. The *Bellum Judaicum* (or *Jewish War*) was written in 85 CE, while the *Antiquitates* (or *Jewish Antiquities*) was completed some ten years later. Both were written in Rome, where Josephus spent his final years as a retainer of the Flavian emperors. A few differences occur between the two, which some scholars have taken as evidence for a more anti-Herodian tenor to the later work; so Laqueur, 1920, 194–9.

2   All members of the Herodian and Hasmonean families are keyed by number to the genealogical table in Fig. 55. Antipater (2) was Herod's father, who had been the governing power behind the last Hasmonean king until assassinated in 43 BCE (*Ant.* 14.281–285). The reference is to Antipater's support of Julius Caesar in marching on Pompey at Pharsalus in 48; he also supplied reinforcements when Caesar moved against the Ptolemaic armies after Pompey's death (cf. *Ant.* 14.123–136).

3   *B.J.* 1.284 has Octavian himself convene the Senate instead of Messalla (*Ant.* 14.384), but Messalla accompanied Antony to Antioch in 41 BCE and had defended Herod (*Ant.* 14.324; *B.J.* 1.243), suggesting instead that Antony was behind the move (cf. Strabo 16.2.46).

4   For an account of these earlier stages of the Hasmonean civil war and the arrival of Roman rule, see Goodman (1996); Bickerman (1962) 166–77; Grabbe (1992) 1.306–11; 2.320–24; and, Richardson (1999) 52–108.

5   Under Simon (143–134 BCE), youngest brother of Judas the Maccabee, both titles had been accorded the Hasmonean ruler, but some Jews (notably the Essenes) resented this "usurpation" of the high priesthood. See further discussion below and VanderKam (2004).

6   For the background and relationship to earlier Israelite and Jewish cultures, see Edelman 1995. The principal tribal god of the Idumeans was Cos (or Qos), probably a close kin to the pre-Israelite Hadad/YHWH (so Dearman, 1995, 127).

7   See especially Kasher (1988) 46–78. A further indication that some of their tribal culture persisted into the Roman period can be seen in Herodian family names, notably Costobar, husband of Herod's sister Salome (6); cf. Richardson (1999) 52–67.

8   See also Dio 49.22.6; Plutarch, *Anton.* 36. For C. Sosius (consul in 32 BCE, who defended Antony's right flank at Actium) see also Velleius Paterculus 2.85–6; Dio 49.22–51.2; and *CIL* IX.4855.

9   See Magie (1950) 1.433–436; Syme (1939) 259–275; and Millar (1993a) 27–39.

10 *Ant.* 14.465–67. Herod had been betrothed to Mariamne (G) earlier, probably in 42, perhaps as an effort on the part of Hyrcanus II to consolidate his position by integrating Herod into his family. Cf. Richardson (1999) 121f.

11 For Herod's titles in inscriptions see *OGIS* 414, 427 (*CIAtt.* 3.550–51), *IG* II².3440, and *SEG* 12 (1955) 150 (all from Athens); *Israel Exploration Journal* 20 (1970) 97–98 (from Jerusalem); and *ZPE* 105 (1995) 81–84 (from Ashdod); cf. Richardson (1999) 203–11.

12 In 25 Herod reinforced the armies of Aelius Gallus for his campaign to southern Arabia (*Ant.* 15.317; Strabo 16.4.22–24; Dio 53.29; Pliny, *Nat. Hist.* 6.160).

13 Dio 53.32.1. For discussion, see Magie (1908) 145–147; and Magie (1950) 1.468; I2.1330.

14 One of the gates of the Herodian Temple complex in Jerusalem came to be known as the "Agrippa Gate" (*B.J.* 1.416; cf. Richardson [1999] 15–18).

15 Richardson (1999) 174–202 provides a useful catalogue of the major projects along with extensive bibliography.

16 *Ant.* 16.300–10; *B.J.* 1.513–30; cf. Richardson (1999) 285–6. Because of his various political machinations, Eurycles soon lost favor with Augustus, who exiled him. See Strabo 8.5.3, 366; Plutarch *Mor.* 207–8; cf. Cartledge and Spawforth (1989) 100–101; Bowersock (1961) 111–18; (1984) 176–8.

17 See especially Dessau, *ILS* 2683 (which mentions a census of Apamea); for discussion see White (2004) 32–34; Fitzmyer (1981) 1.399–405; Brown (1977) 547–56; Potter (1991) 588f.; Levick (1967) 203–214; and Syme (1934) 122–48.

18 For the text and discussion see Stern (1974b) 315–318; he proposes that there was a change of title to *procurator* during the reign of Claudius.

19 It is in the context of Pilate's tenure (*Ant.* 18.63–4) that Josephus may include a brief reference to Jesus; however, the passage, if genuine at all, was elaborated by later Christian interpolations. For discussion see Feldman (1992) 990f; White (2004) 97.

20 On Agrippa's earlier years in Rome see Grabbe (1992) 2.431.

21 In dealing with the last years of Antipas' reign Josephus (*Ant.* 18.116–19) mentions the case of his ordering the execution of John the Baptist; however, Josephus (in contrast to the accounts in the Christian gospels) makes Antipas' own fear of revolution the primary cause instead of a plot by Herodias (16). There is also a

problem with the Gospels' account in that Herodias (16) was not the wife of Philip the Tetrarch (so Matthew 14:3, Mark 6:17) but of another brother, Herod Boethus (13). See Fig. 55.

22 So *Ant.* 19.1–273 and Dio 60.8.2; but compare *B.J.* 2.204–217.

23 The ensuing passage (*Acts* 12.20–23) attributes Agrippa's death to divine vengeance over his public behavior.

24 Born shortly after Agrippa I returned to Judea (37–38), she was apparently named in honor of Caligula's sister; see Braund (1984a) 111.

SELECT BIBLIOGRAPHY AND WORKS CITED

Adams, J. N. (2003). *Bilingualism and the Latin Language* (Cambridge).

Alcock, S. E. (1993). *Graecia Capta. The Landscapes of Roman Greece* (Cambridge).

Alcock, S. E., et al., eds. (2001). *Empires. Perspectives from Archaeology and History* (Cambridge).

Ameling, W. (1994). "Augustus und Agrippa. Bemerkungen zu PKöln VI 249," *Chiron* 24.1–28.

Ando, C. (2000). *Imperial Ideology and Provincial Loyalty in the Roman Empire* (Berkeley).

Badian, E. (1982). "Crisis Theories and the Beginning of the Principate," in Wirth, G., ed., *Romanitas–Christianitas. Festschrift für J. Straub* (Berlin) 18–41.

Baldwin Bowsky, M. W. (1999). "The business of being Roman: The prosopographical evidence," in Chaniotis, A., ed., *From Minoan Farmers to Roman Traders: Sidelights on the Economy of Ancient Crete* (Stuttgart) 349–52.

Barbantani, S. (1998). "Un epigramma encomiastico 'alessandrino' per Augusto," *Aevum Antiquum* 11.255–344.

Barchiesi, A. (1997). *The Poet and the Prince* (Berkeley).

———. (1999). "Venus' Masterplot: Ovid and the Homeric Hymns," in Hardie, Barchiesi, and Hinds, 112–26.

Barrett, A. (2002). *Livia. First Lady of Imperial Rome* (New Haven).

Bartman, E. (1999). *Portraits of Livia. Imaging the Imperial Woman in Augustan Rome* (Cambridge).

Barton, T. S. (1994). *Power and Knowledge: Astrology, Physiognomics, and Medicine under the Roman Empire* (Ann Arbor).

Bartsch, S. (1989). *Decoding the Ancient Novel: The Reader and the Role of Description in Heliodorus and Achilles Tatius* (Princeton).

Beacham, R. (1992). *The Roman Theatre and its Audience* (Cambridge, Mass.).

———. (1999). *Spectacle Entertainments of Early Imperial Rome* (New Haven).

Beard, M. (1986). "Cicero and divination: The formation of a Latin discourse," *JRS* 76.33–46.

Beard, M. and North, J., eds. (1990). *Pagan Priests: Religion and Power in the Ancient World* (London).

Beard, M., North, J., and Price, S. (1998). *Religions of Rome*, 2 vols. (Cambridge).

Beyen, H. G. (1938–60). *Pompejanische Wanddekoration vom zweiten bis zum vierten Stil*, vols. 1 and 2 (The Hague).

Bickerman, E. (1962). *From Ezra to the Last of the Maccabees: Foundations of Postbiblical Judaism* (New York).

Blanckenhagen, P. H. von, and Alexander, C. (1990). *The Augustan Villa at Boscotrecase* (Mainz).

Bonner, S. (1969). *Roman Declamation in the Late Republic and Early Empire* (Liverpool).

Bosworth, A. (1972). "Asinius Pollio and Augustus," *Historia* 21.441–473.

Bowersock, G. W. (1961). "Eurycles of Sparta," *JRS* 51.111–18.

———. (1965). *Augustus and the Greek World* (Oxford).

———. (1983). *Roman Arabia* (Cambridge, Mass.).

———. (1984). "Augustus and the east: The problem of the succession," in Millar and Segal, 169–188.

Bowman, A. K. (1996). "Provincial Administration and Taxation," *CAH²X*.344–70.

Bowman, A. K., and Rathbone, D. W. (1992). "Cities and administration in Roman Egypt," *JRS* 82.107–27.

Bragantini, I., and de Vos, M., eds. (1982). *Le decorazioni della Villa Romana della Farnesina* (Rome).

Braund, D. C. (1984a). *Rome and the Friendly King: The Character of Client Kingship* (New York).

———. (1984b). "Berenice in Rome," *Historia* 33.120–23.

Bringmann, K., and Schäfer, T. (2002). *Augustus und die Begründung des römischen Kaisertums* (Berlin).

Brown, R. E. (1977). *The Birth of the Messiah* (New York).

———. (1994). *The Death of the Messiah*, 2 vols. (New York).

Brunt, P. A. (1976). "The Romanization of the local ruling classes in the Roman empire," in D. M. Pippidi, ed. *Assimilation et résistance à la culture gréco-romaine dans le monde ancien* (Paris 1976) 161–73; repr. in *Roman Imperial Themes* (Oxford 1990) 267–81.

———. (1978). "Laus imperii" in P. Garnsey and C. R. Whittaker, eds. *Imperialism in the Ancient World* (Cambridge) 159–91.

———. (1982). "Nobilitas and novitas," *JRS* 72.1–17.

———. (1988). *The Fall of the Roman Republic* (Oxford).

Buchner, E. (1982). *Die Sonnenuhr des Augustus* (Mainz).

Burkhardt, L. A. (1990). "The Political Elite of the Roman Republic: Comments on Recent Discussion of the Concepts *Nobilitas* and *Homo Novus*," *Historia* 39.77–99.

Burns, J. M. (1978). *Leadership* (New York).

Cairns, F. (1989). *Virgil's Augustan Epic* (Cambridge).

Campbell, J. B. (1984). *The Emperor and the Roman Army* (Oxford).

Cannadine, D. (2001). *Ornamentalism. How the British Saw Their Empire* (London).

Carettoni, G. (1983). "La decorazione pittorica della Casa di Augusto sul Palatino," *MDAI(R)* 90.323–419.

Cartledge, P., and Spawforth, A. (1989). *Hellenistic and Roman Sparta: A Tale of Two Cities* (London).

Cherry, D. (1998). *Frontier and Society in Roman North Africa.* (Oxford).

Chilver, G. E. F. (1950). "Augustus and the Roman Constitution, 1939–50," *Historia* 1.408–435.

Clark, D. (1996). *Urban World/Global City* (London).

Clarke, J. R. (1987). "The Early Third Style at the Villa of Oplontis," *MDAI(R)* 94.267–294.

———. (1991). *The Houses of Roman Italy, 100 B.C.–A.D. 250: Ritual, Space, and Decoration* (Berkeley).

Clarke, K. (1999). *Between Geography and History. Hellenistic Constructions of the Roman World* (Oxford).

Clausen, W. (1987). *Virgil's* Aeneid *and the Tradition of Hellenistic Poetry* (Berkeley).

Coarelli, F. (1987). I *santuari del Lazio in età repubblicana* (Rome).

———. (1988). "Die Stadtplanung von Caesar bis Augustus," in Hofter, 68–80.

Conlin, D. (1997). *The Artists of the Ara Pacis* (Chapel Hill and London).

Conte, G. B. (1994). *Latin Literature. A History* (Baltimore).

Corbeill, A. (2001). "Education in the Roman Republic: creating traditions," in Too, Y. L., ed., *Education in Greek and Roman Antiquity* (Leiden) 261–87.

Corbett, J. H. (1974). "The Succession Policy of Augustus," *Latomus* 33.88–97.

Courtney, E. (1993). *The Fragmentary Latin Poets* (Oxford).

Crook, J. A. (1967). *Law and Life of Rome* (London).

———. (1996a). "Political History, 30 B.C. to A.D. 14," in *CAH²X*.70–112.

———. (1996b). "Augustus: Power, Authority, Achievement," in *CAH²X*.113–146.

Cuff, P. J. (1973). "The Settlement of 23 B.C.," *RivFilol* 101.466–477.

de Vos, M. (1980). *L'egittomania in pitture e mosaici romano-campani della prima età imperiale* (Leiden).

Dearman, J. A. (1995). "Edomite Religion: A Survey and Examination of Some Recent Contributions," in Edelman, 137–58.

Dench, E. (1995). *From Barbarians to New Men. Greek, Roman and Modern Perceptions of Peoples from the Central Apennines* (Oxford).

Dettenhofer, M. H. (1990). *Herrschaft und Widerstand im Augusteischen Principat* (Stuttgart).

Dixon, S. (1988). *The Roman Mother* (London).

Dougherty, C. (2001). *The Raft of Odysseus. The Ethnographic Imagination of Homer's* Odyssey (Oxford and New York).

Eck, W. (1984). "Senatorial self-representation: Developments in the Augustan period," in Millar and Segal (1984) 129–67.

———. (2003). *The Age of Augustus* (Oxford).

Edelman, D. V., ed. (1995). *"You shall not abhor an Edomite, for he is your brother": Edom and Seir in History and Tradition* (Atlanta).

Eder, W. (1990). "Augustus and the Power of Tradition: The Augustan Principate as Binding Link between Republic and Empire," in Raaflaub and Toher, 71–122.

Edwards, C. (1993). *The Politics of Immorality in Ancient Rome* (Cambridge).

———. (1996). *Writing Rome. Textual Approaches to the City* (Cambridge).

Edwards, C., and Woolf, G. D., eds. (2003). *Rome the Cosmopolis* (Cambridge).

Ehrenberg, V., and Jones, A. H. M., eds. (1955). *Documents Illustrating the Reigns of Augustus & Tiberius*, 2nd ed. (Oxford).

Eich, A. (2000). *Politische Literatur in der römischen Gesellschaft: Studien zum Verhältnis von politischer und literarischer Öffentlichkeit in der späten Republik und frühen Kaiserzeit* (Cologne).

Engels, J. (1999). *Augusteische Oikumenegeographie und Universalhistorie im Werk Strabons von Amaseia* (Stuttgart).

Fadinger, V. (1969). *Die Bedeutung des Prinzipats: quellenkritische und staatsrechtliche Untersuchungen zu Cassius Dio und der Parallelüberlieferung* (Berlin).

Fantham, E. (1997). "Images of the city: Propertius' new-old Rome," in Habinek and Schiesaro, 122–35.

Fantham, E., et al., eds. (1994). *Women in the Classical World* (New York and Oxford).

Favro, D. (1992). "*Pater urbis*: Augustus as City Father of Rome," *Journal of the Society of Architectural Historians* 51.61–84.

———. (1993). "Reading the Augustan City," in P. Holliday, ed., *Narrative and Event in Ancient Art* (Cambridge) 230–57.

———. (1996). *The Urban Image of Augustan Rome* (Cambridge).

Feldman, L. H. (1992). "Josephus," in Freedman (1992) 3.981–98.

Fentress, L., ed. (2000). *Romanization and the City. Creation, Transformations, and Failures.* JRA suppl. 38.

Ferrary, J.-L. (1997). "The Hellenistic world and Roman political patronage," in Cartledge, P., Garnsey, P., and Gruen, E., eds., *Hellenistic Constructs: Essays in Culture, History and Historiography* (Berkeley) 105–19.

———. (1999). "A propos de deux passages des *Philippiques* (1, 11–13 et 2, 110). Remarques sur les honneurs religieux rendus à César en 45–44 et sur la politique d'Antoine après les Ides de Mars," *Archiv für Religionsgeschichte* 1.215–32.

Fitzmyer, J. (1981). *The Gospel according to Luke*. 2 vols. *The Anchor Bible* (Garden City).

Fittschen, K. (1976). "Zur Herkunft und Entstehung des 2. Stils. Probleme und Argumente," in *Hellenismus in Mittelitalien*, Zanker, P., ed. (Göttingen) 539–63.

Flory, M. B. (1984). "*Sic exempla parantur*: Livia's shrine to Concordia and the Porticus Liviae," *Historia* 33.309–30.

———. (1993). "Livia and the history of public honorific statues for women in Rome," *Transactions of the Amer. Philol. Assoc.* 123.287–308.

Flower, H. I. (1996). *Roman Ancestor Masks and Aristocratic Power in Roman Culture* (Oxford).

Foucault, M. (1971). *The Order of Things: An Archaeology of the Human Sciences* (New York).

———. (1977). *Discipline and Punish. The Birth of the Prison* (New York).

Fraenkel, E. (1957). *Horace* (Oxford).

Fraschetti, A. (1990). *Roma e il principe* (Bari).

Freedman, D. N., ed. (1992). *The Anchor Bible Dictionary*, 6 vols. (New York).

Frier, B. (1985). *The Rise of the Roman Jurists* (Princeton).

Gabba, E. (1991). *Dionysius and the History of Archaic Rome* (Berkeley).

Galinsky, K. (1969). *Aeneas, Sicily and Rome* (Princeton).

———. (1975). *Ovid's* Metamorphoses. *An Introduction to the Basic Aspects* (Oxford).

———. (1996). *Augustan Culture* (Princeton).

———. (1999). "Ovid's *Metamorphoses* and Augustan Cultural Thematics," in Hardie, Barchiesi and Hinds, 103–11.

———. (2003). "Greek and Roman Drama and the *Aeneid*," in Gill, C. J., et al., eds., *Myth, History and Performance in Republican Rome* (Exeter) 275–94.

Ganzert, J. (2000). *Im Allerheiligsten des Augustusforums. Fokus "Oikumenischer Akkulturation"* (Mainz).

Gardner, J. (1996). *Women in Roman Law and Society* (London).

Gelzer, M. (1969). *The Roman Nobility*, trans. R. Seager (Oxford).

Giovannini, A., ed. (2000). *La Révolution Romaine après Ronald Syme. Bilans et Perspectives.* Entretiens Fondation Hardt, vol. 46 (Vandoeuvres/Geneva).

Girardet, K. (1990). "Der Rechtstatus Oktavians im Jahre 32 v. Chr.," *RhM* 133.322–50.

Goldenberg, R. (1979). "The Jewish Sabbath in the Roman World up to the Time of Constantine the Great," in *ANRW* II.19.1, 414–47.

Goodman, M. E. (1987). *The Ruling Class of Judea: The Origins of the Jewish Revolt against Rome AD 66–70.* (Cambridge).

———. (1996). "Judaea," in *CAH²X*.737–81.

Goudineau, C., and Rebourg, A., eds. (1991). *Les villes Augustéennes de Gaule.* Actes du Colloque International d'Autun 6–8 Juin 1985 (Autun).

Grabbe, L. L. (1992). *Judaism from Cyrus to Hadrian*, 2 vols. (Minneapolis).

Gray, E. W. (1970). "The Imperium of M. Agrippa," *ZPE* 6.227–238.

Gros, P. (1976). *Aurea Templa: Recherches sur l'architecture religieuse de Rome à l'époque d'Auguste* (Rome).

Gruen, E. (1990). *Studies in Greek Culture and Roman Policy* (Leiden).

———. (1992). *Culture and National Identity in Republican Rome* (Ithaca).

———. (1996). "The expansion of the empire under Augustus," *CAH²X*.147–97.

———. (2002). *Diaspora: Jews Amidst Greeks and Romans* (Cambridge, Mass.).

Guarducci, M., ed. (1935–1950). *Inscriptiones Creticae*, 4 vols. (Rome).

Gurval, R. (1995). *Actium and Augustus* (Ann Arbor).

Habinek, T. (1998). *The Politics of Latin Literature. Writing, Identity and Empire in Ancient Rome* (Princeton).

Habinek, T., and Schiesaro, A., eds. (1997). *The Roman Cultural Revolution* (Cambridge).

Hanson, J. A. (1959). *Roman Theater Temples* (Princeton).

Hardie, P., Barchiesi, A., and Hinds, S., eds. (1999). *Ovidian Transformations* (Cambridge).

Harris, W. V. (1979). *War and Imperialism in Republican Rome 327–70 B.C.* (Oxford).

Haselberger, L., ed. (2002). *Mapping Augustan Rome. JRA* suppl. 50.

Hemelrijk, E. (1999). *Matrona docta. Educated Women in the Roman Élite* (London).

Herbert-Brown, G., ed. (2002). *Ovid's* Fasti (Oxford).

Hiller von Gärtringen, F., ed. (1904). *Inschriften von Priene* (Berlin).

Hinds, S. (1998). *Allusion and Intertext. Dynamics of Appropriation in Roman Poetry* (Cambridge).

Hölkeskamp, K. J. (1987). *Die Entstehung der Nobilität* (Stuttgart).

———. (1996). "*Exempla* und *mos maiorum*: Überlegungen zum kollektiven Gedächtnis der Nobilität," in Gerke, H. J., and Möller, H., eds., *Vergangenheit und Lebenswelt. Soziale Kommunikation, Traditionsbildung und historisches Bewusstsein* (Tübingen) 301–38.

Hofter, M., ed. (1988). *Kaiser Augustus und die Verlorene Republik* (Mainz).

Holum, K., ed. (1988). *King Herod's Dream: Caesarea on the Sea* (New York).

Hopkins, K. (1978a). *Conquerors and Slaves. Sociological Studies in Roman History I* (Cambridge).

———. (1978b). "Economic growth and towns in classical antiquity," in Abrams, P., and Wrigley, E. A., eds., *Towns in Societies. Essays in Economic History and Historical Sociology* (Cambridge) 35–77.

———. (1983). *Death and Renewal* (Cambridge).

Horden, P., and Purcell, N. (2000). *The Corrupting Sea. A Study of Mediterranean History* (Oxford).

Horsfall, N. (1982). "Allia Potestas and Murdia, two Roman women," *Ancient Society* 12.27–33.

———. (1995). "Virgil's Impact at Rome: The Non-Literary Evidence," in *A Companion to the Study of Virgil* (Leiden) 248–55.

Horsley, R. and Hanson, J. (1985). *Bandits, Prophets, and Messiahs* (Minneapolis).

Iacopi, I. (1997). *La decorazione pittorica della Aula Isiaca* (Rome).

Jenkyns, R. (1998). *Virgil's Experience* (Oxford).

Jones, C. (1993). "Greek Drama in the Roman Empire," in Scodel, R., ed., *Theater and Society in the Classical World* (Ann Arbor) 39–52.

Jones, R. F. J. (1987). "A false start? The Roman urbanization of western Europe," *World Archaeology* 19.1. 47–57.

Jory, E. (1981). "The Literary Evidence for the Beginnings of Imperial Pantomime," *Bulletin of the Institute of Classical Studies* 28.147–61.

———. (1984). "The Early Pantomime Riots," in Moffatt, A., ed., *Maistor: Classical Byzantine Studies for Robert Browning* (Canberra) 57–66.

———. (1996). "The Drama of the Dance," in Slater, W., ed., *Roman Theater and Society* (Ann Arbor) 1–28.

Judge, E. A. (1974). "'*Res Publica Restituta*.' A Modern Illusion?" in Evans, J. A. S., ed., *Polis and Imperium. Studies in Honor of Edward Togo Salmon* (Toronto) 279–311.

Kasher, A. (1985). *Jews in Hellenistic and Roman Egypt* (Tübingen).

———. (1988). *Jews, Idumaeans, and Ancient Arabs* (Tübingen).

Kaster, R. (1988). *Guardians of Language: The Grammarian and Society in Late Antiquity* (Berkeley).

Keay, S., and Terrenato, N., eds. (2001). *Italy and the West. Comparative Issues in Romanization* (Oxford).

Kellum, B. A. (1990). "The City Adorned: Pragmatic Display at the *Aedes Concordiae Augustae*," in Raaflaub and Toher, 276–307.

Kelly, H. (1979). "Tragedy and the Performance of Tragedy in Late Roman Antiquity," *Traditio* 35.21–44.

Kennedy, D. F. (1992). "'Augustan' and 'Anti-Augustan': Reflections on Terms of Reference," in Powell, 26–58.

Kenney, E. J., ed. (1982). *The Cambridge History of Classical Literature*. Vol. 2: *Latin Literature* (Cambridge).

Kent, J. P. C. (1978). *Roman Coins* (London).

Kienast, D. (1999). *Augustus: Prinzeps und Monarch*, 3rd ed. (Darmstadt).

Kleiner, D. E. E. (1977). *Roman Group Portraiture: The Funerary Reliefs of the Late Republic and Early Empire* (New York).

———. (1992). *Roman Sculpture* (New York and London).

———. (2005). *Cleopatra and Rome* (Cambridge, Mass.).

Kleiner, D. E. E., and Matheson, S., eds. (1996). *I Clavdia: Women in Ancient Rome* (New Haven).

———. (2000). *I Clavdia II. Women in Roman Art and Society* (Austin).

Koenen, L. (1970). "Die *Laudatio Funebris* des Augustus für Agrippa," *ZPE* 5.217–283.

Kraabel, A. T. (1979). "The Diaspora Synagogue: Archaeological and Epigraphic Evidence since Sukenik," in *ANRW* II.19.1.477–510.

Kubler, G. (1962). *The Shape of Time: Remarks on the History of Things* (New Haven).

Lacey, W. K. (1979). "*Summi Fastigii Vocabulum*: The Story of a Title," *JRS* 69.28–34.

———. (1985). "Augustus and the Senate, 23 B.C," *Antichthon* 19.57–68.

————. (1996). *Augustus and the Principate: The Evolution of the System* (Liverpool).

Laqueur, R. (1920). *Die jüdische Historiker Flavius Josephus* (Giessen).

Leach, E. W. (1982). "Patrons, Painters, and Patterns: The Anonymity of Romano-Campanian Painting and the Transition from the Second to the Third Style," in Gold, B. K., ed., *Literary and Artistic Patronage in Ancient Rome* (Austin) 135–73.

————. (1988). *The Rhetoric of Space* (Princeton).

Leon, H. J. (1960). *The Jews of Ancient Rome* (New York).

Leppin, H. (1992). *Histrionen: Untersuchungen zur sozialen Stellung von Bühnenkünstlern im Westen des Römischen Reiches zur Zeit der Republik und des Principats* (Bonn).

Levick, B. M. (1967). *Roman Colonies in Southern Asia Minor* (Oxford).

————. (1996). "Greece (including Crete and Cyprus) and Asia," *CAH²* X.641–75.

Lewis, R. W. B. (1950). "Homer and Virgil: The Double Themes," *Furioso* 5.47–59.

Ling, R. (1977). "Studius and the Beginnings of Roman Landscape Painting," *JRS* 67.1–16.

————. (1991). *Roman Painting* (Cambridge).

————. (1997). *The Insula of the Menander at Pompeii*. vol. I: *The Structures* (Oxford).

Lott, J. B. (2004). *The Neighborhoods of Augustan Rome* (Cambridge).

Lynch, K. (1960). *The Image of the City* (Cambridge, Mass.).

Lyne, O. (1994). "Vergil's *Aeneid*: Subversion by Intertextuality," *G&R* 41.187–204.

MacDonald, W. L. (1985). "Empire Imagery in Augustan Architecture," in Winkes, R., ed., *The Age of Augustus* (Louvain) 137–48.

MacMullen, R. (2000). *Romanization in the Age of Augustus* (New Haven).

Magie, D. (1908). "The Mission of Agrippa to the Orient in 23 bc," in *CP* 3.145–57.

————. (1950). *Roman Rule in Asia Minor* (Princeton).

Mau, A. (1882). *Die Geschichte der Dekorativen Wandmalerei in Pompeji* (Leipzig).

McCrum, M., and Woodhead, A. G., eds. (1961). *Select Documents of the Principates of the Flavian Emperors* (Cambridge).

Meyers, E. M., and Strange, J. F. (1981). *Archaeology, the Rabbis, and Early Christianity* (Nashville).

Michels, A. K. (1967). *The Calendar of the Roman Republic* (Princeton).

Mierse, W. (1990). "Augustan Building Programs in the Western Provinces," in Raaflaub and Toher, 308–33.

Millar, F. (1973). "Triumvirate and Principate," *JRS* 63.50–67.

————. (1977). *The Emperor in the Roman World* (London).

————. (1993a). "The Greek City in the Roman Period," in Hansen, M. H., ed., *The Ancient Greek City State* (Copenhagen) 232–60.

————. (1993b). *The Roman Near East: 31 BC–AD 337* (Cambridge, Mass.).

————. (1998). *The Crowd in Rome in the Late Republic* (Ann Arbor).

————. (2000). "The first Revolution: Imperator Caesar, 36–28 BC," in Giovannini, 1–38.

————. (2001). "Greece and Rome from Mummius Achaicus to St Paul: Reflections on a changing world," in J.-Y. Marc and J.-C. Moretti, eds., *Constructions publiques et programmes édilitaires en Grèce entre le IIe siècle av. J.-C. et le Ier siècle ap. J.-C.: Actes du colloque organisé par l'École Française d'Athènes et le CNRS, Athènes 14–17 mai 1995* (Paris) [= *BCH* Supp. 39] 1–11.

————. (2002). *Rome, the Greek World, and the East. Roman Republic and the Augustan Revolution*, vol. 1, Cotton, H. M., and Rogers, G. R., eds. (Chapel Hill).

Millar, F., and Segal, E., eds. (1984). *Caesar Augustus: Seven Aspects* (Oxford).

Millett, M. (1990). *The Romanization of Britain. An Essay in Archaeological Interpretation* (Cambridge).

Moatti, C. (1997). *La raison de Rome* (Paris).

Moormann, E. M., ed. (1995). *Mani di pittori e botteghe pittoriche nel mondo romano. Papers of the Netherlands Institute in Rome* 54.

Müller, C., and Hasenohr, C., eds. (2002). *Les Italiens dans le monde grec. IIe siécle av. J.-C. – Ier siécle ap. J.-C., circulation, activités, intégration: Actes de la Table Ronde, École Normale Supérieure, Paris 14–16 Mai 1998. BCH* suppl 41.

Nicolet, C. (1984). "Augustus, Government and the Propertied Classes," in Millar and Segal, 169–88.

———. (1991). *Space, Geography and Politics in the Early Roman Empire* (Ann Arbor).

Nielsen, I. (1999). *Hellenistic Palaces: Tradition and Renewal*, 2nd ed. (Aarhus).

Nisbet, R. G. M. (1984). "Some problems of text and interpretation in Horace *Odes* 3,14 (*Herculis ritu*)," *Papers of the Liverpool Latin Seminar* 4 (1983) ARCA 11 (Liverpool: F. Cairns) 105–19.

North, J. (1989). "The Roman Counter-revolution," *JRS* 79.151–6.

———. (1990a). "Democratic Politics in Republican Rome," *Past & Present* 126.3–21.

———. (1990b). "Diviners and divination at Rome," in Beard and North, 49–72.

Nye, J. (1990). *Bound to Lead: the Changing Nature of American Power* (New York).

Pani, M. (2003). *La corte dei Cesari* (Rome/Bari).

Petersen, L. H. (2003). "The Baker, his Tomb, his Wife, and her Breadbasket: The Monument of Eurysaces in Rome," *The Art Bulletin* 85.230–257.

Pollini, J. (1987). *The Portraiture of Gaius and Lucius Caesar* (New York).

———. (1990). "Man or God: Divine Assimilation and Imitation in Late Republic and Early Principate," in Raaflaub and Toher, 334–63.

Potter, D. S. (1991). "Quirinius," in Freedman (1992) 5.588–89.

Powell, A., ed. (1992). *Roman Poetry and Propaganda in the Age of Augustus* (London).

Premerstein, A. von (1937). *Vom Werden und Wesen des Prinzipats* (Munich).

Price, S. (1984). *Rituals and Power. The Roman Imperial Cult in Asia Minor* (Cambridge).

Pritchard, J. B., and White, L. M. (1991). *The Harper Collins Concise Atlas of the Bible* (San Francisco).

Purcell, N. (1986). "Livia and the womanhood of Rome," *Proceedings of the Cambridge Philological Society* 32.78–105.

Quass, F. (1993). *Die Honoratiorenschicht in den Städten des griechischen Ostens* (Stuttgart).

Raaflaub, K., and Samons, L. (1990). "Opposition to Augustus," in Raaflaub and Toher, 417–54.

Raaflaub, K., and Toher, M., eds. (1990). *Between Republic and Empire* (Berkeley).

Radke, G. (1990). *Fasti Romani: Betrachtungen zur Frühgeschichte des römischen Kalenders* (Münster).

Ramage, E. (1987). *The Nature and Purpose of Augustus' "Res Gestae"* (Wiesbaden).

Rawson, E. (1975). "Architecture and sculpture: The activities of the Cossutii," *PBSR* 43.36–47 (= *Roman Culture and Society* [Oxford 1991] 189–203).

Rawson, E. (1985). *Intellectual Life in the Late Roman Republic* (Baltimore).

Redfield, J. (1983). "The Economic Man," in Rubino, C., and Shelmerdine, C., eds., *Approaches to Homer* (Austin) 218–47.

Reed, J. L. (2002). *Archaeology and the Galilean Jesus: A Reexamination of the Evidence* (Harrisburg).

Rich, J. W. (1990). *Cassius Dio, The Augustan Settlement (Roman History 53–55.9)* (Warminster).

Richardson, J. S. (1991). "*Imperium Romanum*: Empire and the language of power," *JRS* 81.1–9.

Richardson, L. (1992). *A New Topographical Dictionary of Ancient Rome* (Baltimore).

Richardson, P. (1998). "Augustan Era Synagogues in Rome," in Donfried, K., and Richardson, P., eds., *Judaism and Christianity in First-Century Rome* (Grand Rapids) 17–29.

———. (1999). *Herod: King of the Jews and Friend of the Romans* (Minneapolis).

Rizakis, A. D., ed. (1996). *Roman Onomastics in the Greek East: Social and Political Aspects. Meletemata* 21 (Athens).

Rose, C. B. (1997). *Dynastic Commemoration and Imperial Portraiture in the Julio-Claudian Period* (Cambridge).

Rudd, N. (1982). "Horace," in Kenney, 370–404.

Rüpke, J. (1995). *Kalender und Öffentlichkeit: die Geschichte der Repräsentation und der religiösen Qualifikation von Zeit in Rom* (Berlin).

Russell, D. A. (1979). "De imitatione," in West, D., and Woodman, T., eds., *Creative Imitation and Latin Literature* (Cambridge) 1–16.

Rutgers, L. V. (1995). *The Jews of Late Ancient Rome* (Leiden).

Safrai, S., and Stern, M., eds. (1974). *The Jewish People in the First Century* (Assen).

Saller, R. (1982). *Personal Patronage under the Early Empire* (Cambridge).

———. (1989). "Patronage in Roman society: From Republic to Empire," in Wallace-Hadrill (1989b) 63–87.

———. (1994). *Patriarchy, Property and Death in the Roman Family* (Cambridge).

Salmon, E. T. (1956). "The Evolution of Augustus' Principate," *Historia* 5.456–78.

Salomies, O., ed. (2001). *The Greek East in the Roman context: Proceedings of a colloquium organised by The Finnish Institute at Athens; May 21 and 22, 1999* (Helsinki).

Sartre, M. (1991). *L'Orient romain: provinces et sociétés provinciales en Méditerranée orientale d'Auguste aux Sévères (31 avant J.-C–235 après J.-C.)* (Paris).

Schallit, A. (1969). *König Herodes: Der Mann und sein Werk* (Berlin).

Scheid, J. (1978). "Les prêtres officiels sous les empereurs julio-claudiens," in *ANRW* II.16.1, 610–54.

———. (1999). "Auguste et le grand pontificat. Politique et droit sacré au début du Principat," *Rev. hist. droit* 77.1–19.

Scherrer, P. (2002). "Römische Handelsniederlassungen im Regnum Noricum," in Kos, M., and Scherrer, P., eds., *The Autonomous Towns of Noricum and Pannonia–Die autonomen Städte in Noricum und Pannonien. Situla* 40.11–70.

Schrapel, T. (1996). *Das Reich der Kleopatra: quellenkritische Untersuchungen zu den "Landschenkungen" des Mark Anton* (Trier).

Sherk, R. (1984). *Rome and the Greek East to the Death of Augustus* (= *Translated Documents of Greece and Rome* 4) (Cambridge).

Smallwood, E. M. (1976). *The Jews under Roman Rule from Pompey to Diocletian* (Leiden).

Smith, R. A. (2005). *The Primacy of Vision in Virgil's Aeneid* (Austin).

Southern, P. (1998). *Augustus* (London).

Spawforth, A. (1996). "Roman Corinth: The formation of a colonial élite," in Rizakis, 167–82.

———. (2002). "Éléments italiens parmi les chevaliers et les sénateurs romains de l''ancienne' Grèce," in Müller and Hasenohr, 101–108.

Spinazzola, V. (1953). *Pompei alla Luce degli Scavi Nuovi di Via dell'Abbondanza* (Rome).

Ste. Croix, G. E. M. de (1981). *The Class Struggle in the Ancient Greek World* (London).

Steel, C. E. W. (2001). *Cicero, Rhetoric and Empire* (Oxford).

Steinby, M. E., ed. (1993–2000). *Lexicon Topographicum Urbis Romae*, 6 vols. (Rome).

Stern, M. (1974a). "The Reign of Herod and the Herodian Dynasty," in Safrai and Stern, 1.216–307.

———. (1974b). "The Province of Judea," in Safrai and Stern, 1.308–76.

Strothmann, M. (2000). *Augustus – Vater der res publica* (Stuttgart).

Sutherland, C. H. V. (1974). *Roman Coins* (London).

Syme, R. (1934). "Galatia and Pamphylia under Augustus: The Governorships of Piso, Quirinius, and Silvanus," *Klio* 27.122–48.

———. (1939). *The Roman Revolution* (Oxford).

———. (1984). *History in Ovid* (Oxford).

———. (1986). *The Augustan Aristocracy* (Oxford).

Treggiari, S. (1991). *Roman Marriage. Iusti coniuges from the Time of Cicero to the Time of Ulpian* (Oxford).

———. (1996a). "Women in Roman Society," in Kleiner and Matheson, 116–25.

———. (1996b). "Social Status and Social Legislation," in *CAH²* X.873–904.

VanderKam, J. (2004). *From Joshua to Caiaphas: High Priests after the Exile* (Minneapolis).

Veyne, P. (1976). *Le pain et le cirque. Sociologie historique d'un pluralisme politique* (Paris).

Ville, G. (1981). *La gladiature en Occident des origines à la mort de Domitien* (Rome).

Walker, S., and Higgs, P., eds. (2001). *Cleopatra of Egypt* (Princeton).

Wallace-Hadrill, A. (1983). *Suetonius: The scholar and his Caesars* (London).

———. (1986). "Image and Authority in the Coinage of Augustus," *JRS* 76.66–87.

———. (1987). "Time for Augustus: Ovid, Augustus and the *Fasti*," in Whitby, 221–30.

———. (1988). "The Social Structure of the Roman House," *PBSR* 56.43–97.

———. (1989a). "Rome's cultural revolution," *JRS* 79.157–64.

———, ed. (1989b). *Patronage in Ancient Society* (London).

———. (1993). *Augustan Rome* (Bristol).

———. (1997). "*Mutatio morum*: The idea of a cultural revolution," in Habinek and Schiesaro, 3–22.

———. (2000). "The Roman revolution and material culture," in Giovannini, 283–321.

Ward-Perkins, J. B. (1970). "From Republic to Empire: Reflections on the early imperial provincial architecture of the Roman West," *JRS* 60.1–19.

———. (1981). *Roman Imperial Architecture* (Harmondsworth).

Weinbrot, H. (1978). *Augustus Caesar in "Augustan" England* (Princeton).

Weinstock, S. (1960). "Pax and the 'Ara Pacis'," *JRS* 50.44–58.

———. (1971). *Divus Iulius* (Oxford).

West, D., transl. (1997). *Horace Odes and Epodes* (Oxford).

Wheeler, S. M. (2001). "Ovid's *Metamorphoses* and Universal History," in Levene, D. S., and Nelis, D. P., eds., *Clio and the Poets: Augustan Poetry and the Traditions of Ancient Historiography* (Leiden) 163–89.

Whitby, M., et al., eds. (1987). *Homo viator: Classical Essays for John Bramble* (Bristol).

White, L. M. (1987). "The Delos Synagogue Revisited: Recent Fieldwork in the Graeco-Roman Diaspora," in *Harvard Theological Review* 80.133–66.

———. (1996–97). *The Social Origins of Christian Architecture* (Harrisburg).

———. (2004). *From Jesus to Christianity: The Story of the New Testament and Christian Origins* (San Francisco).

Wilken, R. L. (1992). *The Land Called Holy: Palestine in Christian History and Thought* (New Haven).

Williams, G. (1968). *Tradition and Originality in Roman Poetry* (Oxford).

Williams, R. D. (1990). "The Purpose of the *Aeneid*," in Harrison, S. J., ed., *Oxford Readings in Vergil's* Aeneid (Oxford) 21–36.

Wilson, A. J. N. (1966). *Emigration from Italy in the Republican Age of Rome*. (Manchester).

Wimmel, W. (1960). *Kallimachos in Rom* (Wiesbaden).

Winkes, R., ed. (1982). *The Age of Augustus* (Louvain).

Winterling (1999). *Aula Caesaris. Studien zur Institutionalisierung des römischen Kaiserhofes in der Zeit von Augustus bis Commodus (31 v. Chr.–192 n. Chr.)* (Munich).

Wissowa, G. (1912). *Religion und Kultus der Römer* (Munich 1912, repr. 1971).

Wolf, E. (1982). *Europe and the People Without History* (Berkeley).

Wood, S. (1999). *Imperial Women. A Study in Public Images, 40 B.C.– A.D. 68* (Leiden).

Woolf, G. D. (1992). "Imperialism, empire and the integration of the Roman economy," *World Archaeology* 23.3.283–93.

———. (1994). "Becoming Roman, Staying Greek: Culture, Identity and the Civilizing Process in the Roman East," *PCPS* 40.116–43.

———. (1997). "The Roman urbanization of the East", in Alcock, S. E., ed., *The Early Roman Empire in the East* (Oxford) 1–14.

———. (1998). *Becoming Roman. The Origins of Provincial Civilization in Gaul* (Cambridge).

———. (2000). "Urbanization and its discontents in early Roman Gaul," in Fentress, E., ed., *Romanization and the City. Creation, Dynamics and Failures. JRA* supplement 38 (2000) 115–32.

———. (2001). "The Roman Cultural Revolution in Gaul," in Keay and Terrenato, 173–86.

Yavetz, Z. (1988). *Plebs and Princeps*, 2nd ed. (Oxford).

Zanker, P. (1968). *Forum Augustum* (Tübingen).

———. (1987). "Drei Stadtbilder aus dem augusteischen Rom," in Pietri, C., ed., *L'Urbs. Espace et histoire, 1er siècle av. J.-C. – IIIe siècle ap. J.-C.* (Rome) 475–89.

———. (1988). *The Power of Images in the Age of Augustus*, trans. A. Shapiro, (Ann Arbor).

Zanker, P., ed. (1976). *Hellenismus in Mittelitalien* (Göttingen).

INDEX

LaVergne, TN USA
20 January 2011
213187LV00003B/7/P